PENGUIN BOOKS

GANDHI

Kazuki Ebine is a young up-and-coming manga artist in Tokyo. His previous works range from science fiction to the everyday life of a rock band. Kazuki has won several highly recognized awards from the major comic book magazines in Japan.

To learn more about his work, please visit:
http://web.me.com/e.kazuki/boukenou/top.html
(in Japanese)

GANDHI

A Manga Biography

KAZUKI EBINE

PENGUIN BOOKS

PENGUIN BOOKS

Published by the Penguin Group
Penguin Group (USA) Inc., 375 Hudson Street, New York, New York 10014, U.S.A.
Penguin Group (Canada), 90 Eglinton Avenue East, Suite 700, Toronto,
Ontario, Canada M4P 2Y3 (a division of Pearson Penguin Canada Inc.)
Penguin Books Ltd, 80 Strand, London WC2R 0RL, England
Penguin Ireland, 25 St Stephen's Green, Dublin 2, Ireland (a division of Penguin Books Ltd)
Penguin Group (Australia), 250 Camberwell Road, Camberwell,
Victoria 3124, Australia (a division of Pearson Australia Group Pty Ltd)
Penguin Books India Pvt Ltd, 11 Community Centre,
Panchsheel Park, New Delhi – 110 017, India
Penguin Group (NZ), 67 Apollo Drive, Rosedale, Auckland 0632,
New Zealand (a division of Pearson New Zealand Ltd)
Penguin Books (South Africa) (Pty) Ltd, 24 Sturdee Avenue,
Rosebank, Johannesburg 2196, South Africa

Penguin Books Ltd, Registered Offices:
80 Strand, London WC2R 0RL, England

First published in the United States of America by Emotional Content LLC, 2010
Published in Penguin Books 2011

1   3   5   7   9   10   8   6   4   2

ISBN 978-0-9817543-3-8 (Emotional Content pbk.)
ISBN 978-0-14-312024-7 (Penguin pbk.)

Printed in the United States of America

The weak can never forgive.
Forgiveness is the attribute of the strong.

—Mahatma Gandhi

GANDHI

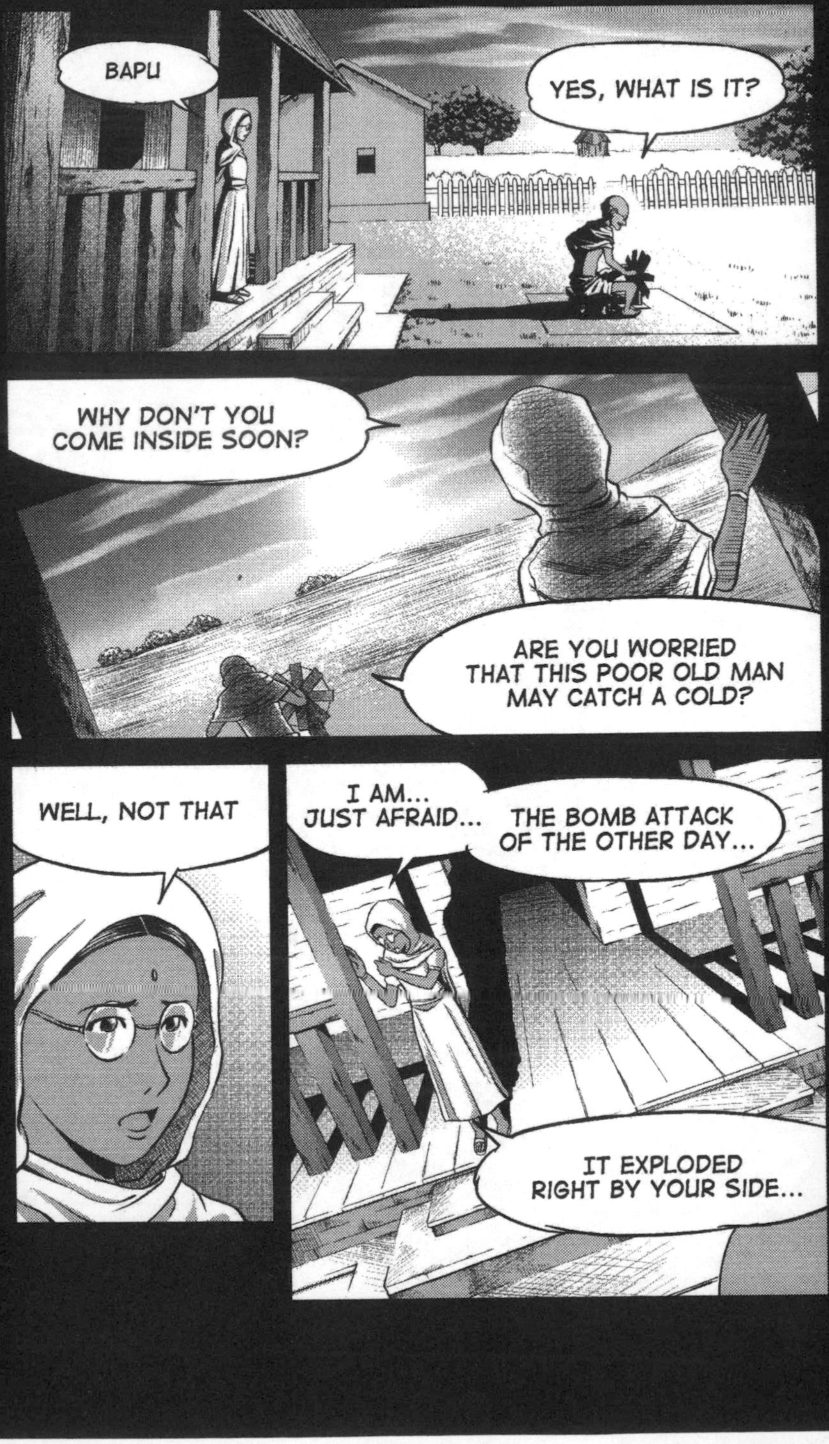
BAPU
YES, WHAT IS IT?
WHY DON'T YOU COME INSIDE SOON?
ARE YOU WORRIED THAT THIS POOR OLD MAN MAY CATCH A COLD?
WELL, NOT THAT
I AM... JUST AFRAID...
THE BOMB ATTACK OF THE OTHER DAY...
IT EXPLODED RIGHT BY YOUR SIDE...

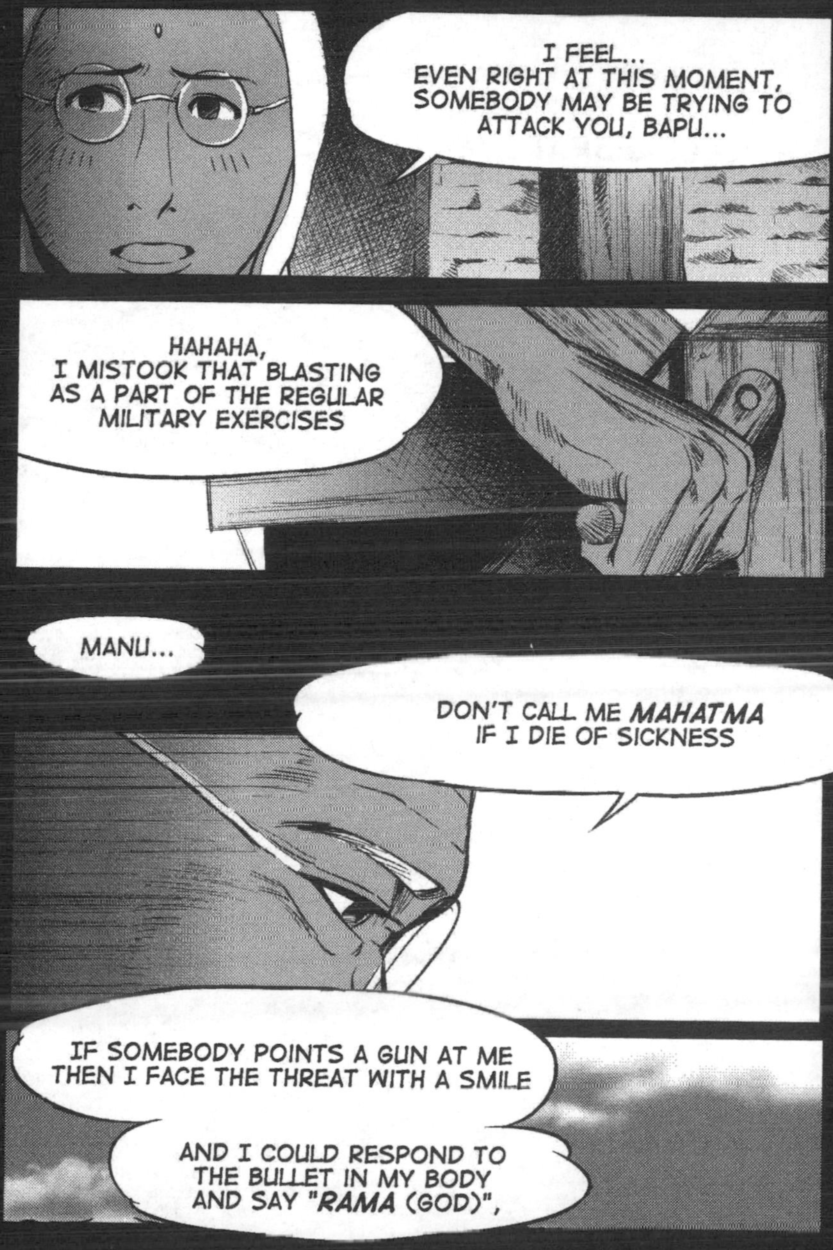
I FEEL... EVEN RIGHT AT THIS MOMENT, SOMEBODY MAY BE TRYING TO ATTACK YOU, BAPU...
HAHAHA, I MISTOOK THAT BLASTING AS A PART OF THE REGULAR MILITARY EXERCISES
MANU...
DON'T CALL ME *MAHATMA* IF I DIE OF SICKNESS
IF SOMEBODY POINTS A GUN AT ME THEN I FACE THE THREAT WITH A SMILE
AND I COULD RESPOND TO THE BULLET IN MY BODY AND SAY "*RAMA* (GOD)",

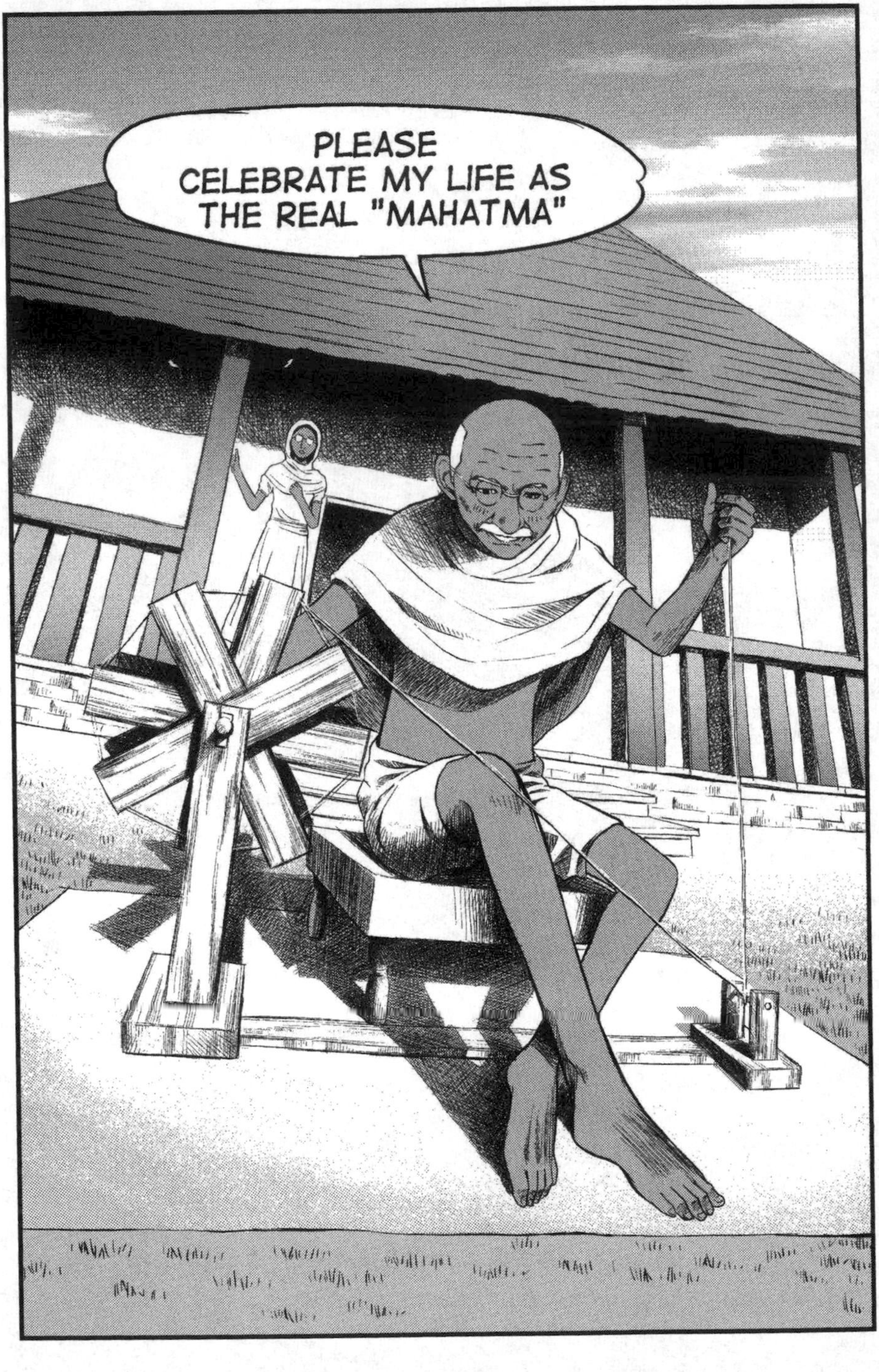
PLEASE CELEBRATE MY LIFE AS THE REAL "MAHATMA"

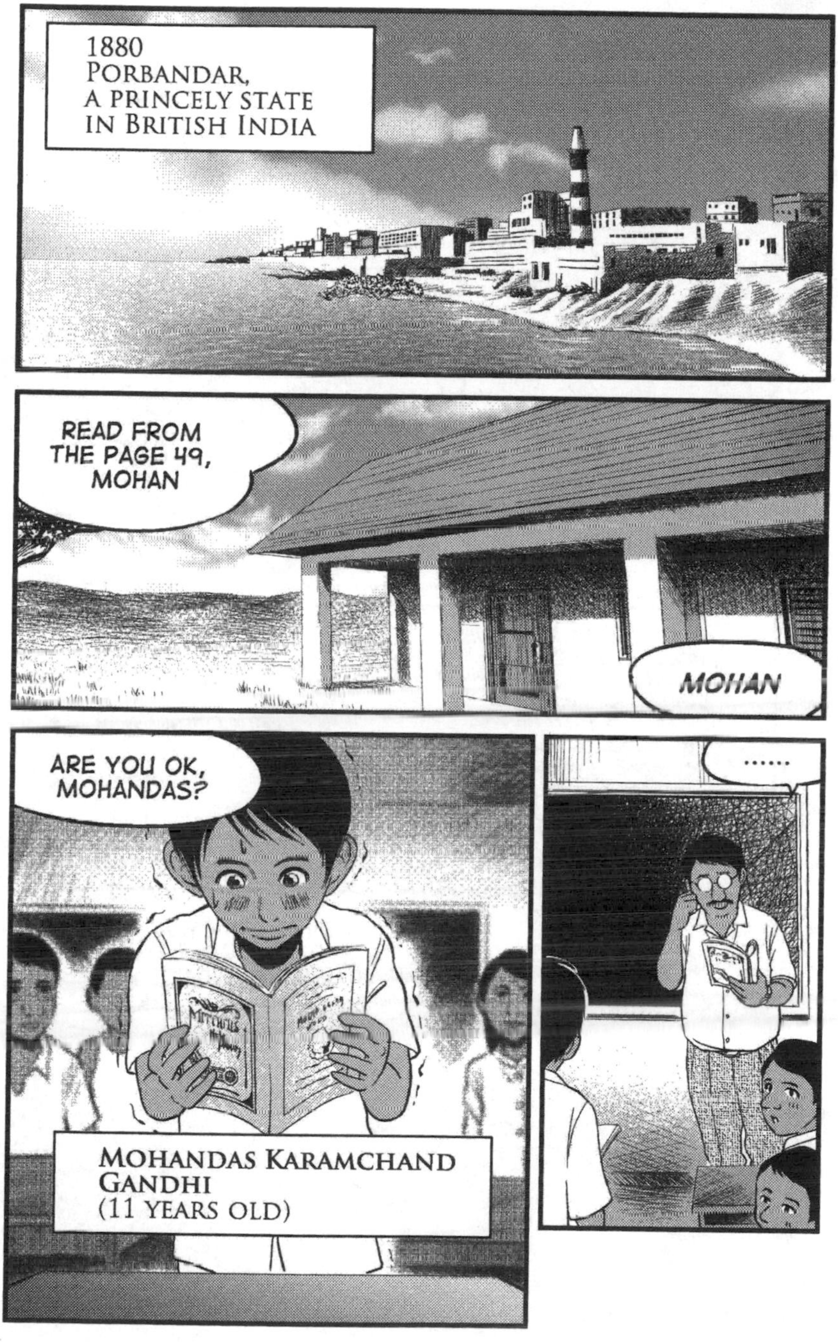
1880
PORBANDAR,
A PRINCELY STATE
IN BRITISH INDIA
READ FROM THE PAGE 49, MOHAN
MOHAN
ARE YOU OK, MOHANDAS?
MOHANDAS KARAMCHAND GANDHI (11 YEARS OLD)
......

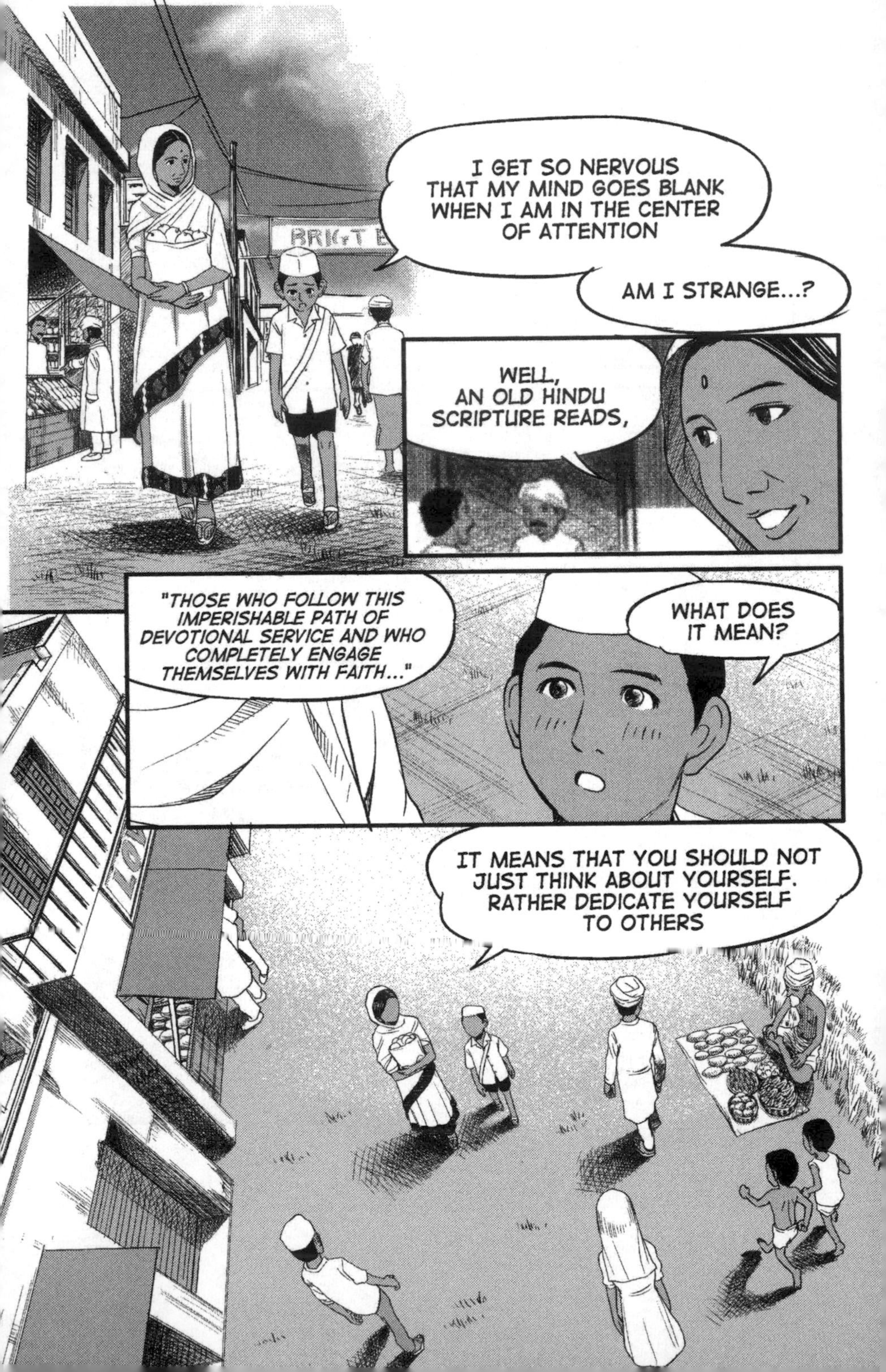
BRIG T E
I GET SO NERVOUS THAT MY MIND GOES BLANK WHEN I AM IN THE CENTER OF ATTENTION
AM I STRANGE...?
WELL, AN OLD HINDU SCRIPTURE READS,
"THOSE WHO FOLLOW THIS IMPERISHABLE PATH OF DEVOTIONAL SERVICE AND WHO COMPLETELY ENGAGE THEMSELVES WITH FAITH..."
WHAT DOES IT MEAN?
IT MEANS THAT YOU SHOULD NOT JUST THINK ABOUT YOURSELF. RATHER DEDICATE YOURSELF TO OTHERS

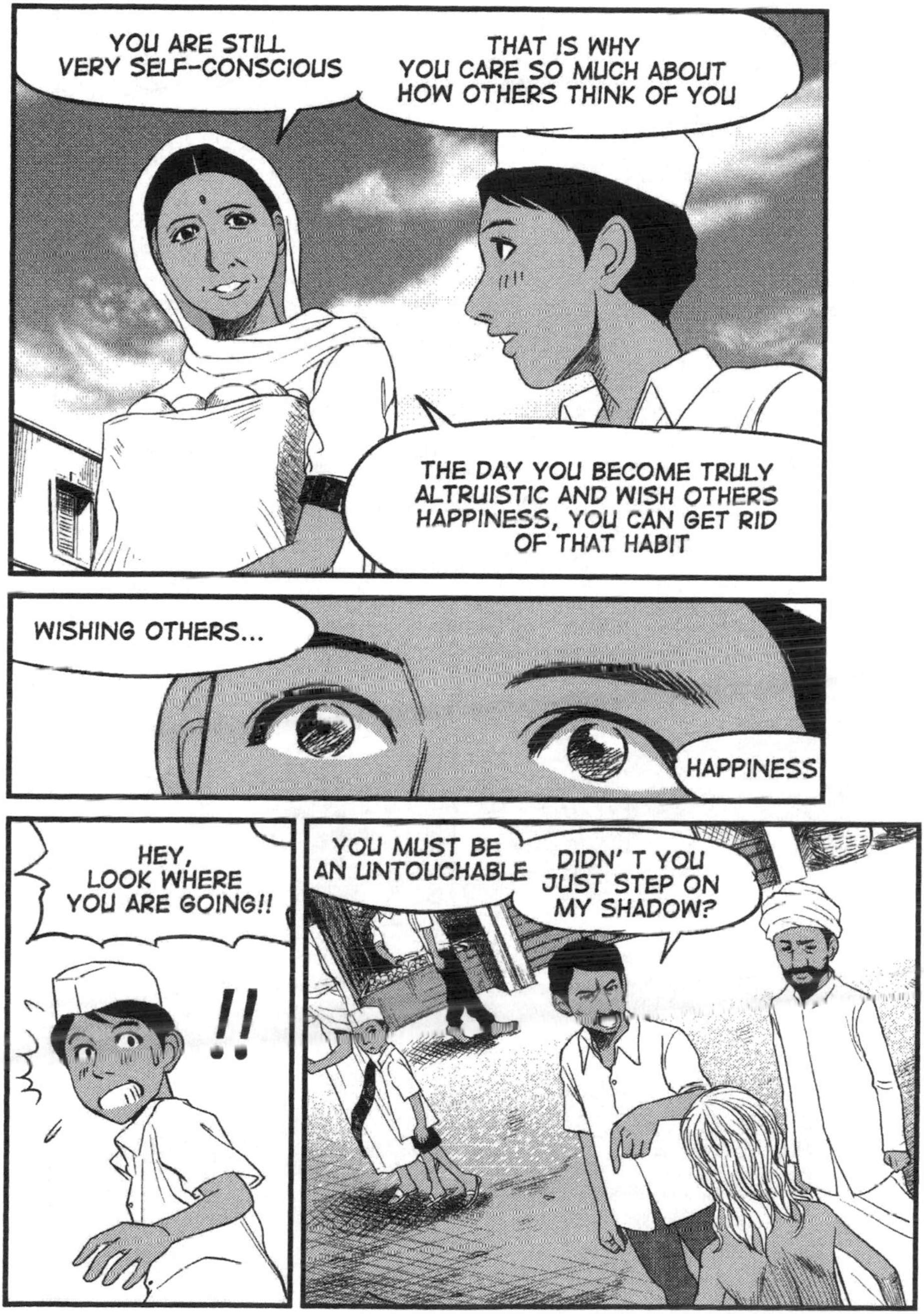
YOU ARE STILL VERY SELF-CONSCIOUS
THAT IS WHY YOU CARE SO MUCH ABOUT HOW OTHERS THINK OF YOU
THE DAY YOU BECOME TRULY ALTRUISTIC AND WISH OTHERS HAPPINESS, YOU CAN GET RID OF THAT HABIT
WISHING OTHERS...
HAPPINESS
HEY, LOOK WHERE YOU ARE GOING!!
!!
DIDN' T YOU JUST STEP ON MY SHADOW?
YOU MUST BE AN UNTOUCHABLE

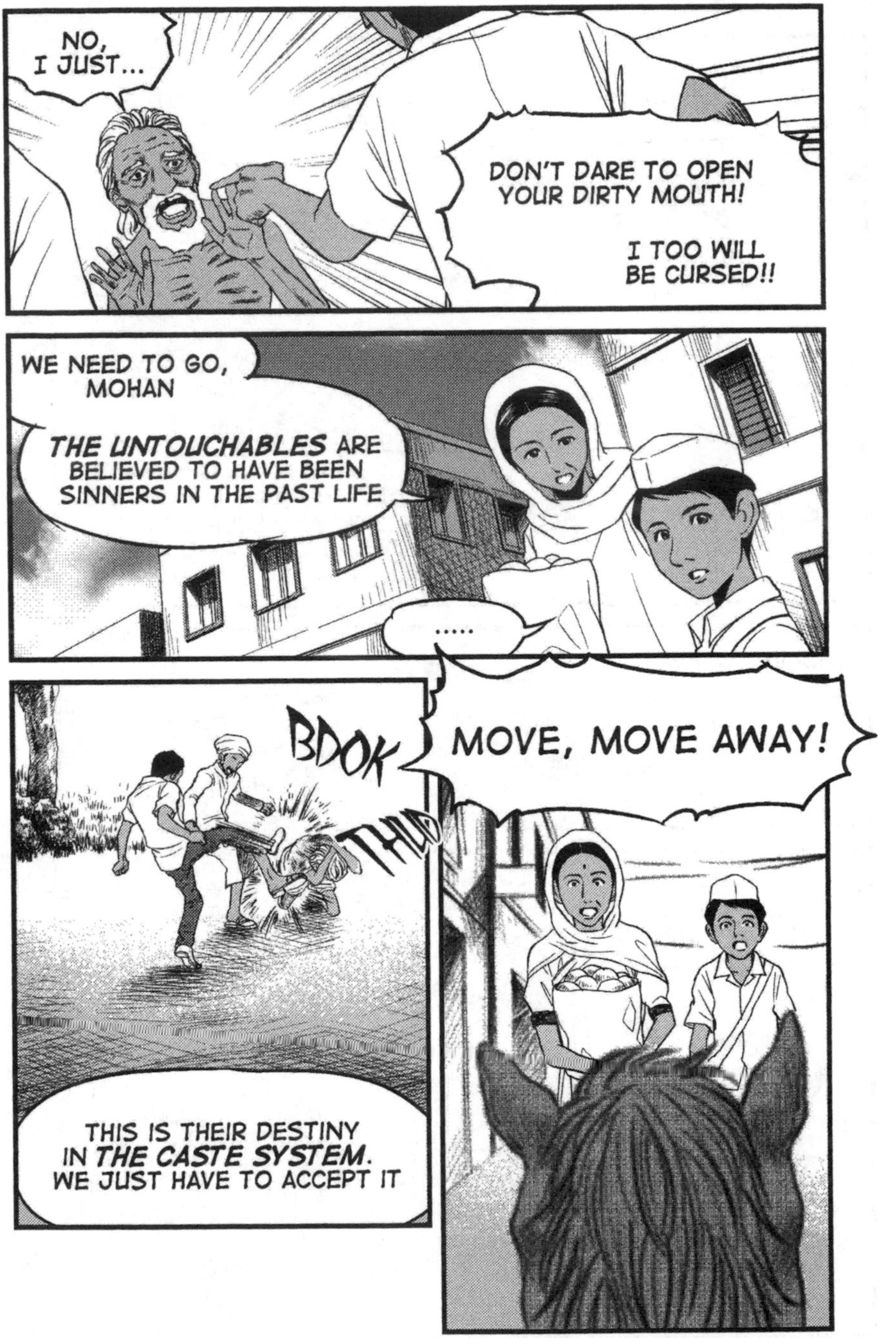
NO, I JUST...
DON'T DARE TO OPEN YOUR DIRTY MOUTH!
I TOO WILL BE CURSED!!
WE NEED TO GO, MOHAN
THE UNTOUCHABLES ARE BELIEVED TO HAVE BEEN SINNERS IN THE PAST LIFE
.....
BDOK
THUD
THIS IS THEIR DESTINY IN THE CASTE SYSTEM. WE JUST HAVE TO ACCEPT IT
MOVE, MOVE AWAY!

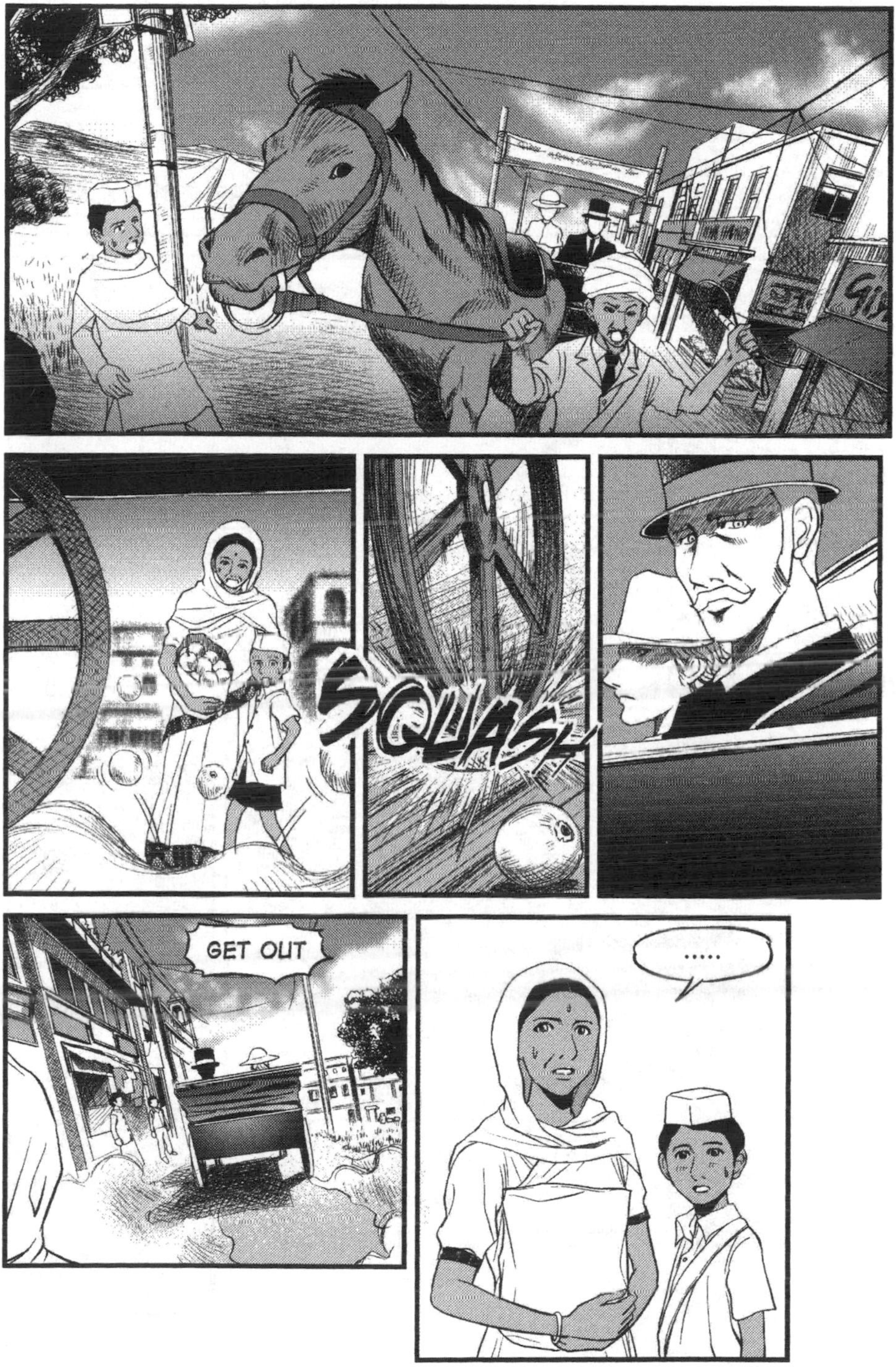
SQUASH
GET OUT
.....

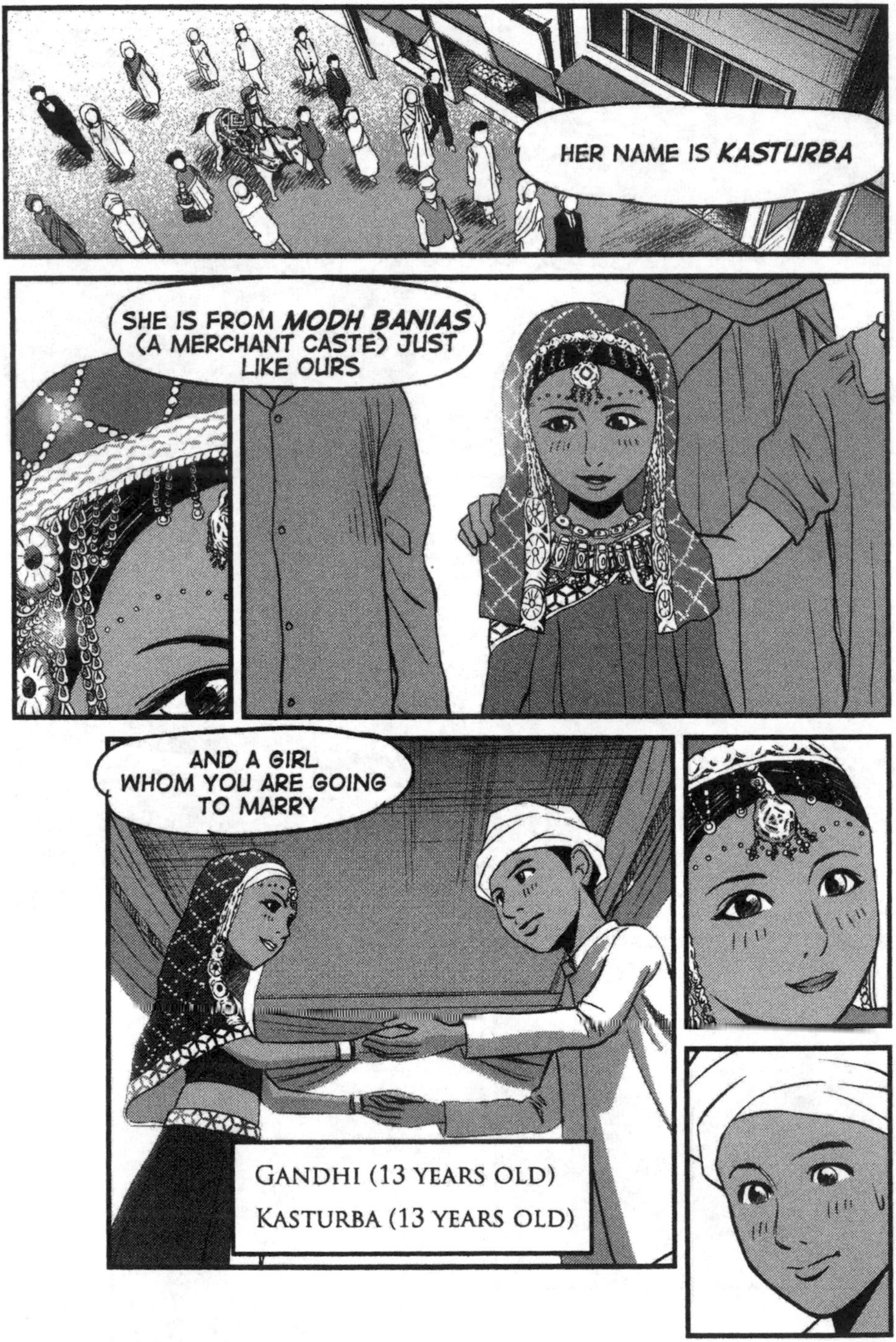
HER NAME IS *KASTURBA*
SHE IS FROM *MODH BANIAS* (A MERCHANT CASTE) JUST LIKE OURS
AND A GIRL WHOM YOU ARE GOING TO MARRY
GANDHI (13 YEARS OLD)
KASTURBA (13 YEARS OLD)

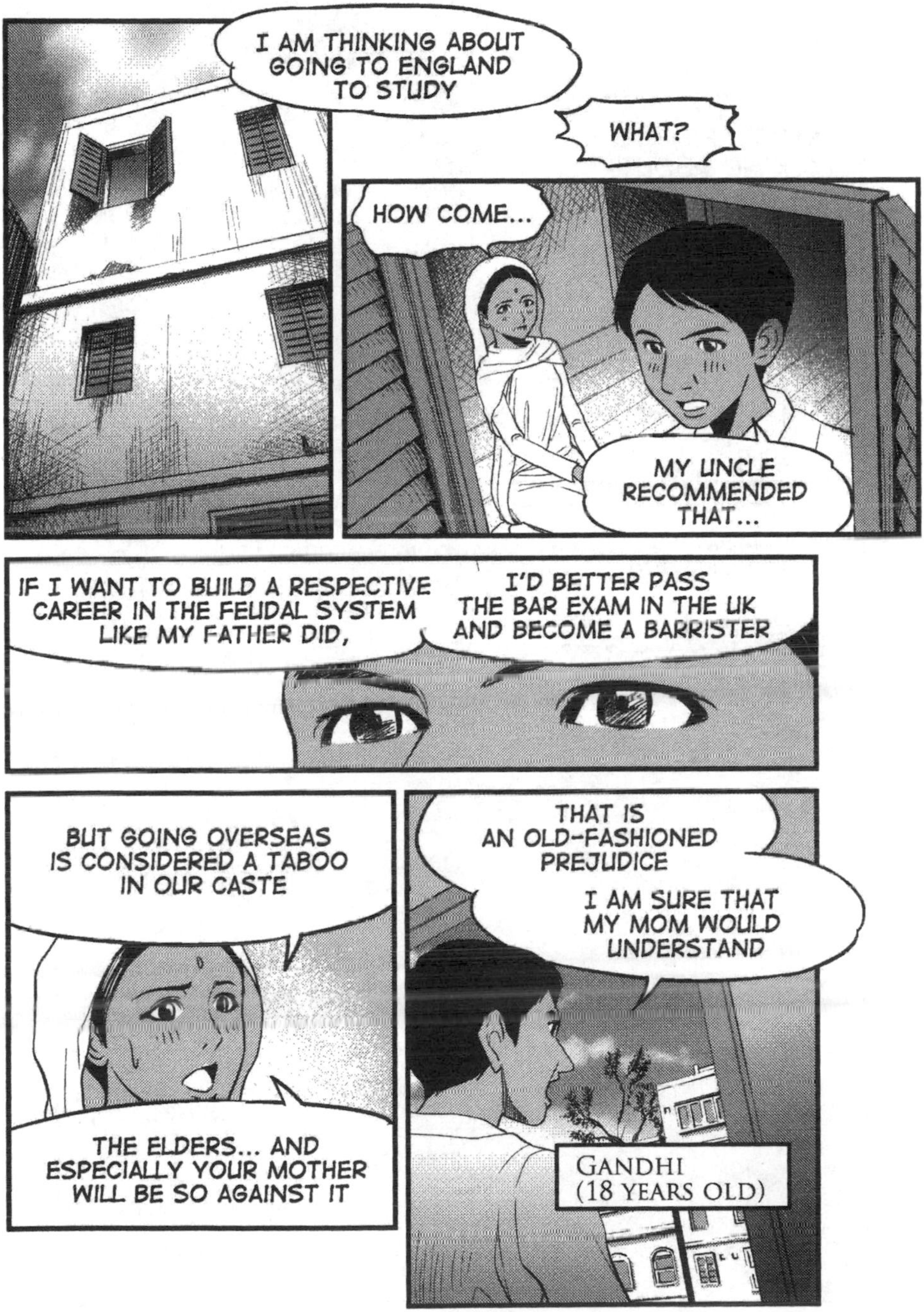
I AM THINKING ABOUT GOING TO ENGLAND TO STUDY
WHAT?
HOW COME...
MY UNCLE RECOMMENDED THAT...
IF I WANT TO BUILD A RESPECTIVE CAREER IN THE FEUDAL SYSTEM LIKE MY FATHER DID,
I'D BETTER PASS THE BAR EXAM IN THE UK AND BECOME A BARRISTER
BUT GOING OVERSEAS IS CONSIDERED A TABOO IN OUR CASTE
THE ELDERS... AND ESPECIALLY YOUR MOTHER WILL BE SO AGAINST IT
THAT IS AN OLD-FASHIONED PREJUDICE
I AM SURE THAT MY MOM WOULD UNDERSTAND
GANDHI (18 YEARS OLD)

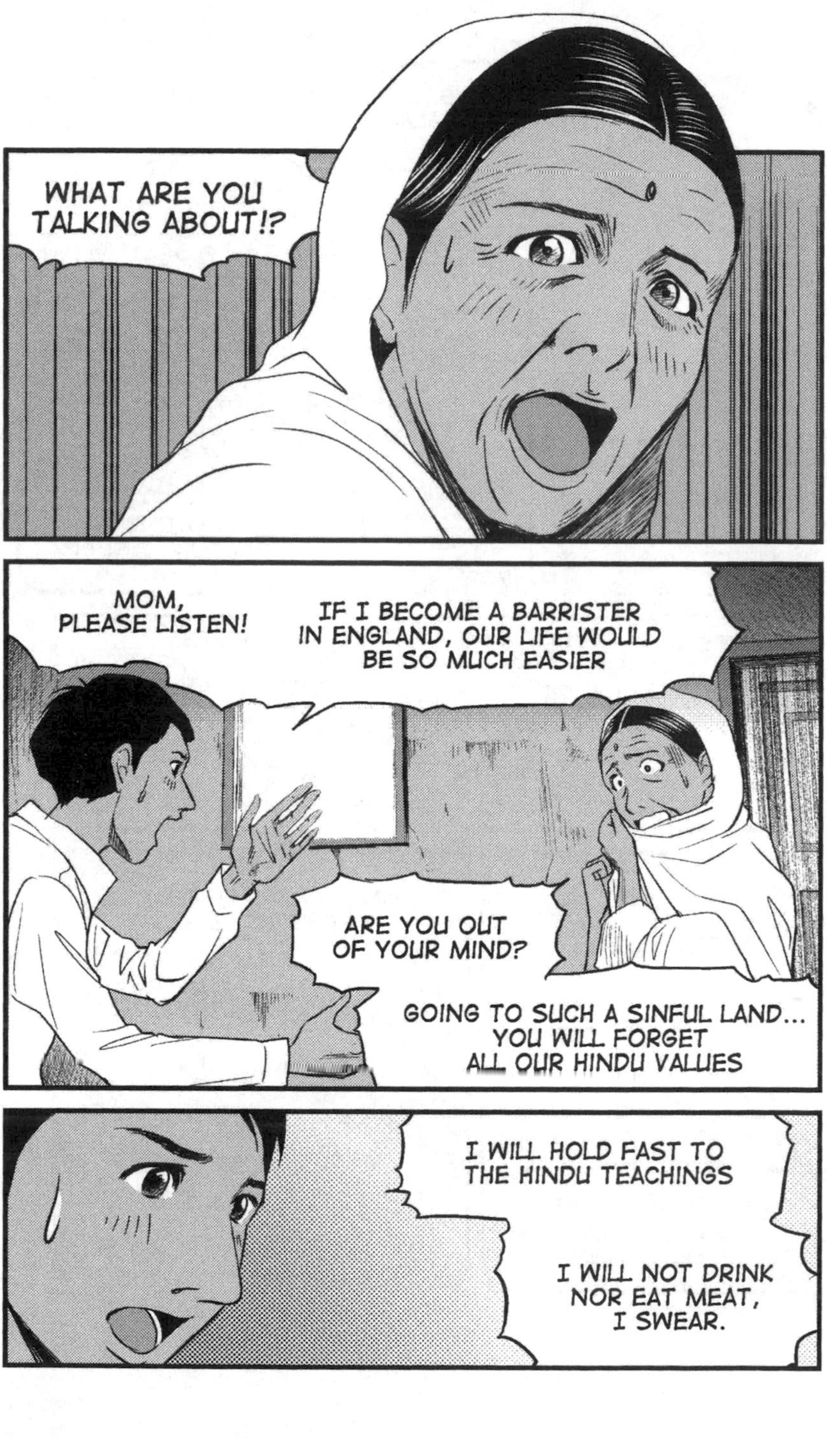
WHAT ARE YOU TALKING ABOUT!?
MOM, PLEASE LISTEN!
IF I BECOME A BARRISTER IN ENGLAND, OUR LIFE WOULD BE SO MUCH EASIER
ARE YOU OUT OF YOUR MIND?
GOING TO SUCH A SINFUL LAND... YOU WILL FORGET ALL OUR HINDU VALUES
I WILL HOLD FAST TO THE HINDU TEACHINGS
I WILL NOT DRINK NOR EAT MEAT, I SWEAR.

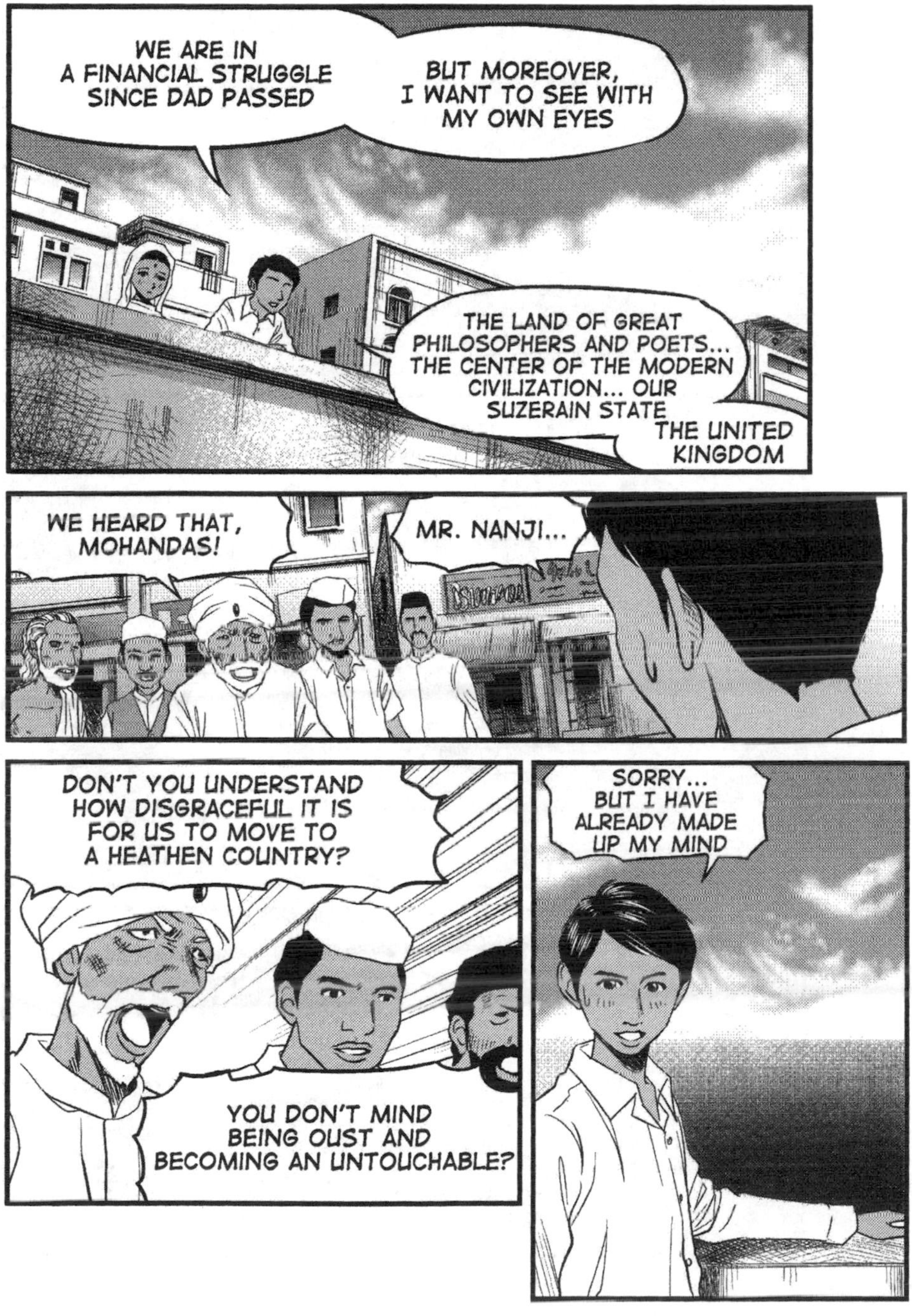
WE ARE IN A FINANCIAL STRUGGLE SINCE DAD PASSED
BUT MOREOVER, I WANT TO SEE WITH MY OWN EYES
THE LAND OF GREAT PHILOSOPHERS AND POETS... THE CENTER OF THE MODERN CIVILIZATION... OUR SUZERAIN STATE
THE UNITED KINGDOM
WE HEARD THAT, MOHANDAS!
MR. NANJI...
DON'T YOU UNDERSTAND HOW DISGRACEFUL IT IS FOR US TO MOVE TO A HEATHEN COUNTRY?
YOU DON'T MIND BEING OUST AND BECOMING AN UNTOUCHABLE?
SORRY... BUT I HAVE ALREADY MADE UP MY MIND

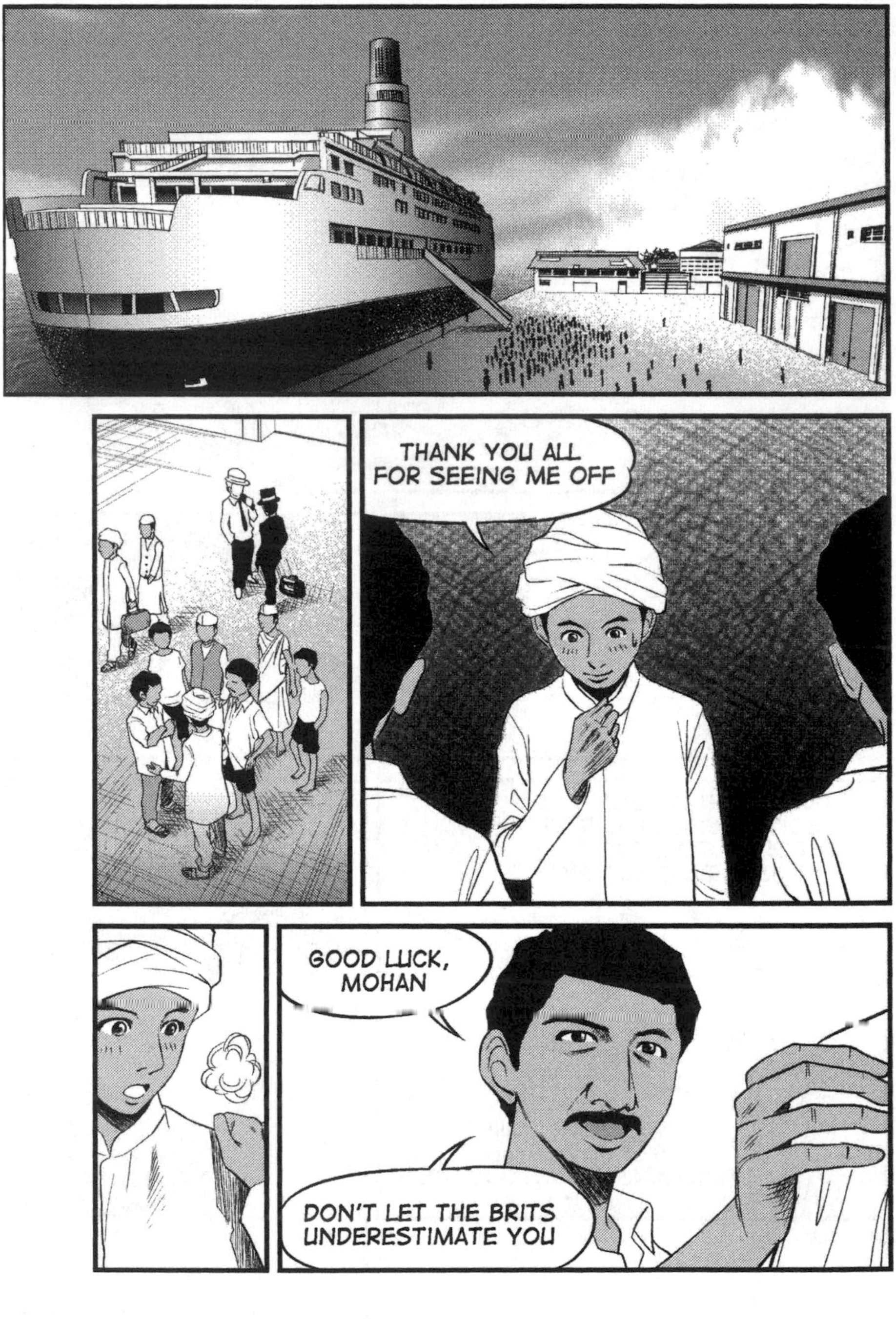
THANK YOU ALL FOR SEEING ME OFF
GOOD LUCK, MOHAN
DON'T LET THE BRITS UNDERESTIMATE YOU

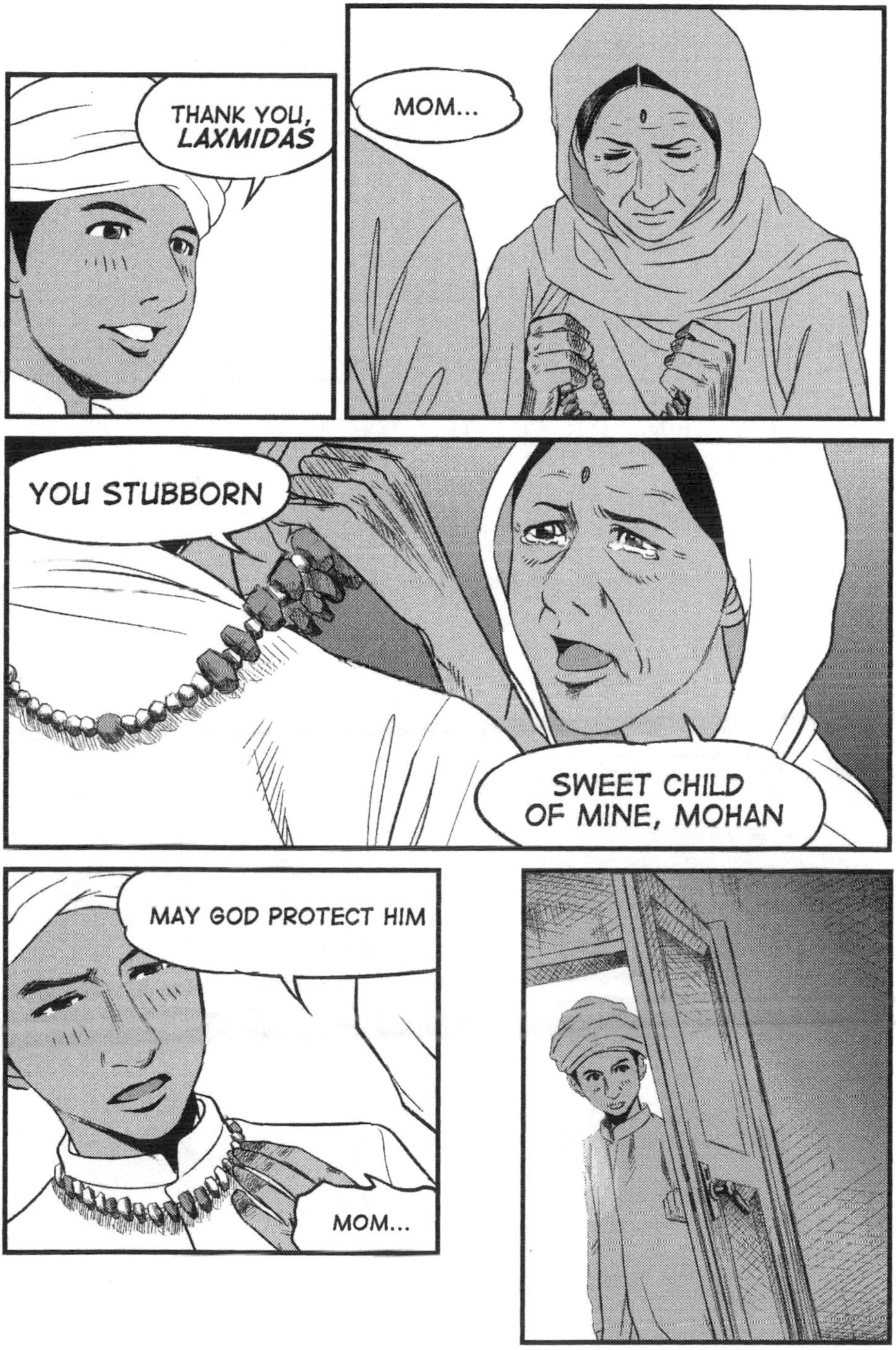
THANK YOU, *LAXMIDAS*
MOM...
YOU STUBBORN
SWEET CHILD OF MINE, MOHAN
MAY GOD PROTECT HIM
MOM...

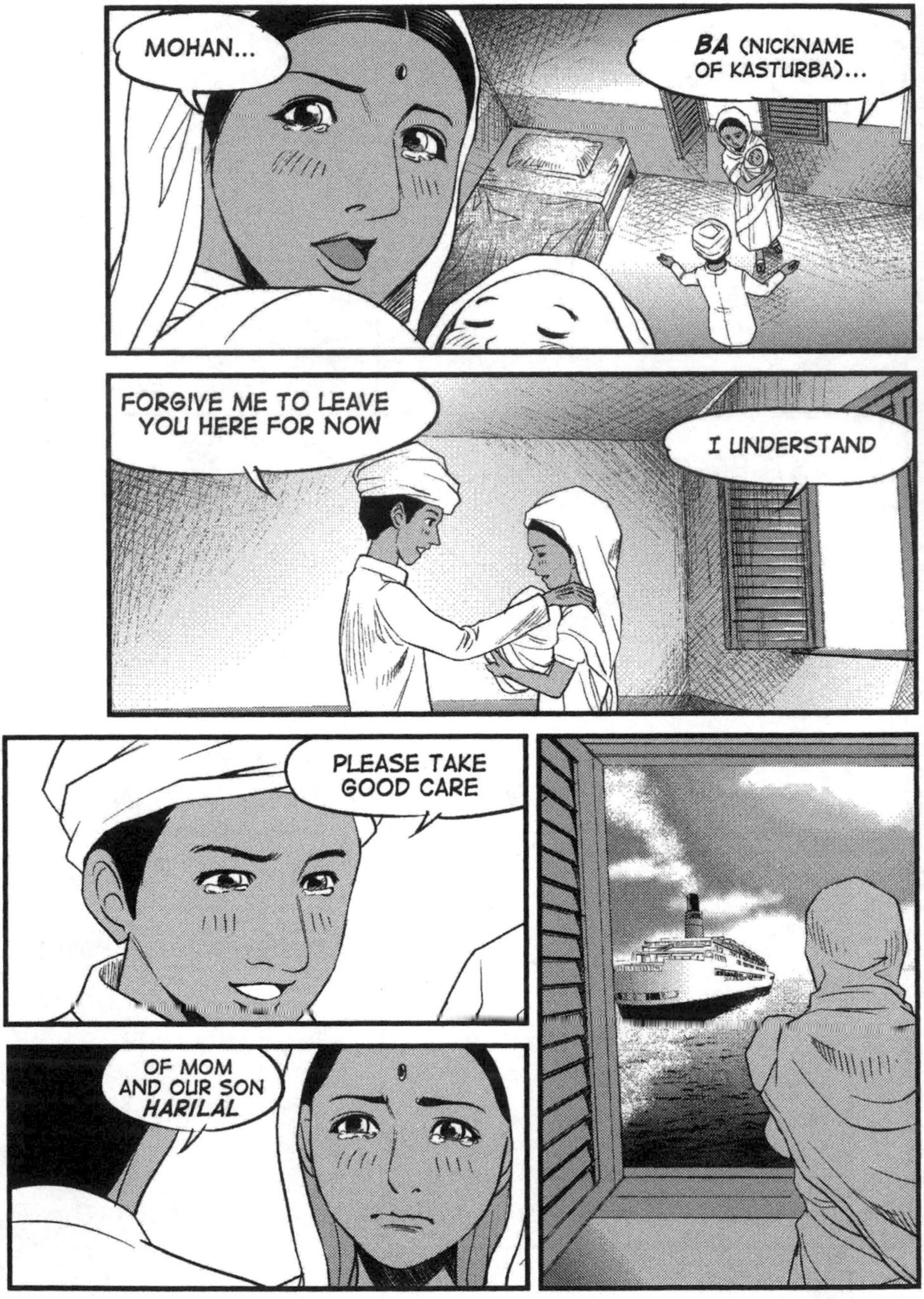
MOHAN...
BA (NICKNAME OF KASTURBA)...
FORGIVE ME TO LEAVE YOU HERE FOR NOW
I UNDERSTAND
PLEASE TAKE GOOD CARE
OF MOM AND OUR SON *HARILAL*

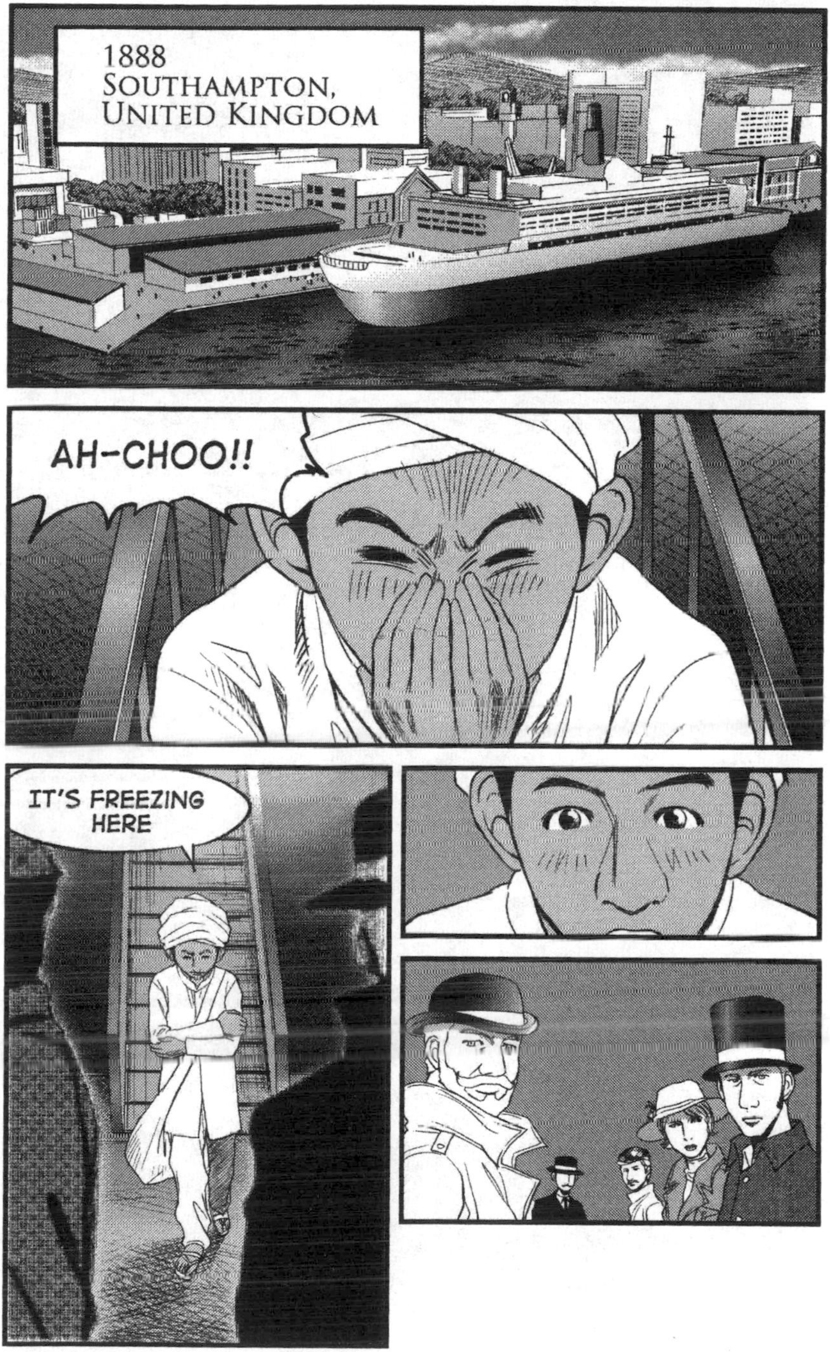
1888
SOUTHAMPTON,
UNITED KINGDOM
AH-CHOO!!
IT'S FREEZING HERE

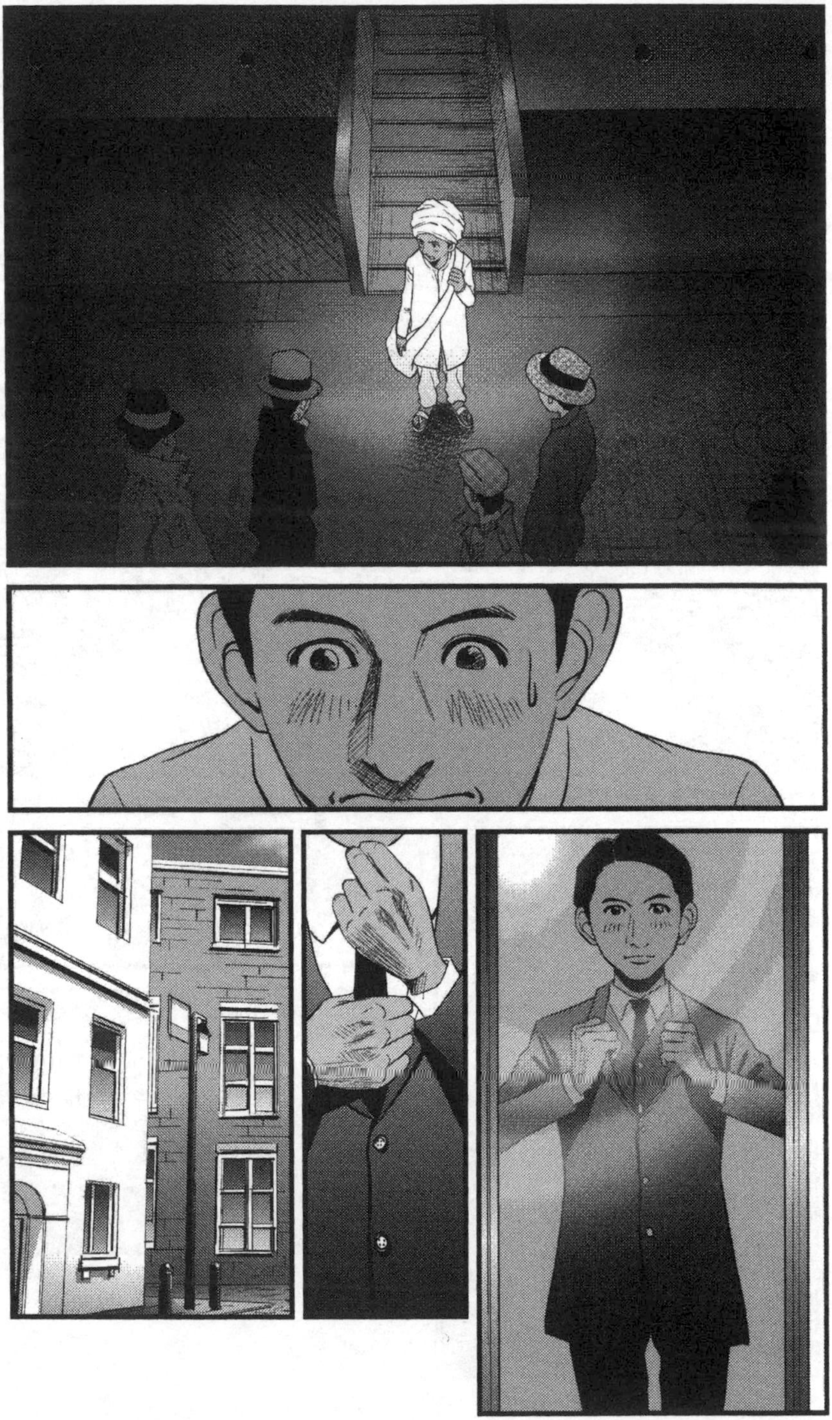

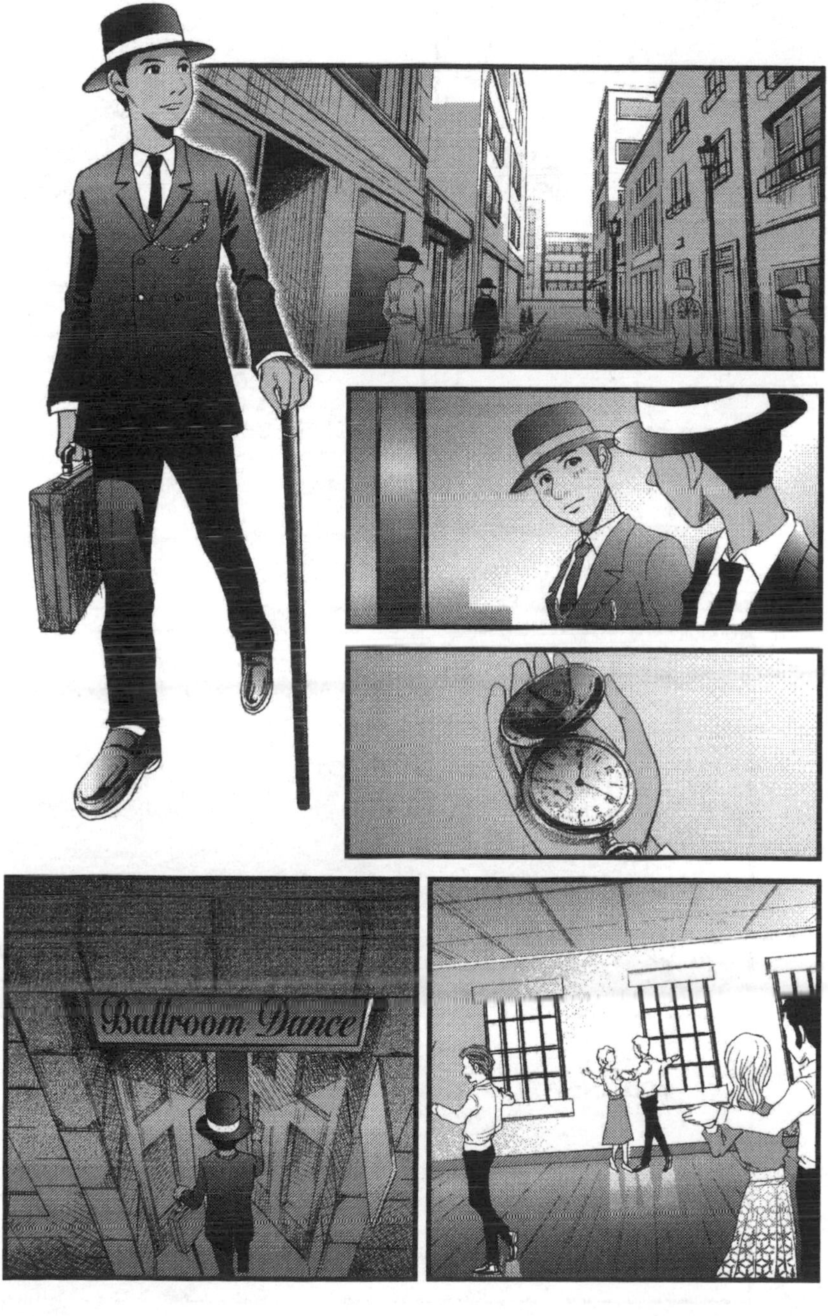
Ballroom Dance

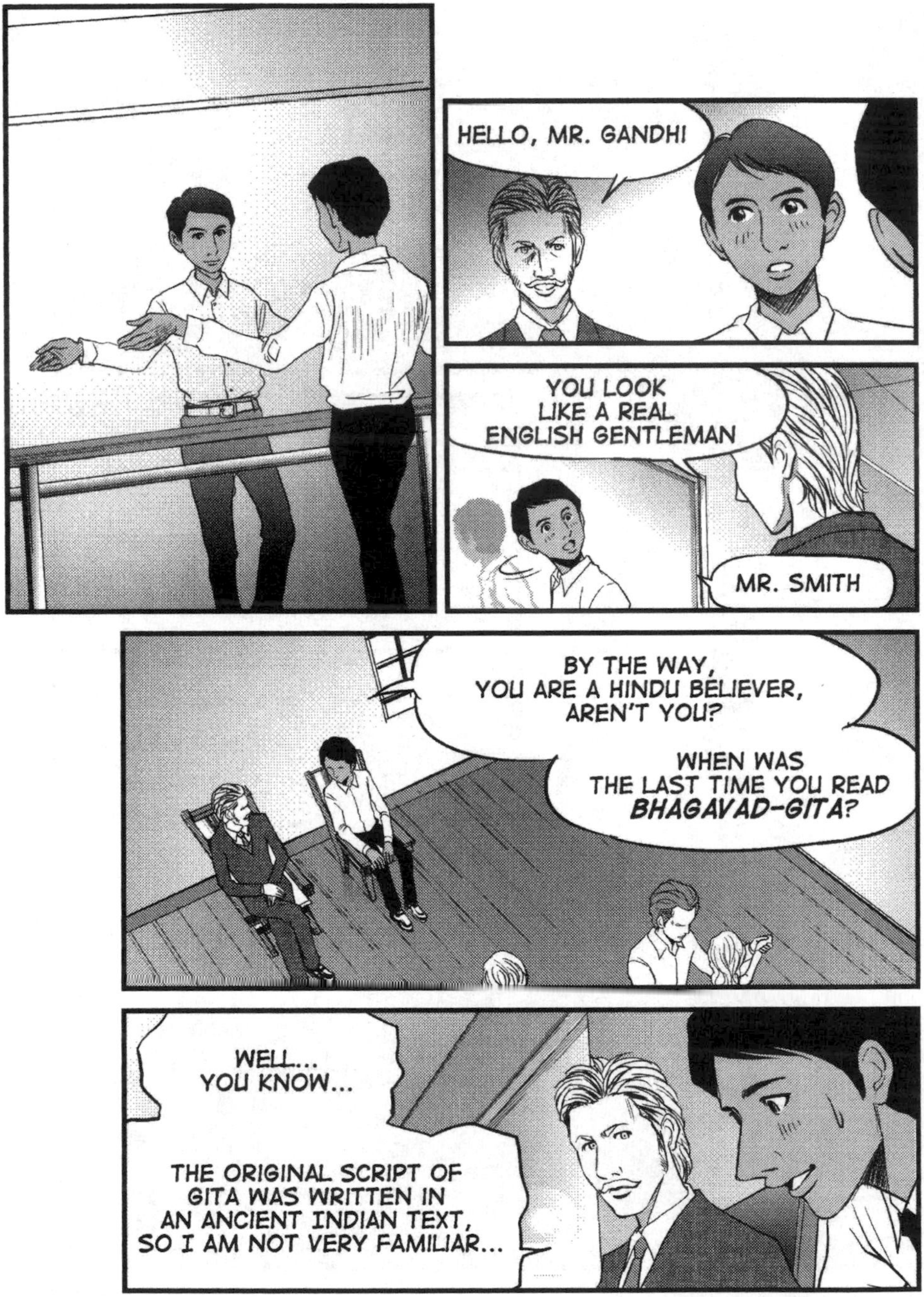
HELLO, MR. GANDHI
YOU LOOK LIKE A REAL ENGLISH GENTLEMAN
MR. SMITH
BY THE WAY, YOU ARE A HINDU BELIEVER, AREN'T YOU?
WHEN WAS THE LAST TIME YOU READ *BHAGAVAD-GITA*?
WELL... YOU KNOW...
THE ORIGINAL SCRIPT OF GITA WAS WRITTEN IN AN ANCIENT INDIAN TEXT, SO I AM NOT VERY FAMILIAR...

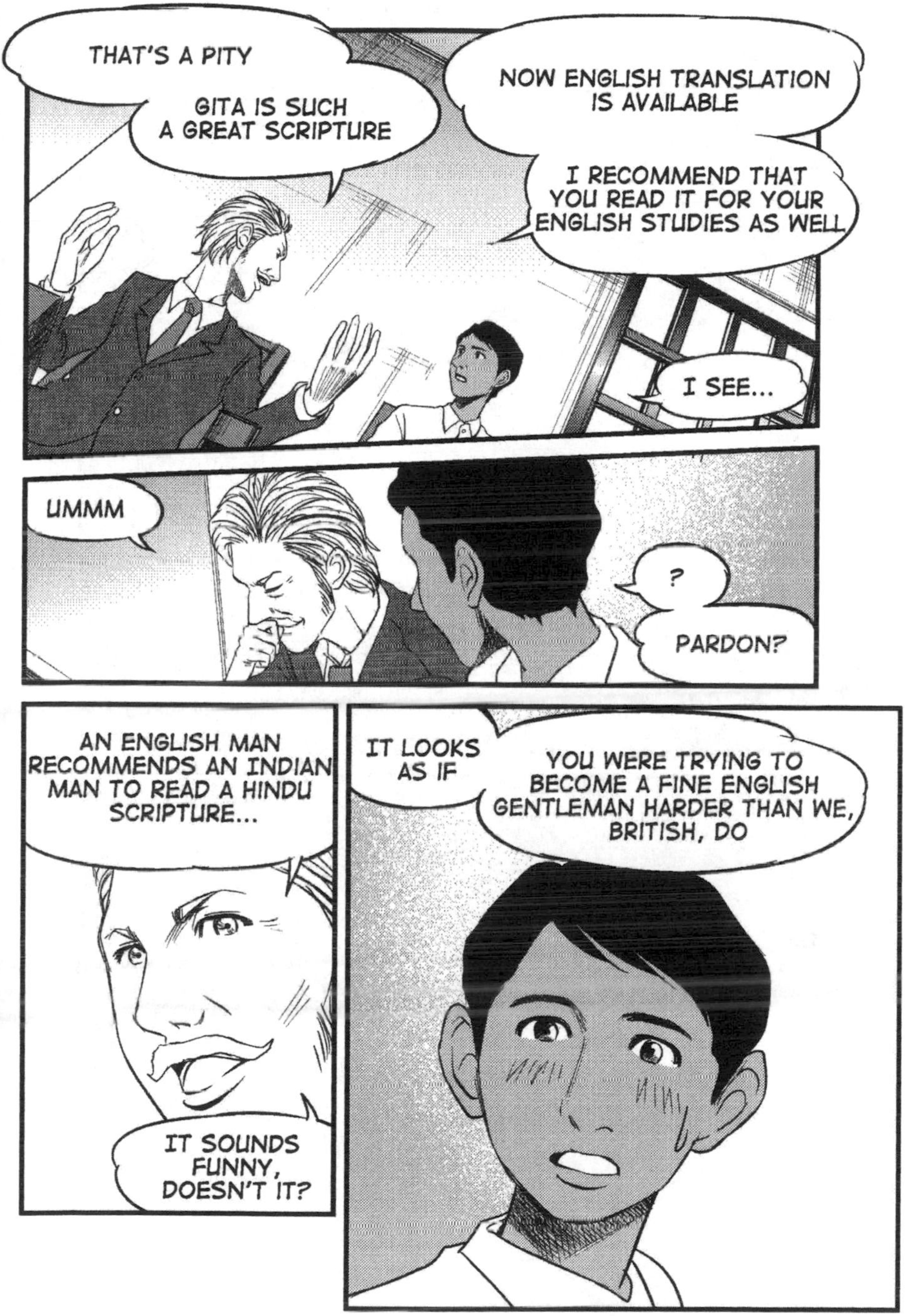
THAT'S A PITY
GITA IS SUCH A GREAT SCRIPTURE
NOW ENGLISH TRANSLATION IS AVAILABLE
I RECOMMEND THAT YOU READ IT FOR YOUR ENGLISH STUDIES AS WELL
I SEE...
UMMM
?
PARDON?
AN ENGLISH MAN RECOMMENDS AN INDIAN MAN TO READ A HINDU SCRIPTURE...
IT SOUNDS FUNNY, DOESN'T IT?
IT LOOKS AS IF
YOU WERE TRYING TO BECOME A FINE ENGLISH GENTLEMAN HARDER THAN WE, BRITISH, DO

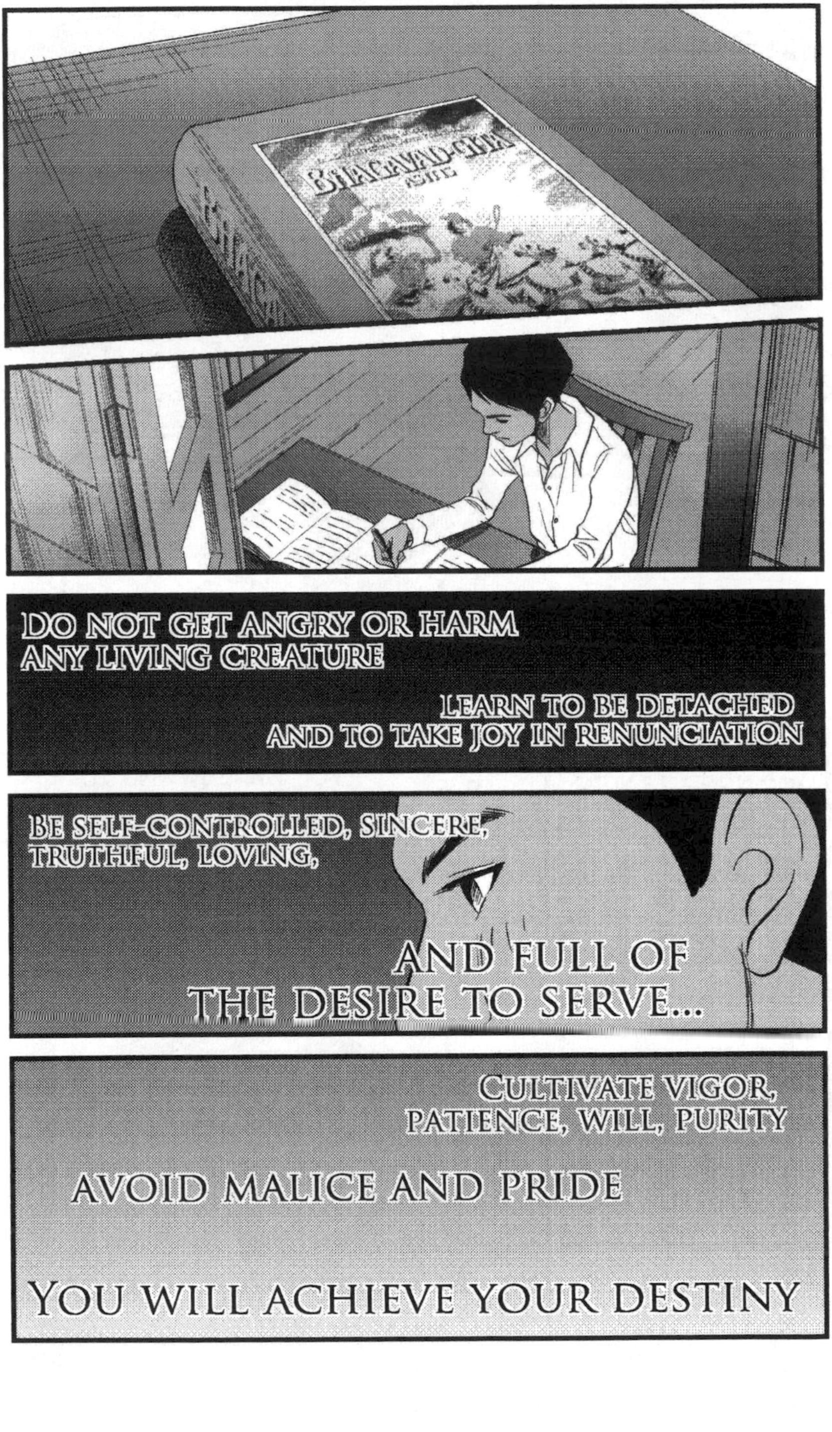
Bhagavad-Gita
DO NOT GET ANGRY OR HARM ANY LIVING CREATURE
LEARN TO BE DETACHED AND TO TAKE JOY IN RENUNCIATION
BE SELF-CONTROLLED, SINCERE, TRUTHFUL, LOVING,
AND FULL OF THE DESIRE TO SERVE...
CULTIVATE VIGOR, PATIENCE, WILL, PURITY
AVOID MALICE AND PRIDE
YOU WILL ACHIEVE YOUR DESTINY

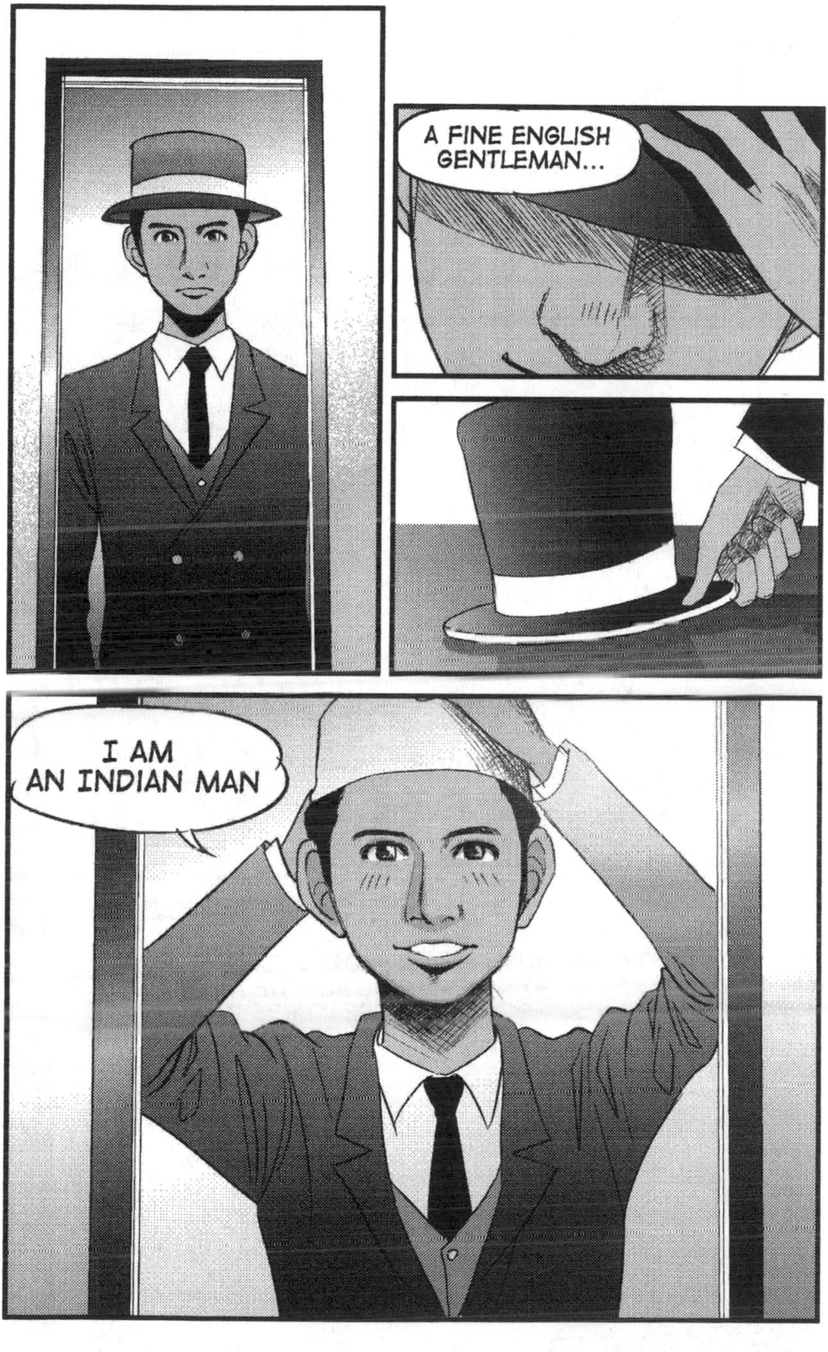
A FINE ENGLISH GENTLEMAN...
I AM AN INDIAN MAN

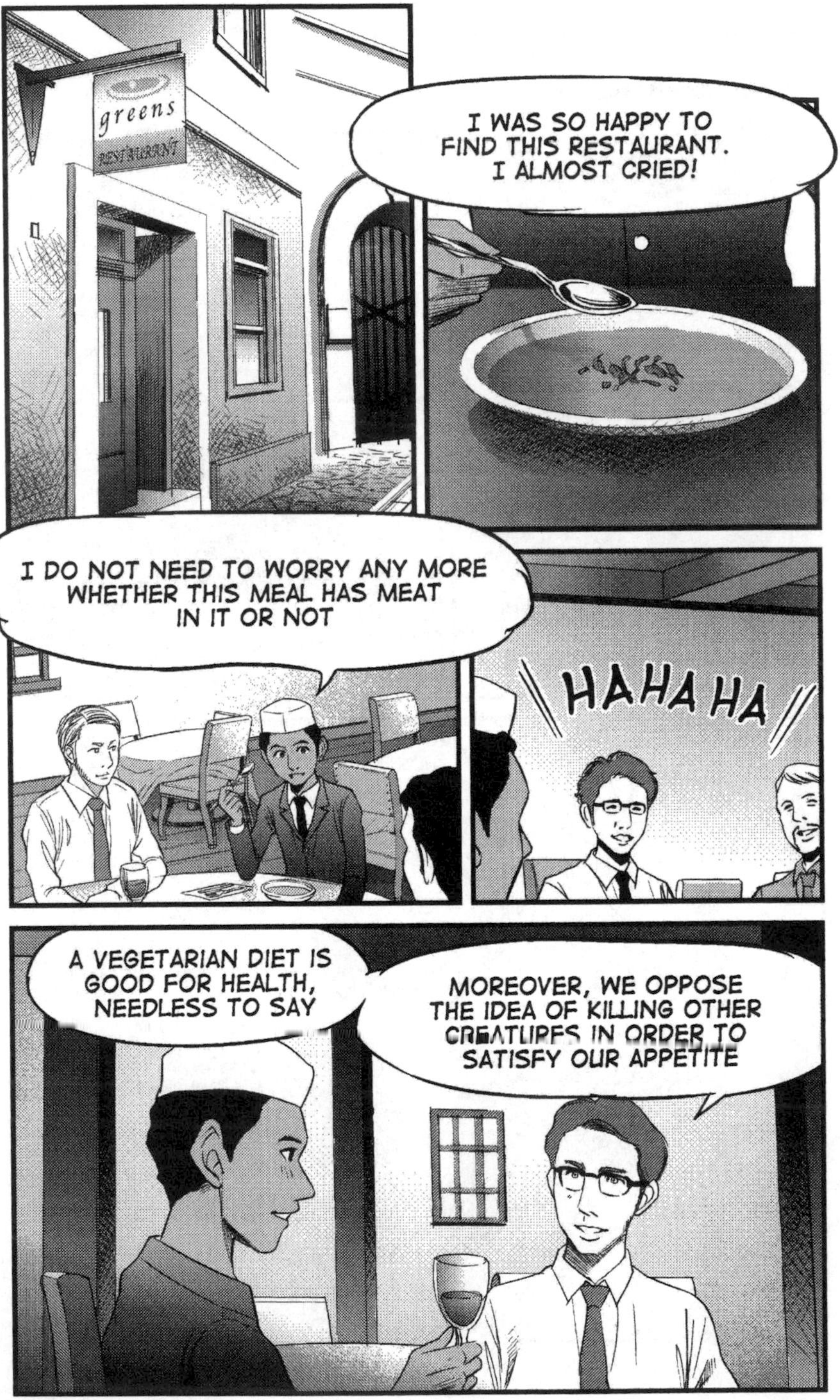
greens
RESTAURANT
I WAS SO HAPPY TO FIND THIS RESTAURANT. I ALMOST CRIED!
I DO NOT NEED TO WORRY ANY MORE WHETHER THIS MEAL HAS MEAT IN IT OR NOT
HAHA HA
A VEGETARIAN DIET IS GOOD FOR HEALTH, NEEDLESS TO SAY
MOREOVER, WE OPPOSE THE IDEA OF KILLING OTHER CREATURES IN ORDER TO SATISFY OUR APPETITE

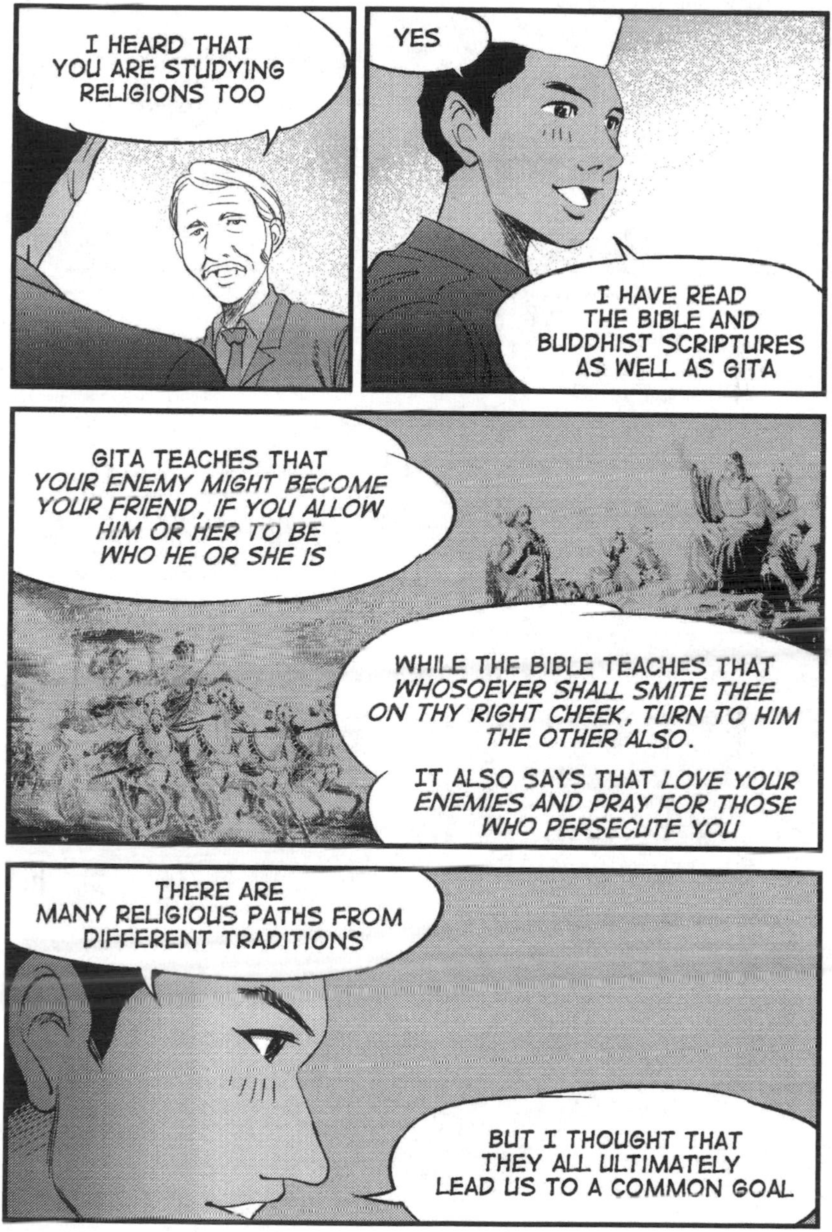
I HEARD THAT YOU ARE STUDYING RELIGIONS TOO
YES
I HAVE READ THE BIBLE AND BUDDHIST SCRIPTURES AS WELL AS GITA
GITA TEACHES THAT *YOUR ENEMY MIGHT BECOME YOUR FRIEND, IF YOU ALLOW HIM OR HER TO BE WHO HE OR SHE IS*
WHILE THE BIBLE TEACHES THAT *WHOSOEVER SHALL SMITE THEE ON THY RIGHT CHEEK, TURN TO HIM THE OTHER ALSO.*
IT ALSO SAYS THAT *LOVE YOUR ENEMIES AND PRAY FOR THOSE WHO PERSECUTE YOU*
THERE ARE MANY RELIGIOUS PATHS FROM DIFFERENT TRADITIONS
BUT I THOUGHT THAT THEY ALL ULTIMATELY LEAD US TO A COMMON GOAL

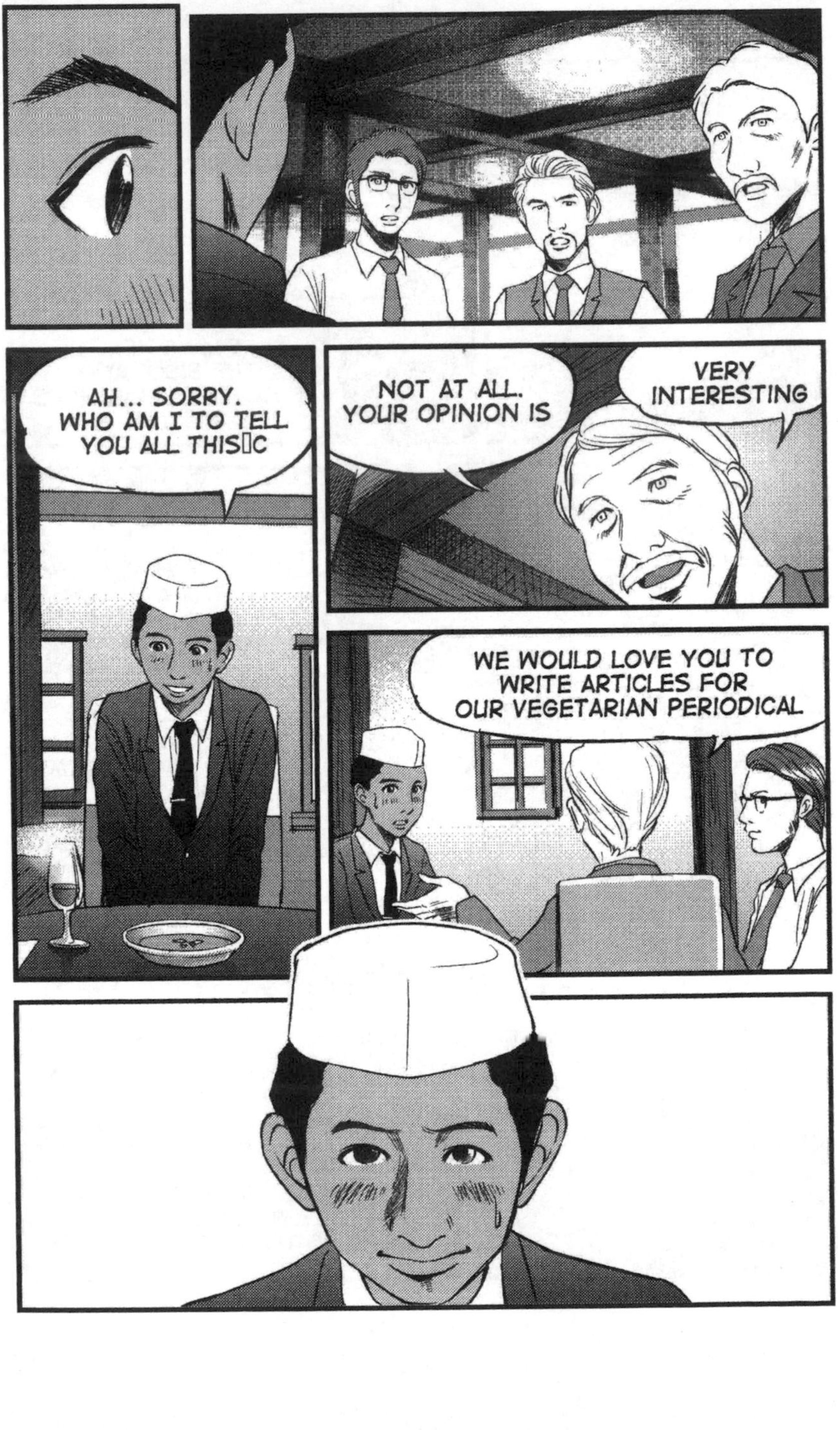
AH... SORRY. WHO AM I TO TELL YOU ALL THIS□C
NOT AT ALL. YOUR OPINION IS
VERY INTERESTING
WE WOULD LOVE YOU TO WRITE ARTICLES FOR OUR VEGETARIAN PERIODICAL

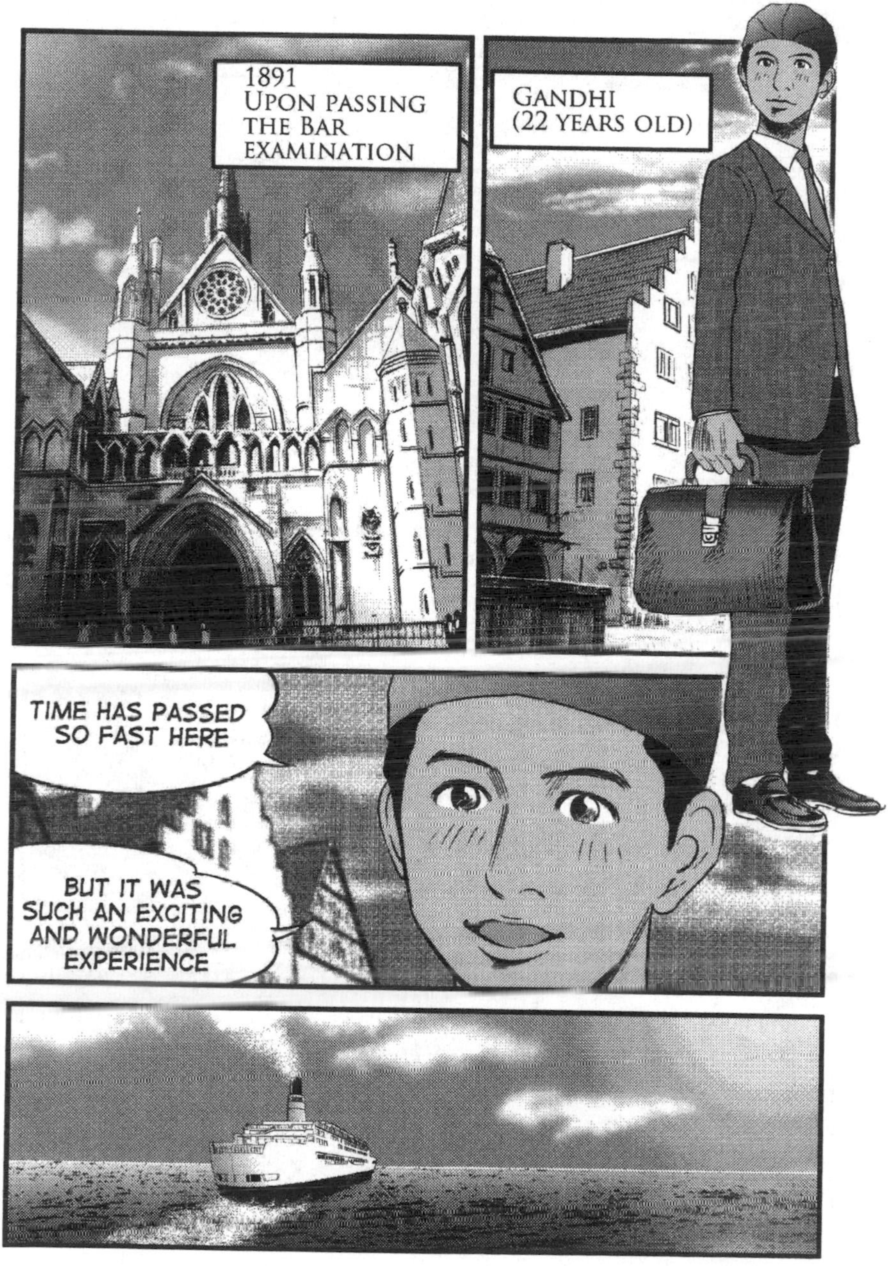
1891
UPON PASSING THE BAR EXAMINATION
GANDHI (22 YEARS OLD)
TIME HAS PASSED SO FAST HERE
BUT IT WAS SUCH AN EXCITING AND WONDERFUL EXPERIENCE

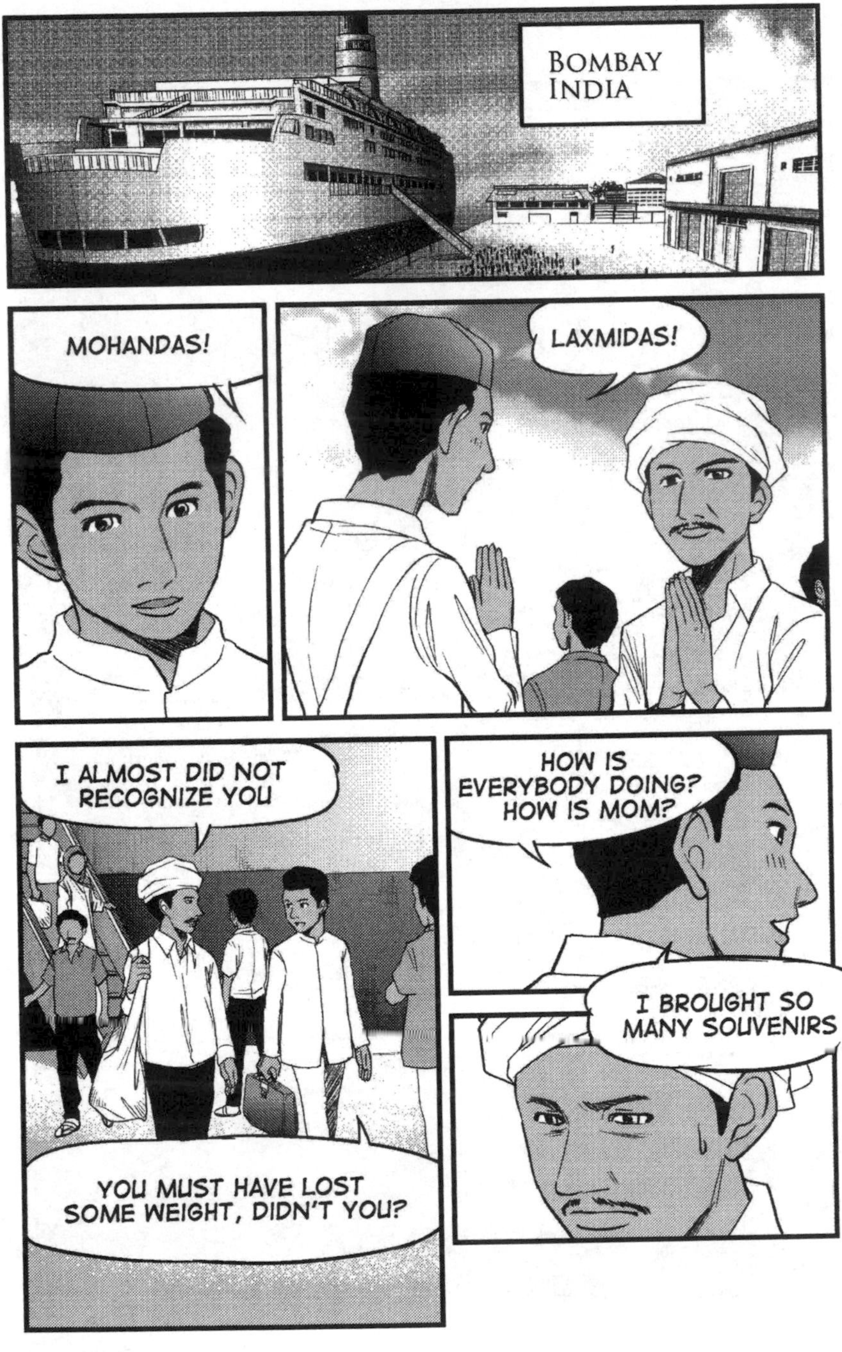
BOMBAY INDIA
MOHANDAS!
LAXMIDAS!
I ALMOST DID NOT RECOGNIZE YOU
YOU MUST HAVE LOST SOME WEIGHT, DIDN'T YOU?
HOW IS EVERYBODY DOING? HOW IS MOM?
I BROUGHT SO MANY SOUVENIRS

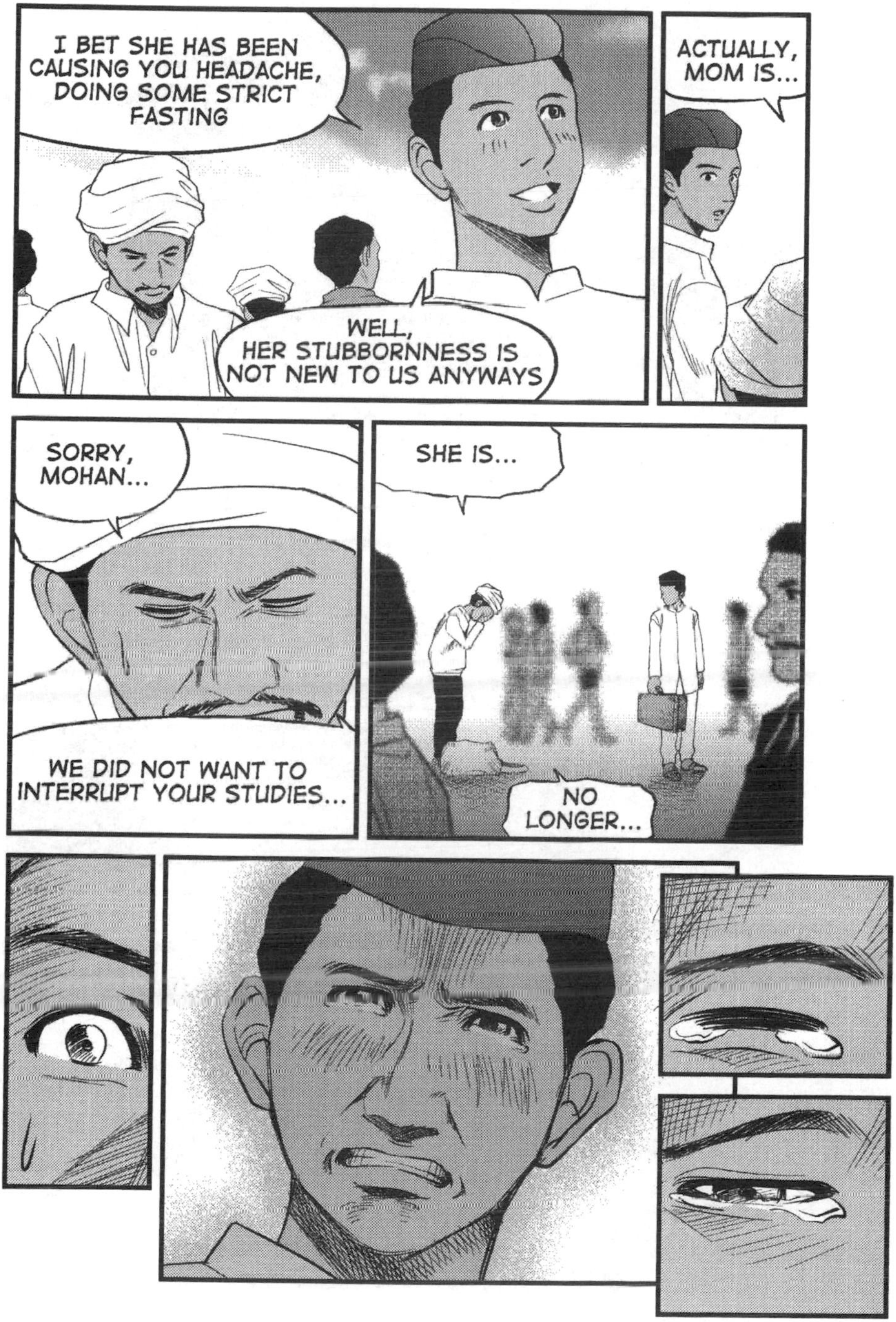

I BET SHE HAS BEEN CAUSING YOU HEADACHE, DOING SOME STRICT FASTING
WELL, HER STUBBORNNESS IS NOT NEW TO US ANYWAYS
ACTUALLY, MOM IS...
SORRY, MOHAN...
WE DID NOT WANT TO INTERRUPT YOUR STUDIES...
SHE IS...
NO LONGER...

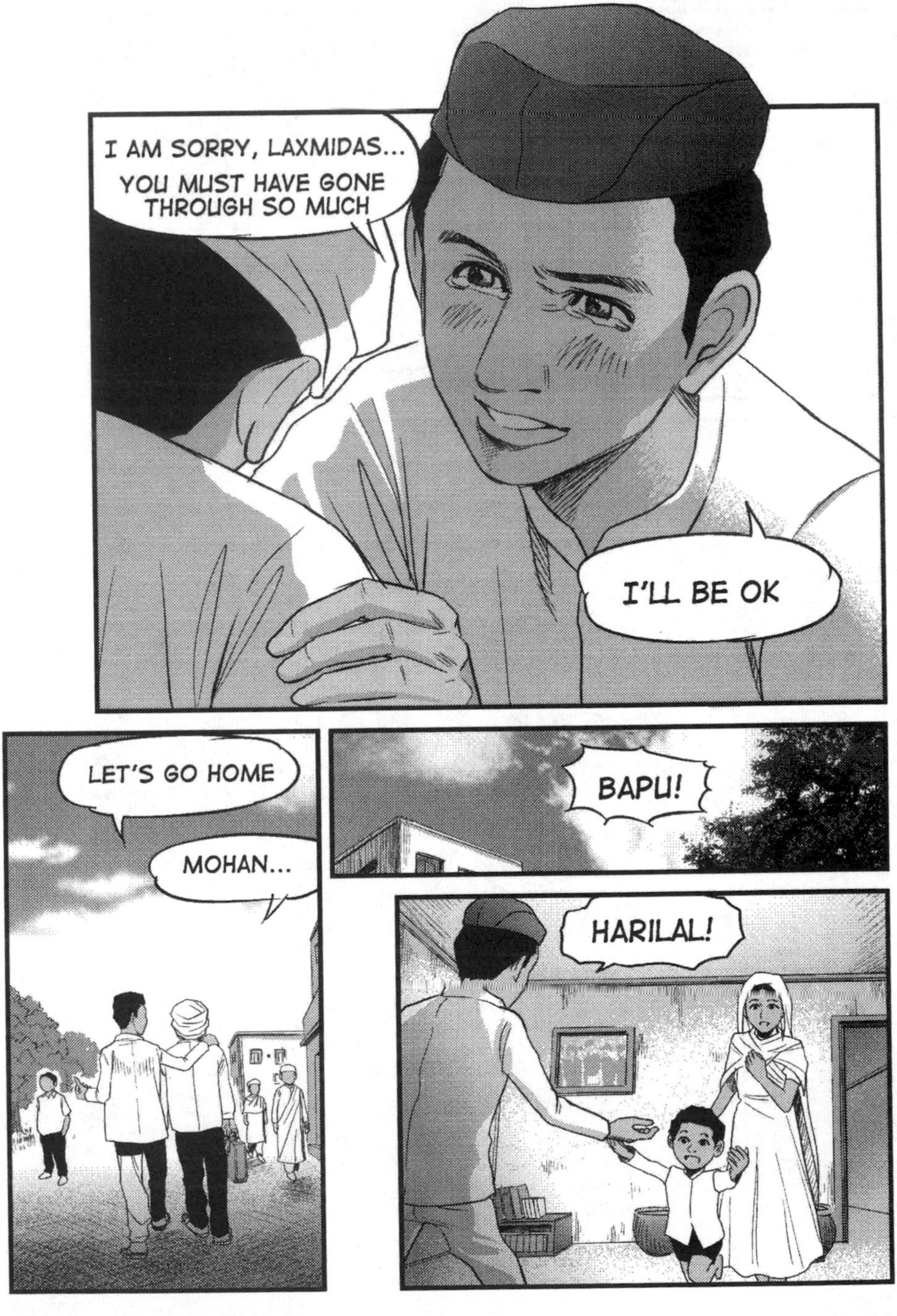
I AM SORRY, LAXMIDAS... YOU MUST HAVE GONE THROUGH SO MUCH
I'LL BE OK
LET'S GO HOME
MOHAN...
BAPU!
HARILAL!

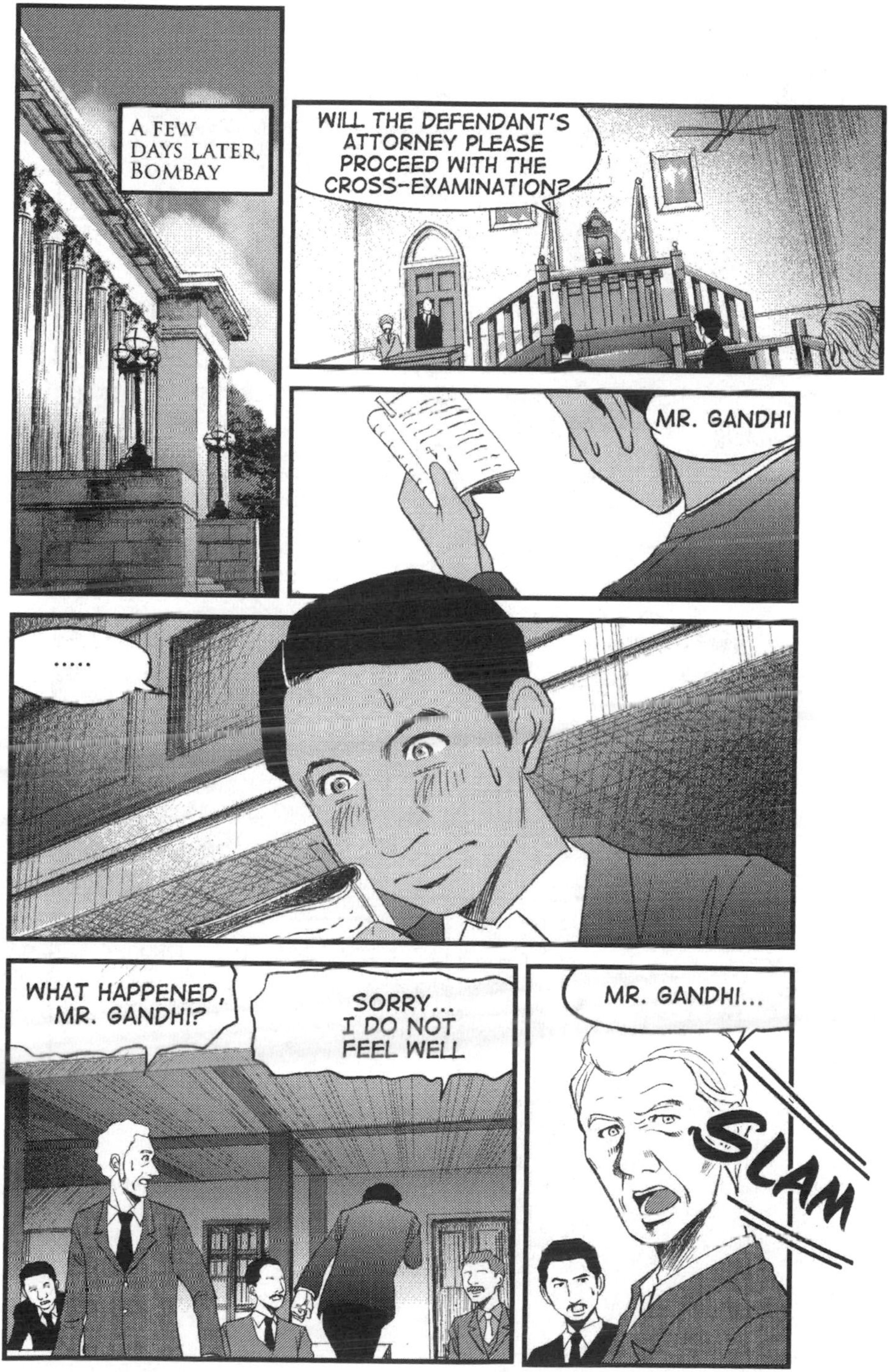
A FEW DAYS LATER, BOMBAY
WILL THE DEFENDANT'S ATTORNEY PLEASE PROCEED WITH THE CROSS-EXAMINATION?
MR. GANDHI
.....
WHAT HAPPENED, MR. GANDHI?
SORRY... I DO NOT FEEL WELL
MR. GANDHI...
SLAM

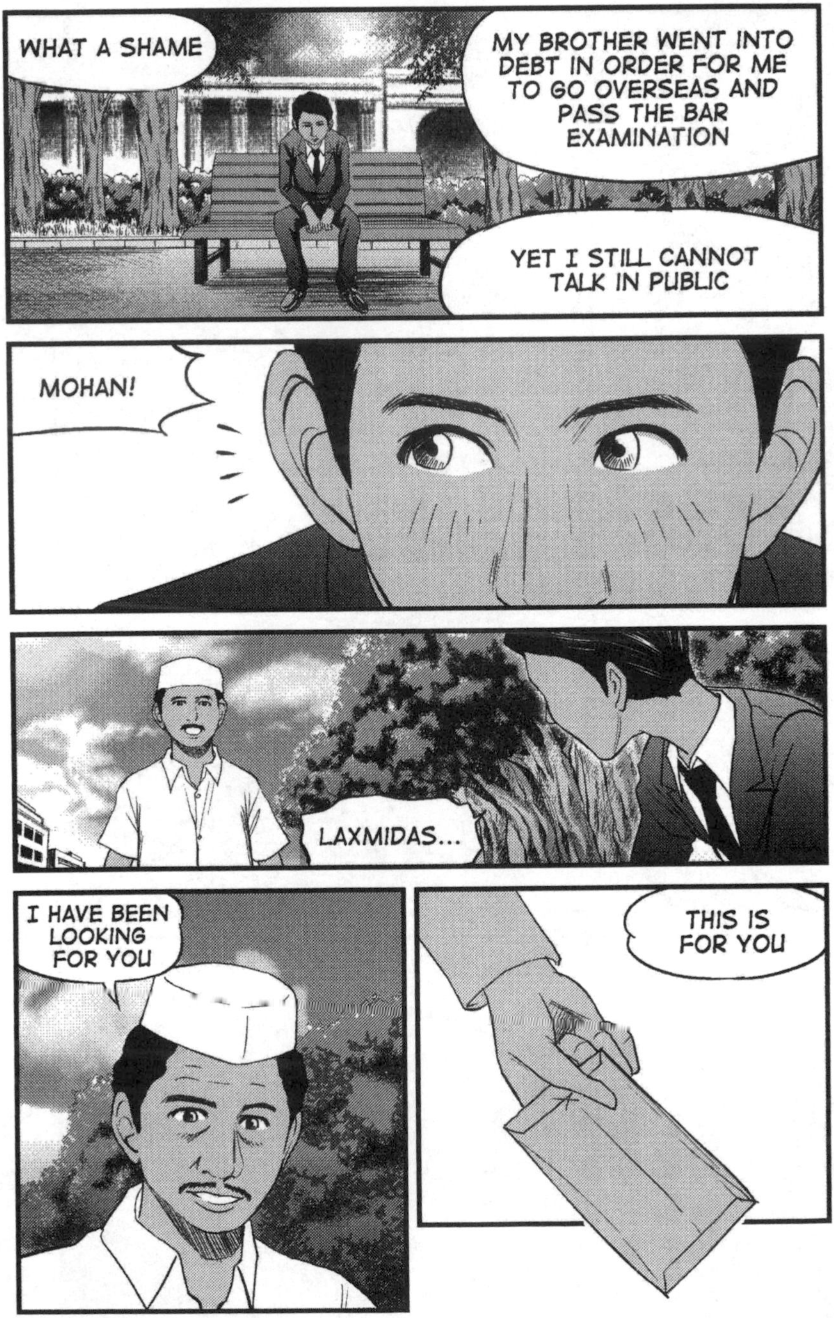
WHAT A SHAME
MY BROTHER WENT INTO DEBT IN ORDER FOR ME TO GO OVERSEAS AND PASS THE BAR EXAMINATION
YET I STILL CANNOT TALK IN PUBLIC
MOHAN!
LAXMIDAS...
I HAVE BEEN LOOKING FOR YOU
THIS IS FOR YOU

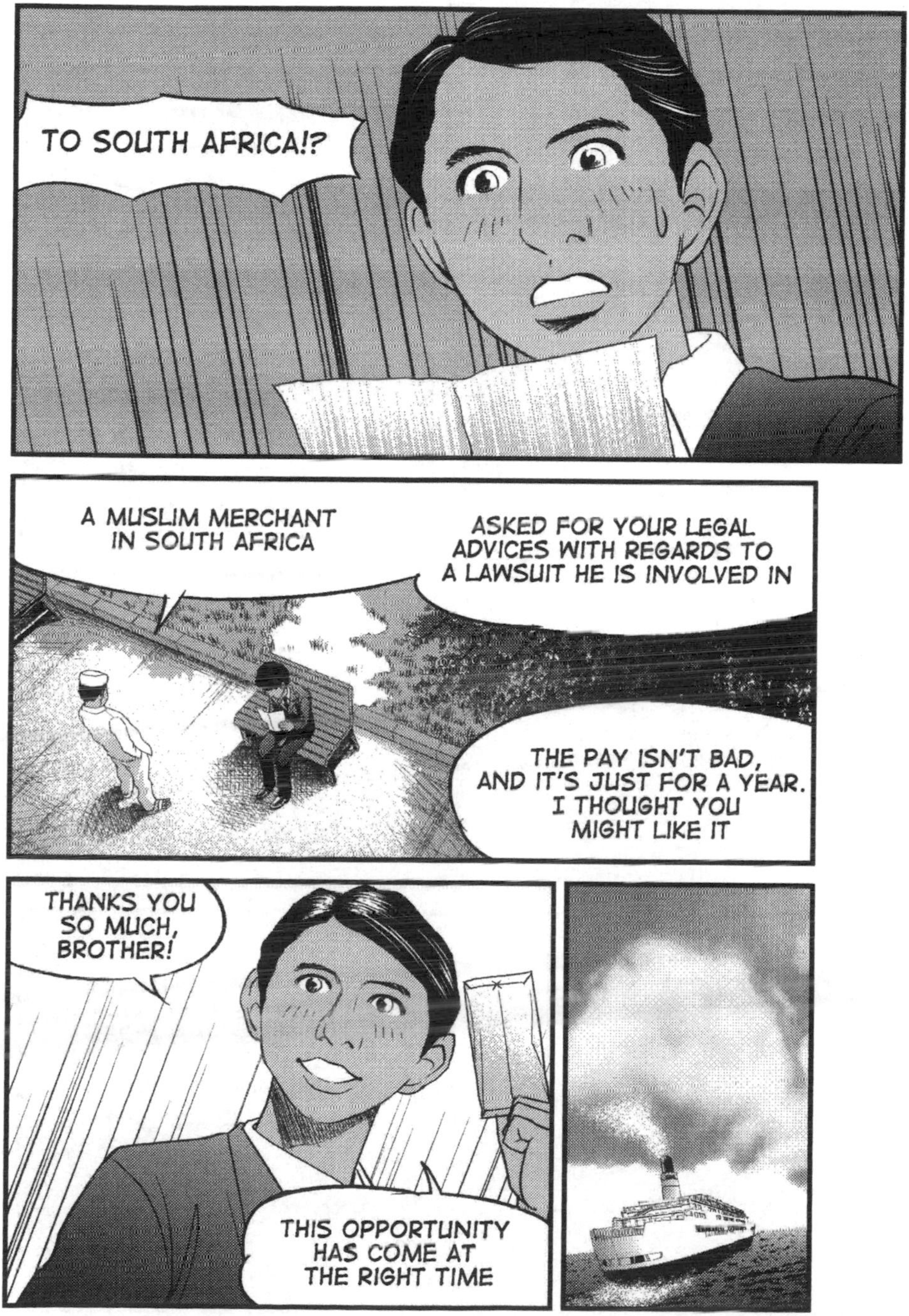
TO SOUTH AFRICA!?
A MUSLIM MERCHANT IN SOUTH AFRICA
ASKED FOR YOUR LEGAL ADVICES WITH REGARDS TO A LAWSUIT HE IS INVOLVED IN
THE PAY ISN'T BAD, AND IT'S JUST FOR A YEAR. I THOUGHT YOU MIGHT LIKE IT
THANKS YOU SO MUCH, BROTHER!
THIS OPPORTUNITY HAS COME AT THE RIGHT TIME

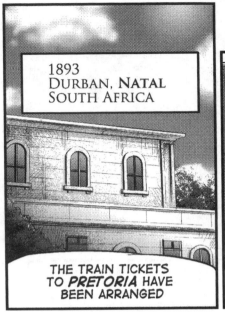

1893
DURBAN, **NATAL**
SOUTH AFRICA

THE TRAIN TICKETS TO *PRETORIA* HAVE BEEN ARRANGED

THANK YOU, MR. ABDULLA

I FEEL BAD TO SEND YOU OFF ALREADY. YOU JUST ARRIVED IN NATAL A WEEK AGO

NOT AT ALL. I REALLY APPRECIATE THE OPPORTUNITY

I HAVE TO REMIND YOU THAT YOU NEED TO BE VERY CAUTIOUS

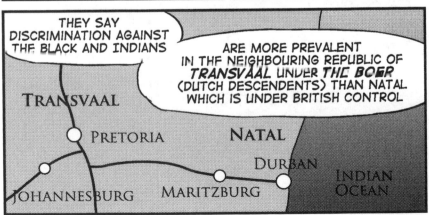

THEY SAY DISCRIMINATION AGAINST THE BLACK AND INDIANS

ARE MORE PREVALENT IN THE NEIGHBOURING REPUBLIC OF *TRANSVAAL* UNDER *THE BOER* (DUTCH DESCENDENTS) THAN NATAL WHICH IS UNDER BRITISH CONTROL

TRANSVAAL

PRETORIA

NATAL

JOHANNESBURG

MARITZBURG

DURBAN

INDIAN OCEAN

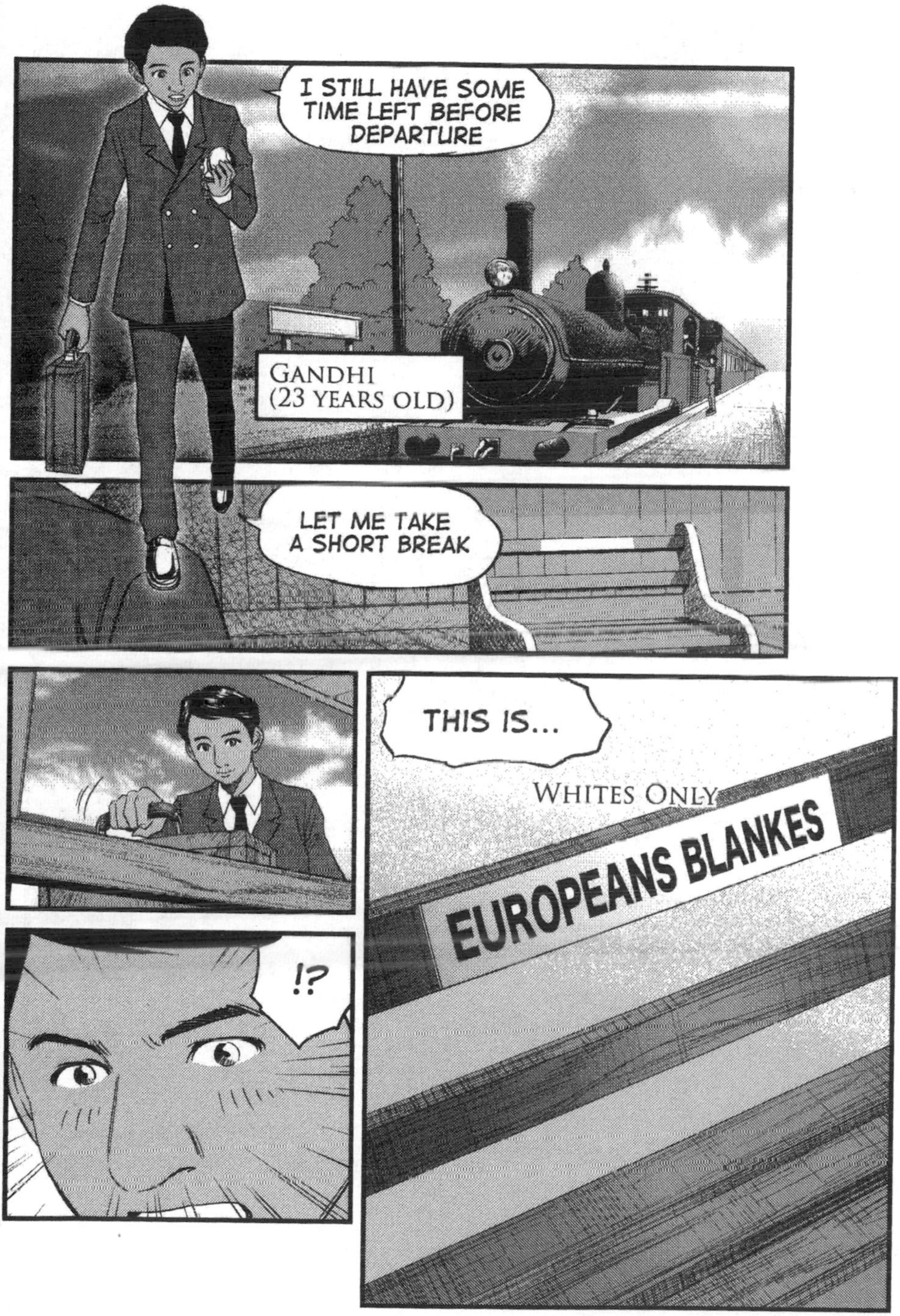
I STILL HAVE SOME TIME LEFT BEFORE DEPARTURE
GANDHI (23 YEARS OLD)
LET ME TAKE A SHORT BREAK
THIS IS...
WHITES ONLY
EUROPEANS BLANKES
!?

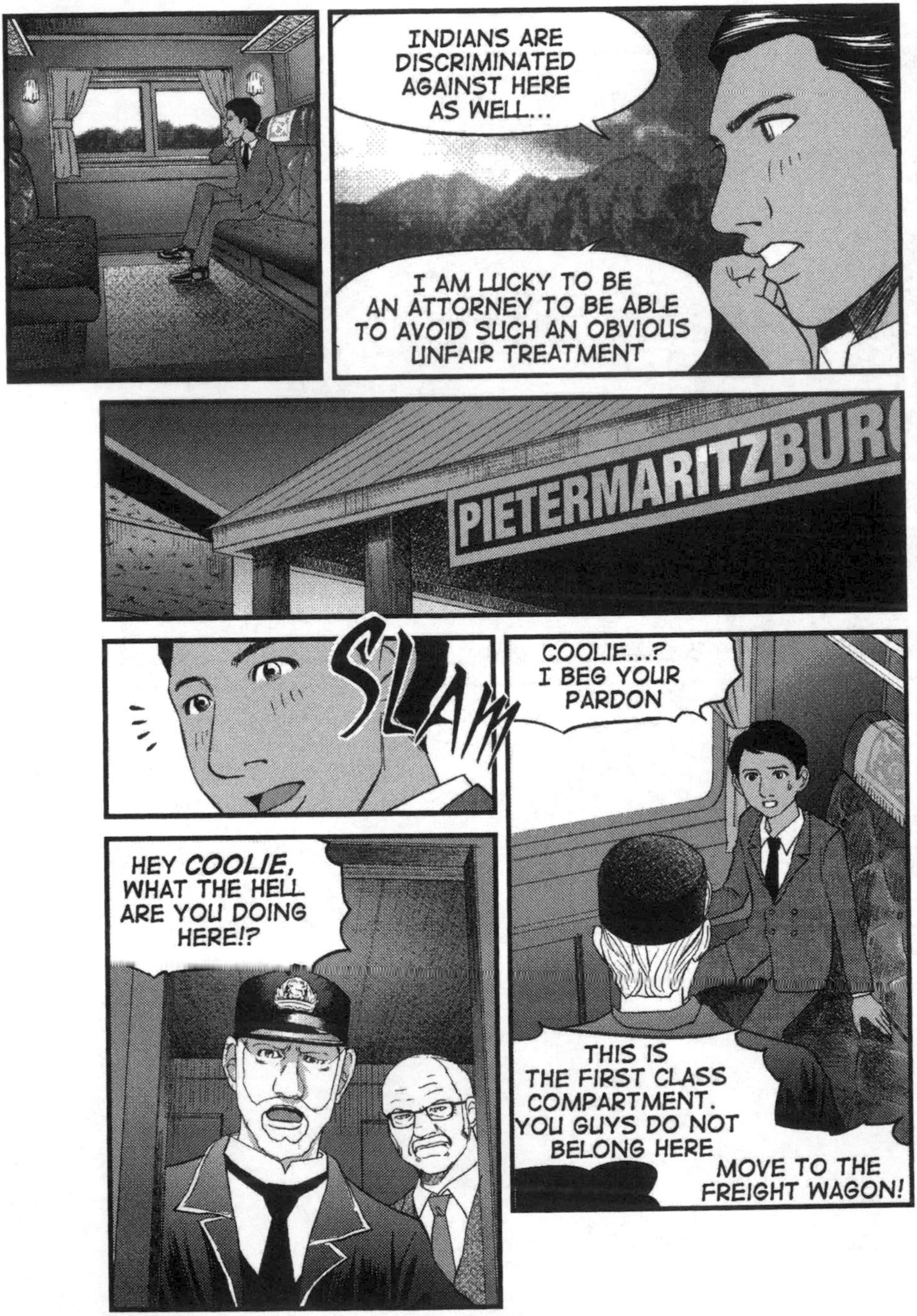

INDIANS ARE DISCRIMINATED AGAINST HERE AS WELL...
I AM LUCKY TO BE AN ATTORNEY TO BE ABLE TO AVOID SUCH AN OBVIOUS UNFAIR TREATMENT
PIETERMARITZBUR
SLAM
HEY *COOLIE*, WHAT THE HELL ARE YOU DOING HERE!?
COOLIE...? I BEG YOUR PARDON
THIS IS THE FIRST CLASS COMPARTMENT. YOU GUYS DO NOT BELONG HERE
MOVE TO THE FREIGHT WAGON!

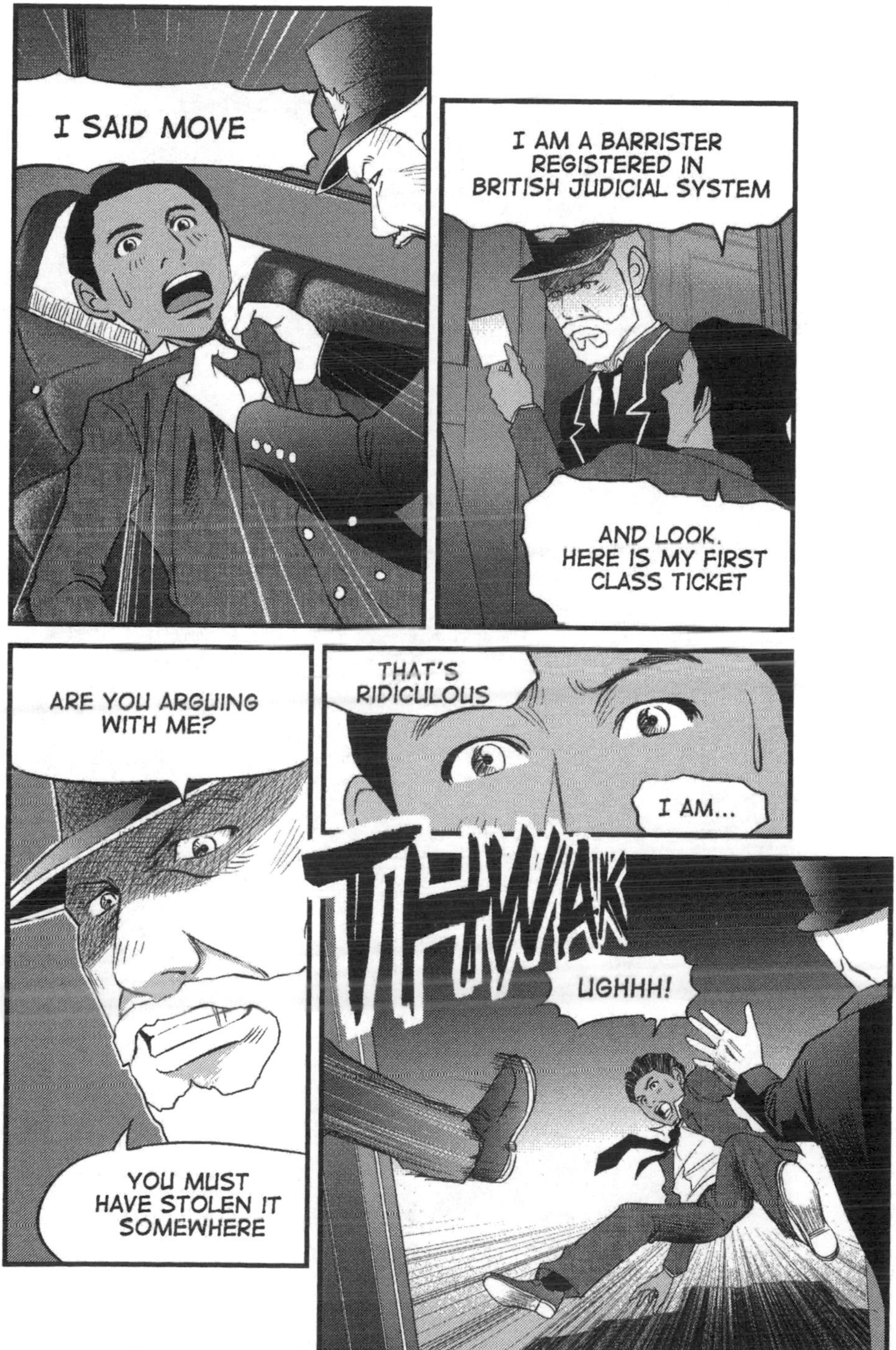
I SAID MOVE
I AM A BARRISTER REGISTERED IN BRITISH JUDICIAL SYSTEM
AND LOOK. HERE IS MY FIRST CLASS TICKET
ARE YOU ARGUING WITH ME?
THAT'S RIDICULOUS
I AM...
YOU MUST HAVE STOLEN IT SOMEWHERE
THWAK
UGHHH!

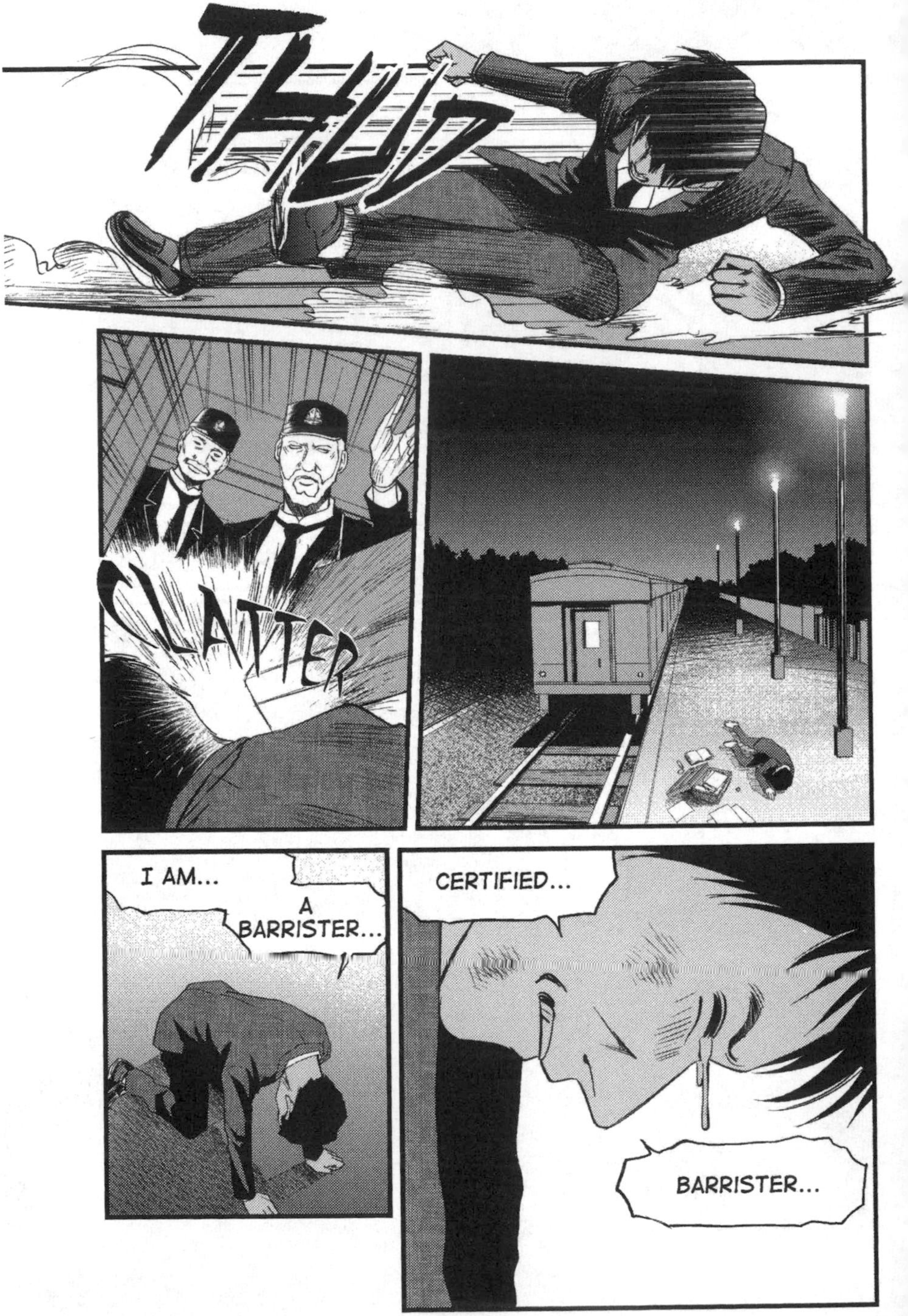
THUD
CLATTER
I AM...
A BARRISTER...
CERTIFIED...
BARRISTER...

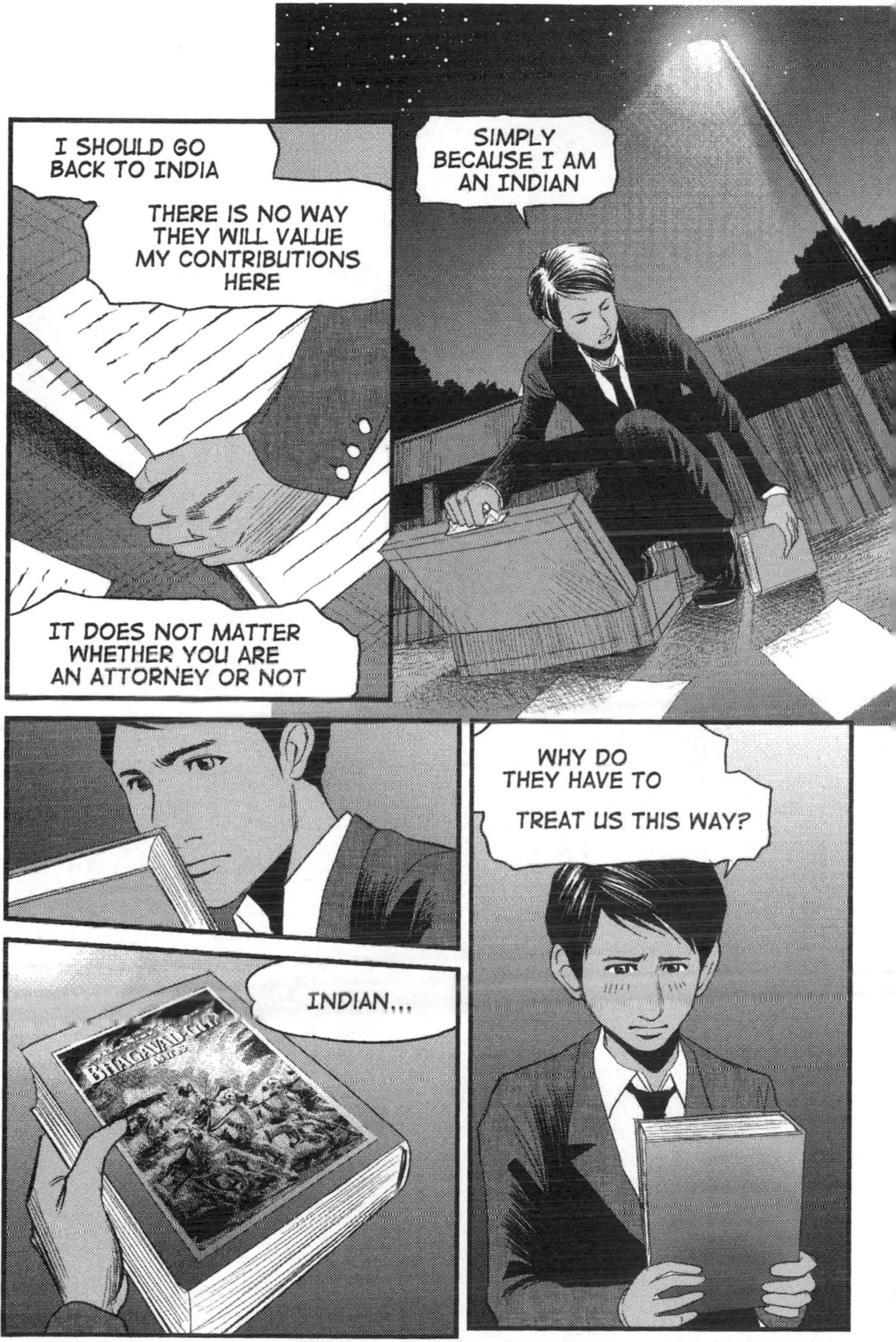
I SHOULD GO BACK TO INDIA
THERE IS NO WAY THEY WILL VALUE MY CONTRIBUTIONS HERE
IT DOES NOT MATTER WHETHER YOU ARE AN ATTORNEY OR NOT
SIMPLY BECAUSE I AM AN INDIAN
WHY DO THEY HAVE TO TREAT US THIS WAY?
INDIAN...
BHAGAVAD GITA

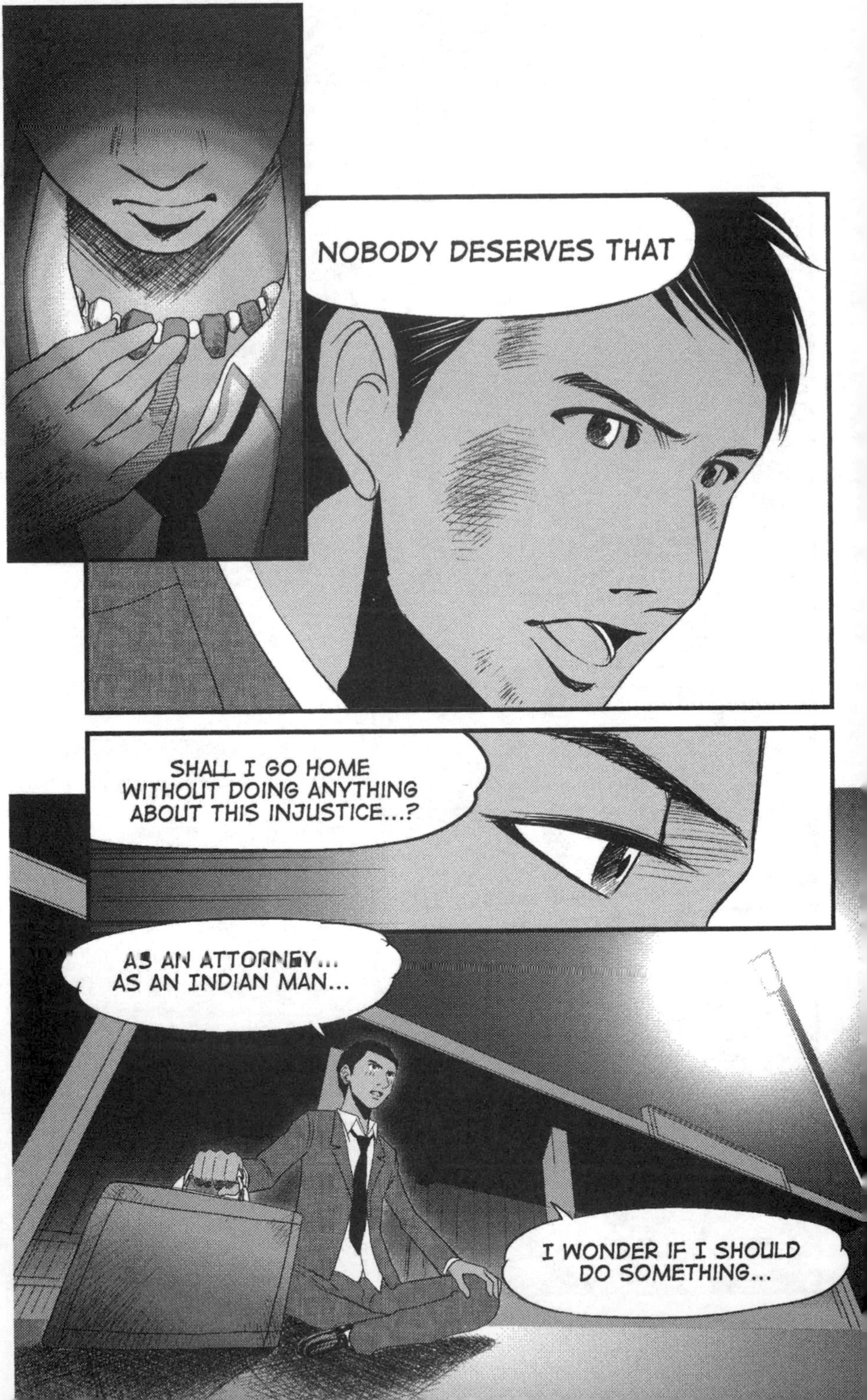
NOBODY DESERVES THAT
SHALL I GO HOME WITHOUT DOING ANYTHING ABOUT THIS INJUSTICE...?
AS AN ATTORNEY... AS AN INDIAN MAN...
I WONDER IF I SHOULD DO SOMETHING...

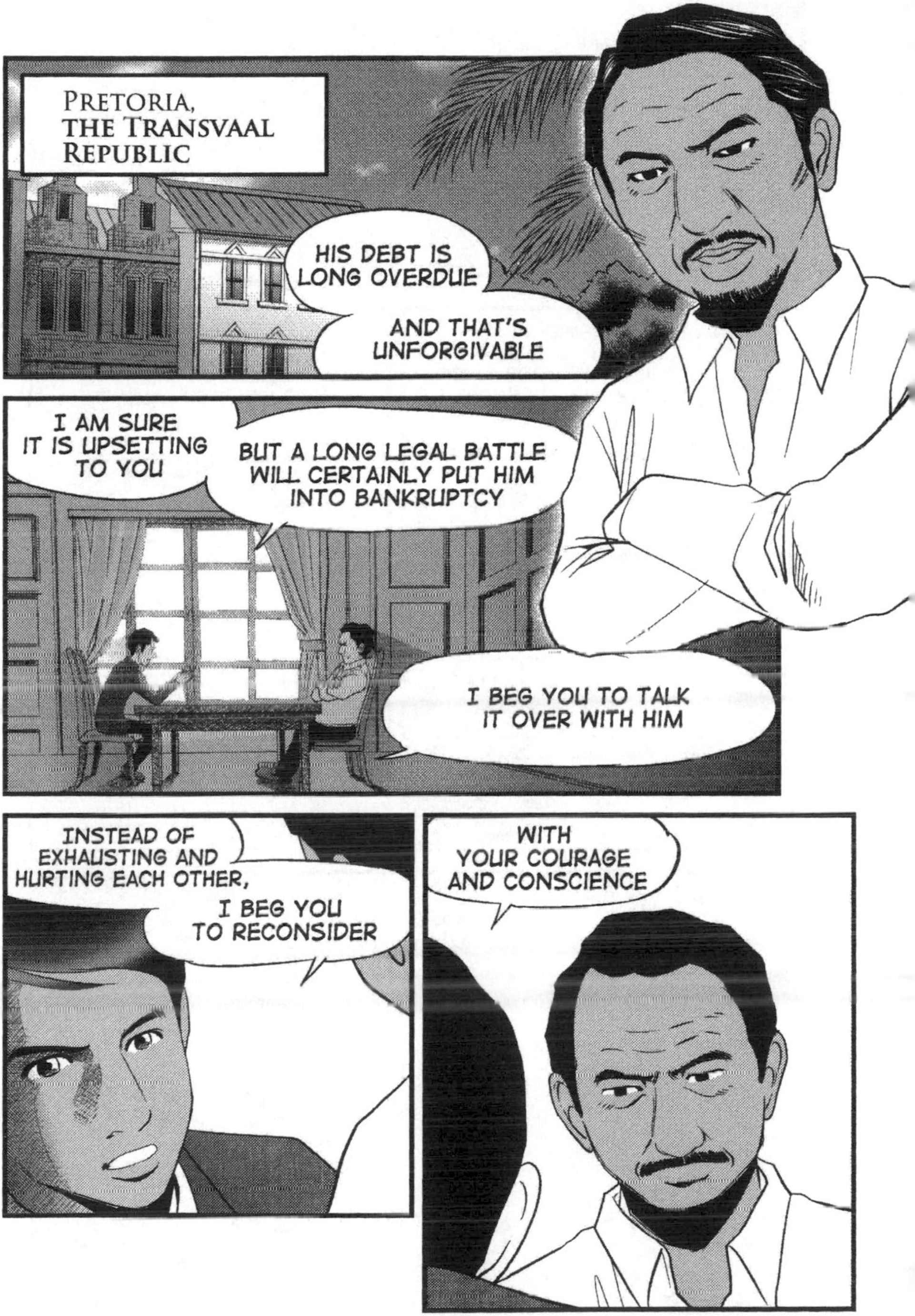
PRETORIA, THE TRANSVAAL REPUBLIC
HIS DEBT IS LONG OVERDUE
AND THAT'S UNFORGIVABLE
I AM SURE IT IS UPSETTING TO YOU
BUT A LONG LEGAL BATTLE WILL CERTAINLY PUT HIM INTO BANKRUPTCY
I BEG YOU TO TALK IT OVER WITH HIM
INSTEAD OF EXHAUSTING AND HURTING EACH OTHER,
I BEG YOU TO RECONSIDER
WITH YOUR COURAGE AND CONSCIENCE

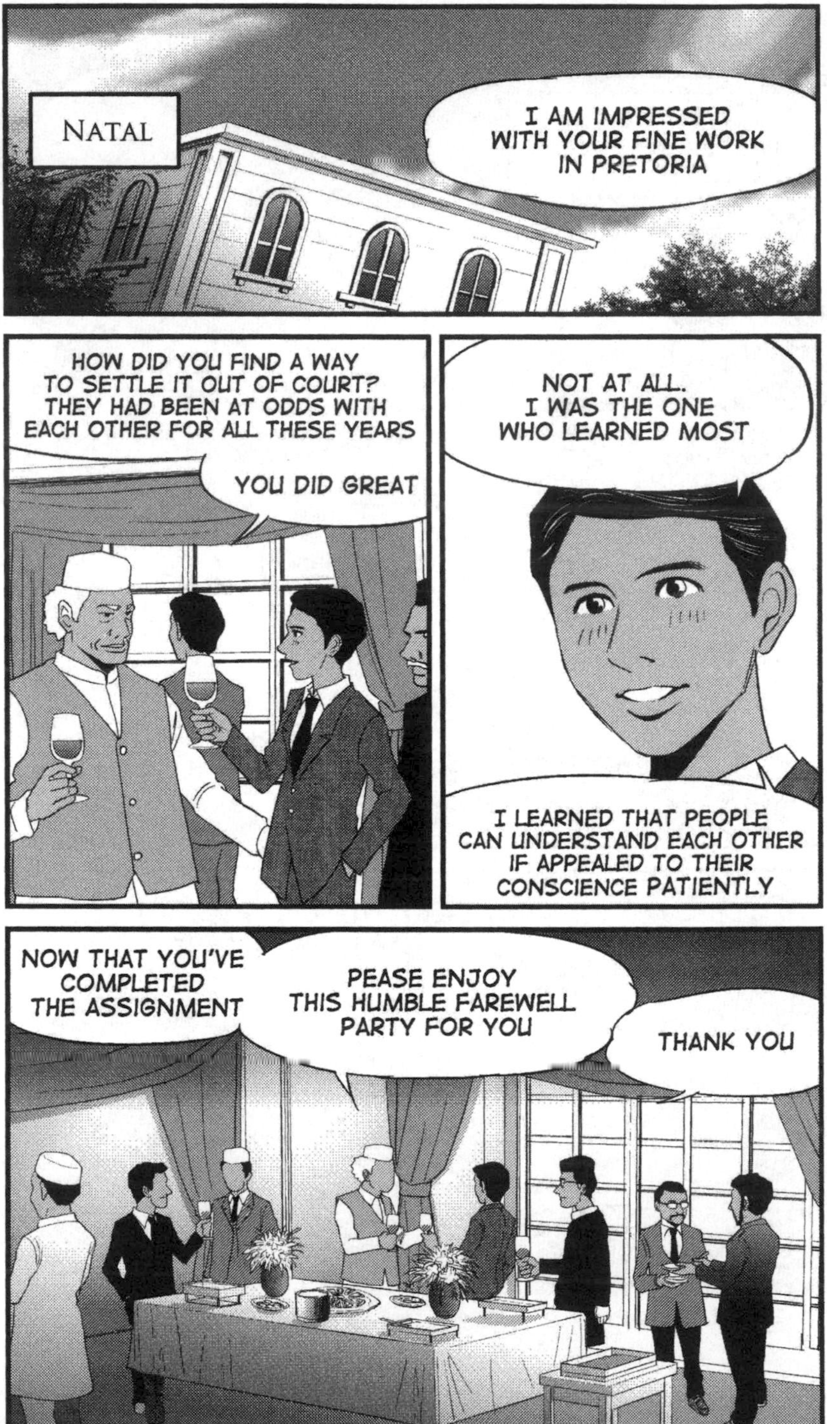
NATAL
I AM IMPRESSED WITH YOUR FINE WORK IN PRETORIA
HOW DID YOU FIND A WAY TO SETTLE IT OUT OF COURT? THEY HAD BEEN AT ODDS WITH EACH OTHER FOR ALL THESE YEARS
YOU DID GREAT
NOT AT ALL. I WAS THE ONE WHO LEARNED MOST
I LEARNED THAT PEOPLE CAN UNDERSTAND EACH OTHER IF APPEALED TO THEIR CONSCIENCE PATIENTLY
NOW THAT YOU'VE COMPLETED THE ASSIGNMENT
PEASE ENJOY THIS HUMBLE FAREWELL PARTY FOR YOU
THANK YOU

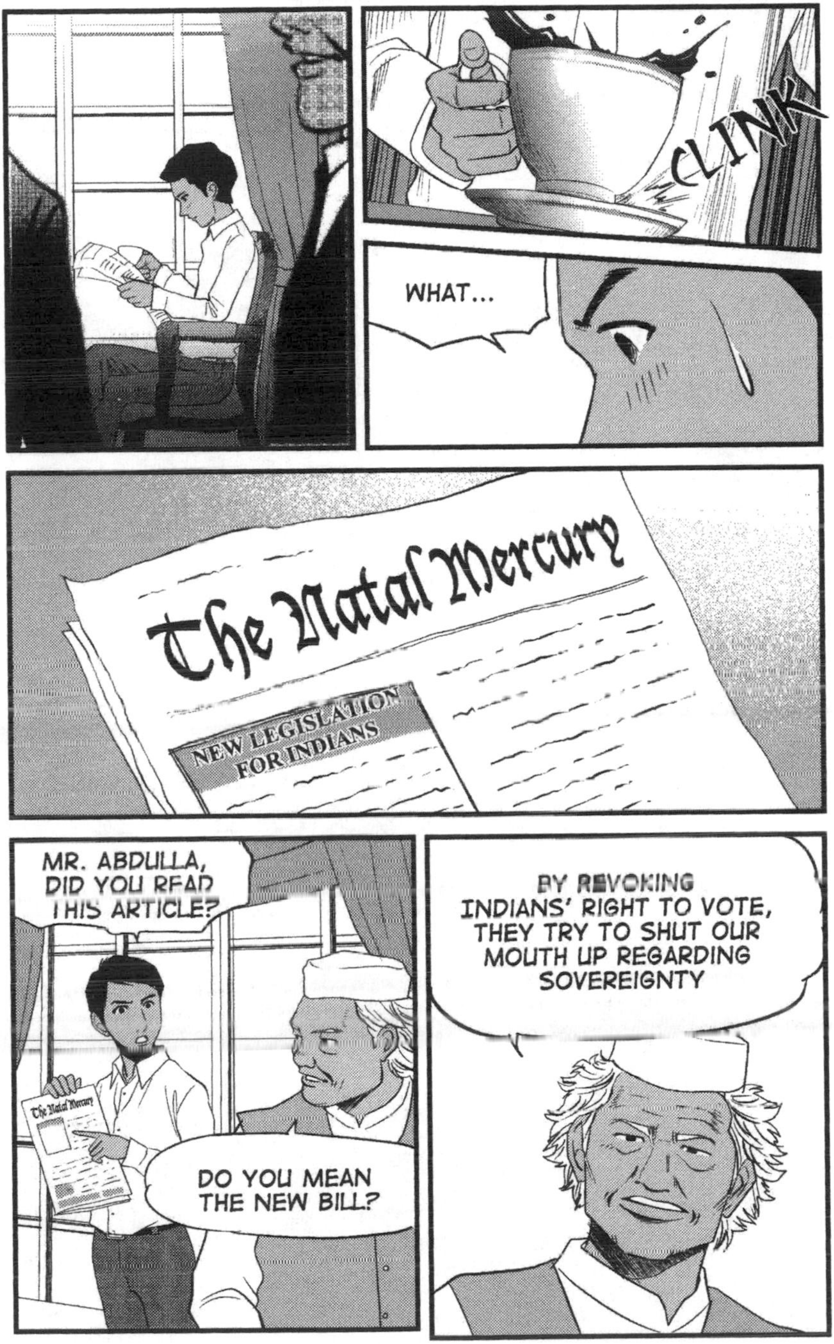
CLINK
WHAT...
The Natal Mercury
NEW LEGISLATION FOR INDIANS
MR. ABDULLA, DID YOU READ THIS ARTICLE?
DO YOU MEAN THE NEW BILL?
BY REVOKING INDIANS' RIGHT TO VOTE, THEY TRY TO SHUT OUR MOUTH UP REGARDING SOVEREIGNTY

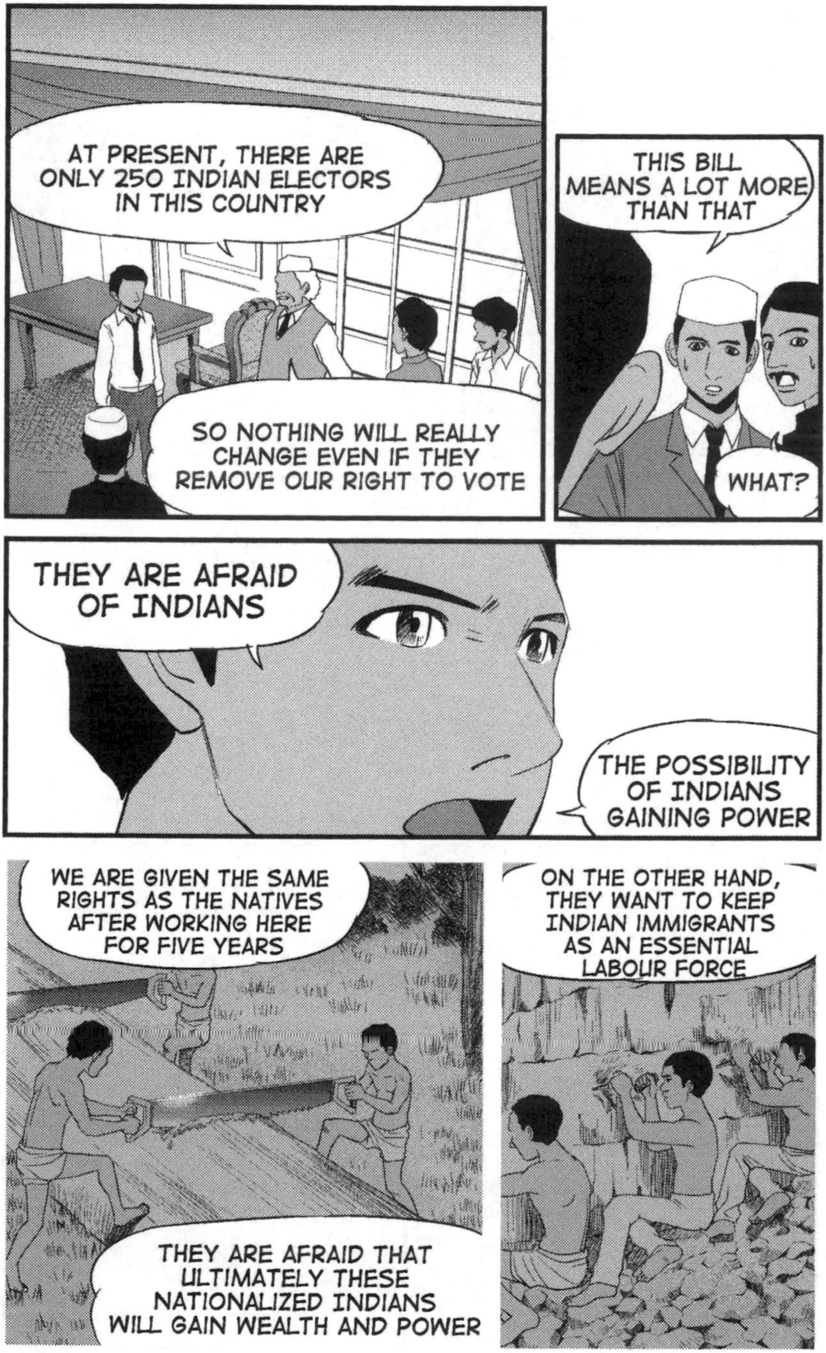
AT PRESENT, THERE ARE ONLY 250 INDIAN ELECTORS IN THIS COUNTRY
SO NOTHING WILL REALLY CHANGE EVEN IF THEY REMOVE OUR RIGHT TO VOTE
THIS BILL MEANS A LOT MORE THAN THAT
WHAT?
THEY ARE AFRAID OF INDIANS
THE POSSIBILITY OF INDIANS GAINING POWER
WE ARE GIVEN THE SAME RIGHTS AS THE NATIVES AFTER WORKING HERE FOR FIVE YEARS
THEY ARE AFRAID THAT ULTIMATELY THESE NATIONALIZED INDIANS WILL GAIN WEALTH AND POWER
ON THE OTHER HAND, THEY WANT TO KEEP INDIAN IMMIGRANTS AS AN ESSENTIAL LABOUR FORCE

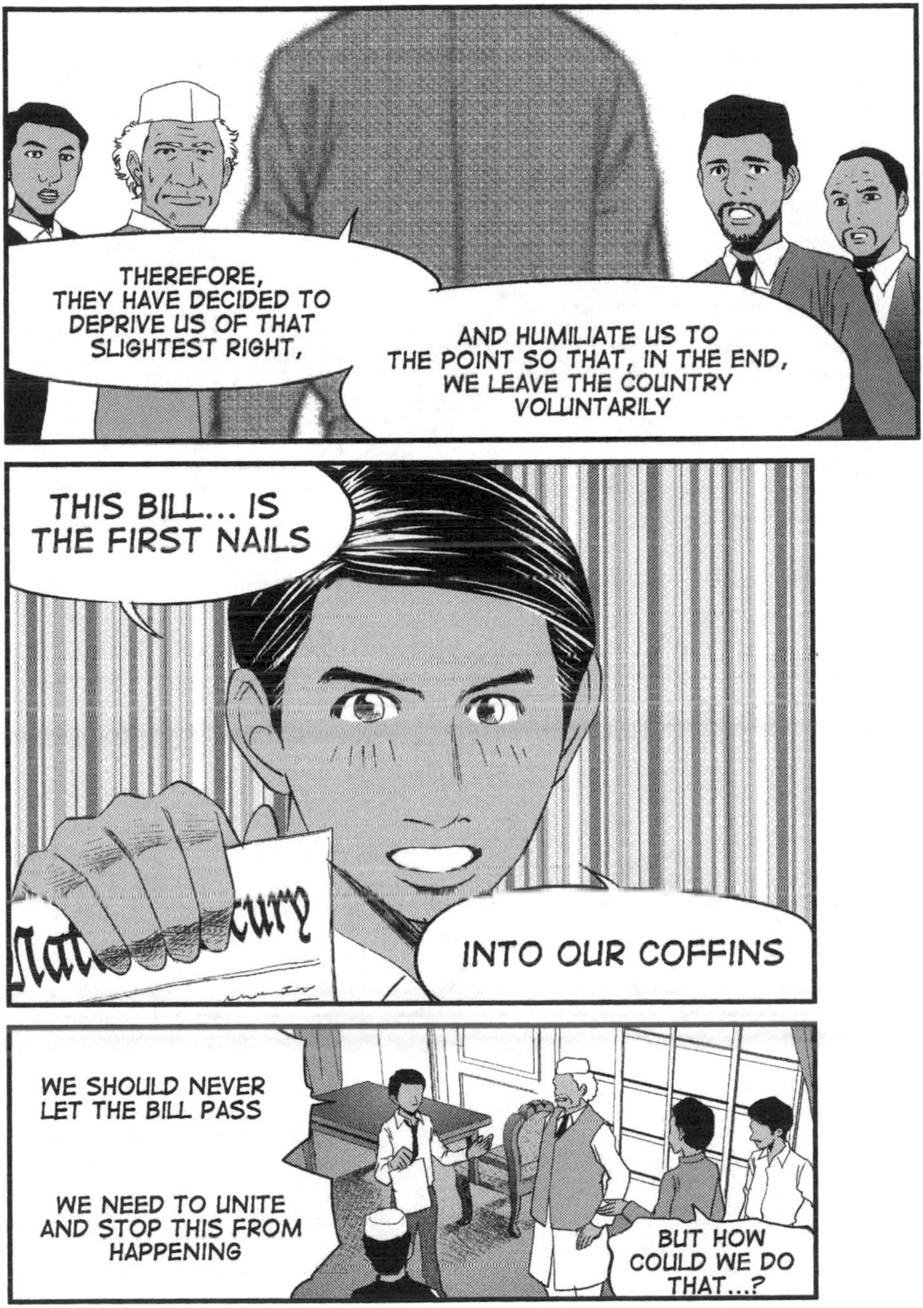
THEREFORE, THEY HAVE DECIDED TO DEPRIVE US OF THAT SLIGHTEST RIGHT,
AND HUMILIATE US TO THE POINT SO THAT, IN THE END, WE LEAVE THE COUNTRY VOLUNTARILY
THIS BILL... IS THE FIRST NAILS
INTO OUR COFFINS
WE SHOULD NEVER LET THE BILL PASS
WE NEED TO UNITE AND STOP THIS FROM HAPPENING
BUT HOW COULD WE DO THAT...?

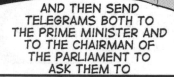

LET'S SEE. FIRST WE DRAFT A PETITION, AND MAKE COPIES

GET THEM SIGNED BY AS MANY PEOPLE AS POSSIBLE

AND THEN SEND TELEGRAMS BOTH TO THE PRIME MINISTER AND TO THE CHAIRMAN OF THE PARLIAMENT TO ASK THEM TO

POSTPONE THE DELIBERATION ON THE BILL WHILE OUR PETITION IS BEING REVIEWED

!

MR. GANDHI. WOULD YOU LEAD THE CAMPAIGN?

WE NEED YOUR HELP

YOUR WORK WILL BE COMPENSATED AS MUCH AS WE COULD AFFORD

PLEASE PUT OFF YOUR DEPARTURE AT LEAST FOR ONE MONTH FOR THIS CAUSE

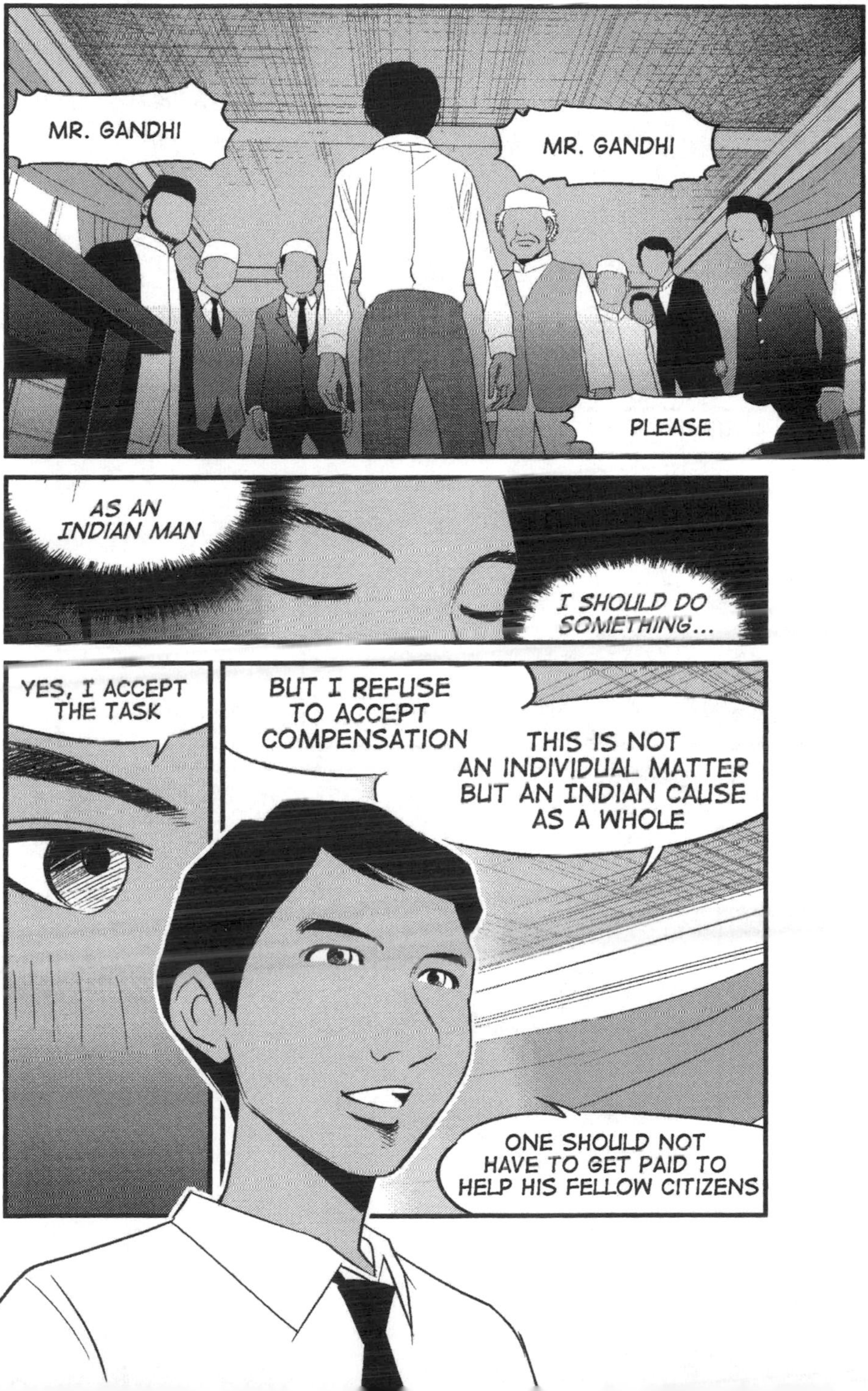
MR. GANDHI
MR. GANDHI
PLEASE
AS AN INDIAN MAN
I SHOULD DO SOMETHING...
YES, I ACCEPT THE TASK
BUT I REFUSE TO ACCEPT COMPENSATION
THIS IS NOT AN INDIVIDUAL MATTER BUT AN INDIAN CAUSE AS A WHOLE
ONE SHOULD NOT HAVE TO GET PAID TO HELP HIS FELLOW CITIZENS

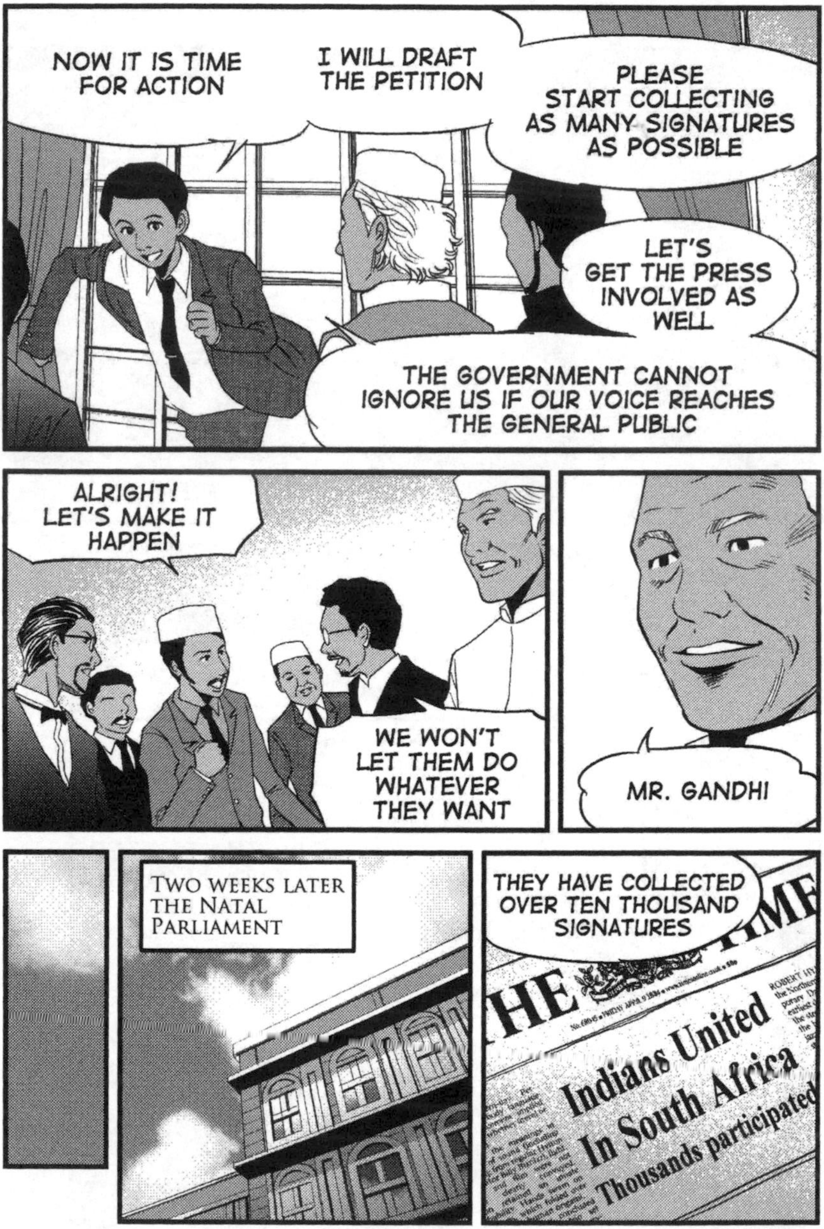
NOW IT IS TIME FOR ACTION
I WILL DRAFT THE PETITION
PLEASE START COLLECTING AS MANY SIGNATURES AS POSSIBLE
LET'S GET THE PRESS INVOLVED AS WELL
THE GOVERNMENT CANNOT IGNORE US IF OUR VOICE REACHES THE GENERAL PUBLIC
ALRIGHT! LET'S MAKE IT HAPPEN
WE WON'T LET THEM DO WHATEVER THEY WANT
MR. GANDHI
TWO WEEKS LATER THE NATAL PARLIAMENT
THEY HAVE COLLECTED OVER TEN THOUSAND SIGNATURES
Indians United
In South Africa
Thousands participated

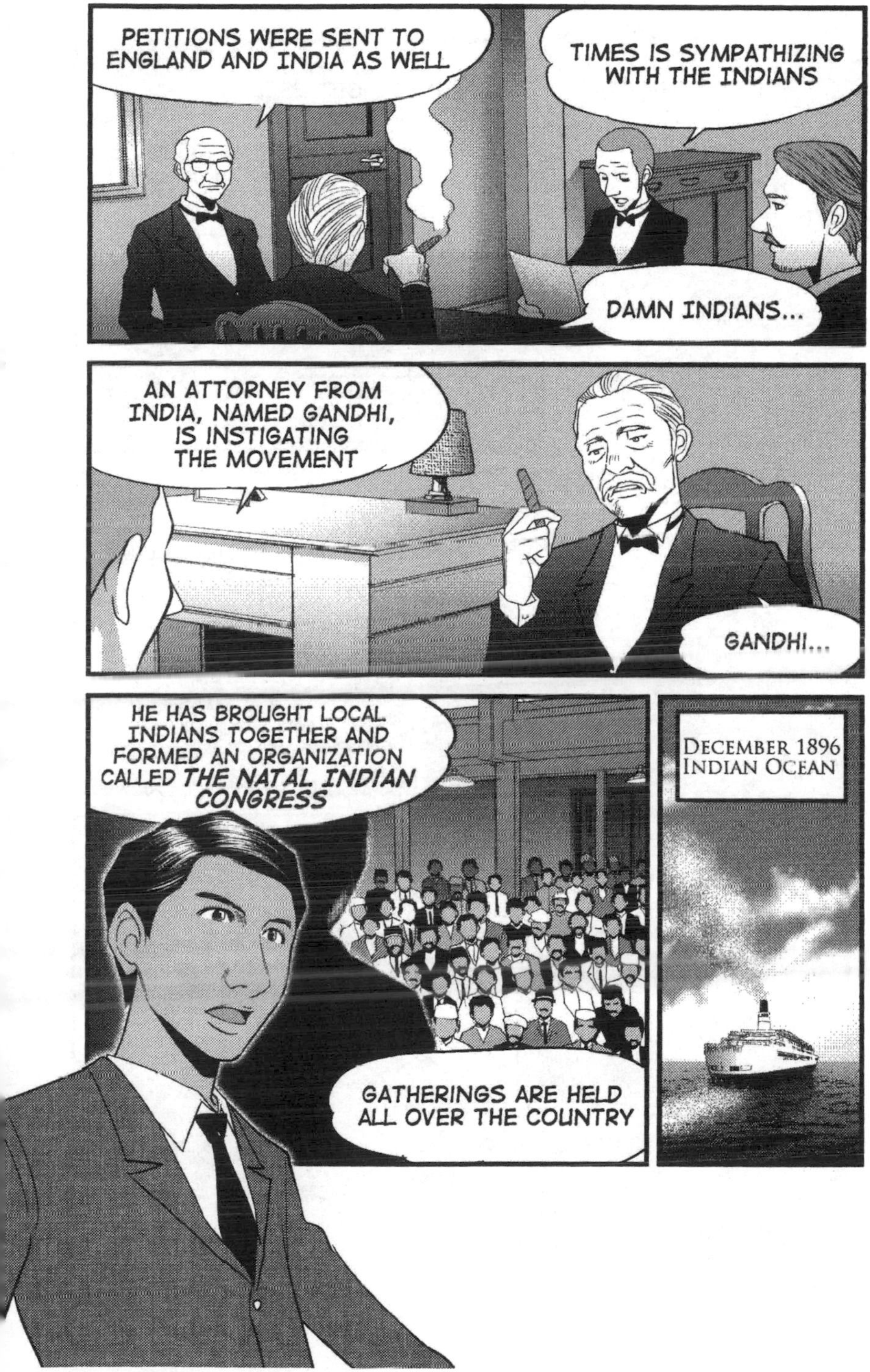
PETITIONS WERE SENT TO ENGLAND AND INDIA AS WELL
TIMES IS SYMPATHIZING WITH THE INDIANS
DAMN INDIANS...
AN ATTORNEY FROM INDIA, NAMED GANDHI, IS INSTIGATING THE MOVEMENT
GANDHI...
HE HAS BROUGHT LOCAL INDIANS TOGETHER AND FORMED AN ORGANIZATION CALLED *THE NATAL INDIAN CONGRESS*
GATHERINGS ARE HELD ALL OVER THE COUNTRY
DECEMBER 1896
INDIAN OCEAN

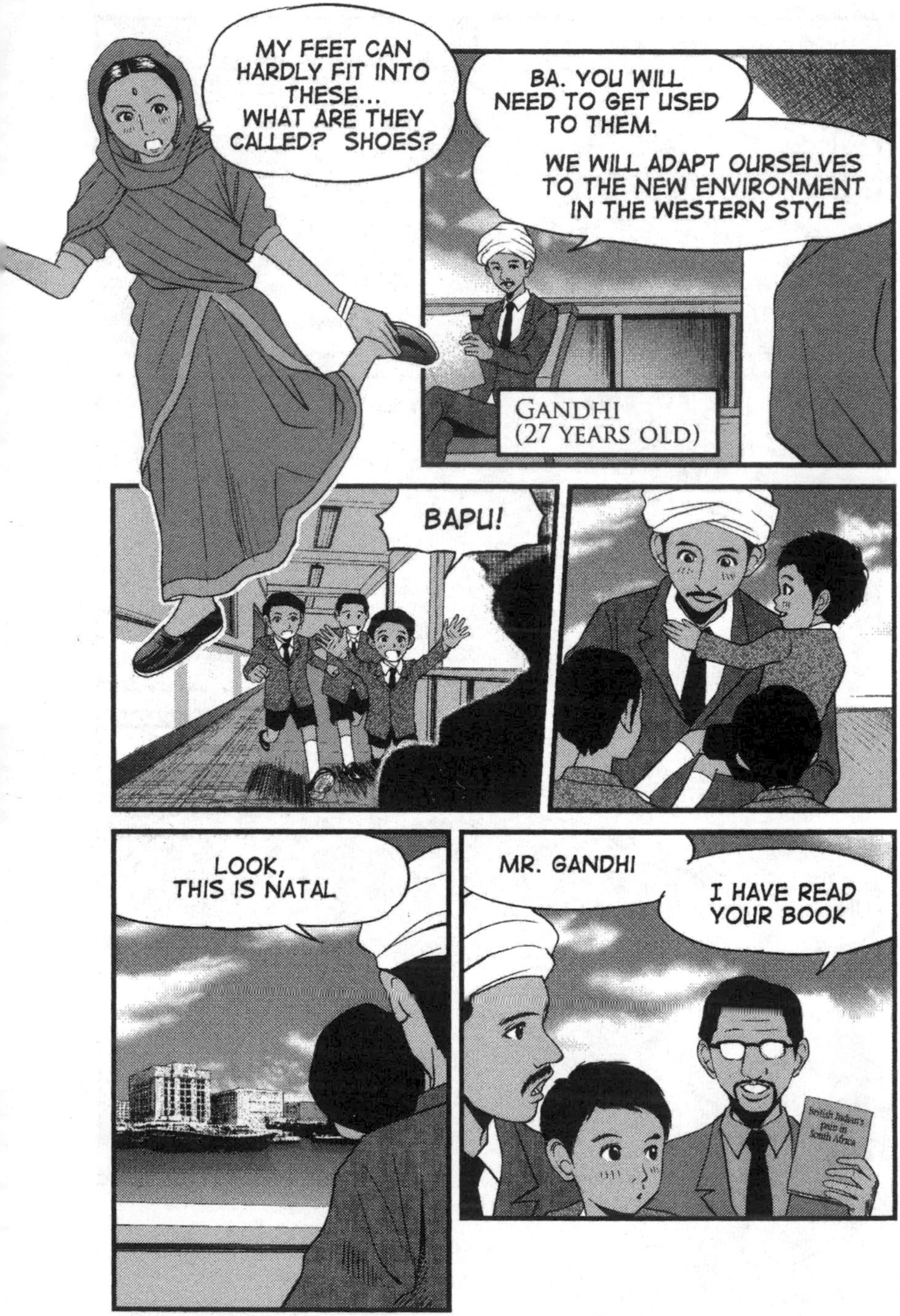
MY FEET CAN HARDLY FIT INTO THESE... WHAT ARE THEY CALLED? SHOES?
BA. YOU WILL NEED TO GET USED TO THEM.
WE WILL ADAPT OURSELVES TO THE NEW ENVIRONMENT IN THE WESTERN STYLE
GANDHI (27 YEARS OLD)
BAPU!
LOOK, THIS IS NATAL
MR. GANDHI
I HAVE READ YOUR BOOK

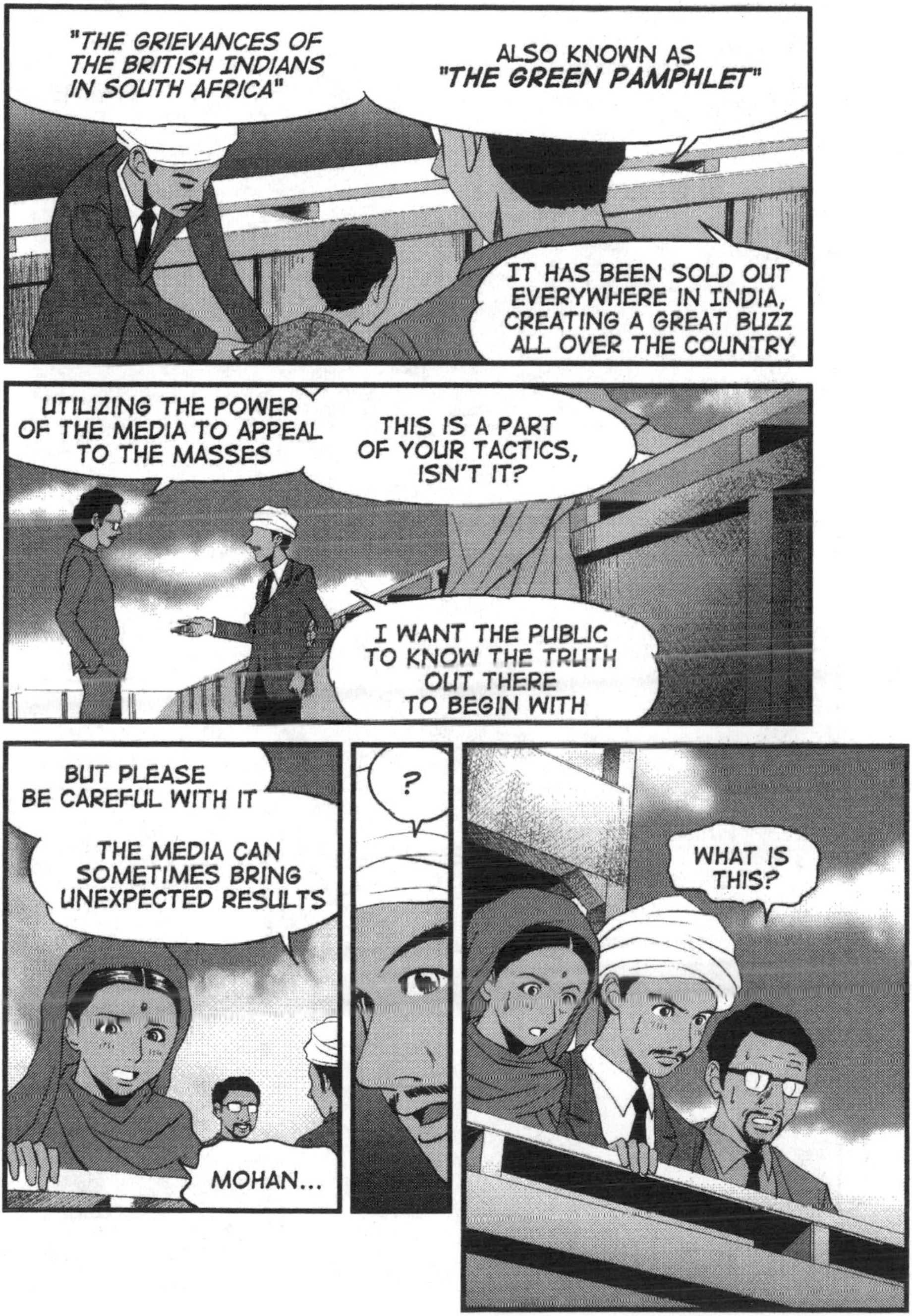
"THE GRIEVANCES OF THE BRITISH INDIANS IN SOUTH AFRICA"
ALSO KNOWN AS "THE GREEN PAMPHLET"
IT HAS BEEN SOLD OUT EVERYWHERE IN INDIA, CREATING A GREAT BUZZ ALL OVER THE COUNTRY
UTILIZING THE POWER OF THE MEDIA TO APPEAL TO THE MASSES
THIS IS A PART OF YOUR TACTICS, ISN'T IT?
I WANT THE PUBLIC TO KNOW THE TRUTH OUT THERE TO BEGIN WITH
BUT PLEASE BE CAREFUL WITH IT
THE MEDIA CAN SOMETIMES BRING UNEXPECTED RESULTS
MOHAN...
?
WHAT IS THIS?

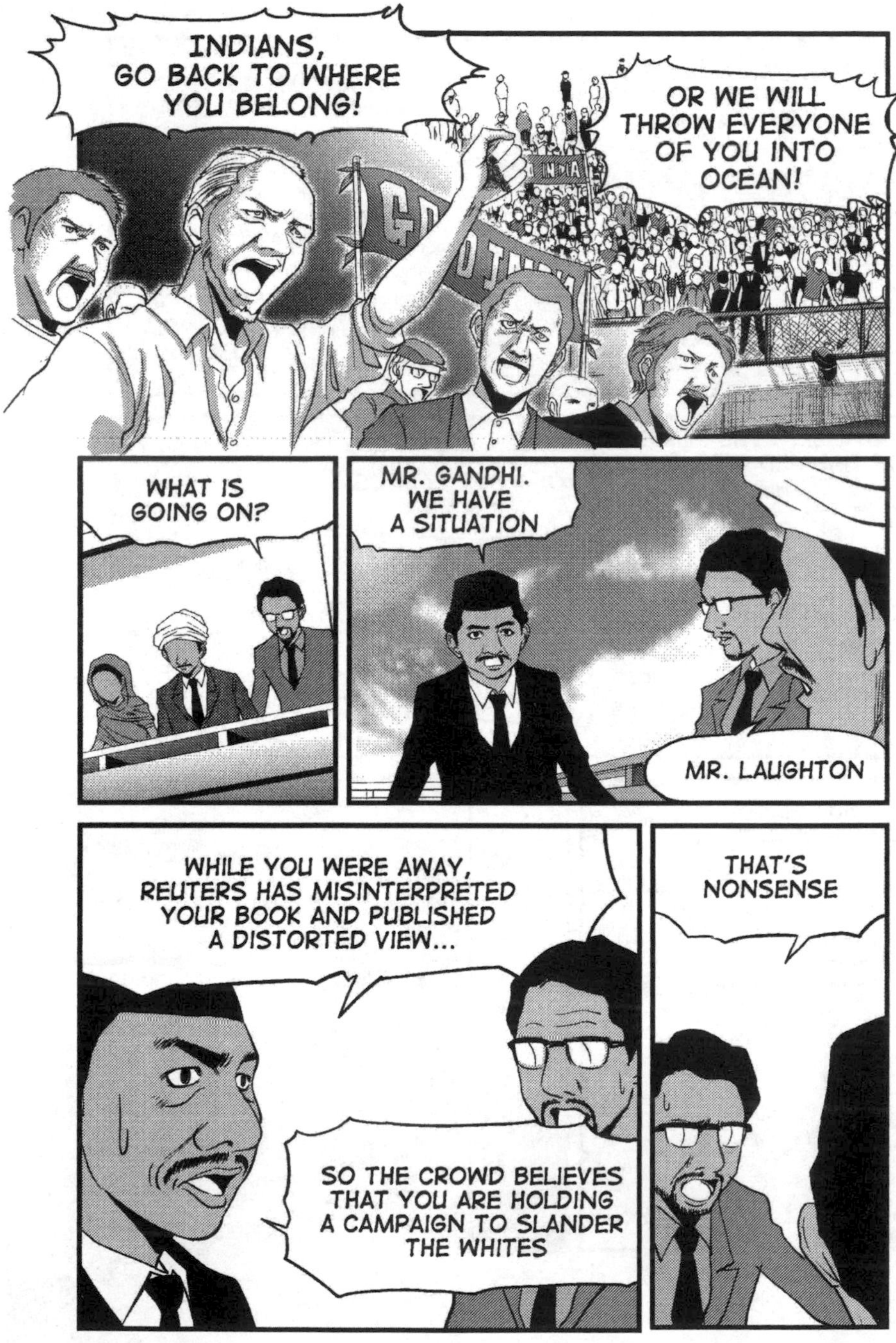
INDIANS, GO BACK TO WHERE YOU BELONG!
OR WE WILL THROW EVERYONE OF YOU INTO OCEAN!
WHAT IS GOING ON?
MR. GANDHI. WE HAVE A SITUATION
MR. LAUGHTON
WHILE YOU WERE AWAY, REUTERS HAS MISINTERPRETED YOUR BOOK AND PUBLISHED A DISTORTED VIEW...
SO THE CROWD BELIEVES THAT YOU ARE HOLDING A CAMPAIGN TO SLANDER THE WHITES
THAT'S NONSENSE

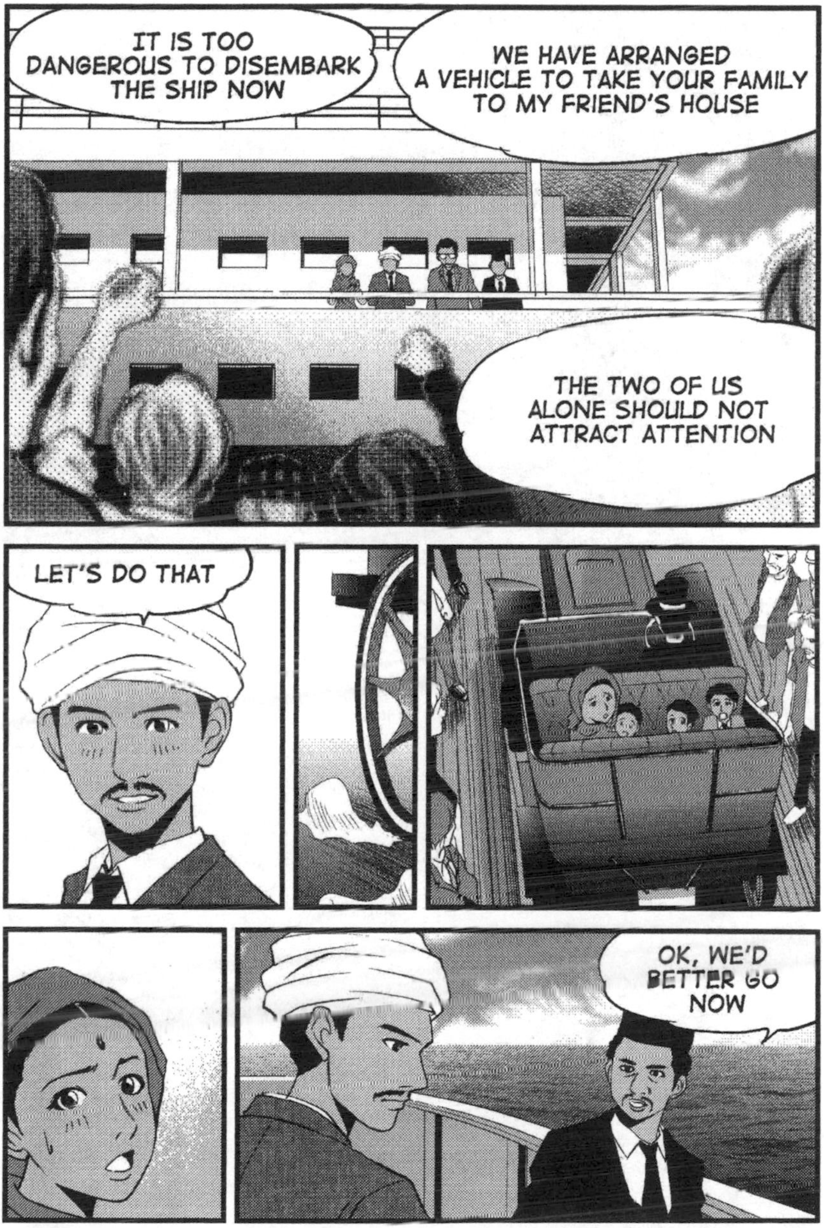
IT IS TOO DANGEROUS TO DISEMBARK THE SHIP NOW
WE HAVE ARRANGED A VEHICLE TO TAKE YOUR FAMILY TO MY FRIEND'S HOUSE
THE TWO OF US ALONE SHOULD NOT ATTRACT ATTENTION
LET'S DO THAT
OK, WE'D BETTER GO NOW

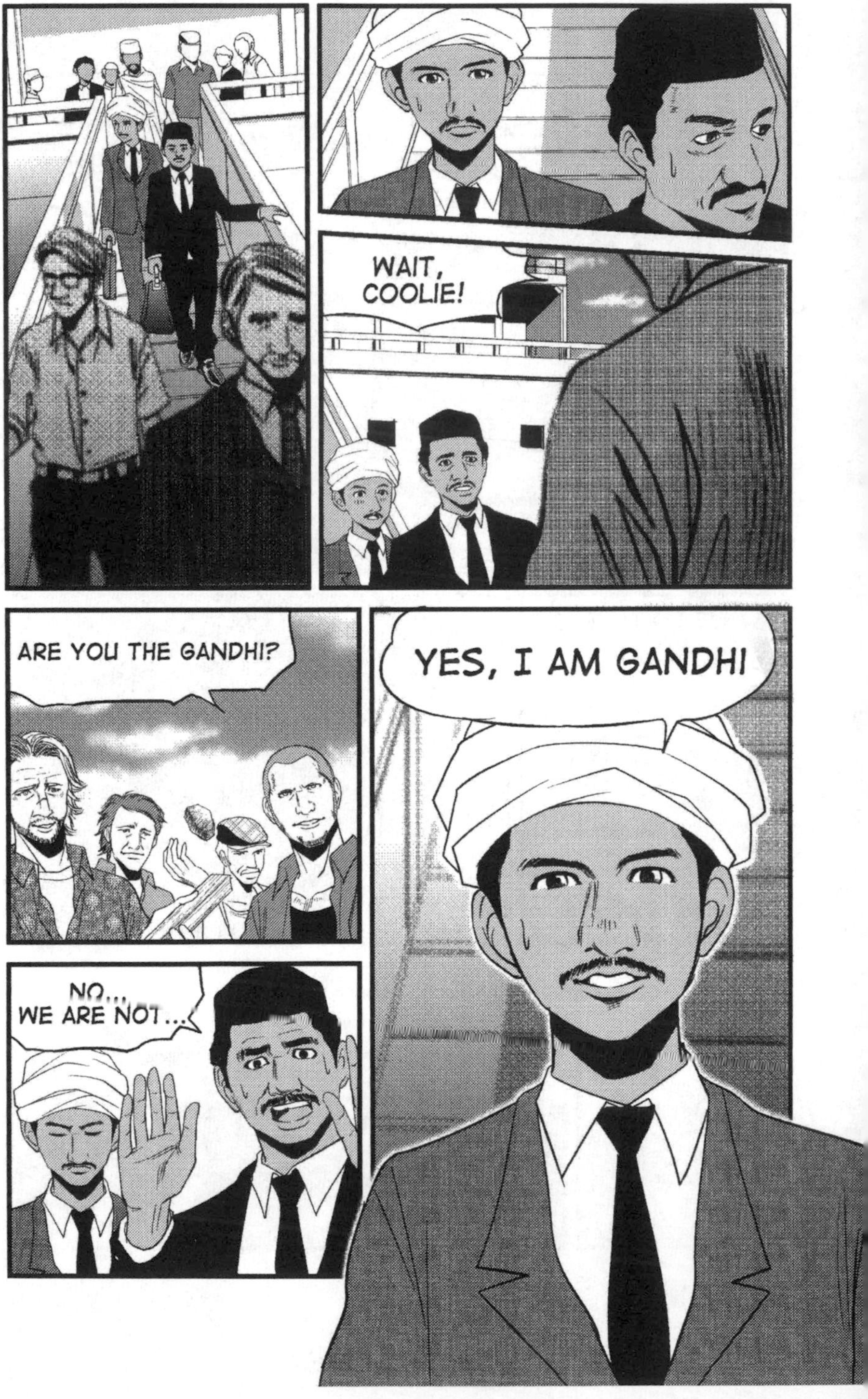
WAIT, COOLIE!
ARE YOU THE GANDHI?
NO... WE ARE NOT...
YES, I AM GANDHI

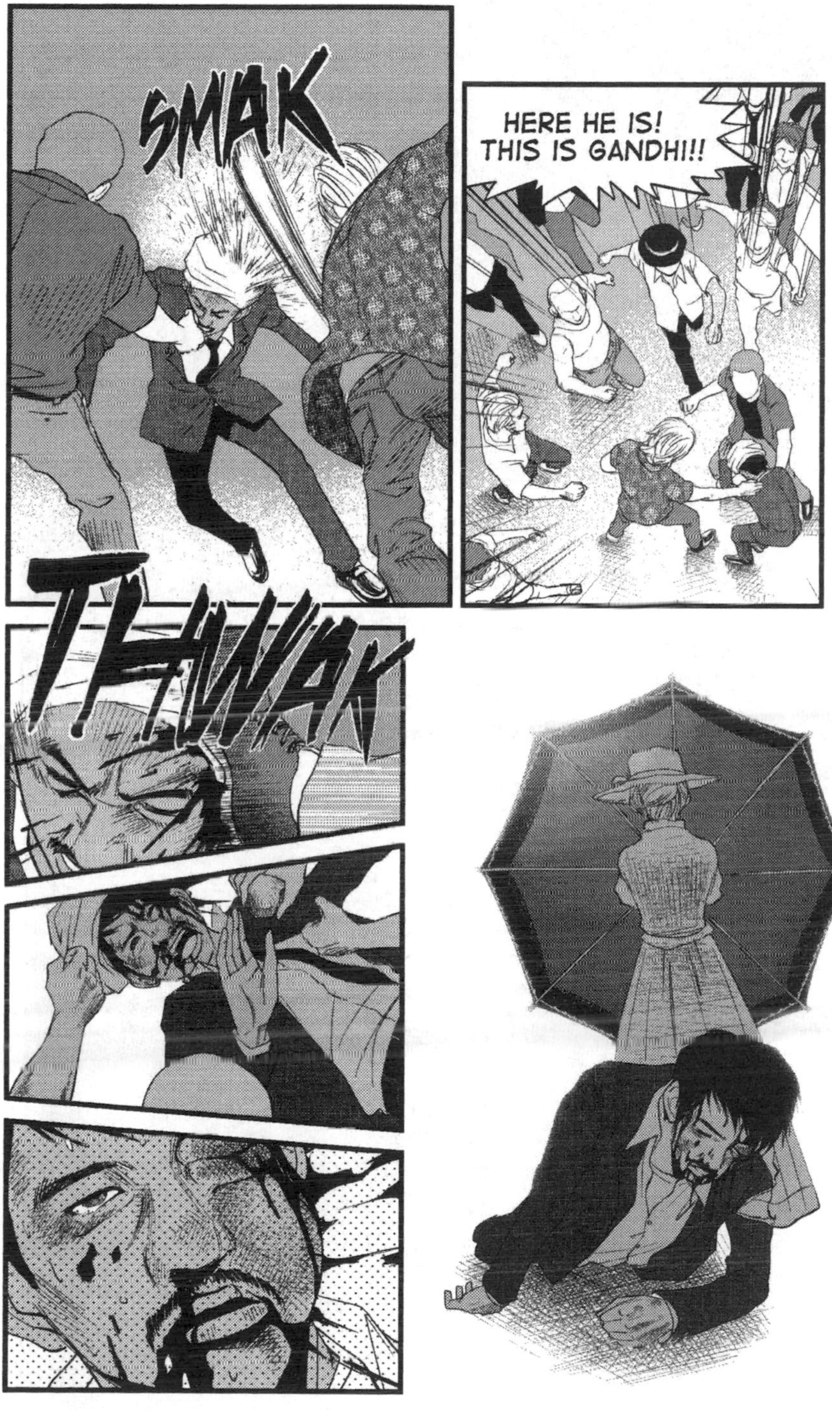
SMAK
HERE HE IS! THIS IS GANDHI!!!
THWAK

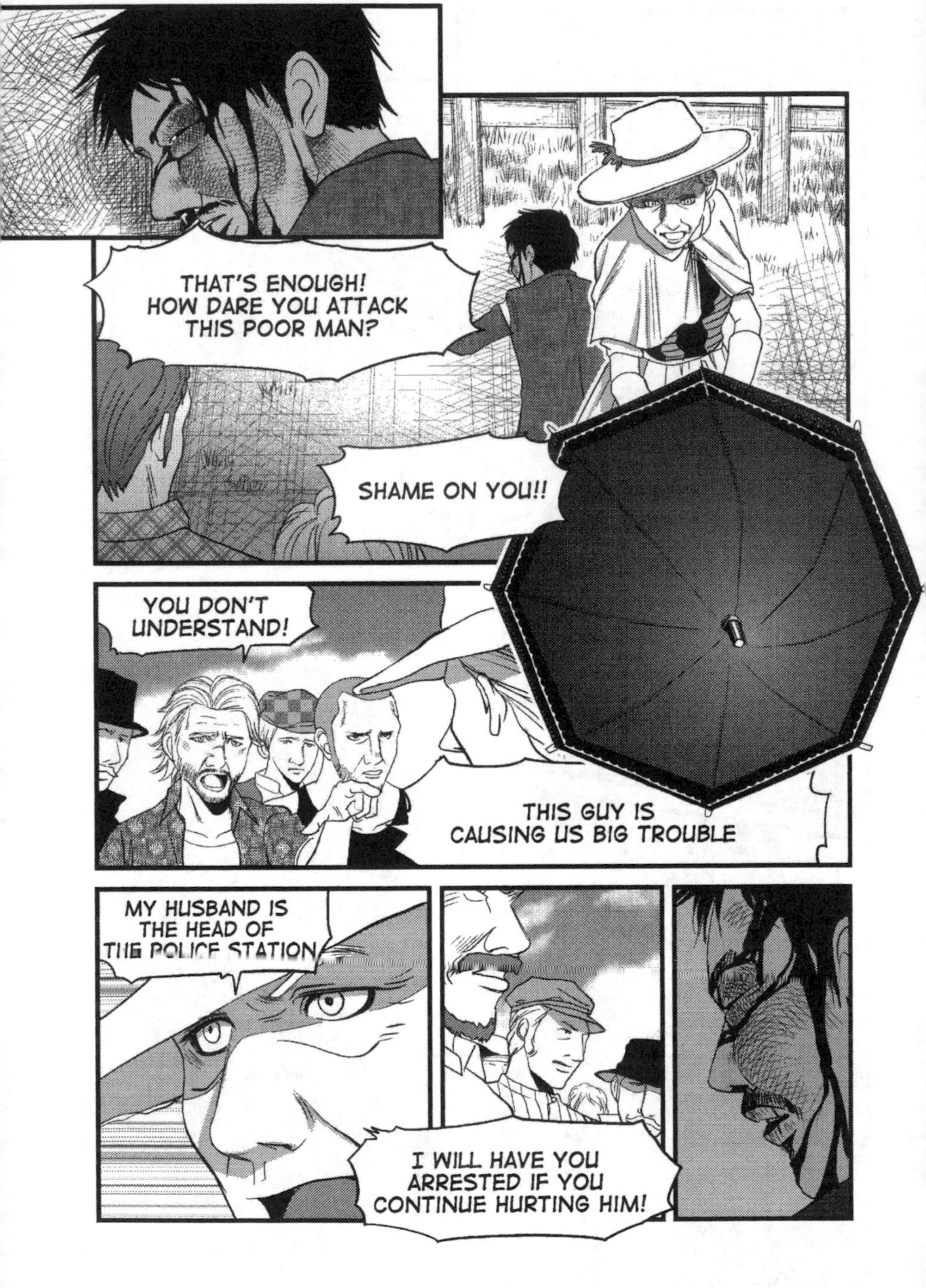
THAT'S ENOUGH! HOW DARE YOU ATTACK THIS POOR MAN?
SHAME ON YOU!!
YOU DON'T UNDERSTAND!
THIS GUY IS CAUSING US BIG TROUBLE
MY HUSBAND IS THE HEAD OF THE POLICE STATION
I WILL HAVE YOU ARRESTED IF YOU CONTINUE HURTING HIM!

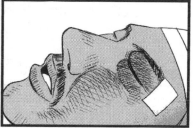

HOW IS HE?

YOU CANNOT KEEP MY MOUTH SHUT EVEN IN THIS CONDITION...

WE, THE ENGLISH GOVERNMENT, DEEPLY REGRET THIS INCIDENT

THE COLONIAL SECRETARY, CHAMBERLAIN, HAS ORDERED US TO ARRANGE PROPER LEGAL ACTIONS TO BRING CHARGES AGAIST THE OFFENDERS

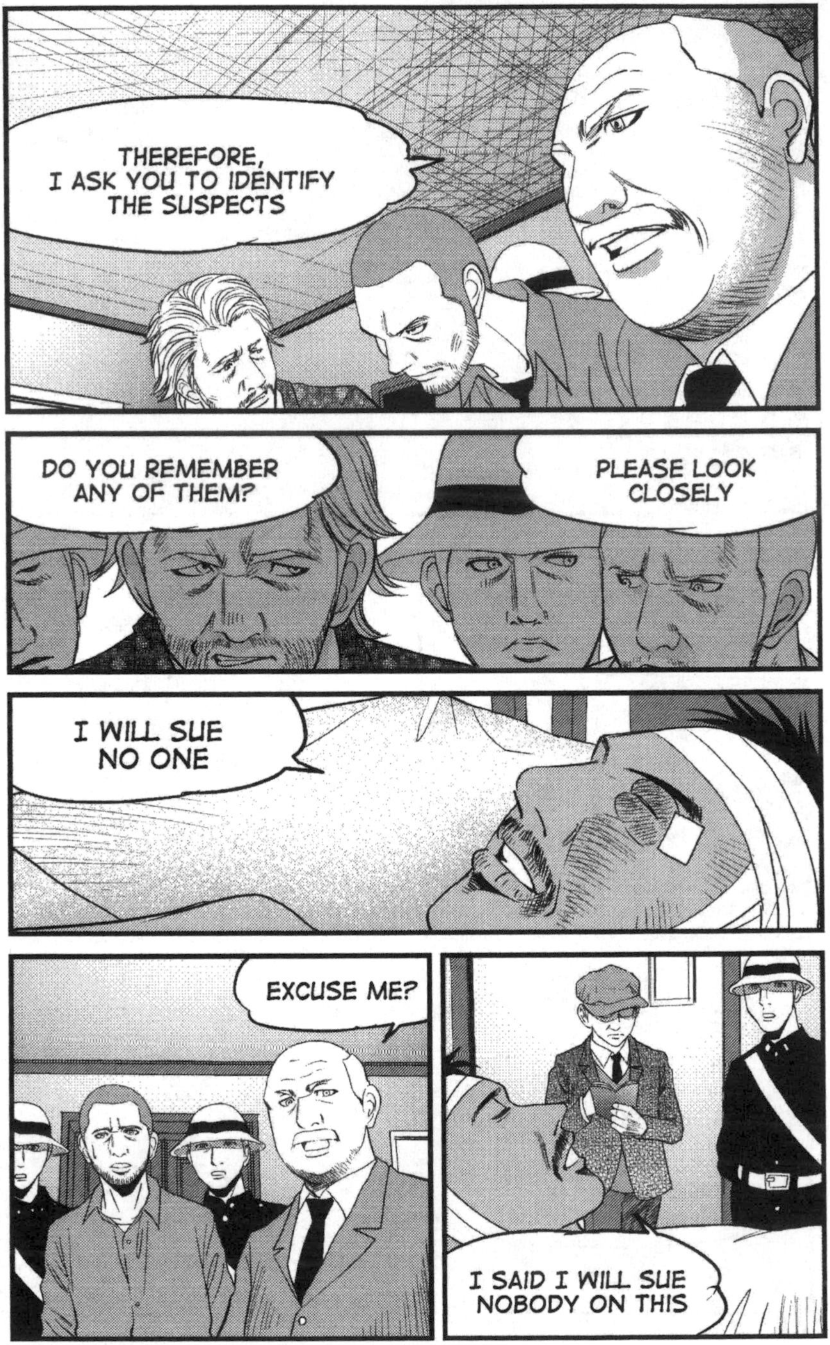
THEREFORE, I ASK YOU TO IDENTIFY THE SUSPECTS
DO YOU REMEMBER ANY OF THEM?
PLEASE LOOK CLOSELY
I WILL SUE NO ONE
EXCUSE ME?
I SAID I WILL SUE NOBODY ON THIS

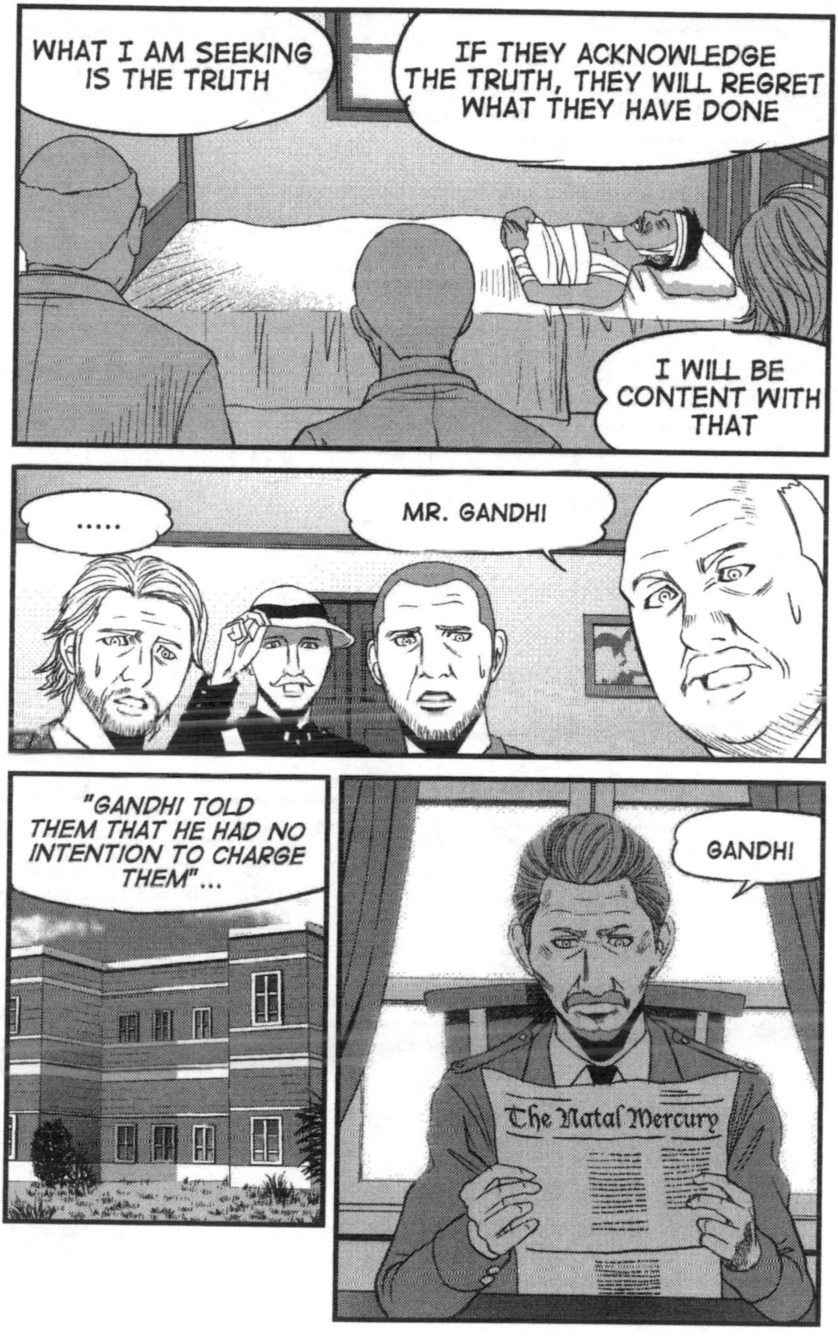
WHAT I AM SEEKING IS THE TRUTH
IF THEY ACKNOWLEDGE THE TRUTH, THEY WILL REGRET WHAT THEY HAVE DONE
I WILL BE CONTENT WITH THAT
.....
MR. GANDHI
"GANDHI TOLD THEM THAT HE HAD NO INTENTION TO CHARGE THEM"...
GANDHI
The Natal Mercury

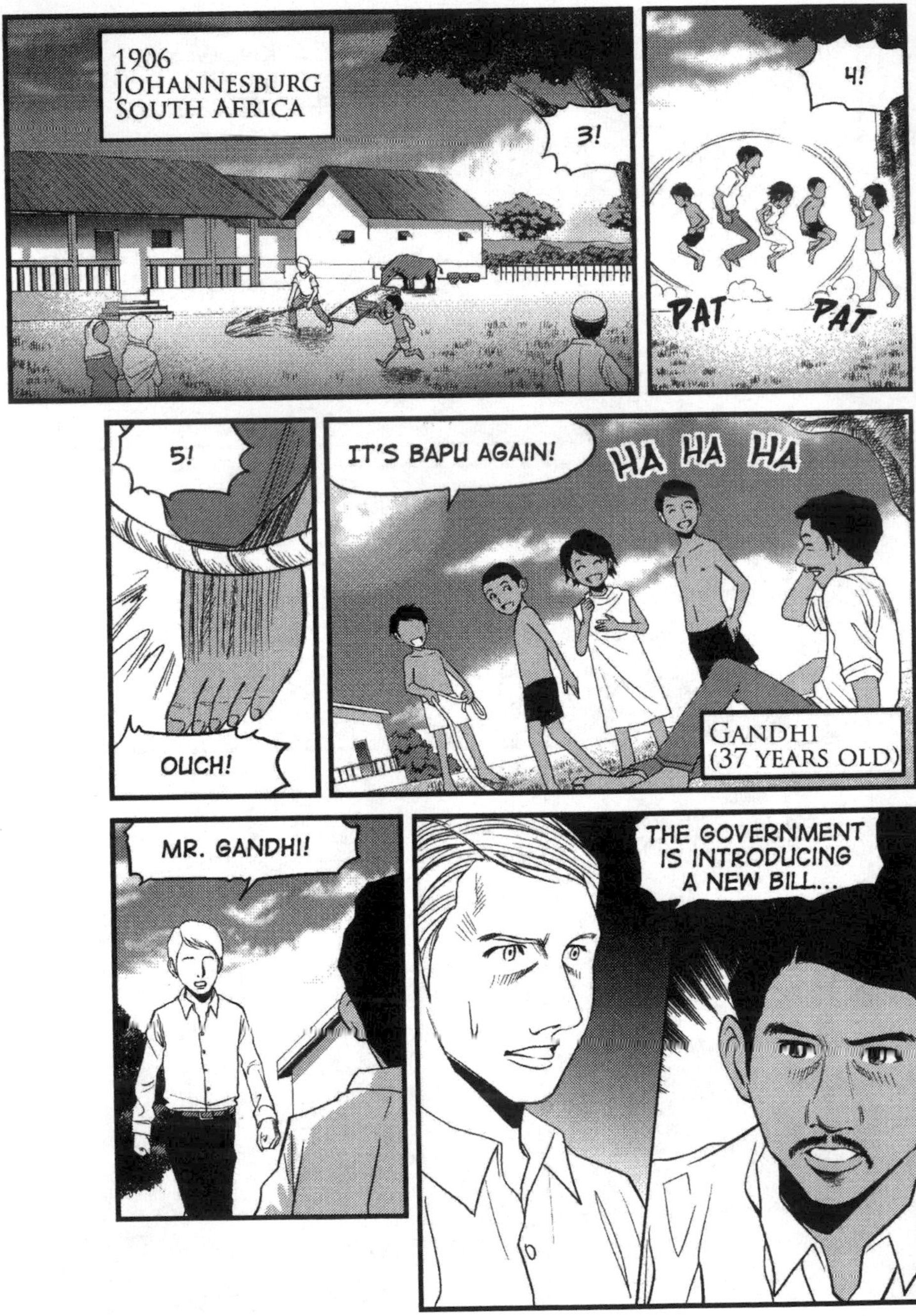
1906
JOHANNESBURG
SOUTH AFRICA
3!
4!
PAT
PAT
5!
OUCH!
IT'S BAPU AGAIN!
HA HA HA
GANDHI
(37 YEARS OLD)
MR. GANDHI!
THE GOVERNMENT IS INTRODUCING A NEW BILL...

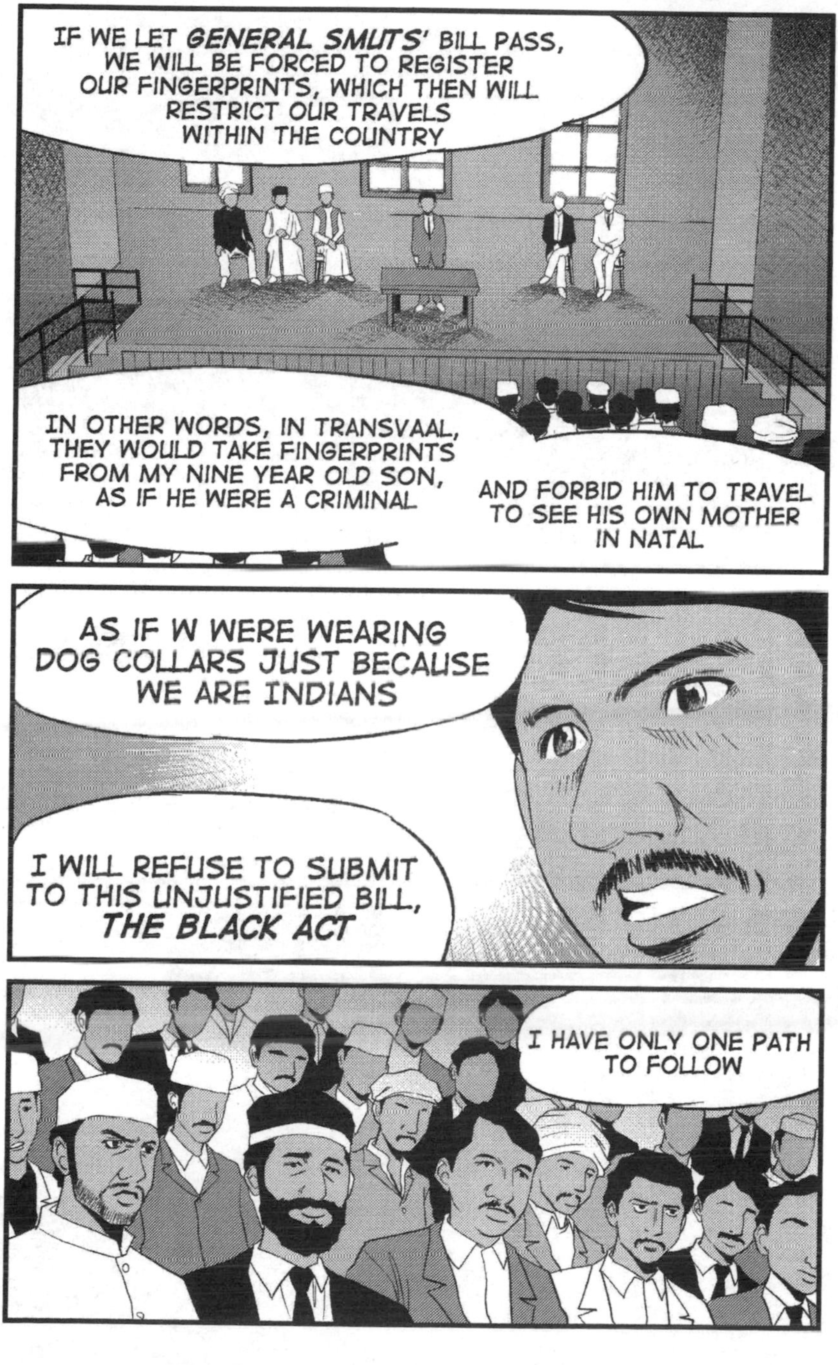
IF WE LET GENERAL SMUTS' BILL PASS, WE WILL BE FORCED TO REGISTER OUR FINGERPRINTS, WHICH THEN WILL RESTRICT OUR TRAVELS WITHIN THE COUNTRY
IN OTHER WORDS, IN TRANSVAAL, THEY WOULD TAKE FINGERPRINTS FROM MY NINE YEAR OLD SON, AS IF HE WERE A CRIMINAL
AND FORBID HIM TO TRAVEL TO SEE HIS OWN MOTHER IN NATAL
AS IF W WERE WEARING DOG COLLARS JUST BECAUSE WE ARE INDIANS
I WILL REFUSE TO SUBMIT TO THIS UNJUSTIFIED BILL, THE BLACK ACT
I HAVE ONLY ONE PATH TO FOLLOW

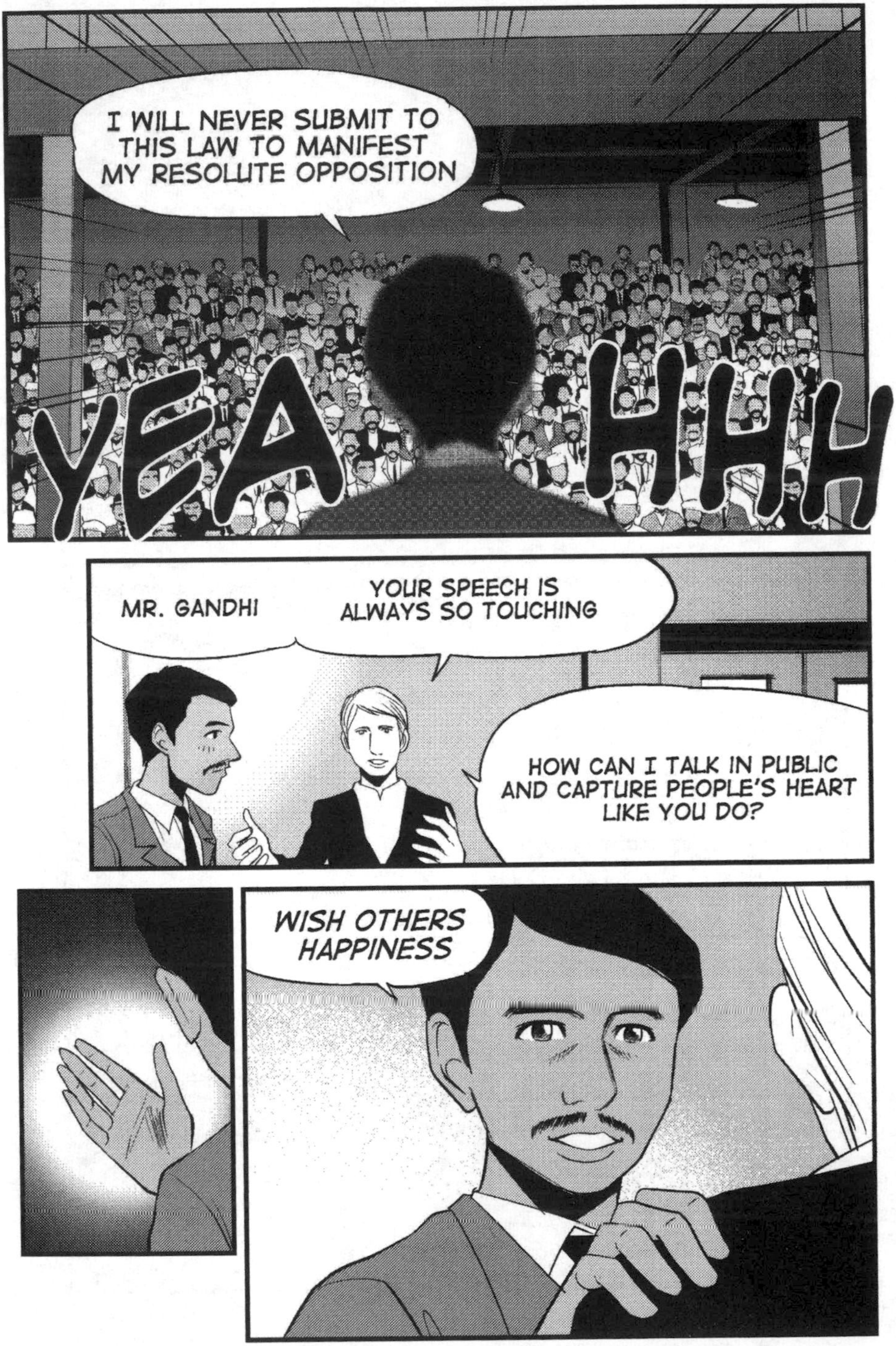
I WILL NEVER SUBMIT TO THIS LAW TO MANIFEST MY RESOLUTE OPPOSITION
YEAHHHH
MR. GANDHI
YOUR SPEECH IS ALWAYS SO TOUCHING
HOW CAN I TALK IN PUBLIC AND CAPTURE PEOPLE'S HEART LIKE YOU DO?
WISH OTHERS HAPPINESS

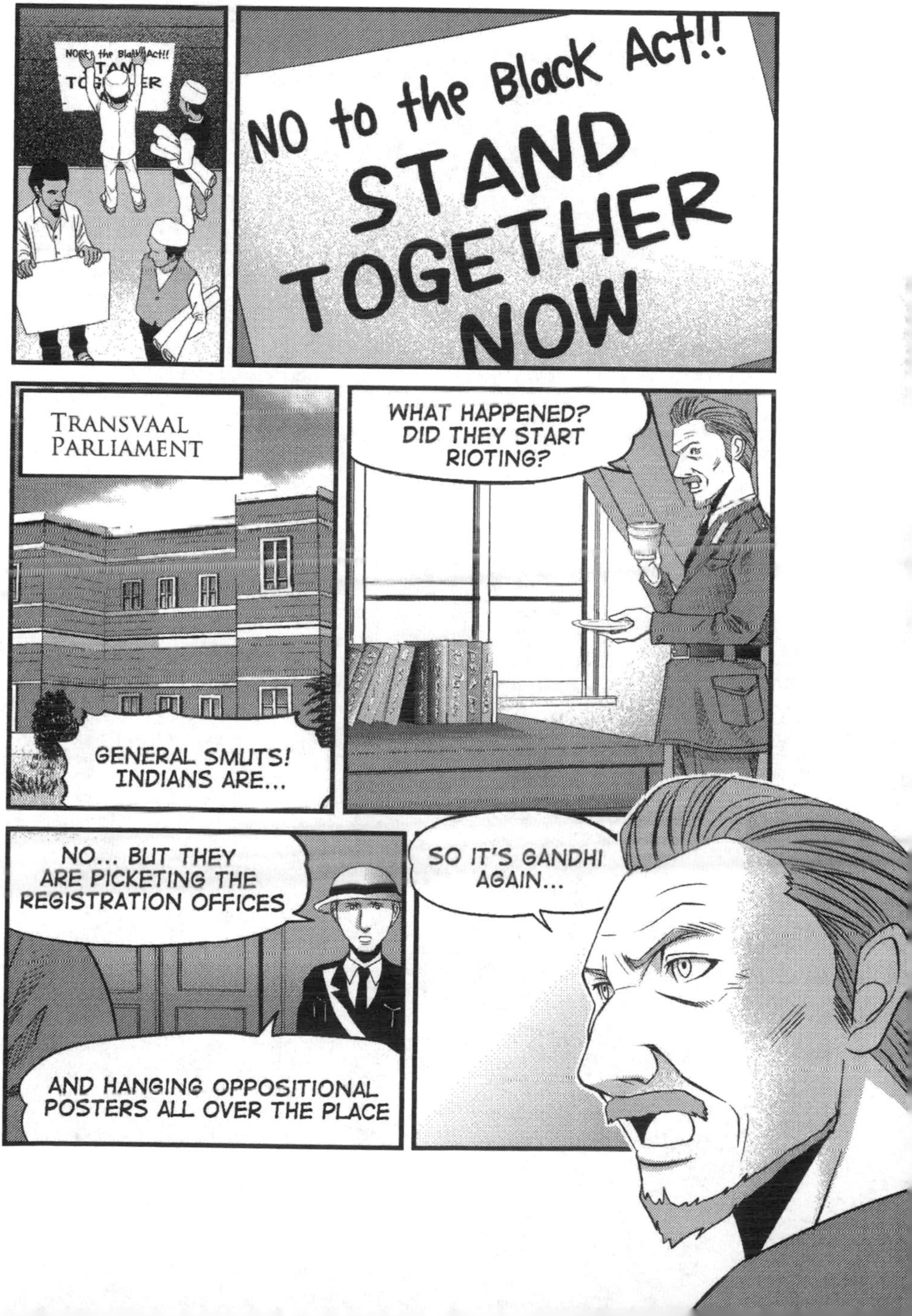
NO to the Black Act!!
STAND TOGETHER NOW
TRANSVAAL PARLIAMENT
GENERAL SMUTS! INDIANS ARE...
WHAT HAPPENED? DID THEY START RIOTING?
NO... BUT THEY ARE PICKETING THE REGISTRATION OFFICES
AND HANGING OPPOSITIONAL POSTERS ALL OVER THE PLACE
SO IT'S GANDHI AGAIN...

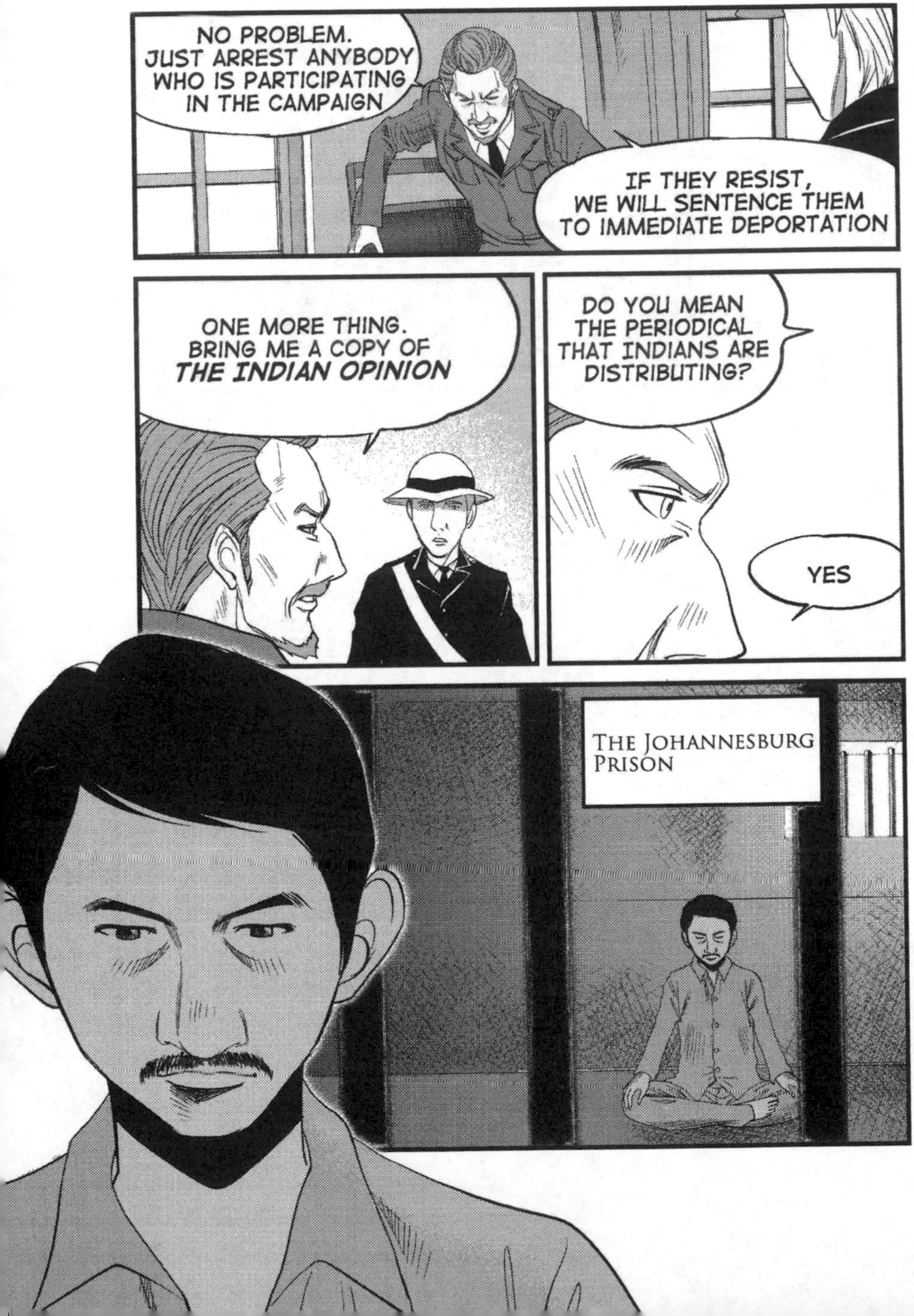
NO PROBLEM. JUST ARREST ANYBODY WHO IS PARTICIPATING IN THE CAMPAIGN
IF THEY RESIST, WE WILL SENTENCE THEM TO IMMEDIATE DEPORTATION
ONE MORE THING. BRING ME A COPY OF THE INDIAN OPINION
DO YOU MEAN THE PERIODICAL THAT INDIANS ARE DISTRIBUTING?
YES
THE JOHANNESBURG PRISON

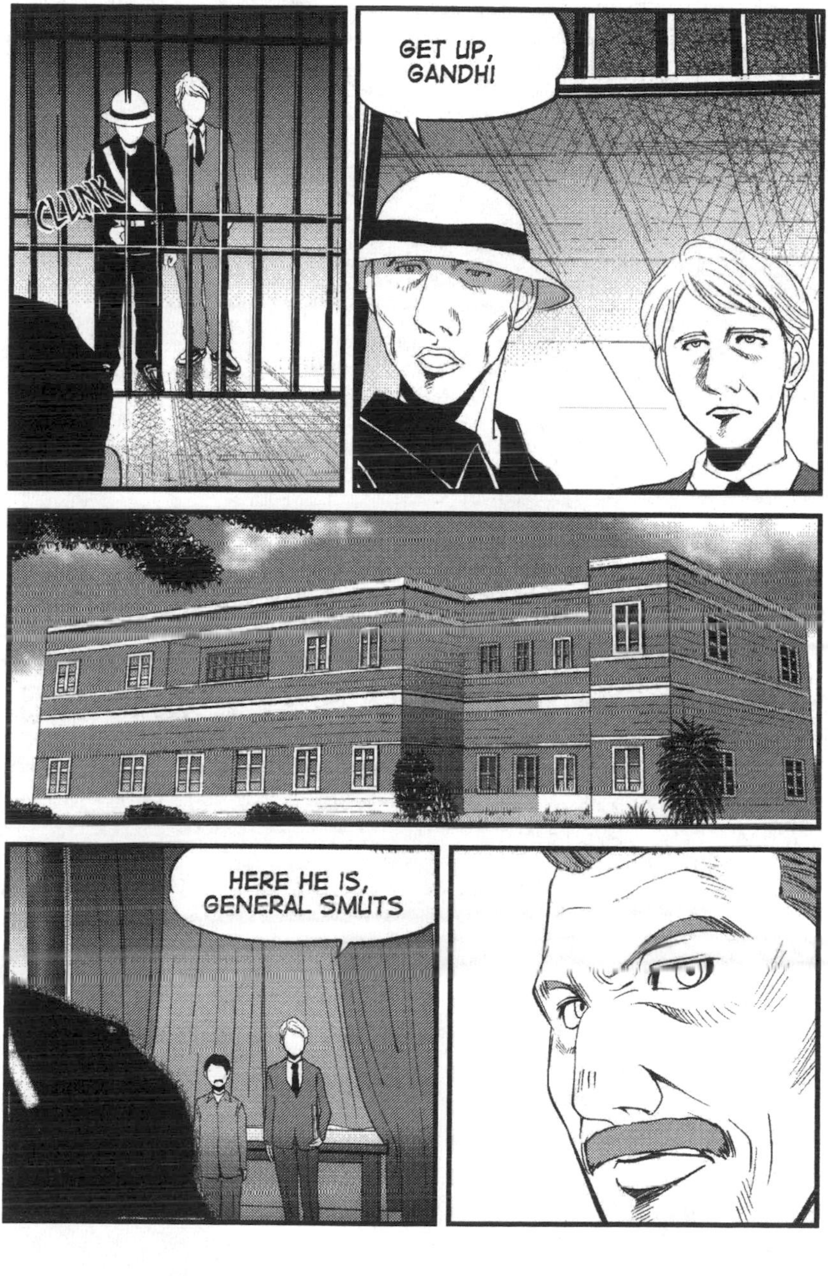
CLLINK
GET UP, GANDHI
HERE HE IS, GENERAL SMUTS

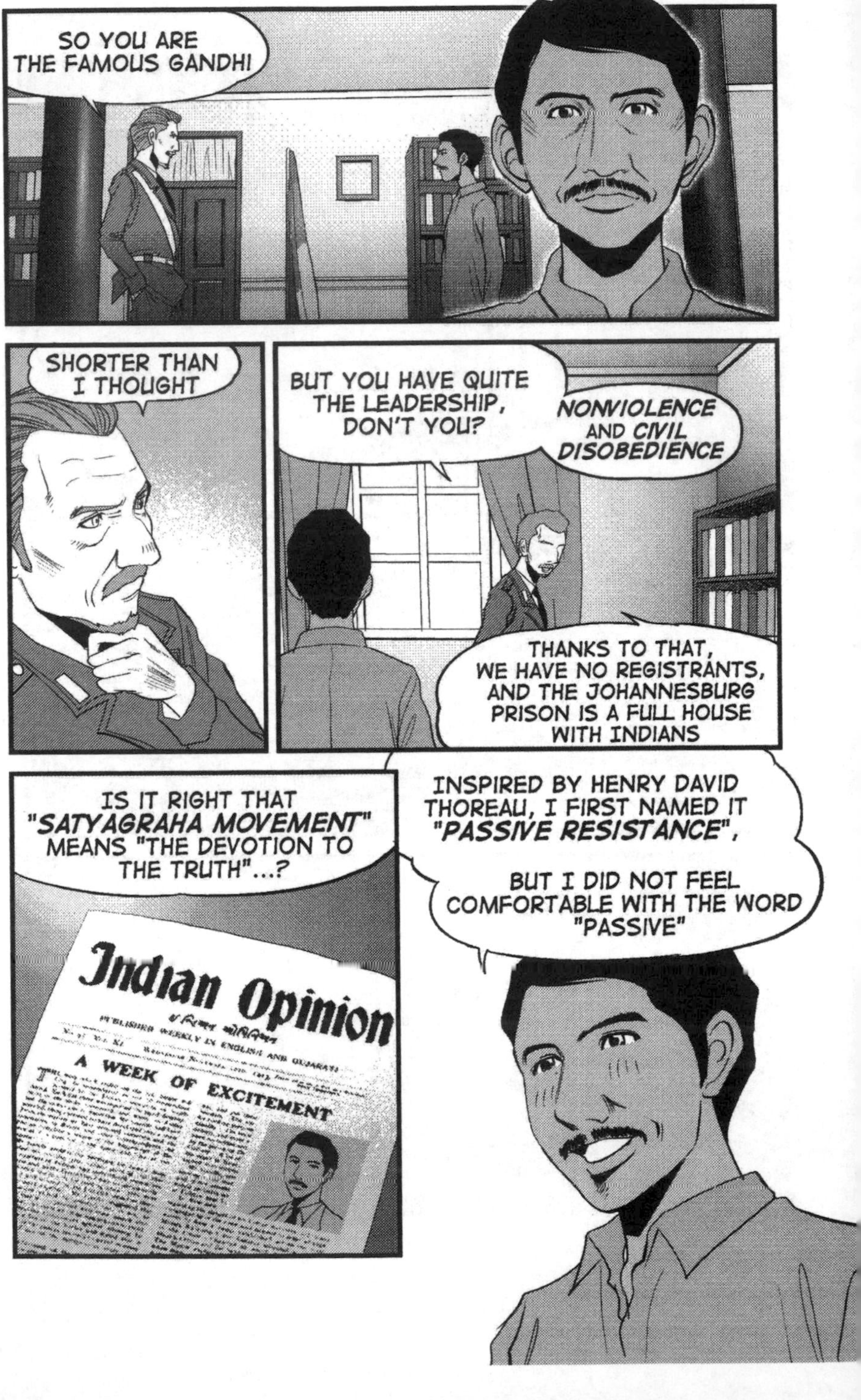
SO YOU ARE THE FAMOUS GANDHI
SHORTER THAN I THOUGHT
BUT YOU HAVE QUITE THE LEADERSHIP, DON'T YOU?
NONVIOLENCE AND CIVIL DISOBEDIENCE
THANKS TO THAT, WE HAVE NO REGISTRANTS, AND THE JOHANNESBURG PRISON IS A FULL HOUSE WITH INDIANS
IS IT RIGHT THAT "SATYAGRAHA MOVEMENT" MEANS "THE DEVOTION TO THE TRUTH"...?
Indian Opinion
PUBLISHED WEEKLY IN ENGLISH AND GUJARATI
A WEEK OF EXCITEMENT
INSPIRED BY HENRY DAVID THOREAU, I FIRST NAMED IT "PASSIVE RESISTANCE",
BUT I DID NOT FEEL COMFORTABLE WITH THE WORD "PASSIVE"

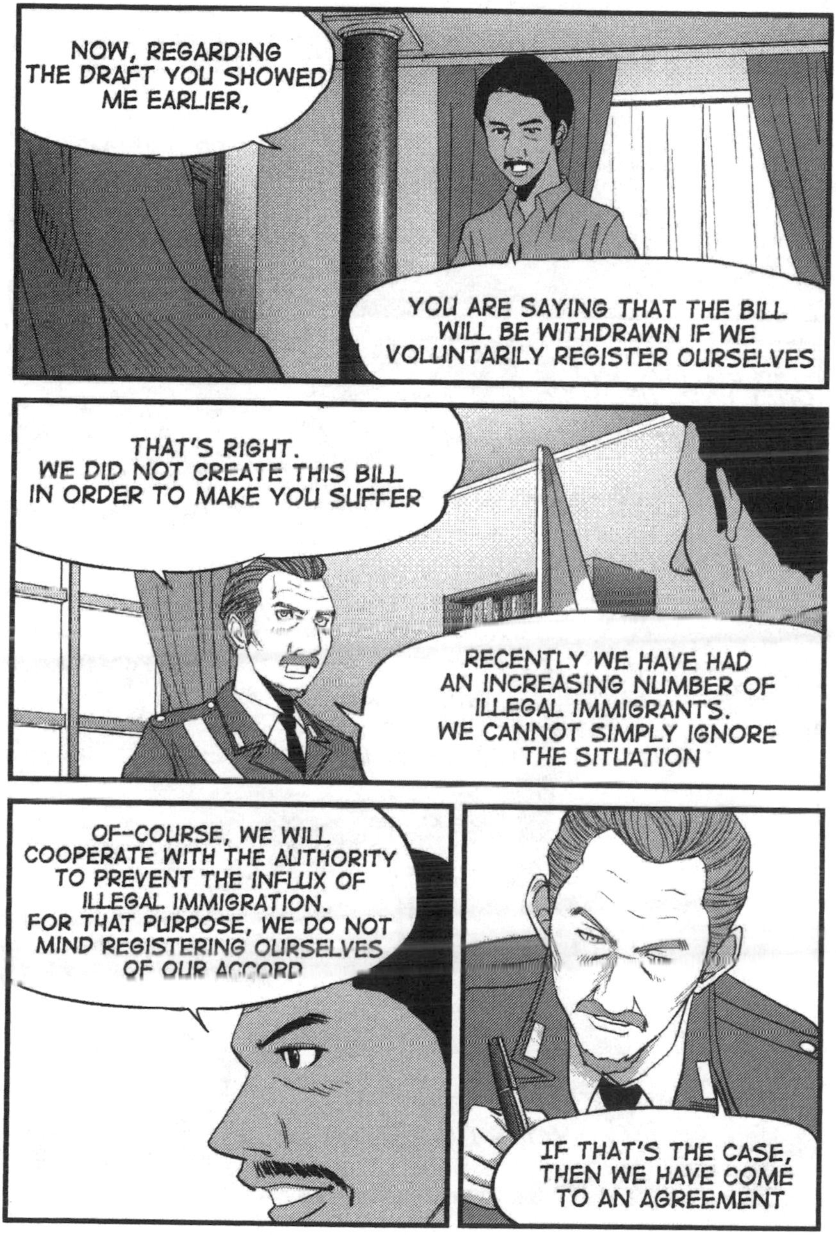
NOW, REGARDING THE DRAFT YOU SHOWED ME EARLIER,
YOU ARE SAYING THAT THE BILL WILL BE WITHDRAWN IF WE VOLUNTARILY REGISTER OURSELVES
THAT'S RIGHT. WE DID NOT CREATE THIS BILL IN ORDER TO MAKE YOU SUFFER
RECENTLY WE HAVE HAD AN INCREASING NUMBER OF ILLEGAL IMMIGRANTS. WE CANNOT SIMPLY IGNORE THE SITUATION
OF-COURSE, WE WILL COOPERATE WITH THE AUTHORITY TO PREVENT THE INFLUX OF ILLEGAL IMMIGRATION. FOR THAT PURPOSE, WE DO NOT MIND REGISTERING OURSELVES OF OUR ACCORD
IF THAT'S THE CASE, THEN WE HAVE COME TO AN AGREEMENT

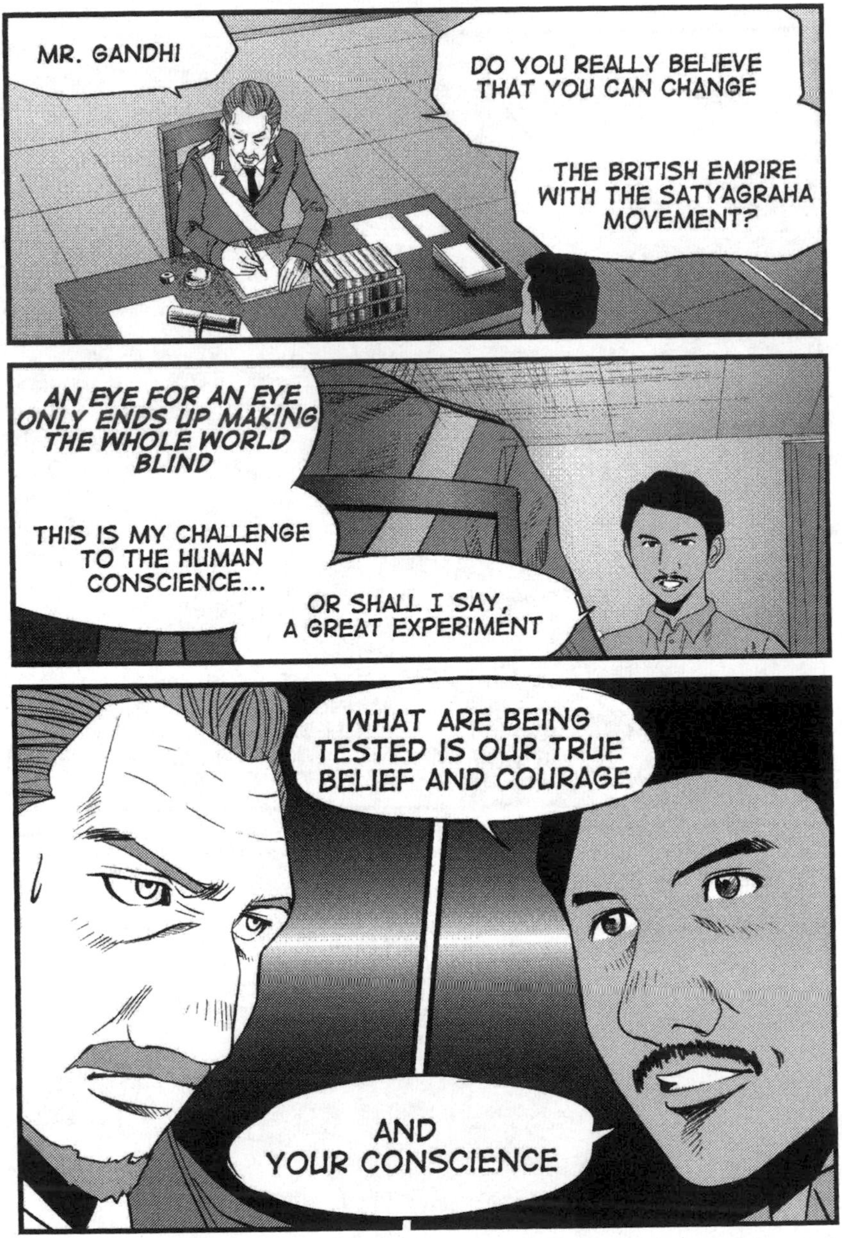
MR. GANDHI
DO YOU REALLY BELIEVE THAT YOU CAN CHANGE
THE BRITISH EMPIRE WITH THE SATYAGRAHA MOVEMENT?
AN EYE FOR AN EYE ONLY ENDS UP MAKING THE WHOLE WORLD BLIND
THIS IS MY CHALLENGE TO THE HUMAN CONSCIENCE...
OR SHALL I SAY, A GREAT EXPERIMENT
WHAT ARE BEING TESTED IS OUR TRUE BELIEF AND COURAGE
AND YOUR CONSCIENCE

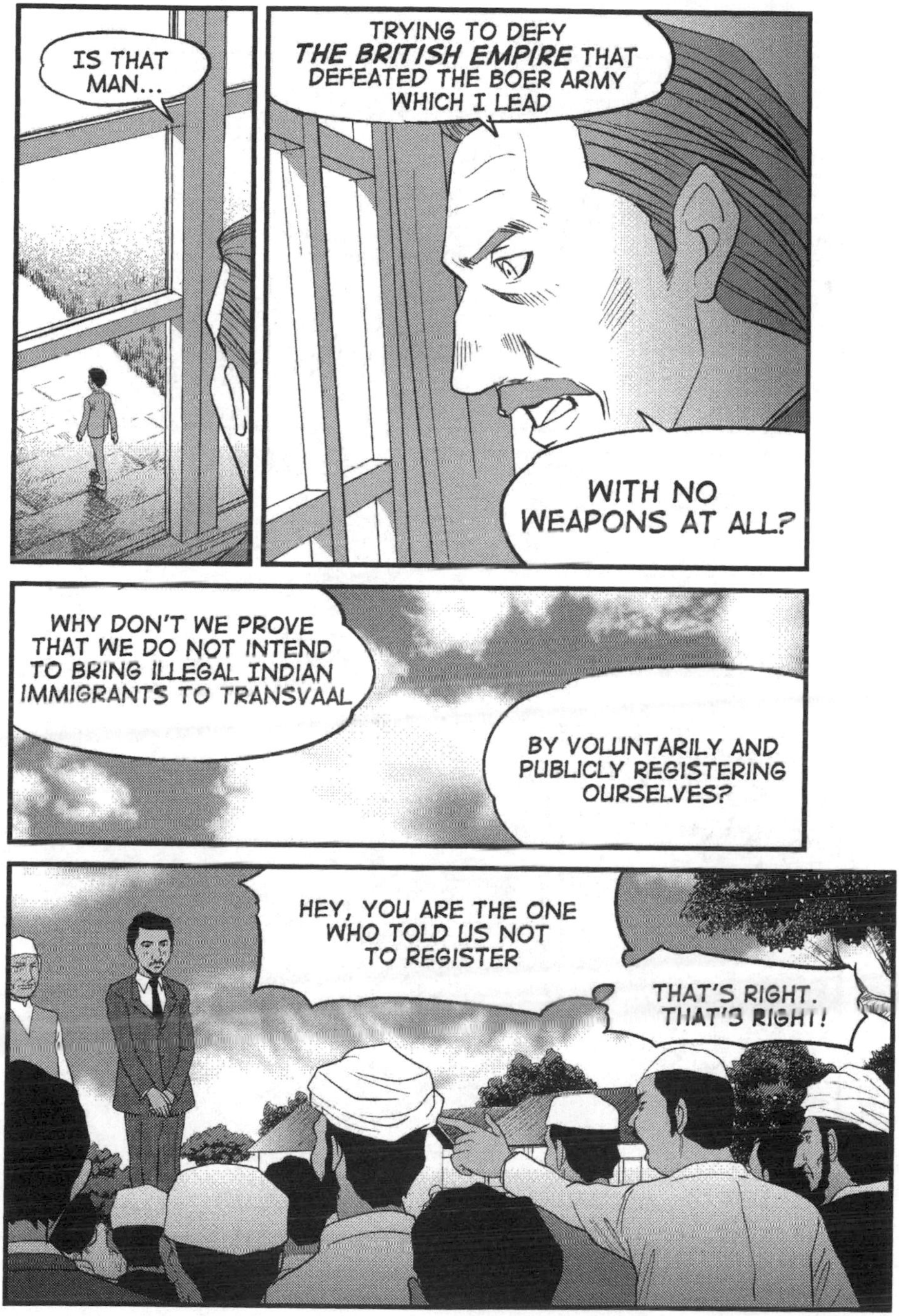
IS THAT MAN...
TRYING TO DEFY *THE BRITISH EMPIRE* THAT DEFEATED THE BOER ARMY WHICH I LEAD
WITH NO WEAPONS AT ALL?
WHY DON'T WE PROVE THAT WE DO NOT INTEND TO BRING ILLEGAL INDIAN IMMIGRANTS TO TRANSVAAL
BY VOLUNTARILY AND PUBLICLY REGISTERING OURSELVES?
HEY, YOU ARE THE ONE WHO TOLD US NOT TO REGISTER
THAT'S RIGHT. THAT'S RIGHT!

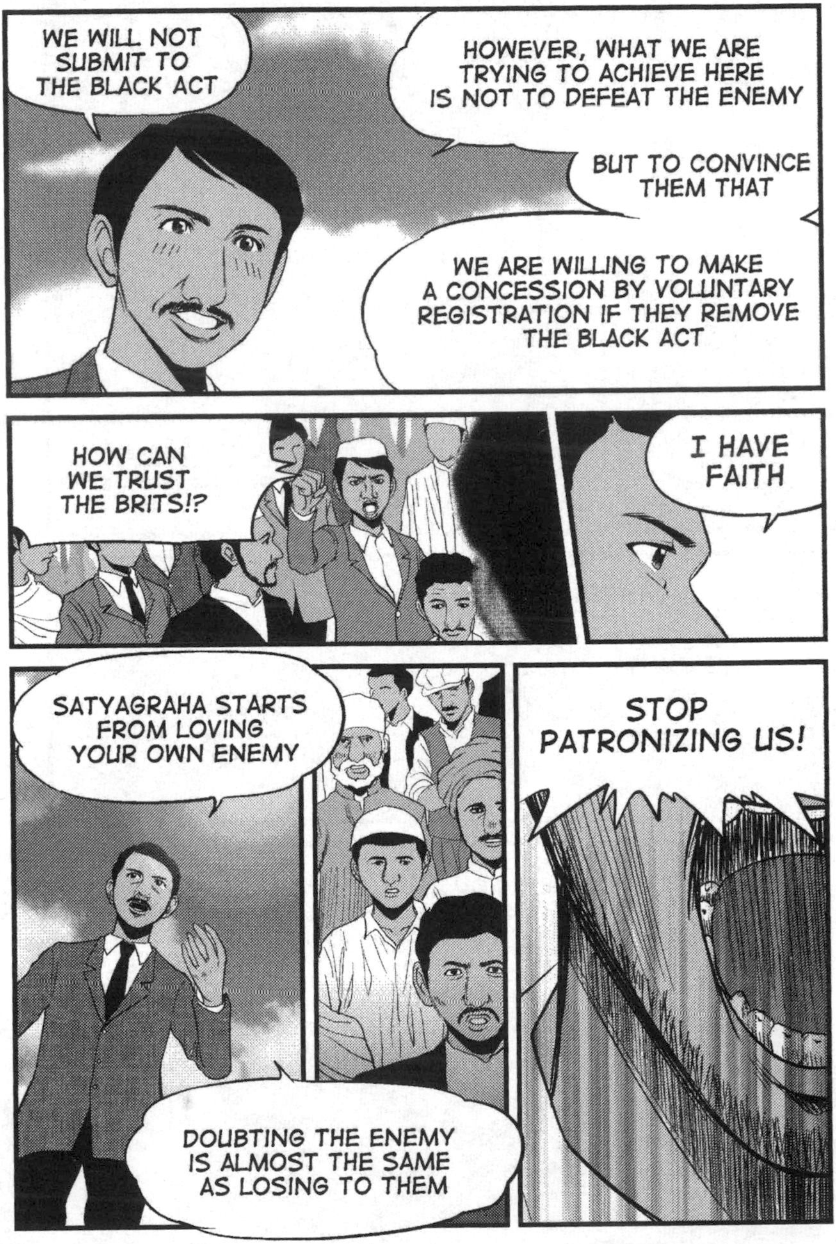
WE WILL NOT SUBMIT TO THE BLACK ACT
HOWEVER, WHAT WE ARE TRYING TO ACHIEVE HERE IS NOT TO DEFEAT THE ENEMY
BUT TO CONVINCE THEM THAT
WE ARE WILLING TO MAKE A CONCESSION BY VOLUNTARY REGISTRATION IF THEY REMOVE THE BLACK ACT
HOW CAN WE TRUST THE BRITS!?
I HAVE FAITH
SATYAGRAHA STARTS FROM LOVING YOUR OWN ENEMY
DOUBTING THE ENEMY IS ALMOST THE SAME AS LOSING TO THEM
STOP PATRONIZING US!

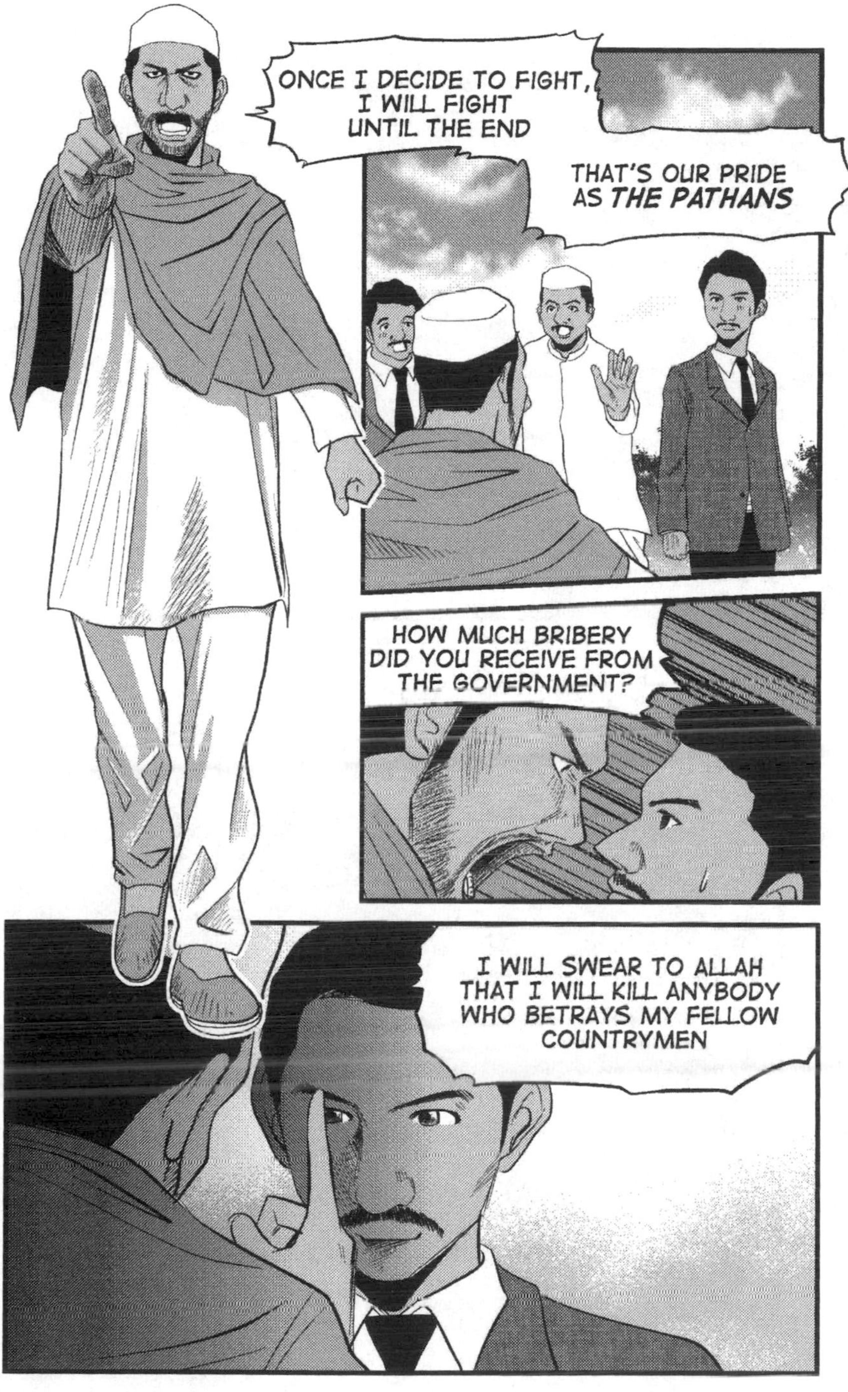
ONCE I DECIDE TO FIGHT, I WILL FIGHT UNTIL THE END
THAT'S OUR PRIDE AS *THE PATHANS*
HOW MUCH BRIBERY DID YOU RECEIVE FROM THE GOVERNMENT?
I WILL SWEAR TO ALLAH THAT I WILL KILL ANYBODY WHO BETRAYS MY FELLOW COUNTRYMEN

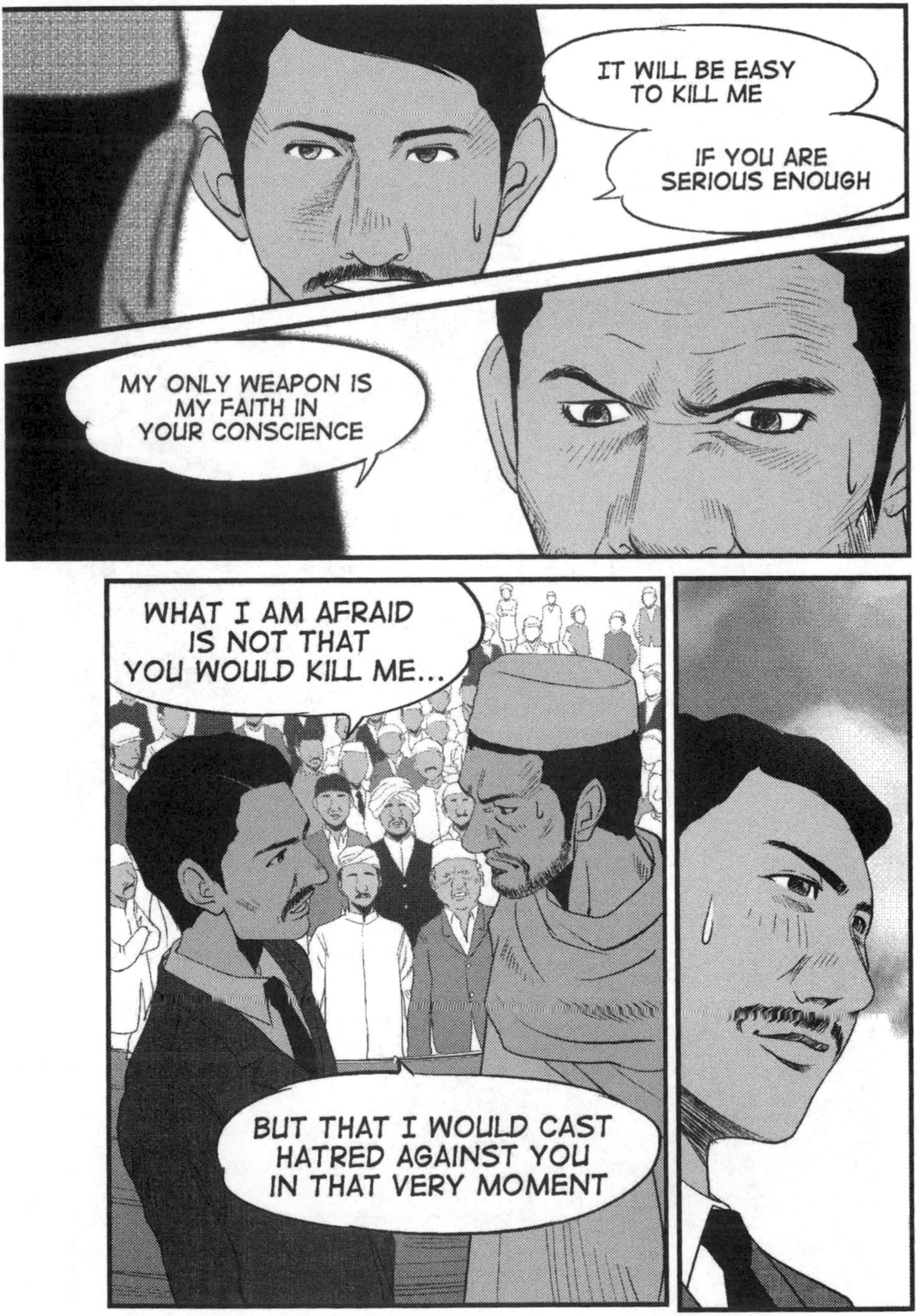
IT WILL BE EASY TO KILL ME
IF YOU ARE SERIOUS ENOUGH
MY ONLY WEAPON IS MY FAITH IN YOUR CONSCIENCE
WHAT I AM AFRAID IS NOT THAT YOU WOULD KILL ME...
BUT THAT I WOULD CAST HATRED AGAINST YOU IN THAT VERY MOMENT

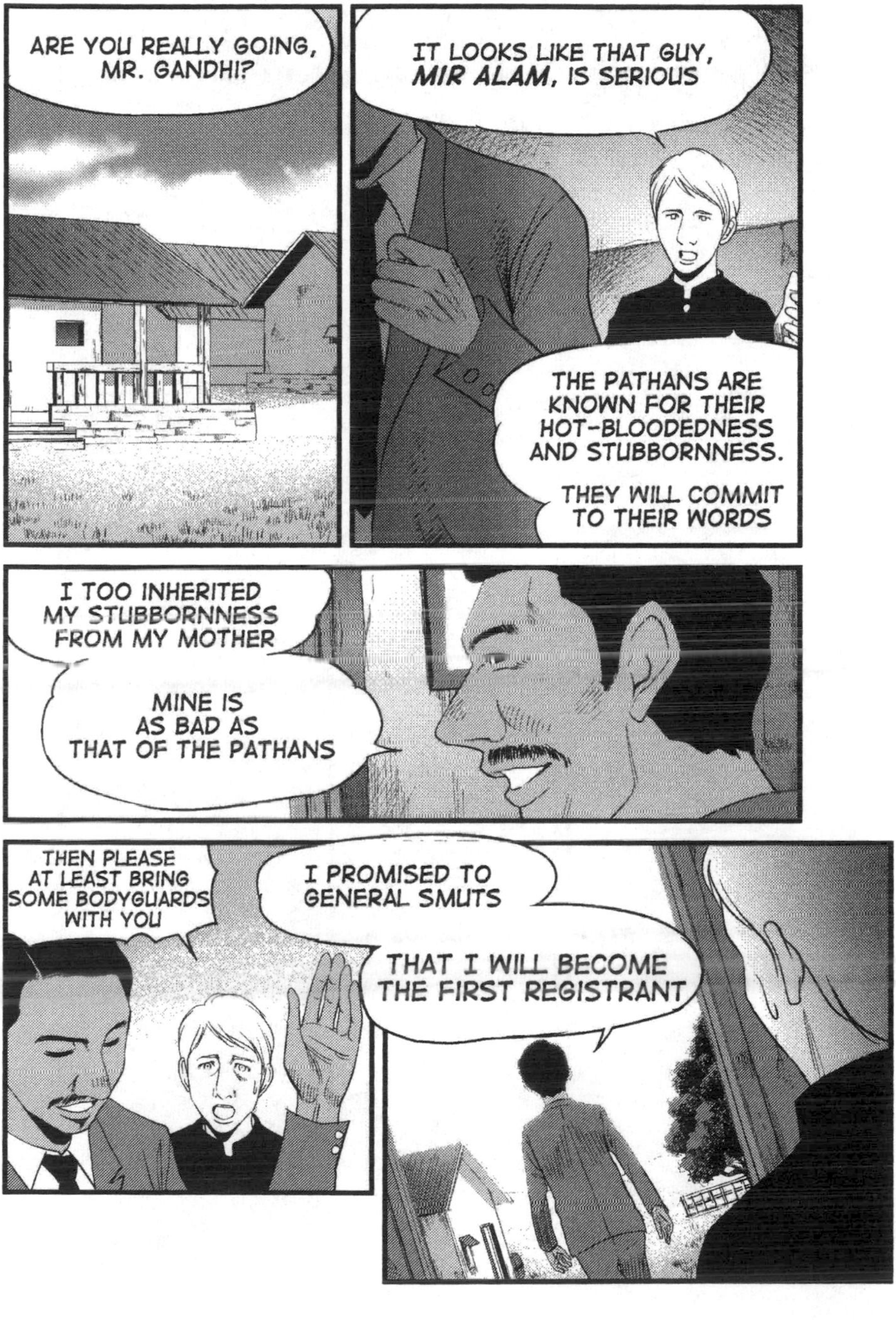
ARE YOU REALLY GOING, MR. GANDHI?
IT LOOKS LIKE THAT GUY, MIR ALAM, IS SERIOUS
THE PATHANS ARE KNOWN FOR THEIR HOT-BLOODEDNESS AND STUBBORNNESS.
THEY WILL COMMIT TO THEIR WORDS
I TOO INHERITED MY STUBBORNNESS FROM MY MOTHER
MINE IS AS BAD AS THAT OF THE PATHANS
THEN PLEASE AT LEAST BRING SOME BODYGUARDS WITH YOU
I PROMISED TO GENERAL SMUTS
THAT I WILL BECOME THE FIRST REGISTRANT

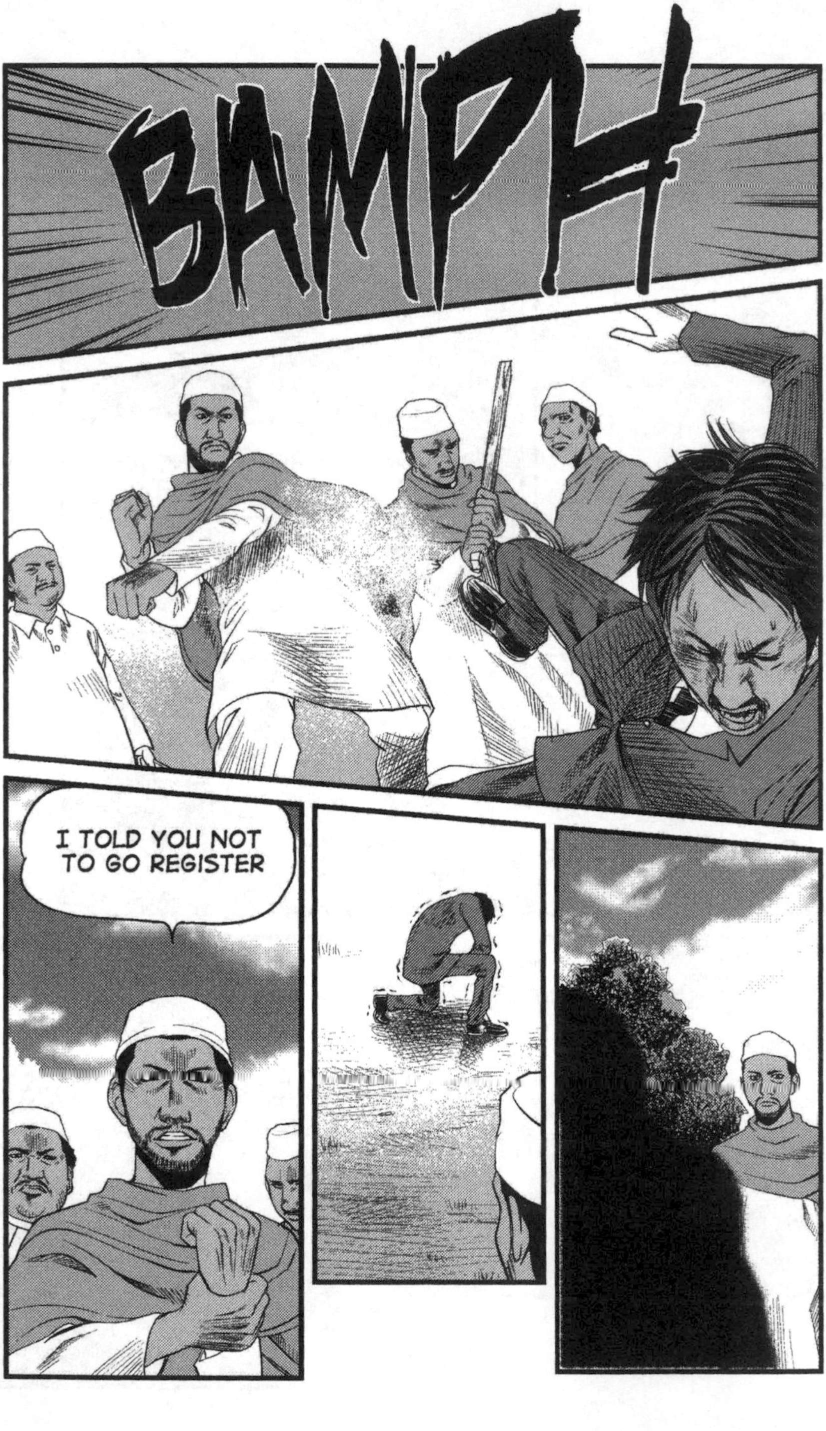
BAMPH
I TOLD YOU NOT TO GO REGISTER

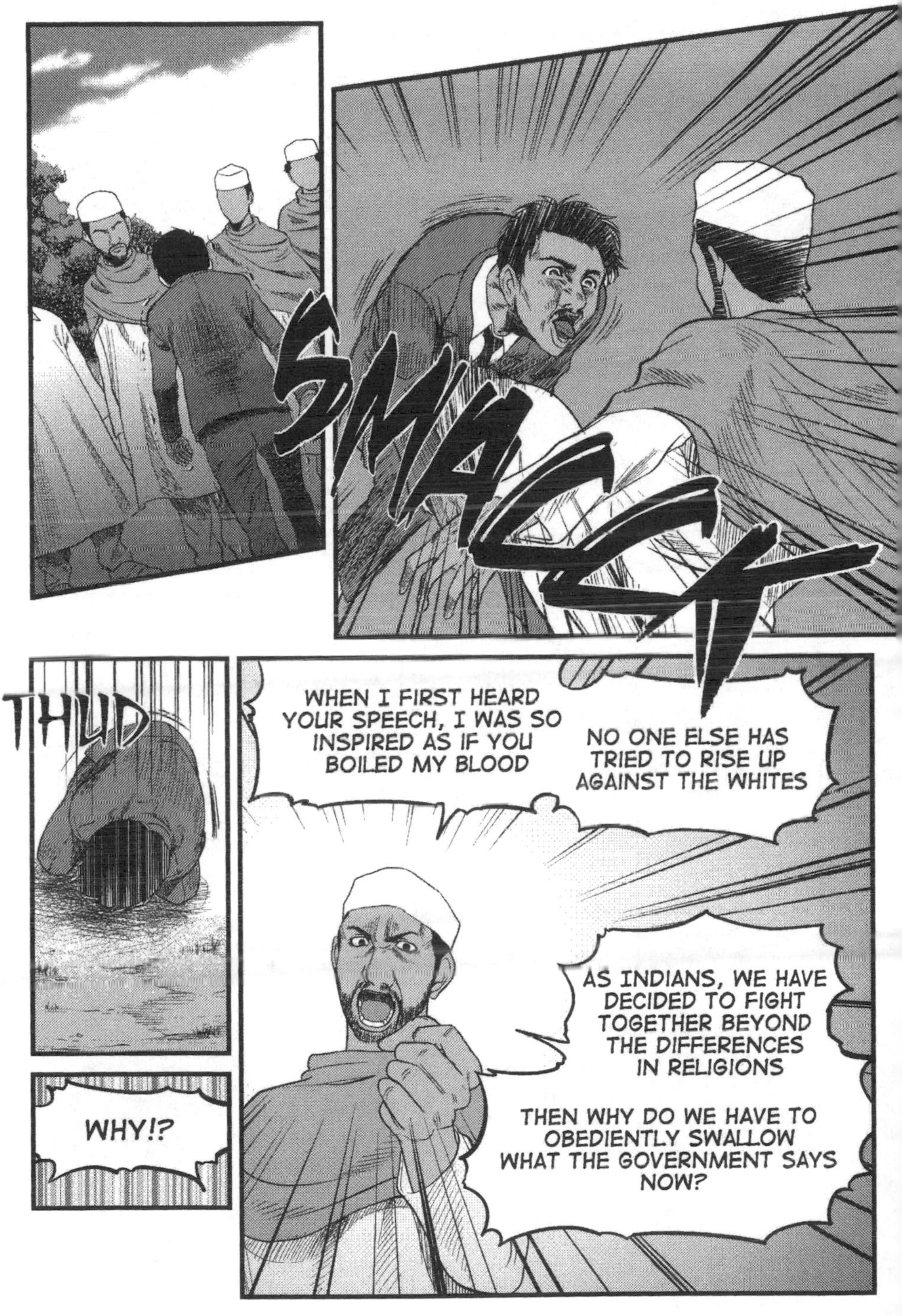
SMACK
THUD
WHEN I FIRST HEARD YOUR SPEECH, I WAS SO INSPIRED AS IF YOU BOILED MY BLOOD
NO ONE ELSE HAS TRIED TO RISE UP AGAINST THE WHITES
WHY!?
AS INDIANS, WE HAVE DECIDED TO FIGHT TOGETHER BEYOND THE DIFFERENCES IN RELIGIONS
THEN WHY DO WE HAVE TO OBEDIENTLY SWALLOW WHAT THE GOVERNMENT SAYS NOW?

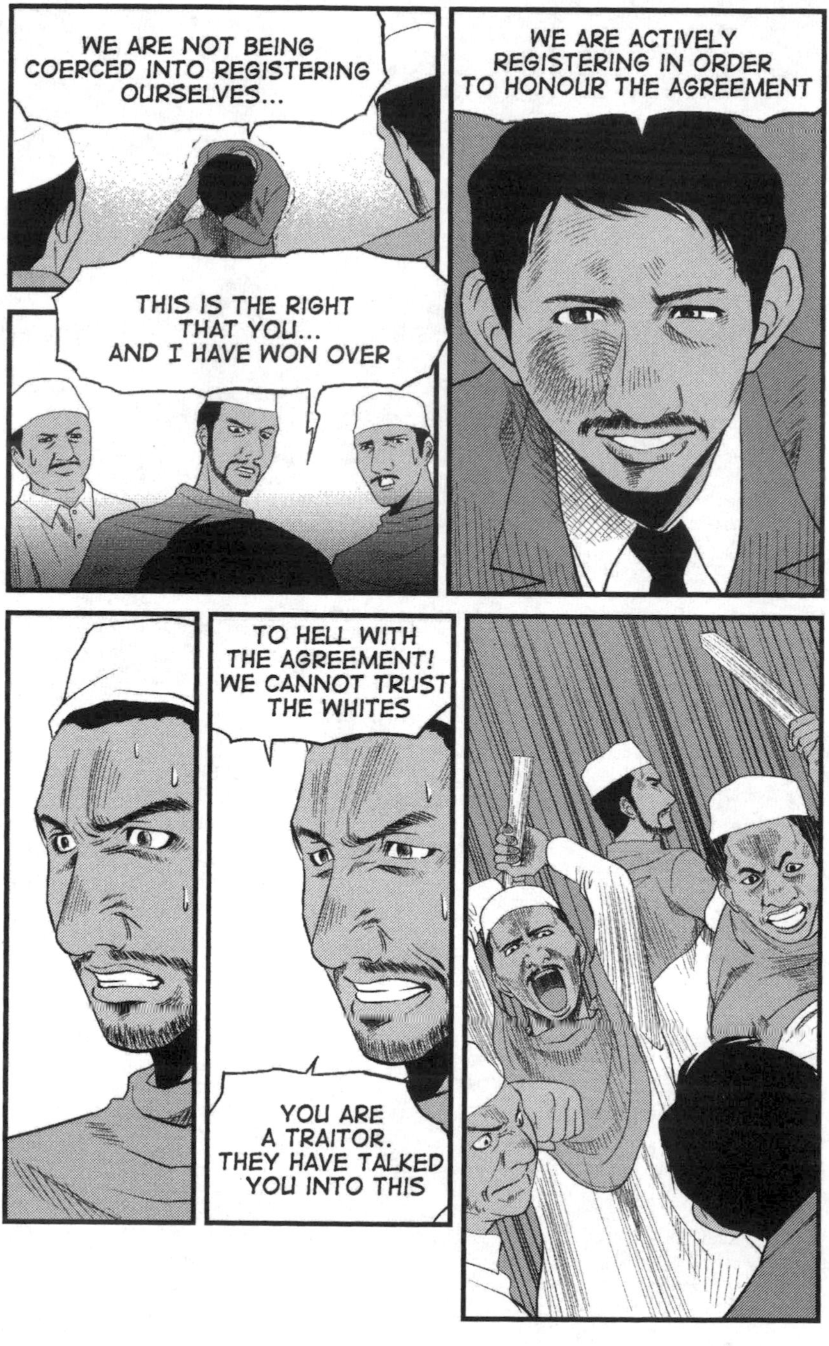
WE ARE NOT BEING COERCED INTO REGISTERING OURSELVES...
WE ARE ACTIVELY REGISTERING IN ORDER TO HONOUR THE AGREEMENT
THIS IS THE RIGHT THAT YOU... AND I HAVE WON OVER
TO HELL WITH THE AGREEMENT! WE CANNOT TRUST THE WHITES
YOU ARE A TRAITOR. THEY HAVE TALKED YOU INTO THIS

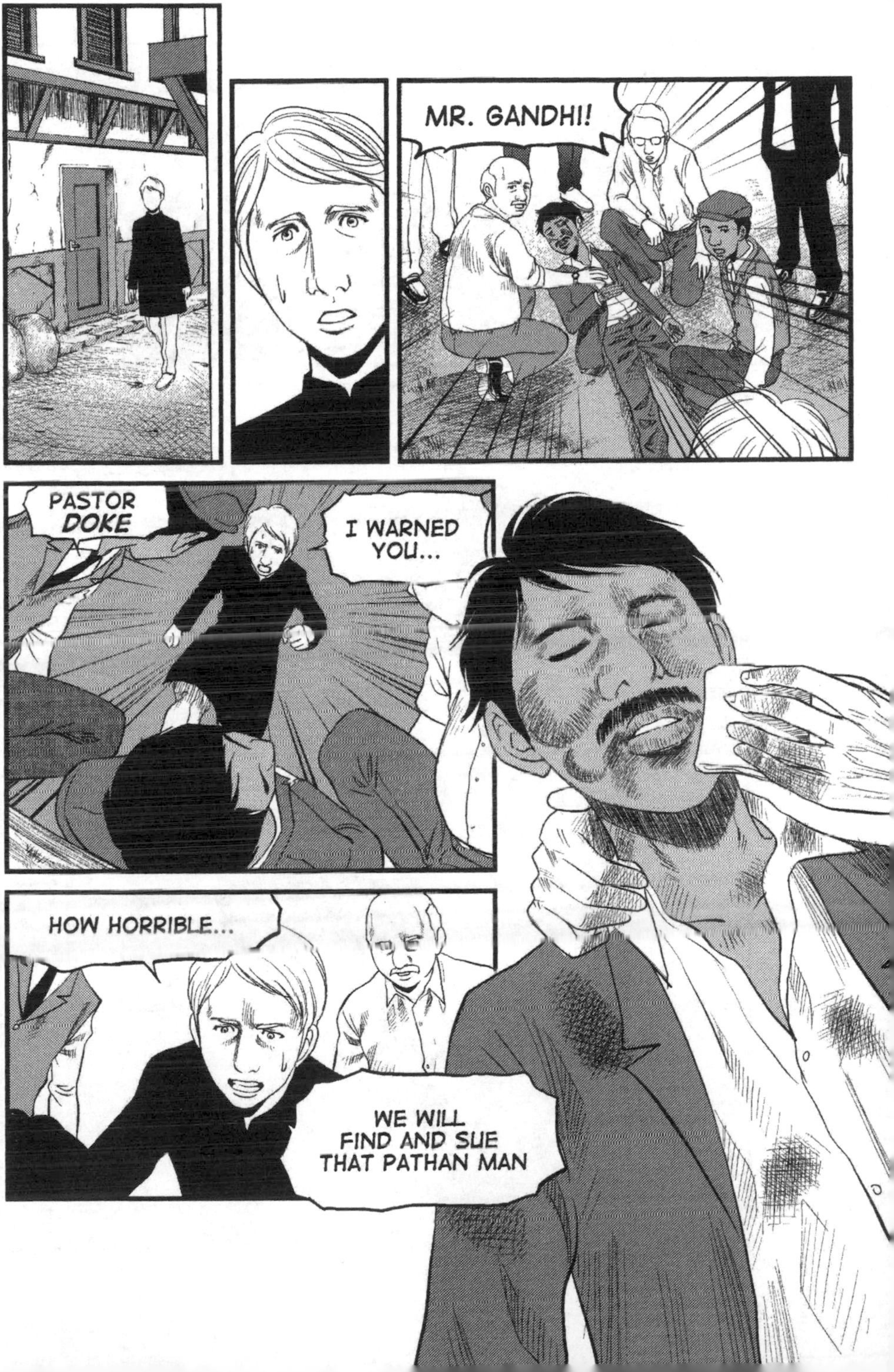
MR. GANDHI!
PASTOR DOKE
I WARNED YOU...
HOW HORRIBLE...
WE WILL FIND AND SUE THAT PATHAN MAN

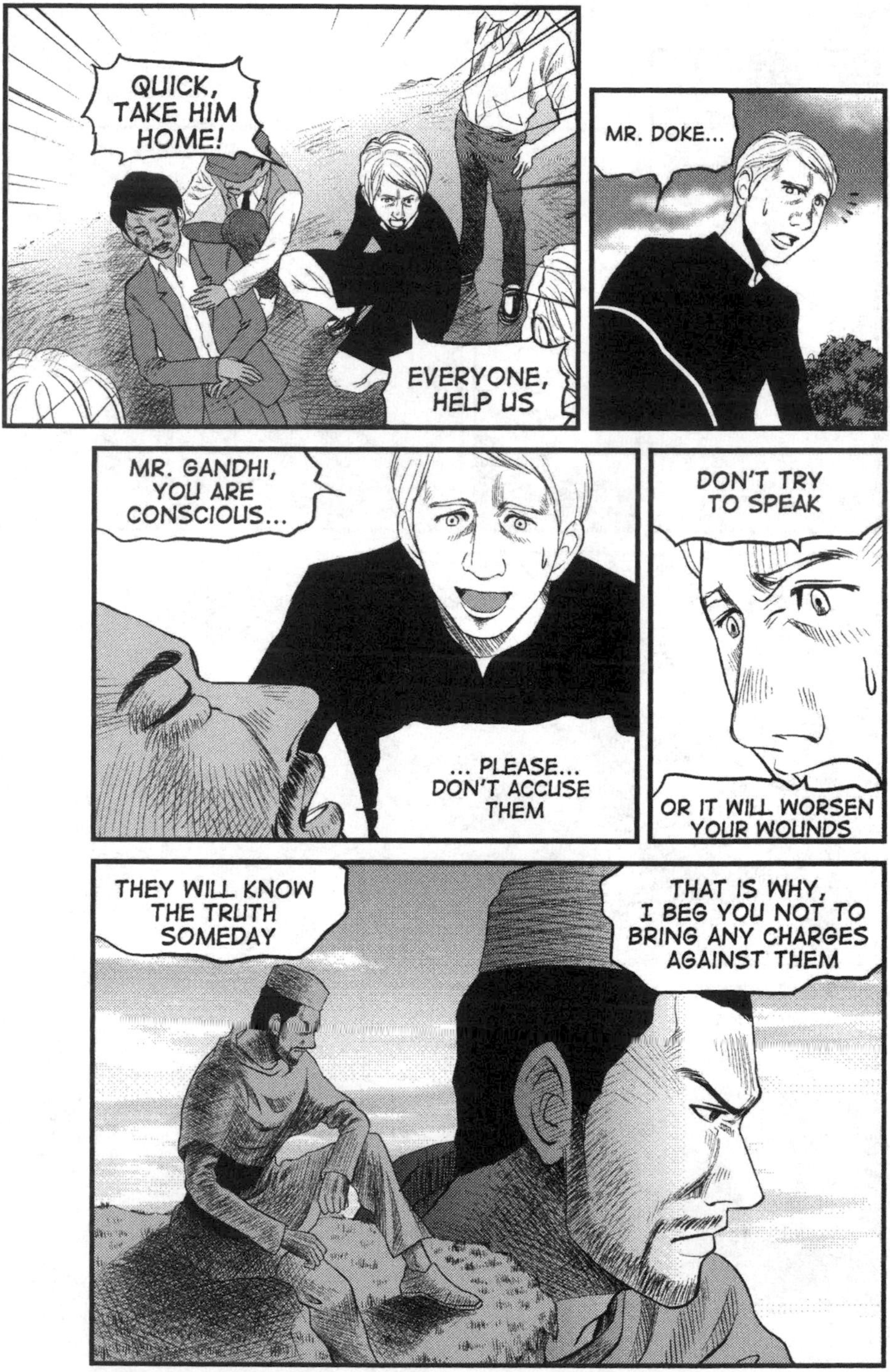
QUICK, TAKE HIM HOME!
EVERYONE, HELP US
MR. DOKE...
MR. GANDHI, YOU ARE CONSCIOUS...
... PLEASE... DON'T ACCUSE THEM
DON'T TRY TO SPEAK
OR IT WILL WORSEN YOUR WOUNDS
THEY WILL KNOW THE TRUTH SOMEDAY
THAT IS WHY, I BEG YOU NOT TO BRING ANY CHARGES AGAINST THEM

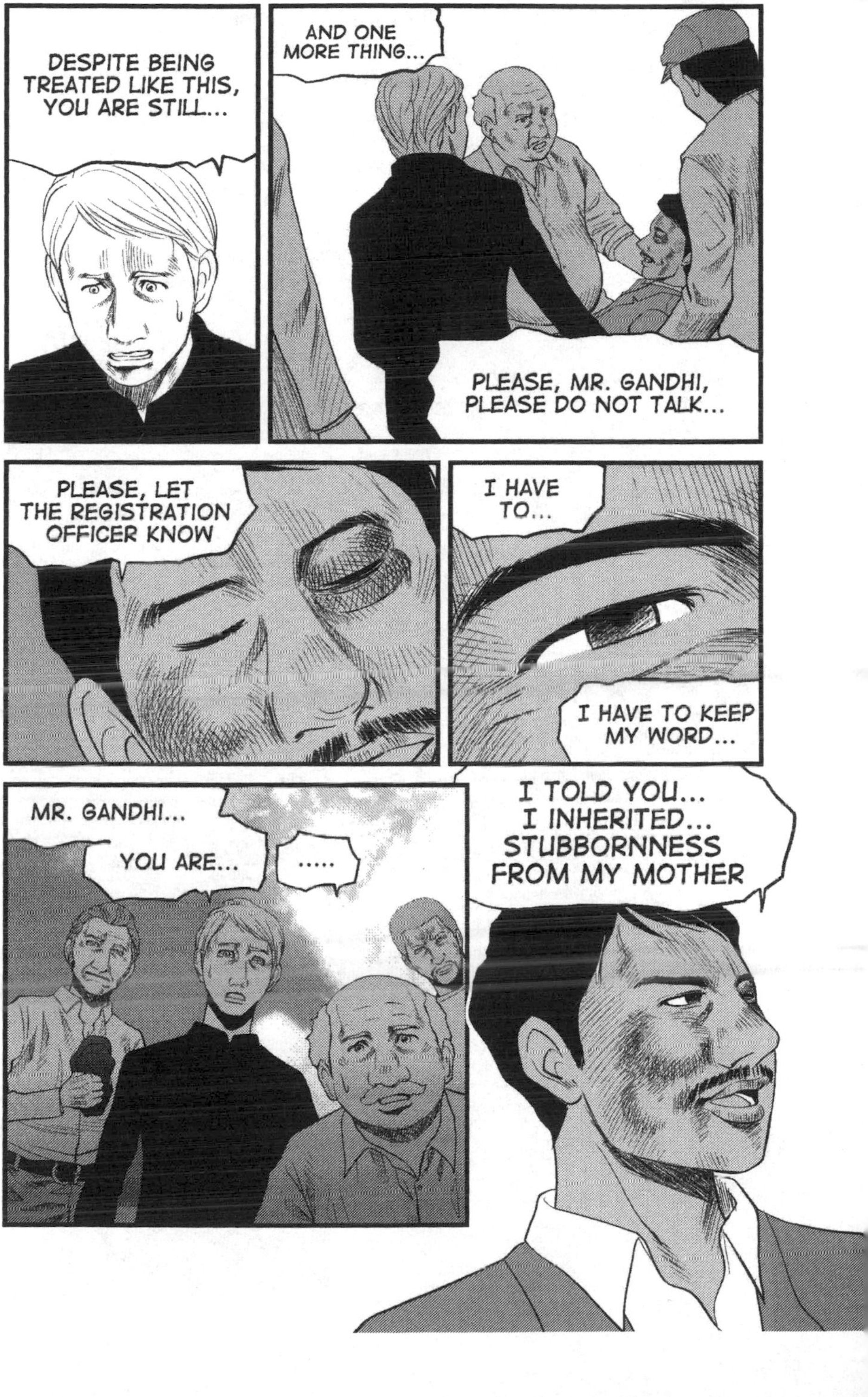
DESPITE BEING TREATED LIKE THIS, YOU ARE STILL...
AND ONE MORE THING...
PLEASE, MR. GANDHI, PLEASE DO NOT TALK...
PLEASE, LET THE REGISTRATION OFFICER KNOW
I HAVE TO...
I HAVE TO KEEP MY WORD...
MR. GANDHI...
YOU ARE...
.....
I TOLD YOU... I INHERITED... STUBBORNNESS FROM MY MOTHER

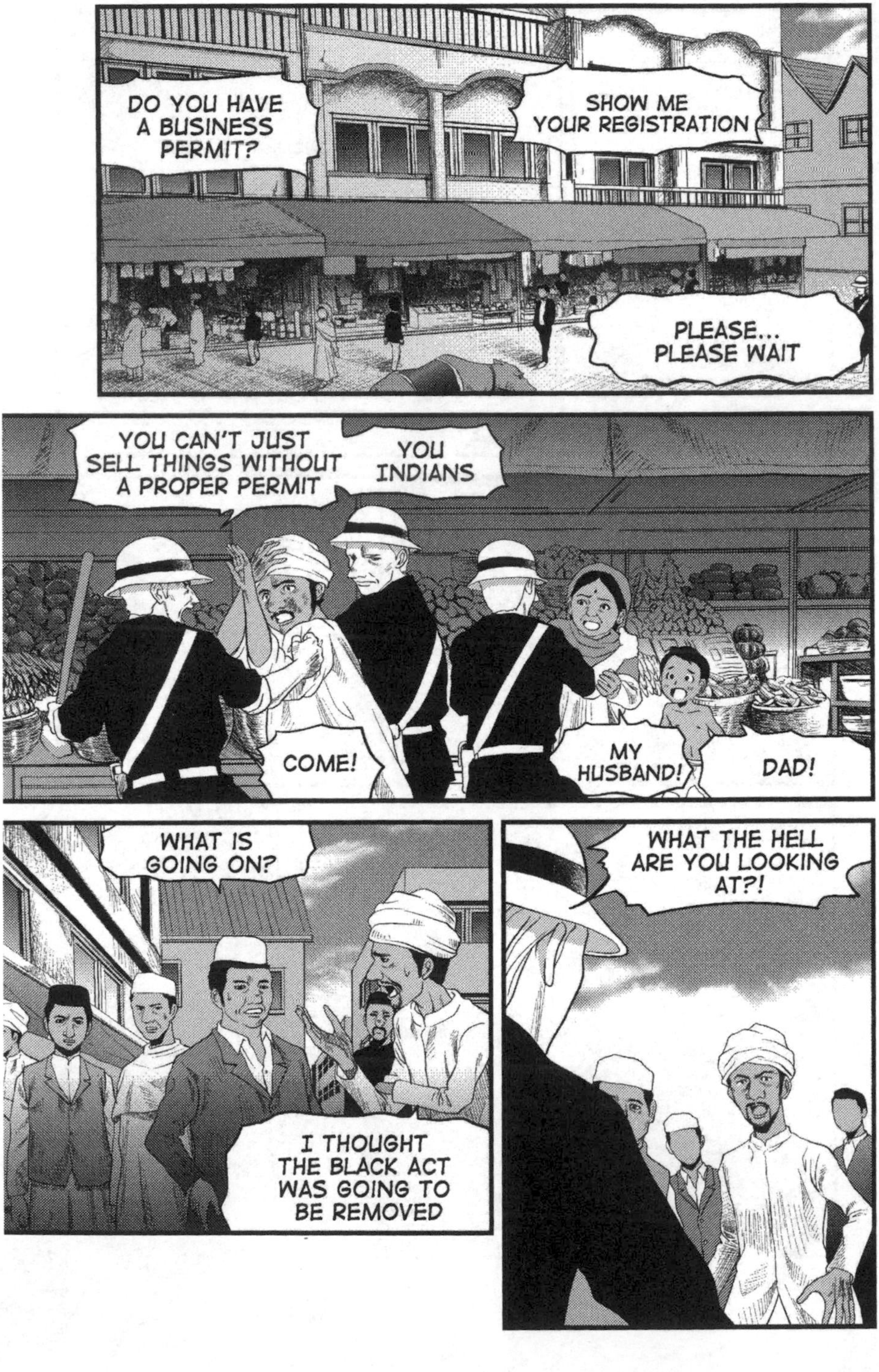
DO YOU HAVE A BUSINESS PERMIT?
SHOW ME YOUR REGISTRATION
PLEASE... PLEASE WAIT
YOU CAN'T JUST SELL THINGS WITHOUT A PROPER PERMIT
YOU INDIANS
COME!
MY HUSBAND!
DAD!
WHAT IS GOING ON?
I THOUGHT THE BLACK ACT WAS GOING TO BE REMOVED
WHAT THE HELL ARE YOU LOOKING AT?!

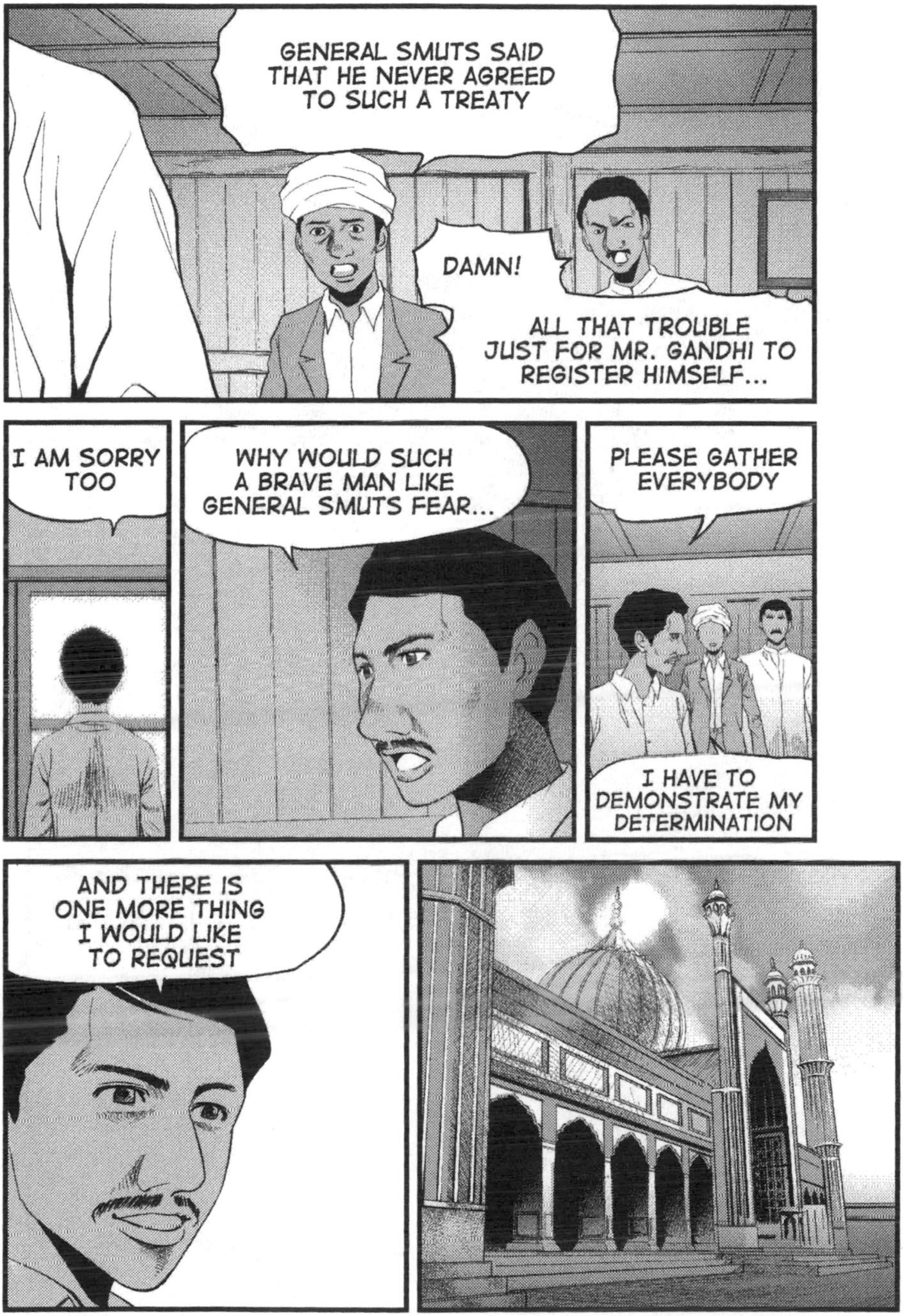
GENERAL SMUTS SAID THAT HE NEVER AGREED TO SUCH A TREATY
DAMN!
ALL THAT TROUBLE JUST FOR MR. GANDHI TO REGISTER HIMSELF...
I AM SORRY TOO
WHY WOULD SUCH A BRAVE MAN LIKE GENERAL SMUTS FEAR...
PLEASE GATHER EVERYBODY
I HAVE TO DEMONSTRATE MY DETERMINATION
AND THERE IS ONE MORE THING I WOULD LIKE TO REQUEST

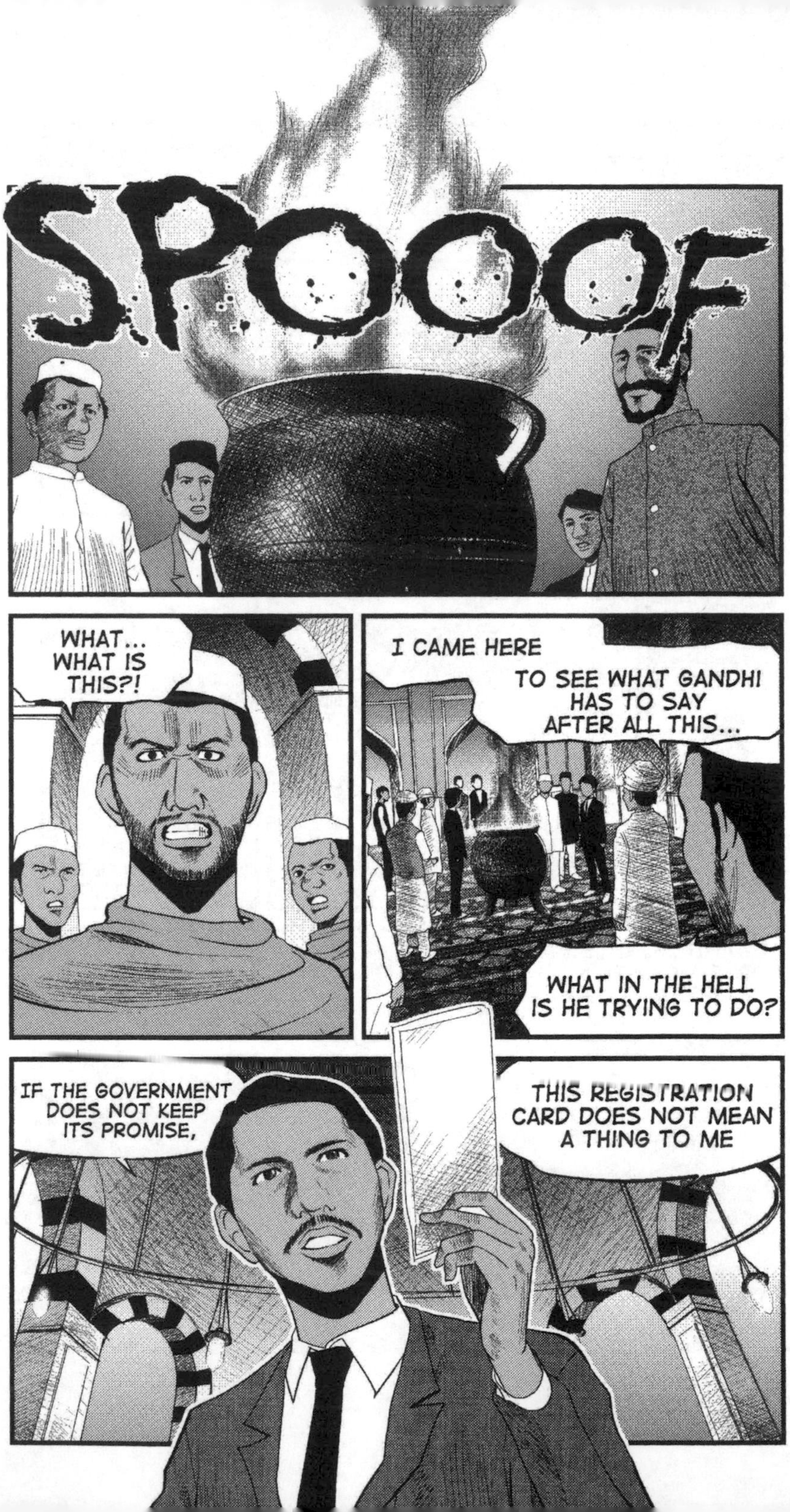
SPOOOF
WHAT... WHAT IS THIS?!
I CAME HERE
TO SEE WHAT GANDHI HAS TO SAY AFTER ALL THIS...
WHAT IN THE HELL IS HE TRYING TO DO?
IF THE GOVERNMENT DOES NOT KEEP ITS PROMISE,
THIS REGISTRATION CARD DOES NOT MEAN A THING TO ME

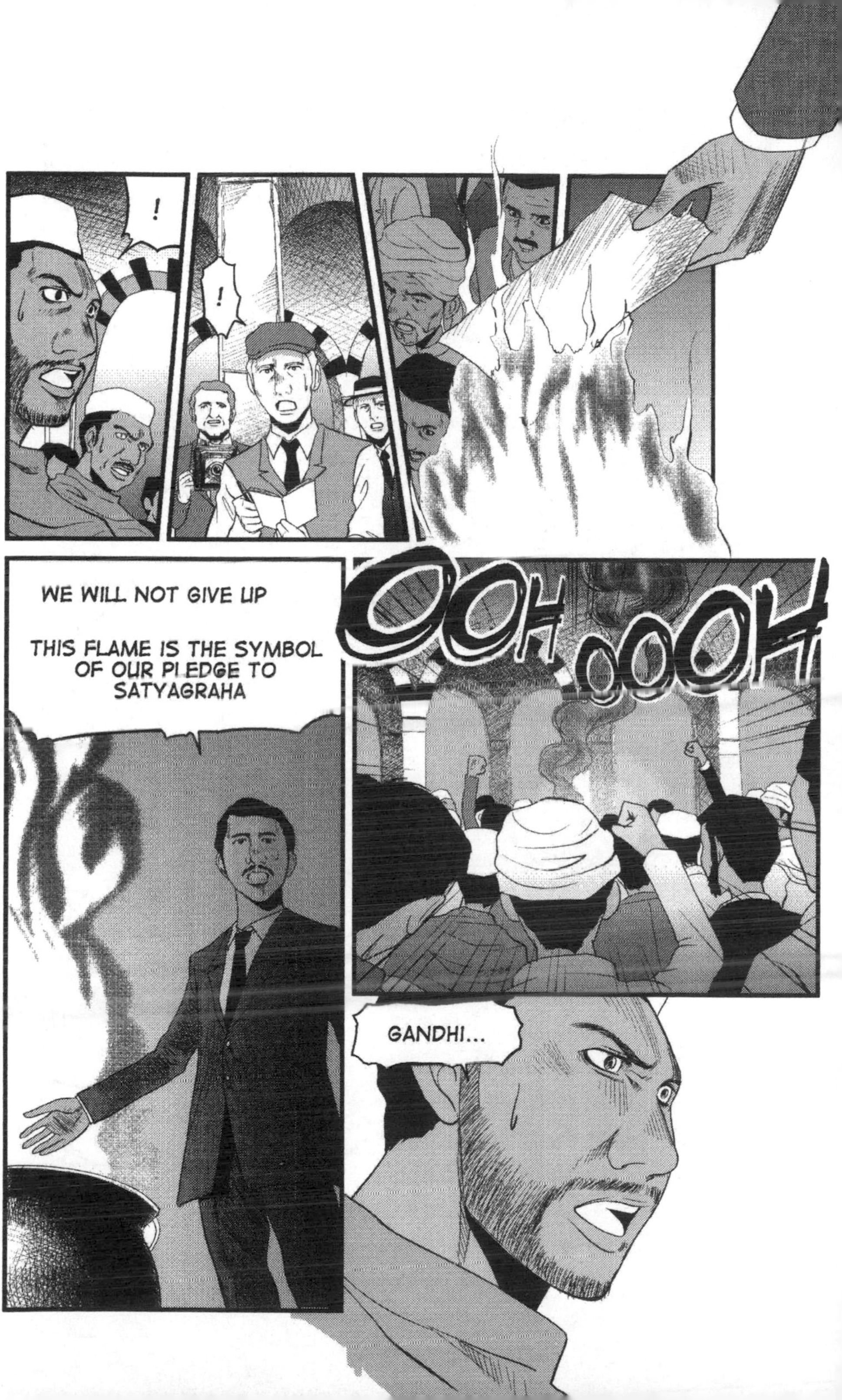
!
!
WE WILL NOT GIVE UP
THIS FLAME IS THE SYMBOL OF OUR PLEDGE TO SATYAGRAHA
OOH OOOH
GANDHI...

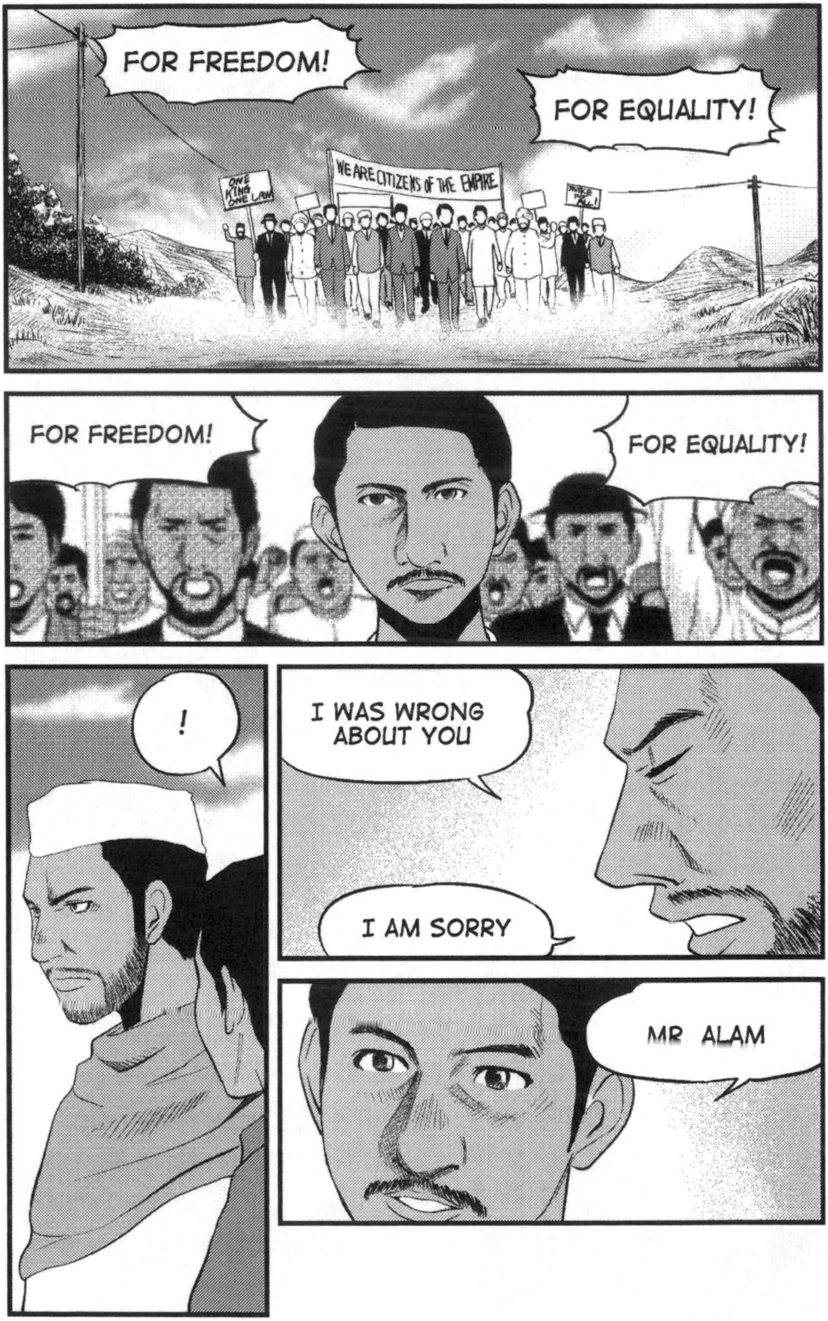
FOR FREEDOM!
FOR EQUALITY!
ONE KING ONE LAW
WE ARE CITIZENS OF THE EMPIRE
FOR FREEDOM!
FOR EQUALITY!
!
I WAS WRONG ABOUT YOU
I AM SORRY
MR ALAM

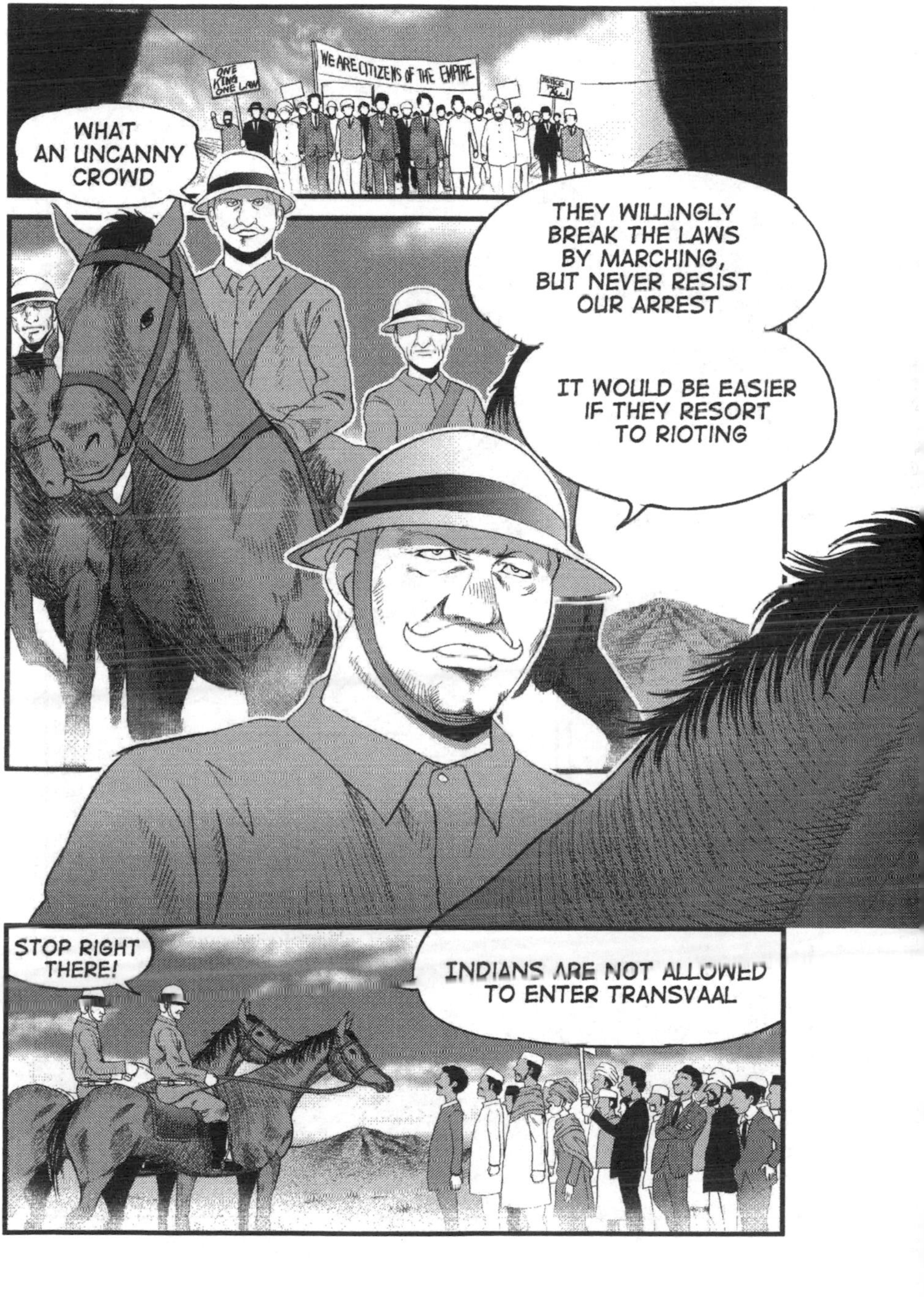
WE ARE CITIZENS OF THE EMPIRE
ONE KING ONE LAW
WHAT AN UNCANNY CROWD
THEY WILLINGLY BREAK THE LAWS BY MARCHING, BUT NEVER RESIST OUR ARREST
IT WOULD BE EASIER IF THEY RESORT TO RIOTING
STOP RIGHT THERE!
INDIANS ARE NOT ALLOWED TO ENTER TRANSVAAL

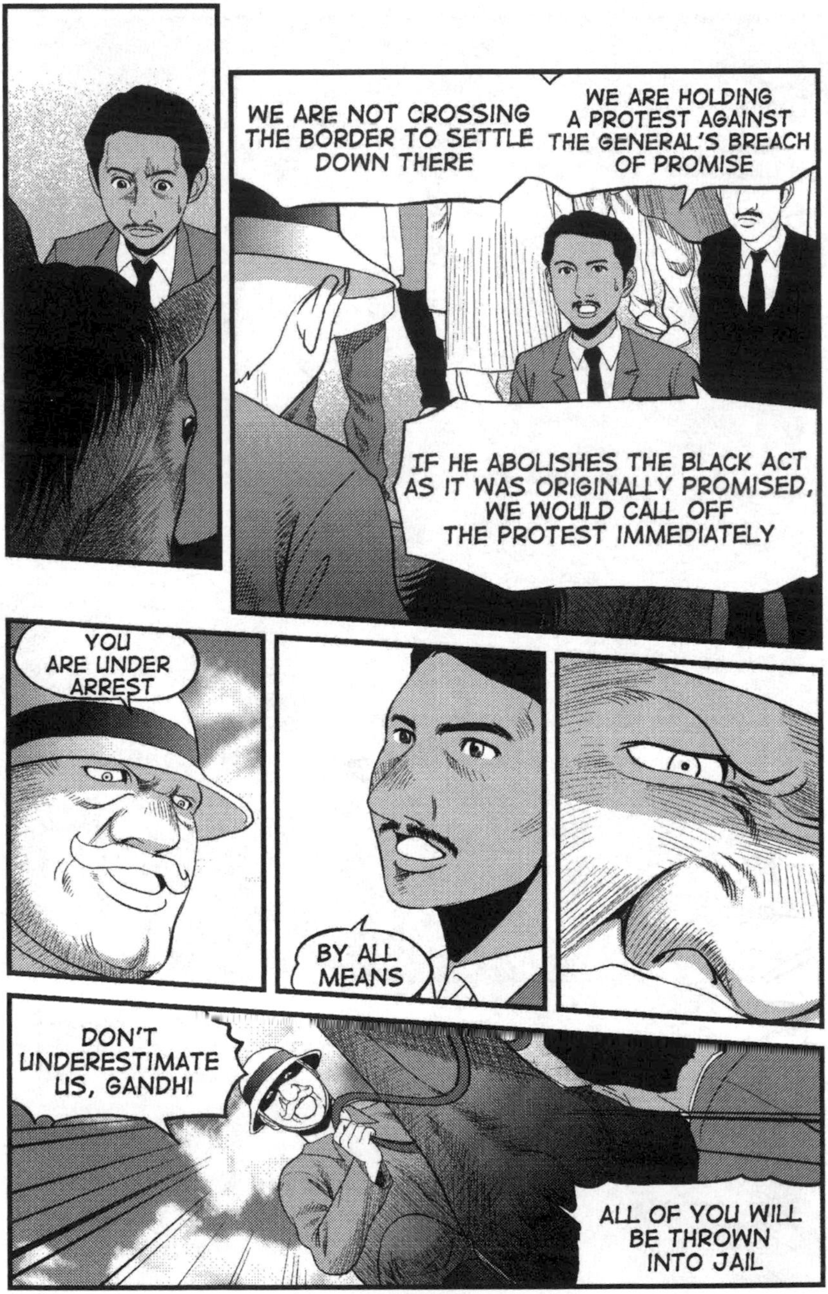
WE ARE NOT CROSSING THE BORDER TO SETTLE DOWN THERE
WE ARE HOLDING A PROTEST AGAINST THE GENERAL'S BREACH OF PROMISE
IF HE ABOLISHES THE BLACK ACT AS IT WAS ORIGINALLY PROMISED, WE WOULD CALL OFF THE PROTEST IMMEDIATELY
YOU ARE UNDER ARREST
BY ALL MEANS
DON'T UNDERESTIMATE US, GANDHI
ALL OF YOU WILL BE THROWN INTO JAIL

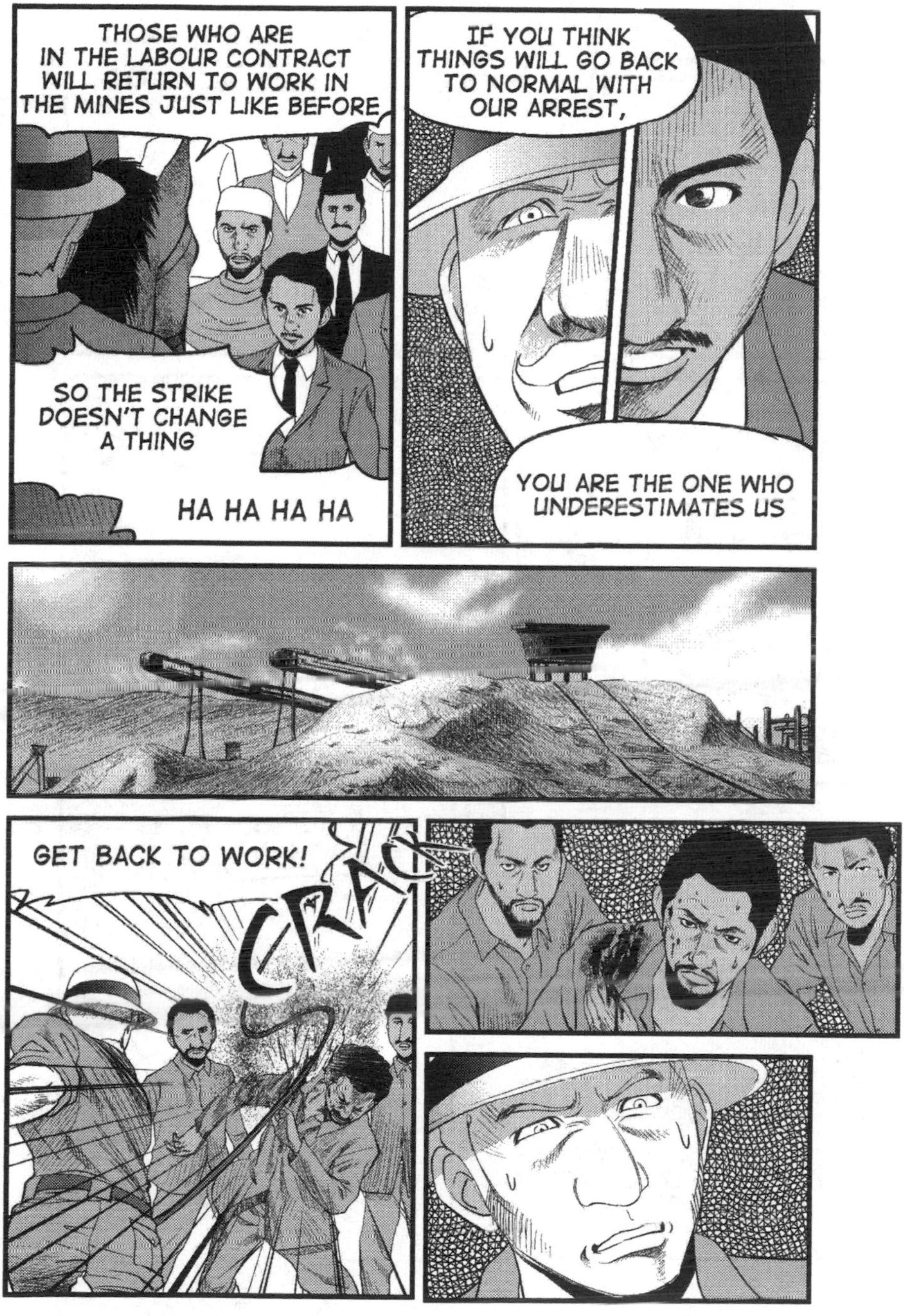
THOSE WHO ARE IN THE LABOUR CONTRACT WILL RETURN TO WORK IN THE MINES JUST LIKE BEFORE
SO THE STRIKE DOESN'T CHANGE A THING
HA HA HA HA
IF YOU THINK THINGS WILL GO BACK TO NORMAL WITH OUR ARREST,
YOU ARE THE ONE WHO UNDERESTIMATES US
GET BACK TO WORK!
CRACK

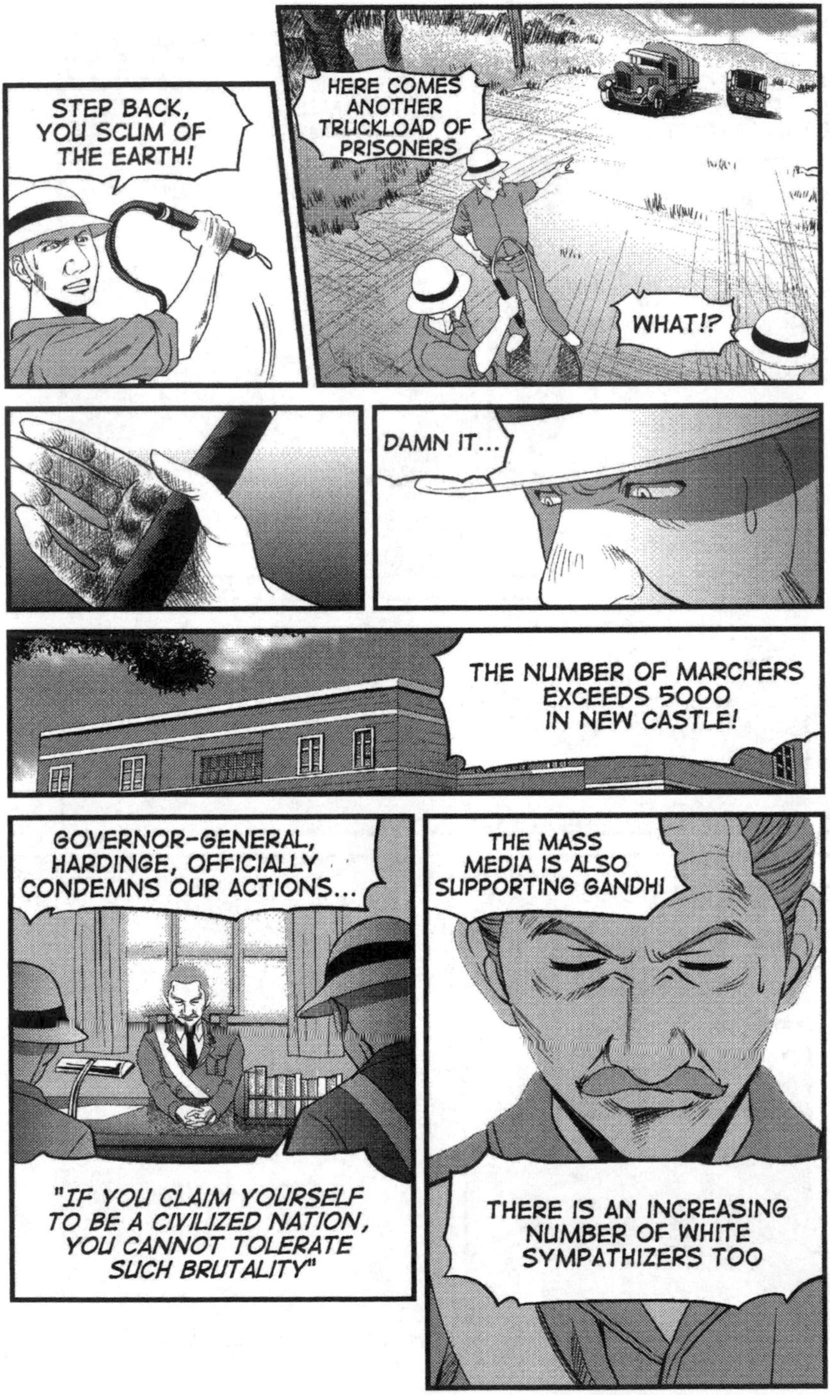
STEP BACK, YOU SCUM OF THE EARTH!
HERE COMES ANOTHER TRUCKLOAD OF PRISONERS
WHAT!?
DAMN IT...
THE NUMBER OF MARCHERS EXCEEDS 5000 IN NEW CASTLE!
GOVERNOR-GENERAL, HARDINGE, OFFICIALLY CONDEMNS OUR ACTIONS...
"IF YOU CLAIM YOURSELF TO BE A CIVILIZED NATION, YOU CANNOT TOLERATE SUCH BRUTALITY"
THE MASS MEDIA IS ALSO SUPPORTING GANDHI
THERE IS AN INCREASING NUMBER OF WHITE SYMPATHIZERS TOO

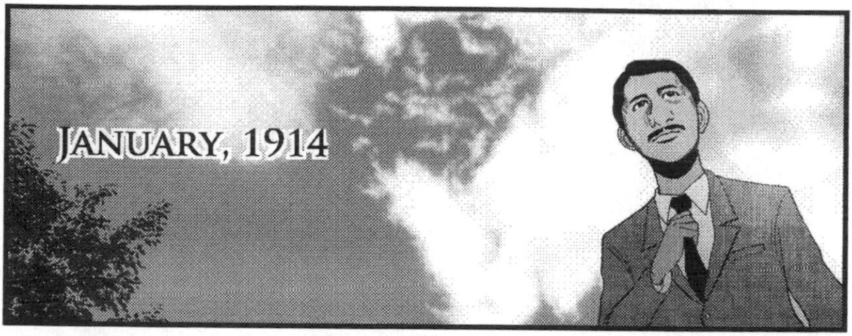
JANUARY, 1914

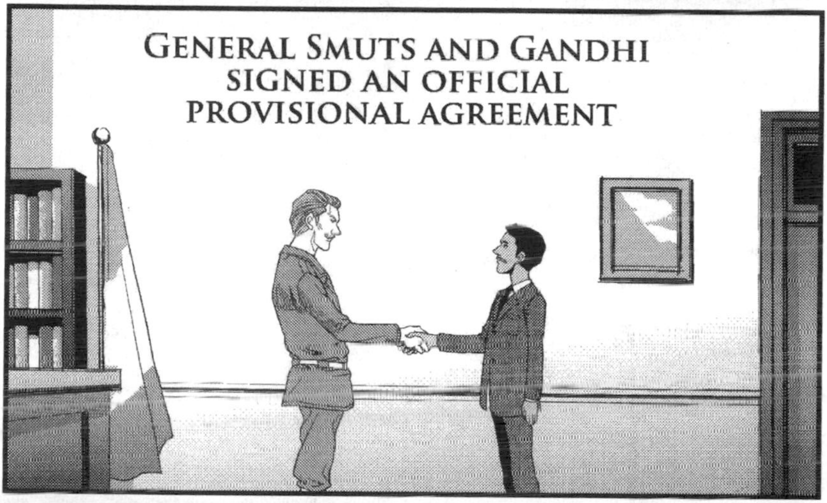
GENERAL SMUTS AND GANDHI SIGNED AN OFFICIAL PROVISIONAL AGREEMENT

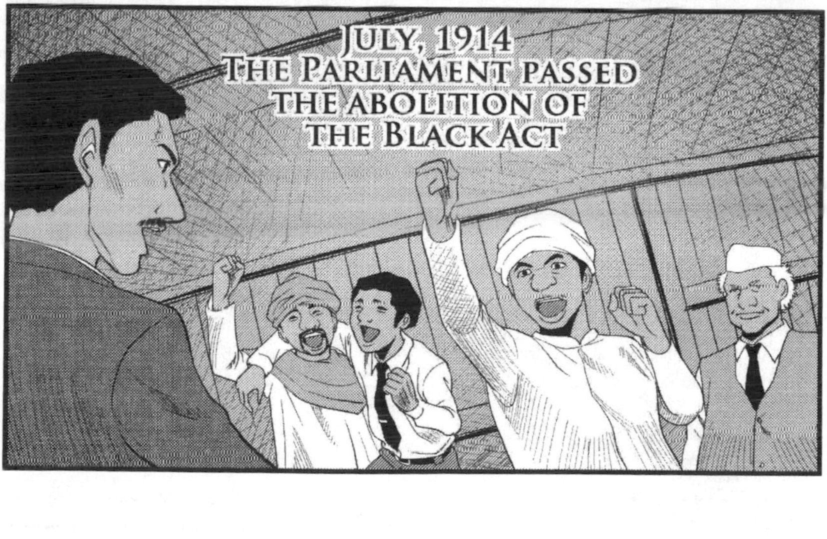
JULY, 1914
THE PARLIAMENT PASSED THE ABOLITION OF THE BLACK ACT

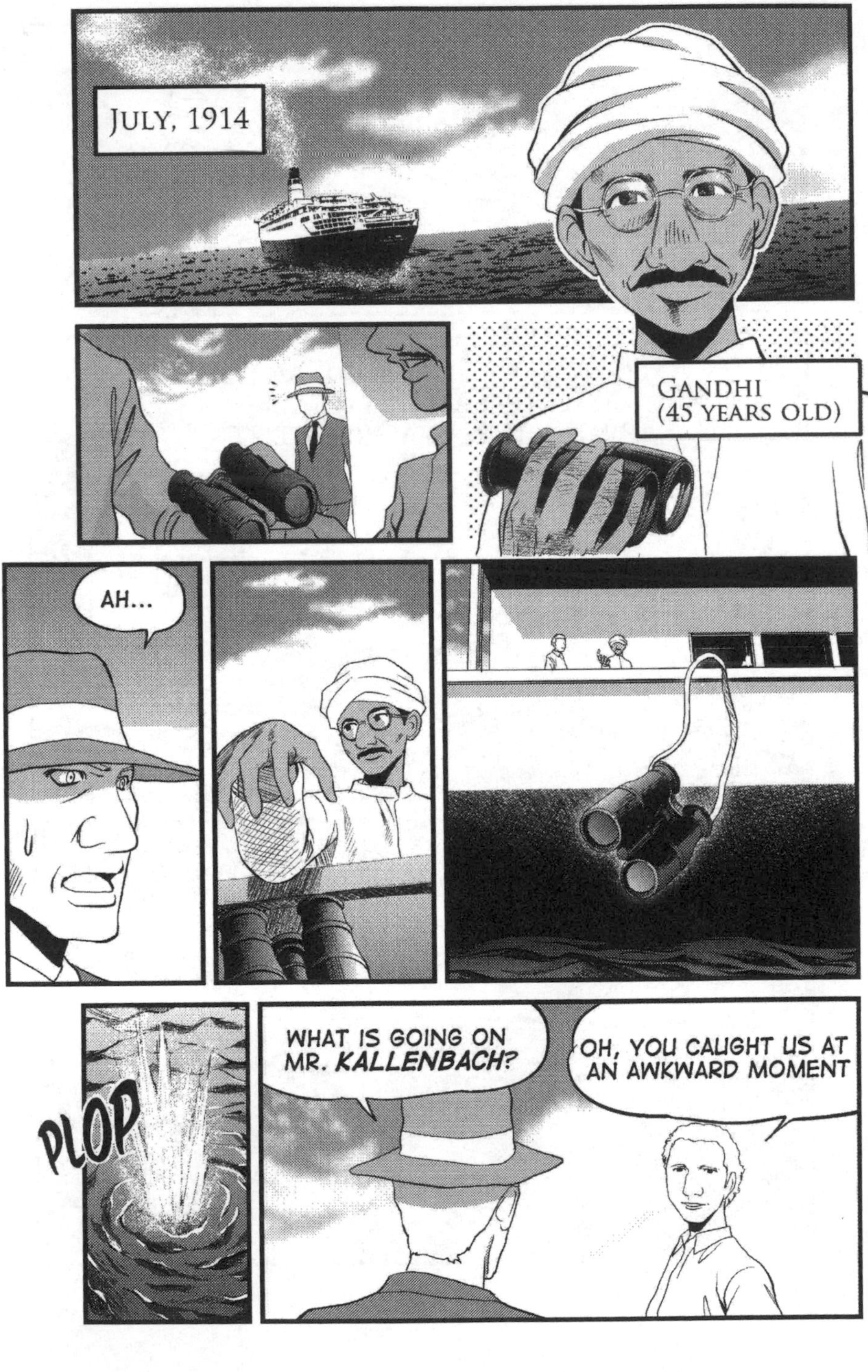

JULY, 1914
GANDHI
(45 YEARS OLD)
AH...
PLOP
WHAT IS GOING ON
MR. KALLENBACH?
OH, YOU CAUGHT US AT
AN AWKWARD MOMENT

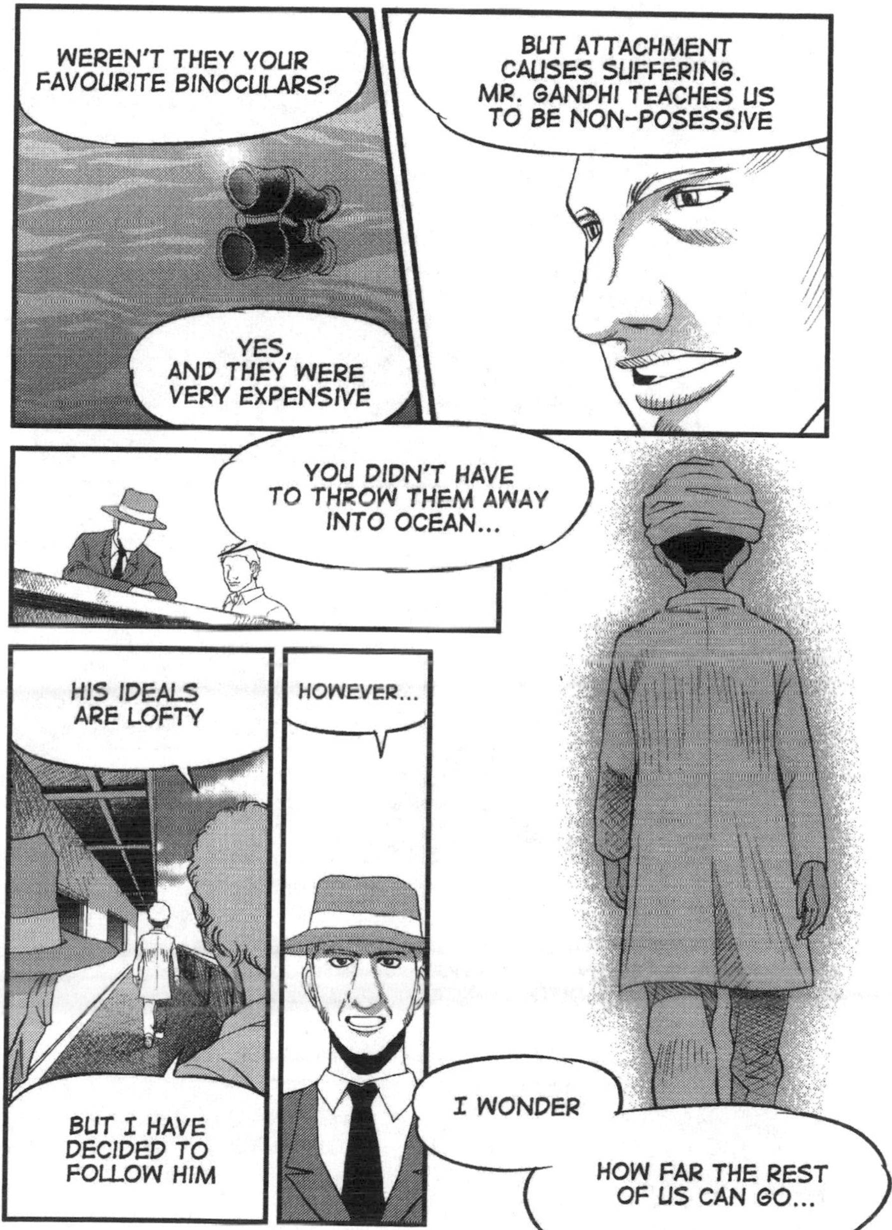
WEREN'T THEY YOUR FAVOURITE BINOCULARS?
YES, AND THEY WERE VERY EXPENSIVE
BUT ATTACHMENT CAUSES SUFFERING. MR. GANDHI TEACHES US TO BE NON-POSESSIVE
YOU DIDN'T HAVE TO THROW THEM AWAY INTO OCEAN...
HIS IDEALS ARE LOFTY
BUT I HAVE DECIDED TO FOLLOW HIM
HOWEVER...
I WONDER
HOW FAR THE REST OF US CAN GO...

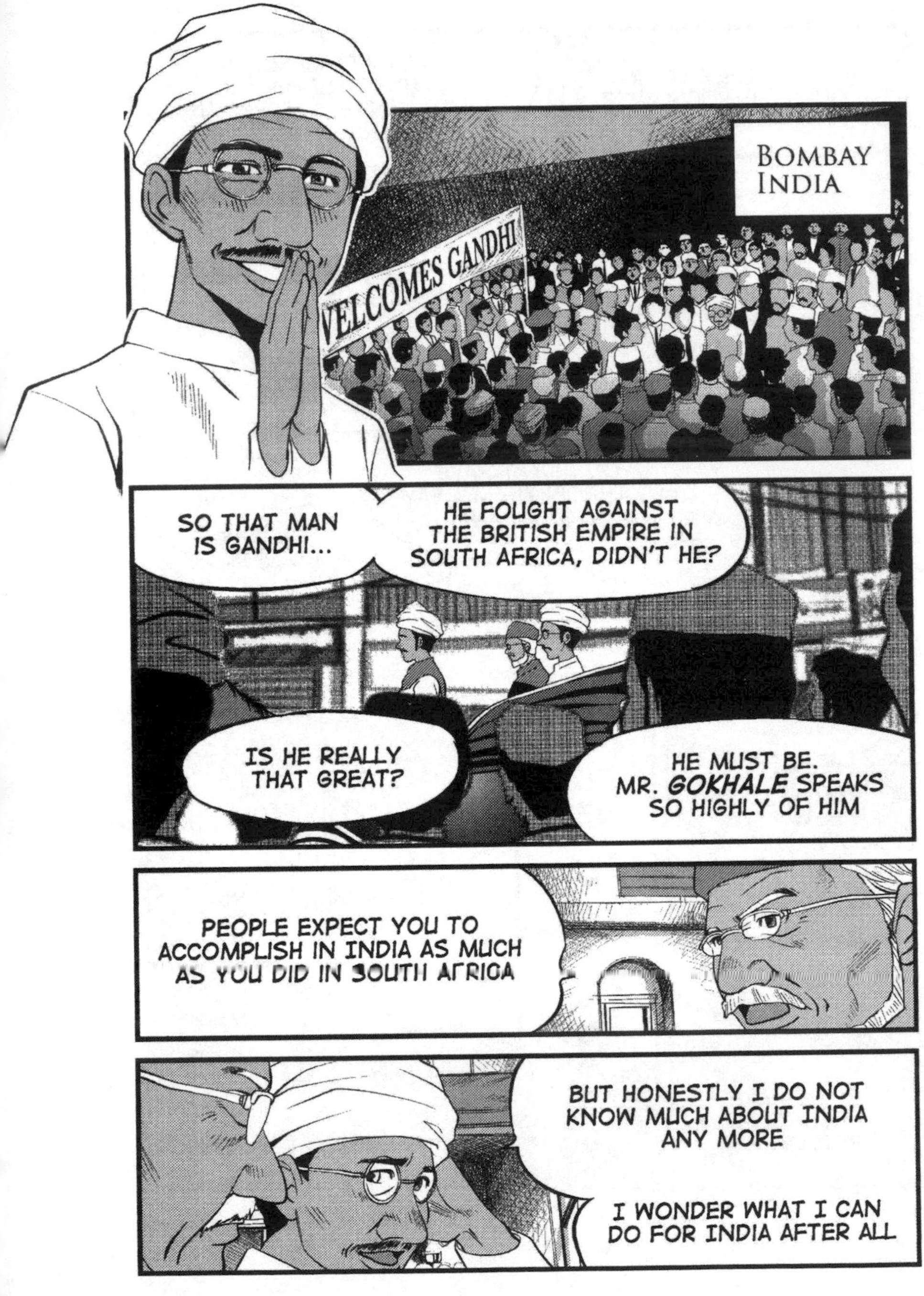
BOMBAY
INDIA
WELCOMES GANDHI
SO THAT MAN IS GANDHI...
HE FOUGHT AGAINST THE BRITISH EMPIRE IN SOUTH AFRICA, DIDN'T HE?
IS HE REALLY THAT GREAT?
HE MUST BE. MR. GOKHALE SPEAKS SO HIGHLY OF HIM
PEOPLE EXPECT YOU TO ACCOMPLISH IN INDIA AS MUCH AS YOU DID IN SOUTH AFRICA
BUT HONESTLY I DO NOT KNOW MUCH ABOUT INDIA ANY MORE
I WONDER WHAT I CAN DO FOR INDIA AFTER ALL

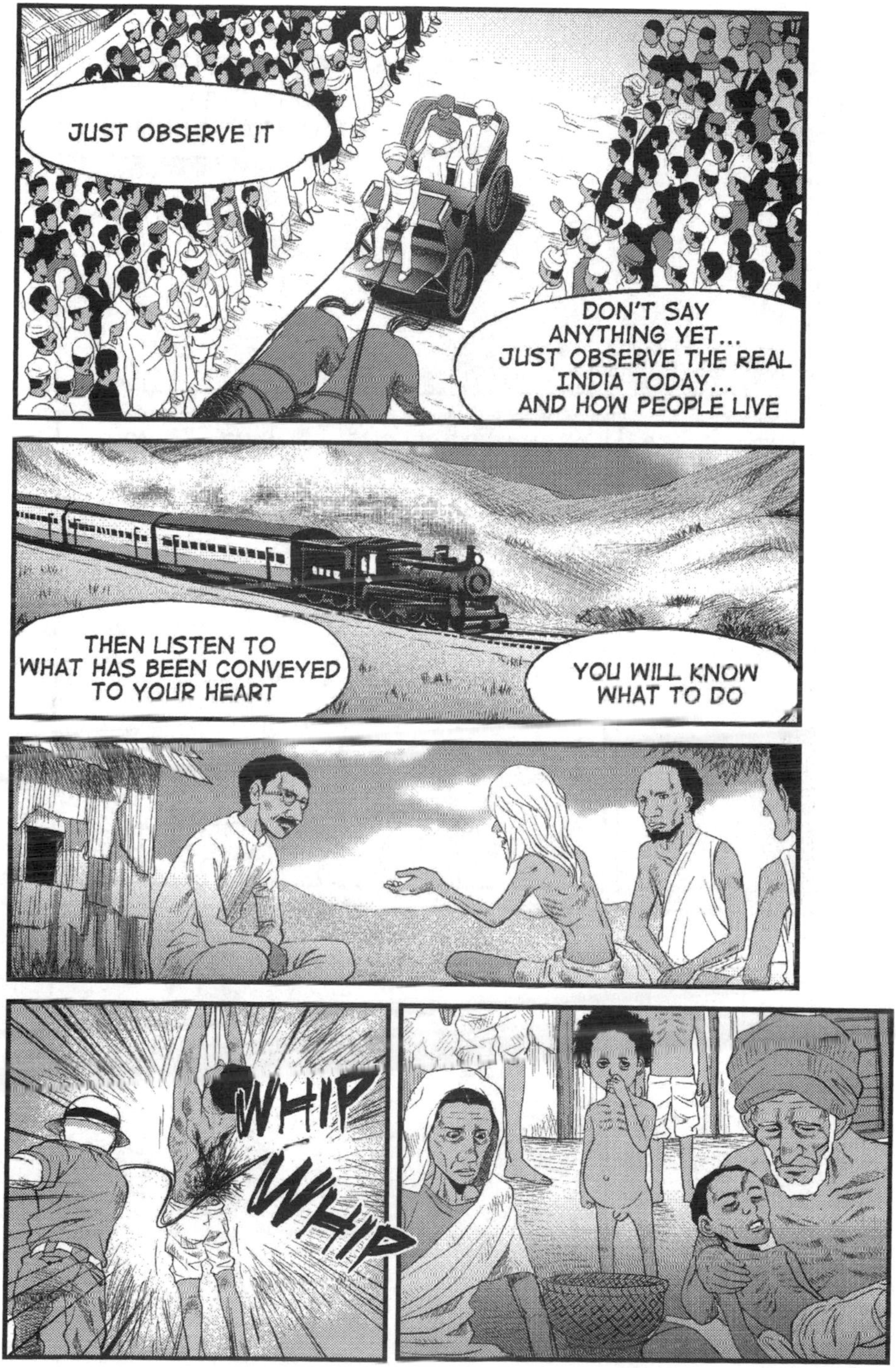
JUST OBSERVE IT
DON'T SAY ANYTHING YET... JUST OBSERVE THE REAL INDIA TODAY... AND HOW PEOPLE LIVE
THEN LISTEN TO WHAT HAS BEEN CONVEYED TO YOUR HEART
YOU WILL KNOW WHAT TO DO
WHIP
WHIP
WHIP

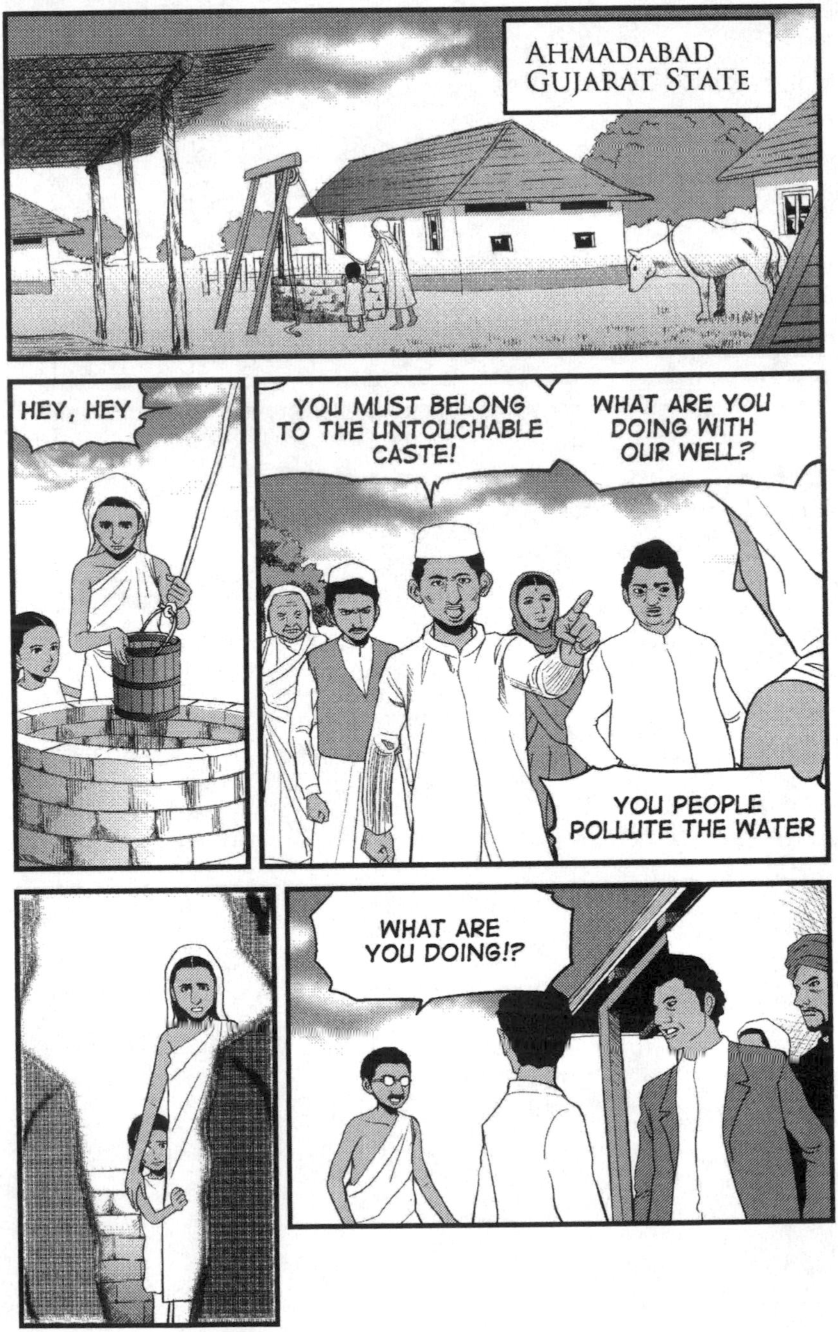
AHMADABAD GUJARAT STATE
HEY, HEY
YOU MUST BELONG TO THE UNTOUCHABLE CASTE!
WHAT ARE YOU DOING WITH OUR WELL?
YOU PEOPLE POLLUTE THE WATER
WHAT ARE YOU DOING!?

MR. GANDHI, WHY DID YOU BRING THE UNTOUCHABLE TO OUR COMMUNITY?

SOME OF OUR PATRONS IN THIS *ASHRAM* ARE SO UPSET THAT

THEY CONSIDER PULLING OUT THEIR FINANCIAL SUPPORT

I JUST CANNOT SHARE THE SAME WELL WITH THESE FOLKS

.....

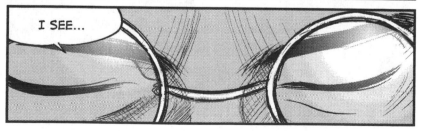

I SEE...

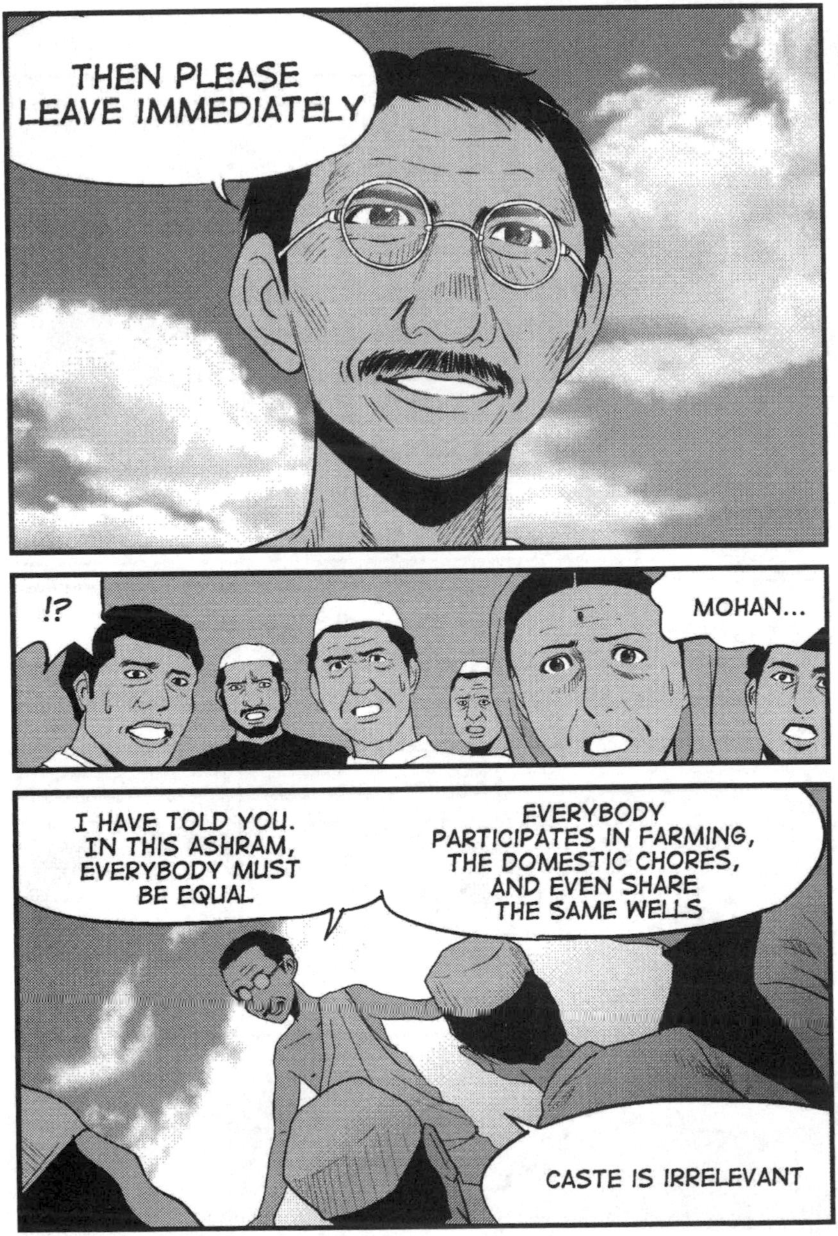
THEN PLEASE LEAVE IMMEDIATELY
!?
MOHAN...
I HAVE TOLD YOU. IN THIS ASHRAM, EVERYBODY MUST BE EQUAL
EVERYBODY PARTICIPATES IN FARMING, THE DOMESTIC CHORES, AND EVEN SHARE THE SAME WELLS
CASTE IS IRRELEVANT

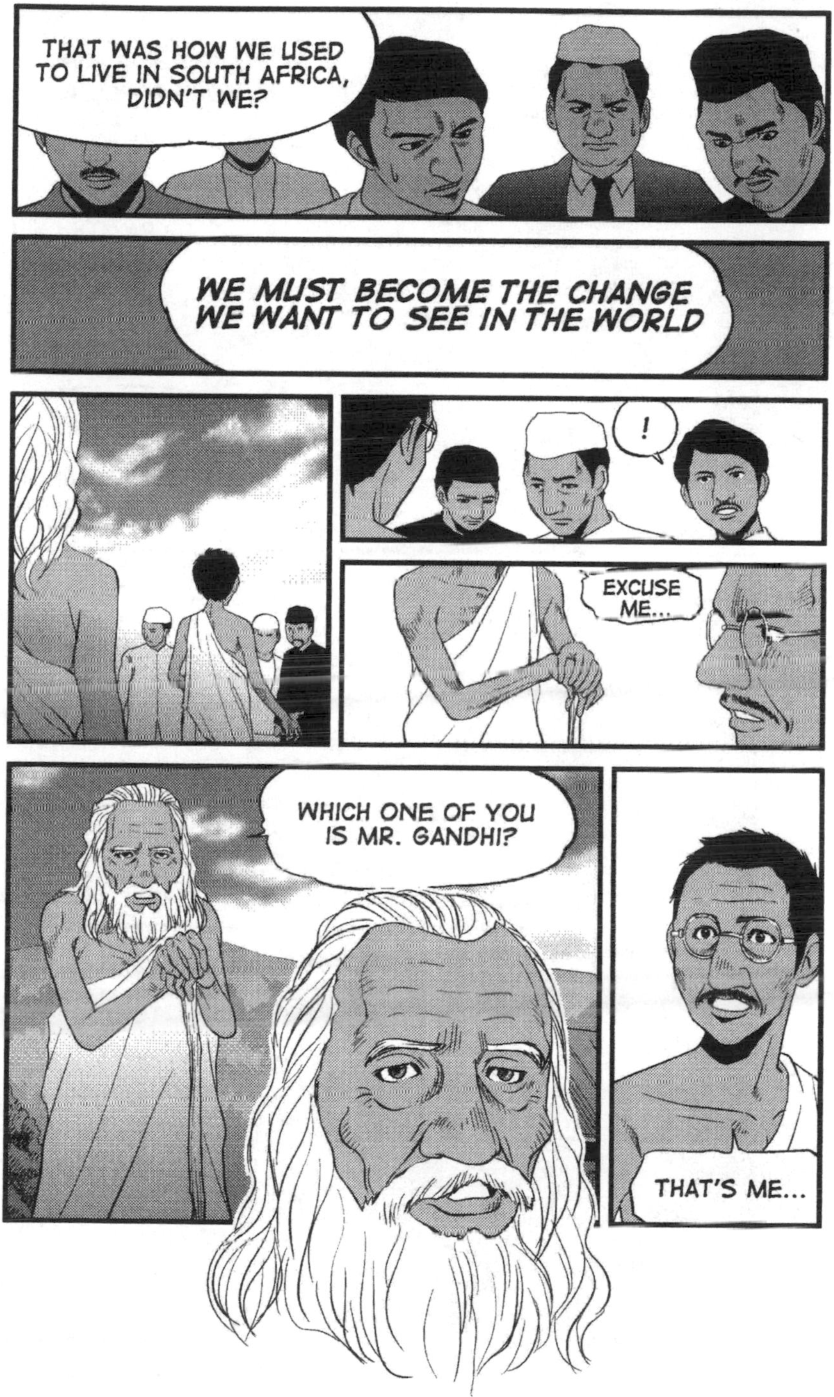
THAT WAS HOW WE USED TO LIVE IN SOUTH AFRICA, DIDN'T WE?
WE MUST BECOME THE CHANGE WE WANT TO SEE IN THE WORLD
!
EXCUSE ME...
WHICH ONE OF YOU IS MR. GANDHI?
THAT'S ME...

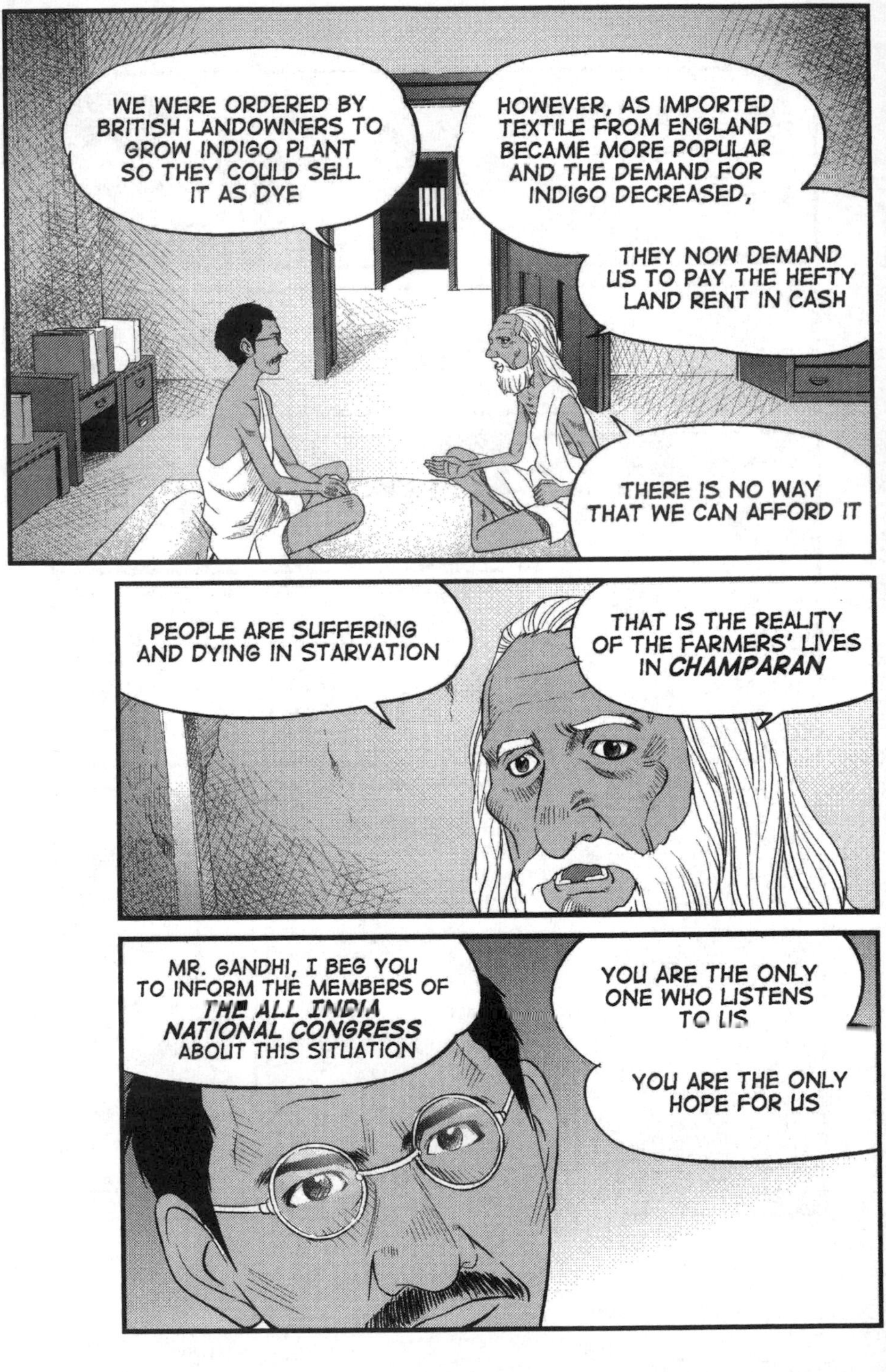
WE WERE ORDERED BY BRITISH LANDOWNERS TO GROW INDIGO PLANT SO THEY COULD SELL IT AS DYE
HOWEVER, AS IMPORTED TEXTILE FROM ENGLAND BECAME MORE POPULAR AND THE DEMAND FOR INDIGO DECREASED,
THEY NOW DEMAND US TO PAY THE HEFTY LAND RENT IN CASH
THERE IS NO WAY THAT WE CAN AFFORD IT
PEOPLE ARE SUFFERING AND DYING IN STARVATION
THAT IS THE REALITY OF THE FARMERS' LIVES IN *CHAMPARAN*
MR. GANDHI, I BEG YOU TO INFORM THE MEMBERS OF *THE ALL INDIA NATIONAL CONGRESS* ABOUT THIS SITUATION
YOU ARE THE ONLY ONE WHO LISTENS TO US
YOU ARE THE ONLY HOPE FOR US

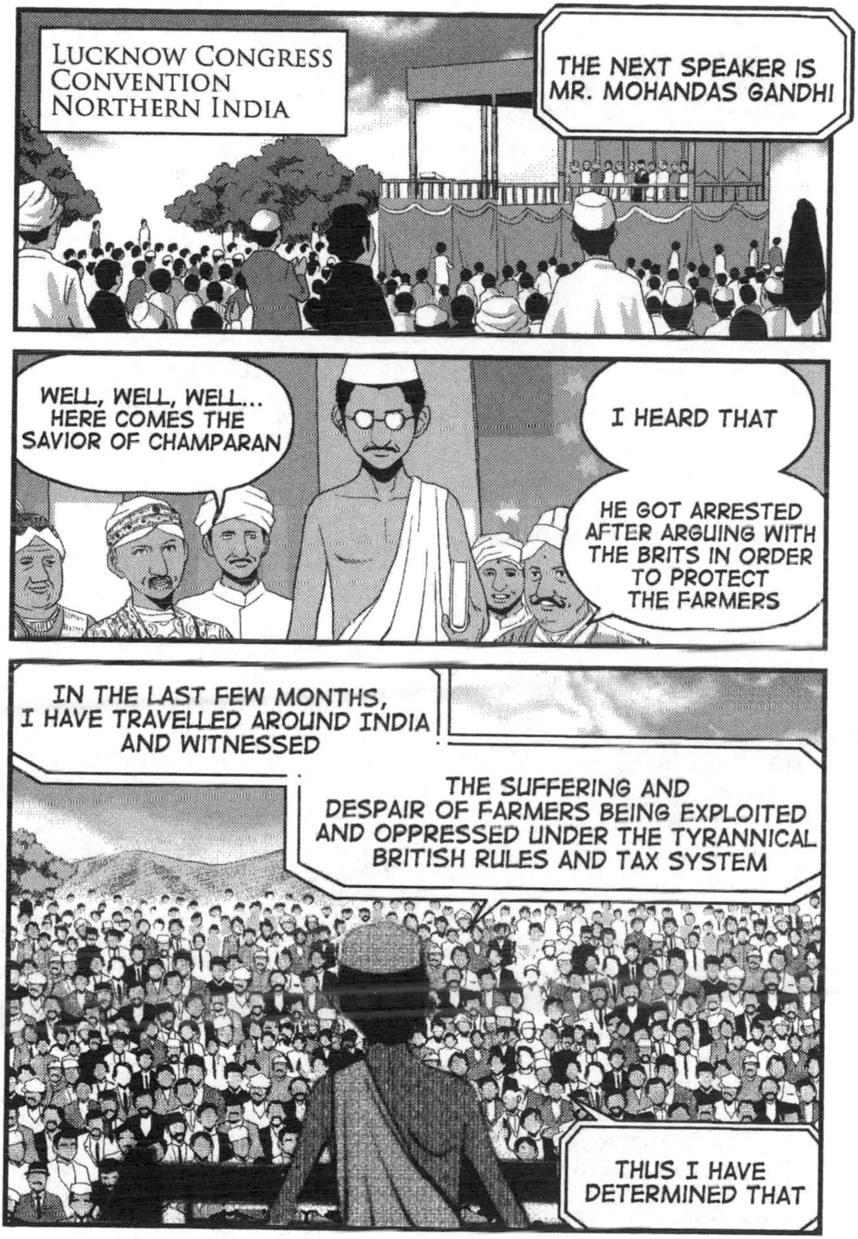
LUCKNOW CONGRESS CONVENTION NORTHERN INDIA
THE NEXT SPEAKER IS MR. MOHANDAS GANDHI
WELL, WELL, WELL... HERE COMES THE SAVIOR OF CHAMPARAN
I HEARD THAT
HE GOT ARRESTED AFTER ARGUING WITH THE BRITS IN ORDER TO PROTECT THE FARMERS
IN THE LAST FEW MONTHS, I HAVE TRAVELLED AROUND INDIA AND WITNESSED
THE SUFFERING AND DESPAIR OF FARMERS BEING EXPLOITED AND OPPRESSED UNDER THE TYRANNICAL BRITISH RULES AND TAX SYSTEM
THUS I HAVE DETERMINED THAT

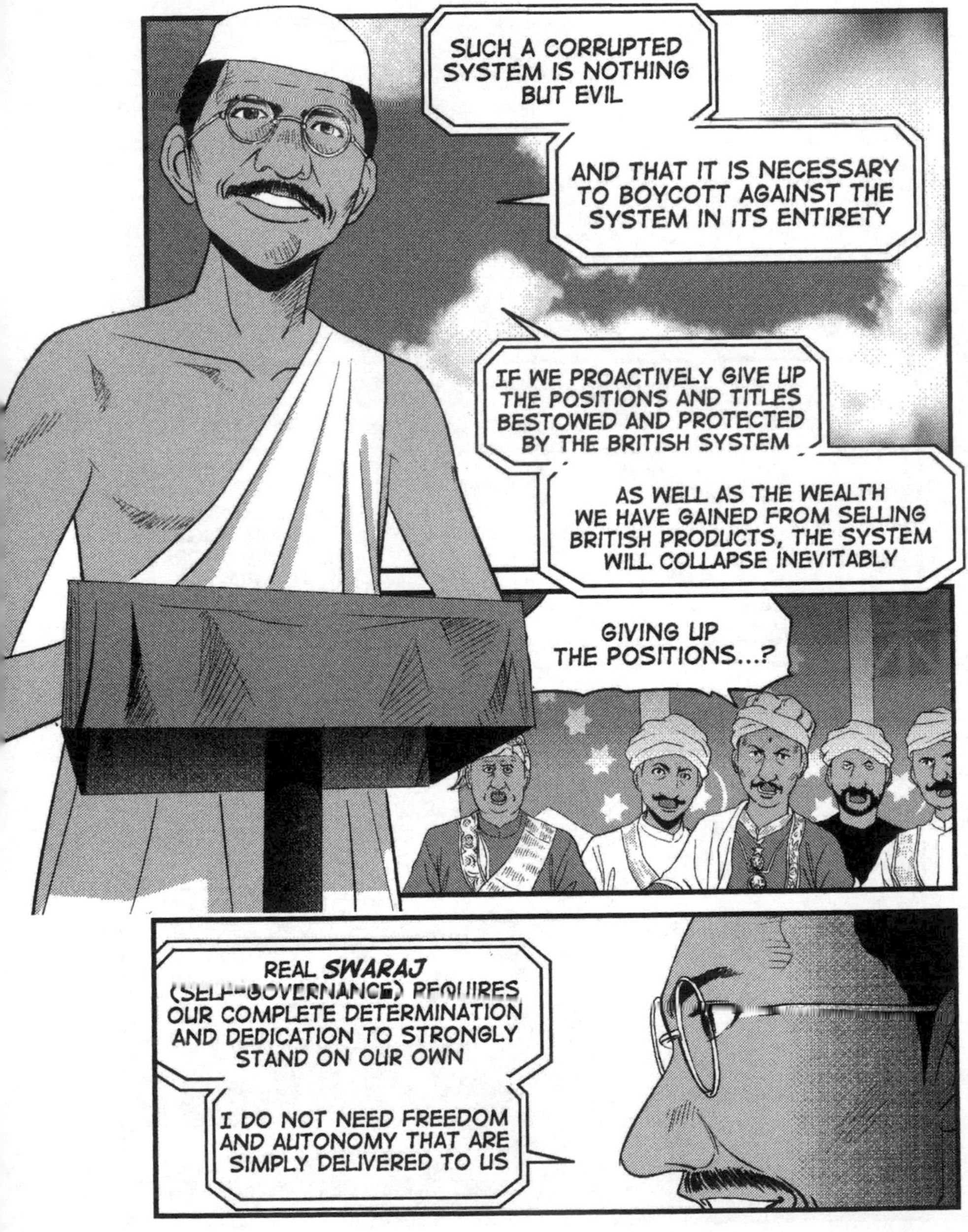
SUCH A CORRUPTED SYSTEM IS NOTHING BUT EVIL
AND THAT IT IS NECESSARY TO BOYCOTT AGAINST THE SYSTEM IN ITS ENTIRETY
IF WE PROACTIVELY GIVE UP THE POSITIONS AND TITLES BESTOWED AND PROTECTED BY THE BRITISH SYSTEM
AS WELL AS THE WEALTH WE HAVE GAINED FROM SELLING BRITISH PRODUCTS, THE SYSTEM WILL COLLAPSE INEVITABLY
GIVING UP THE POSITIONS...?
REAL *SWARAJ* (SELF-GOVERNANCE) REQUIRES OUR COMPLETE DETERMINATION AND DEDICATION TO STRONGLY STAND ON OUR OWN
I DO NOT NEED FREEDOM AND AUTONOMY THAT ARE SIMPLY DELIVERED TO US

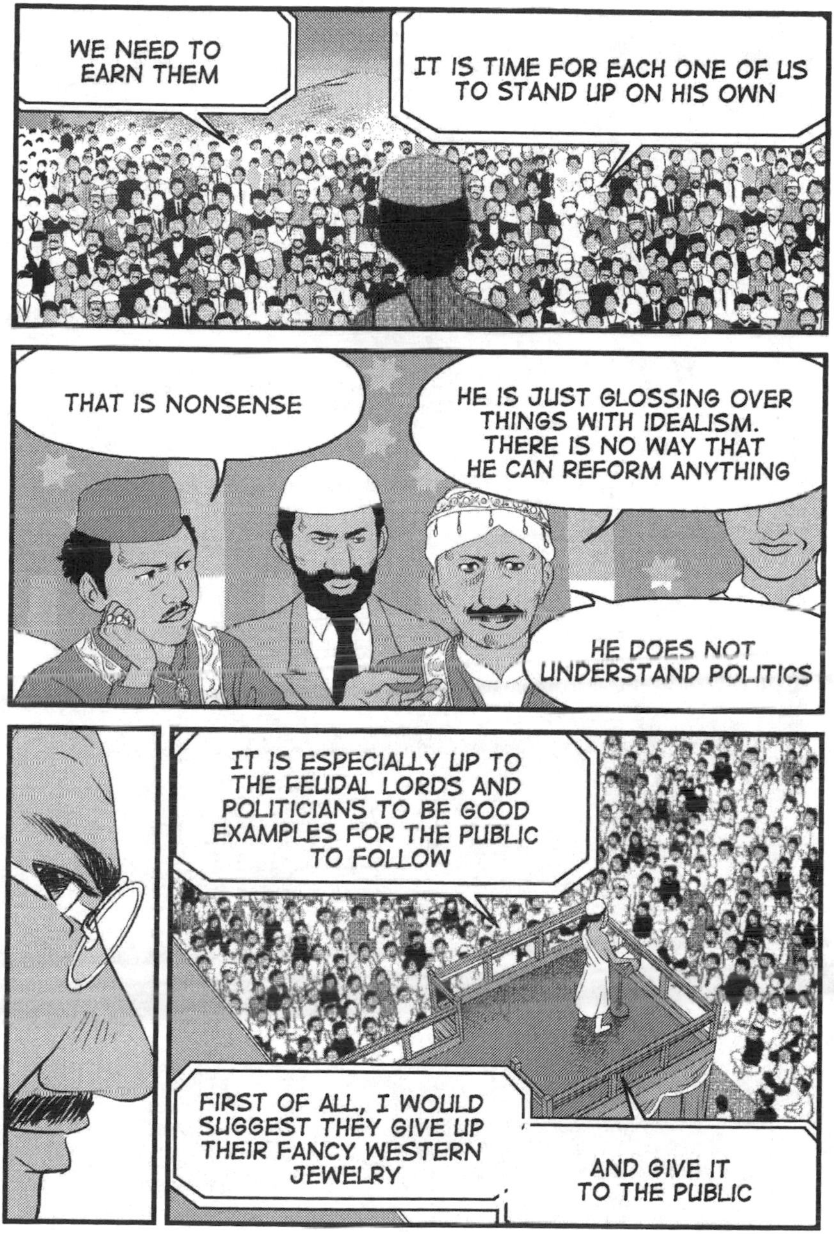
WE NEED TO EARN THEM
IT IS TIME FOR EACH ONE OF US TO STAND UP ON HIS OWN
THAT IS NONSENSE
HE IS JUST GLOSSING OVER THINGS WITH IDEALISM. THERE IS NO WAY THAT HE CAN REFORM ANYTHING
HE DOES NOT UNDERSTAND POLITICS
IT IS ESPECIALLY UP TO THE FEUDAL LORDS AND POLITICIANS TO BE GOOD EXAMPLES FOR THE PUBLIC TO FOLLOW
FIRST OF ALL, I WOULD SUGGEST THEY GIVE UP THEIR FANCY WESTERN JEWELRY
AND GIVE IT TO THE PUBLIC

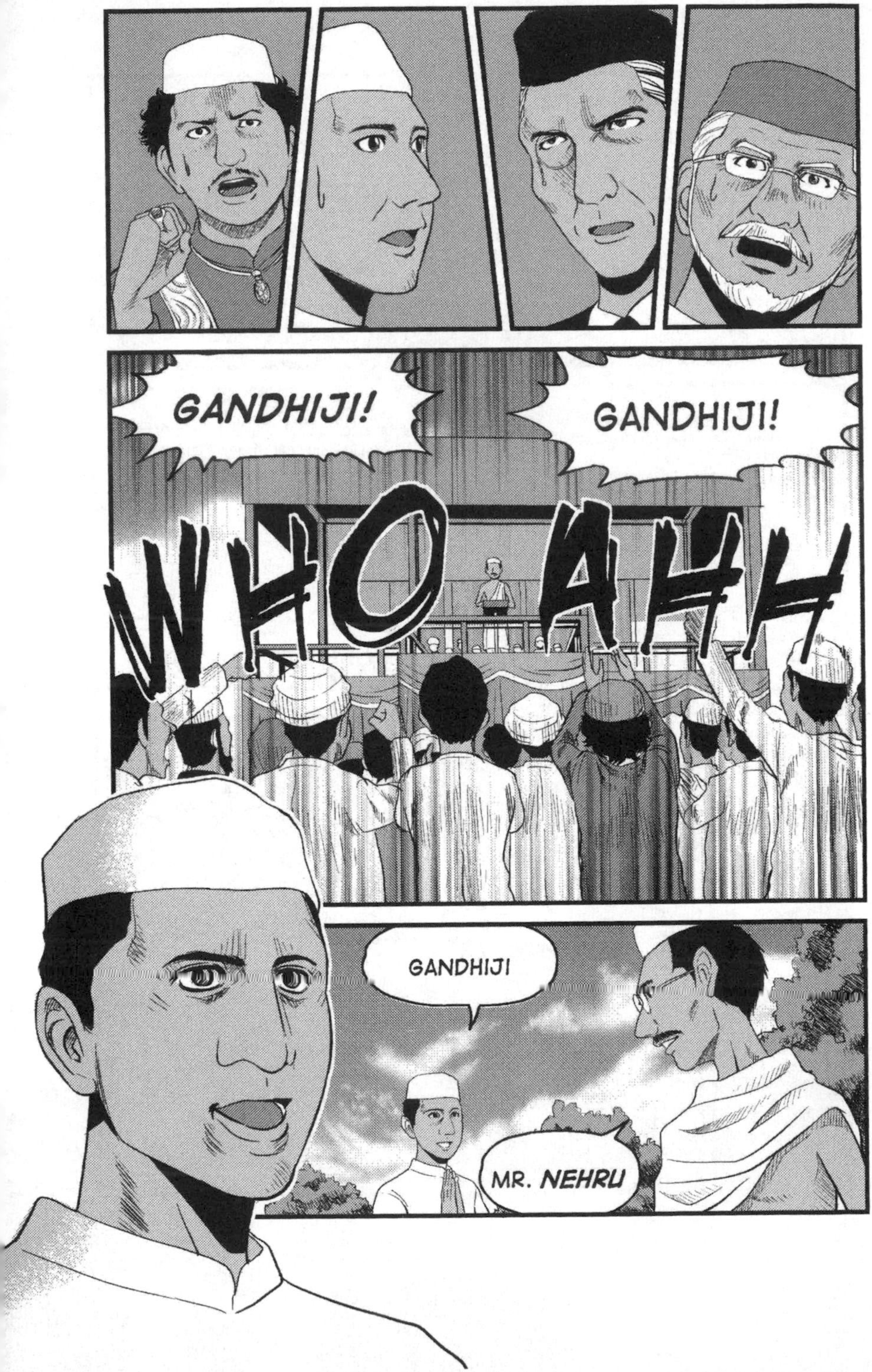
GANDHIJI!
GANDHIJI!
WHOAHH
GANDHIJI
MR. NEHRU

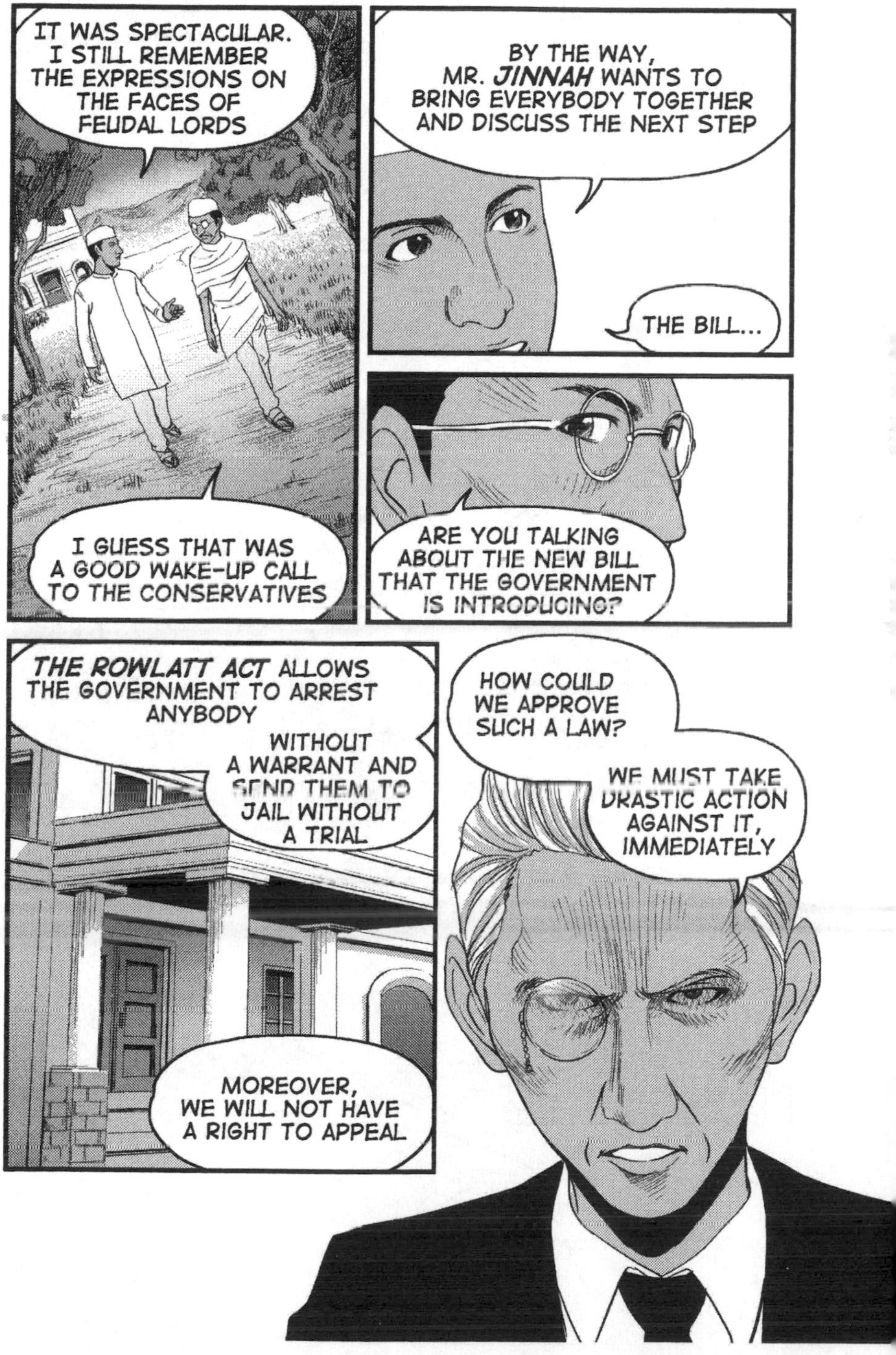
IT WAS SPECTACULAR. I STILL REMEMBER THE EXPRESSIONS ON THE FACES OF FEUDAL LORDS
I GUESS THAT WAS A GOOD WAKE-UP CALL TO THE CONSERVATIVES
BY THE WAY, MR. *JINNAH* WANTS TO BRING EVERYBODY TOGETHER AND DISCUSS THE NEXT STEP
THE BILL...
ARE YOU TALKING ABOUT THE NEW BILL THAT THE GOVERNMENT IS INTRODUCING?
THE ROWLATT ACT ALLOWS THE GOVERNMENT TO ARREST ANYBODY
WITHOUT A WARRANT AND SEND THEM TO JAIL WITHOUT A TRIAL
MOREOVER, WE WILL NOT HAVE A RIGHT TO APPEAL
HOW COULD WE APPROVE SUCH A LAW?
WE MUST TAKE DRASTIC ACTION AGAINST IT, IMMEDIATELY

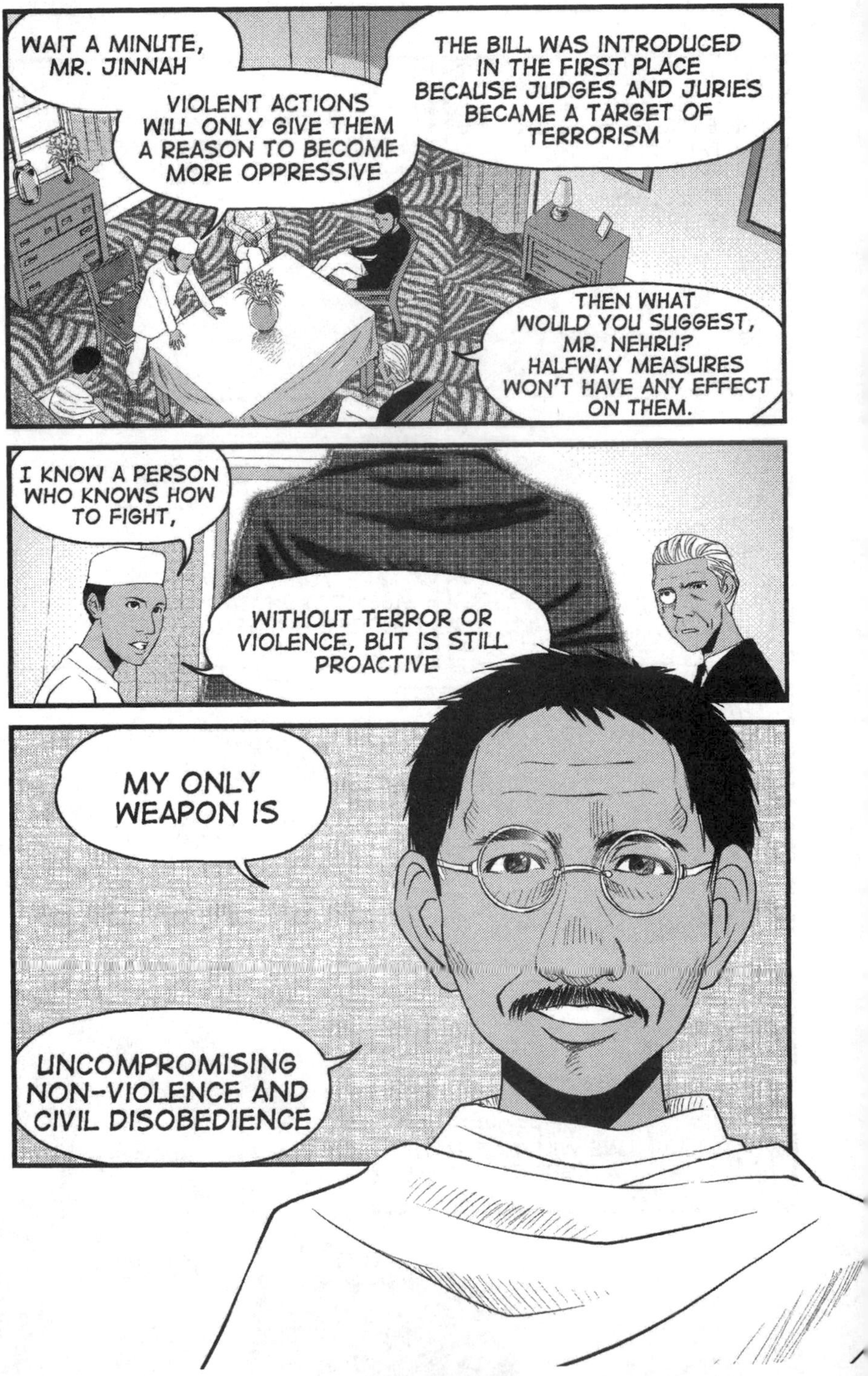

WAIT A MINUTE, MR. JINNAH
VIOLENT ACTIONS WILL ONLY GIVE THEM A REASON TO BECOME MORE OPPRESSIVE
THE BILL WAS INTRODUCED IN THE FIRST PLACE BECAUSE JUDGES AND JURIES BECAME A TARGET OF TERRORISM
THEN WHAT WOULD YOU SUGGEST, MR. NEHRU? HALFWAY MEASURES WON'T HAVE ANY EFFECT ON THEM.
I KNOW A PERSON WHO KNOWS HOW TO FIGHT,
WITHOUT TERROR OR VIOLENCE, BUT IS STILL PROACTIVE
MY ONLY WEAPON IS
UNCOMPROMISING NON-VIOLENCE AND CIVIL DISOBEDIENCE

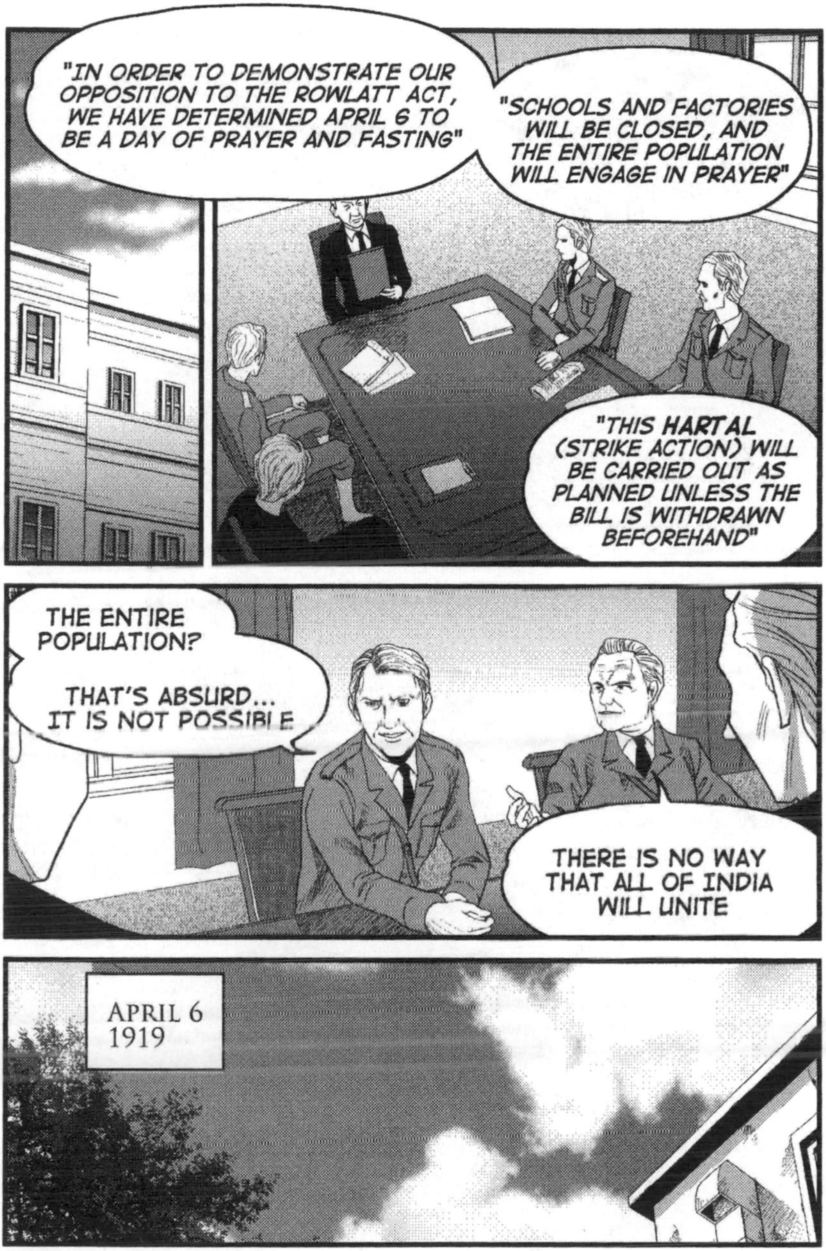
"IN ORDER TO DEMONSTRATE OUR OPPOSITION TO THE ROWLATT ACT, WE HAVE DETERMINED APRIL 6 TO BE A DAY OF PRAYER AND FASTING"
"SCHOOLS AND FACTORIES WILL BE CLOSED, AND THE ENTIRE POPULATION WILL ENGAGE IN PRAYER"
"THIS HARTAL (STRIKE ACTION) WILL BE CARRIED OUT AS PLANNED UNLESS THE BILL IS WITHDRAWN BEFOREHAND"
THE ENTIRE POPULATION?
THAT'S ABSURD... IT IS NOT POSSIBLE
THERE IS NO WAY THAT ALL OF INDIA WILL UNITE
APRIL 6
1919

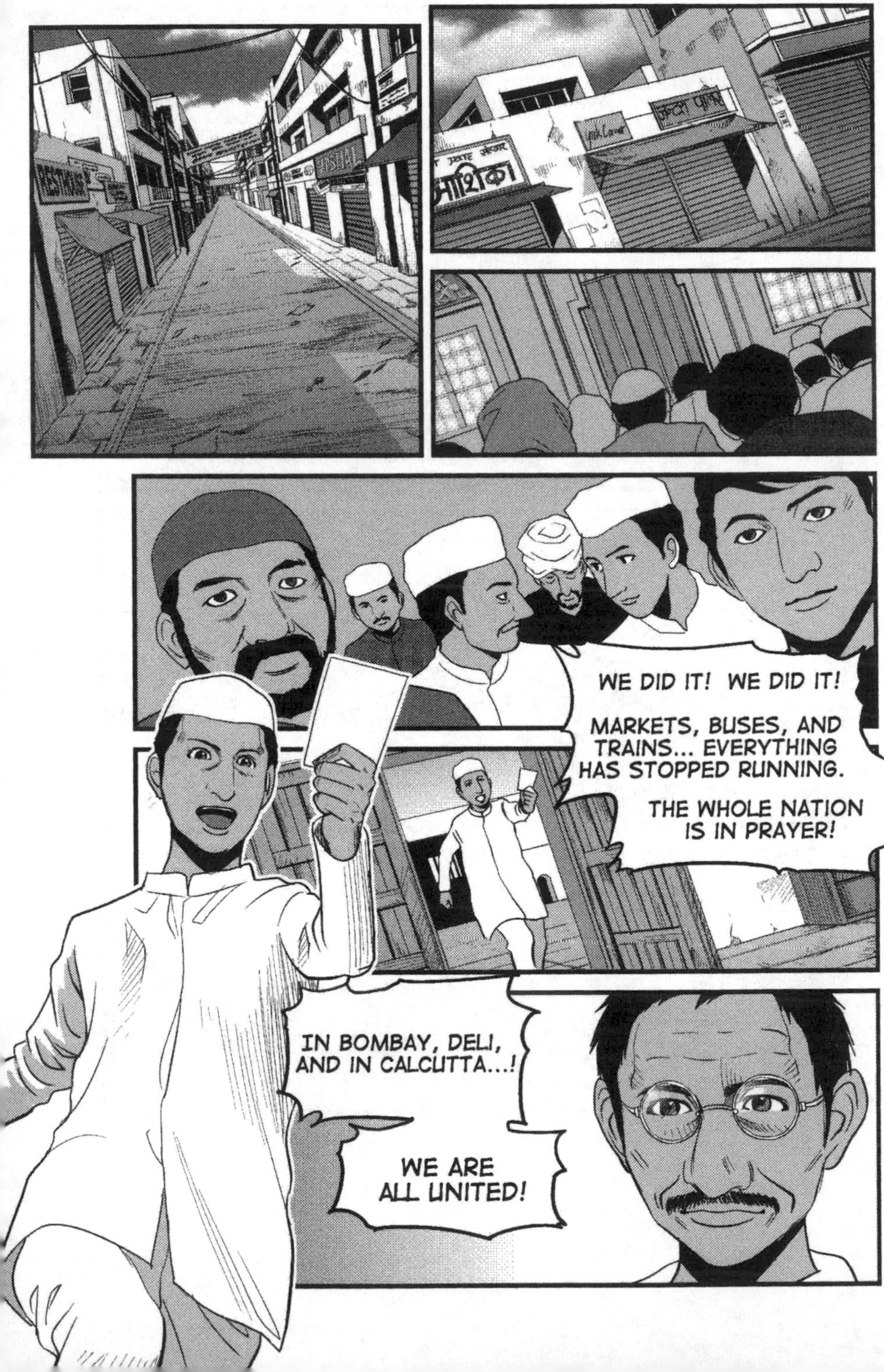
WE DID IT! WE DID IT!
MARKETS, BUSES, AND TRAINS... EVERYTHING HAS STOPPED RUNNING.
THE WHOLE NATION IS IN PRAYER!
IN BOMBAY, DELI, AND IN CALCUTTA...!
WE ARE ALL UNITED!

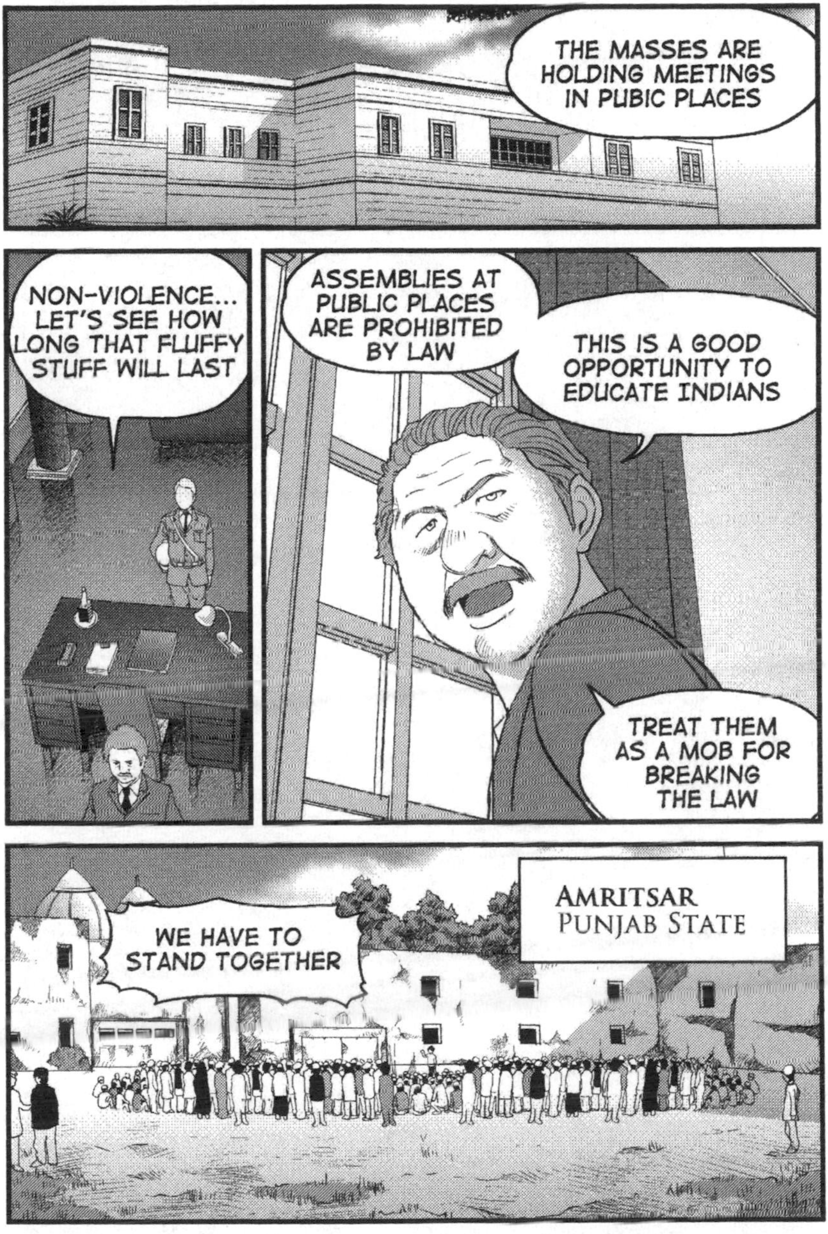
THE MASSES ARE HOLDING MEETINGS IN PUBIC PLACES
NON-VIOLENCE... LET'S SEE HOW LONG THAT FLUFFY STUFF WILL LAST
ASSEMBLIES AT PUBLIC PLACES ARE PROHIBITED BY LAW
THIS IS A GOOD OPPORTUNITY TO EDUCATE INDIANS
TREAT THEM AS A MOB FOR BREAKING THE LAW
AMRITSAR
PUNJAB STATE
WE HAVE TO STAND TOGETHER

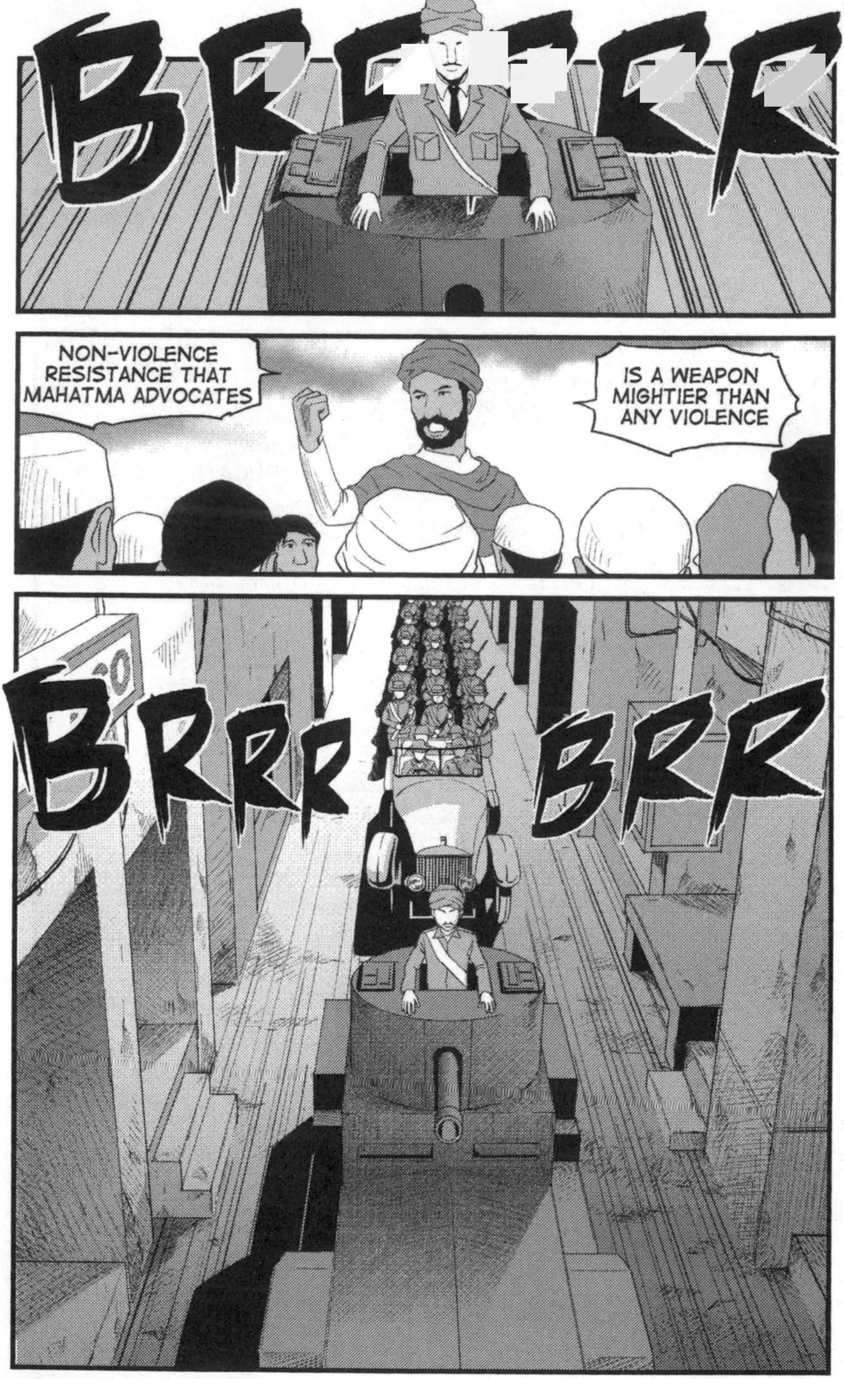
NON-VIOLENCE RESISTANCE THAT MAHATMA ADVOCATES
IS A WEAPON MIGHTIER THAN ANY VIOLENCE
BRRR
BRRR

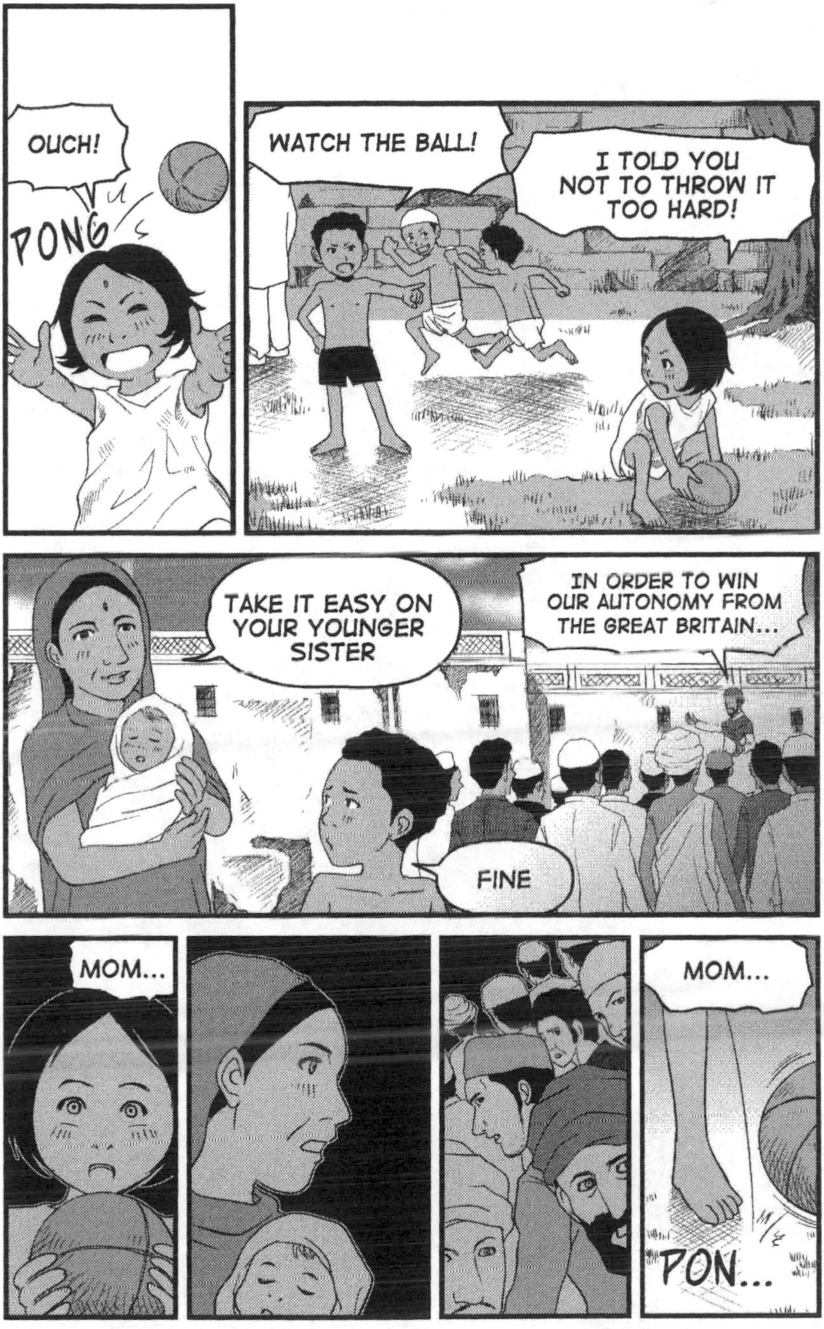
OUCH!
PONG
WATCH THE BALL!
I TOLD YOU NOT TO THROW IT TOO HARD!
TAKE IT EASY ON YOUR YOUNGER SISTER
IN ORDER TO WIN OUR AUTONOMY FROM THE GREAT BRITAIN...
FINE
MOM...
MOM...
PON...

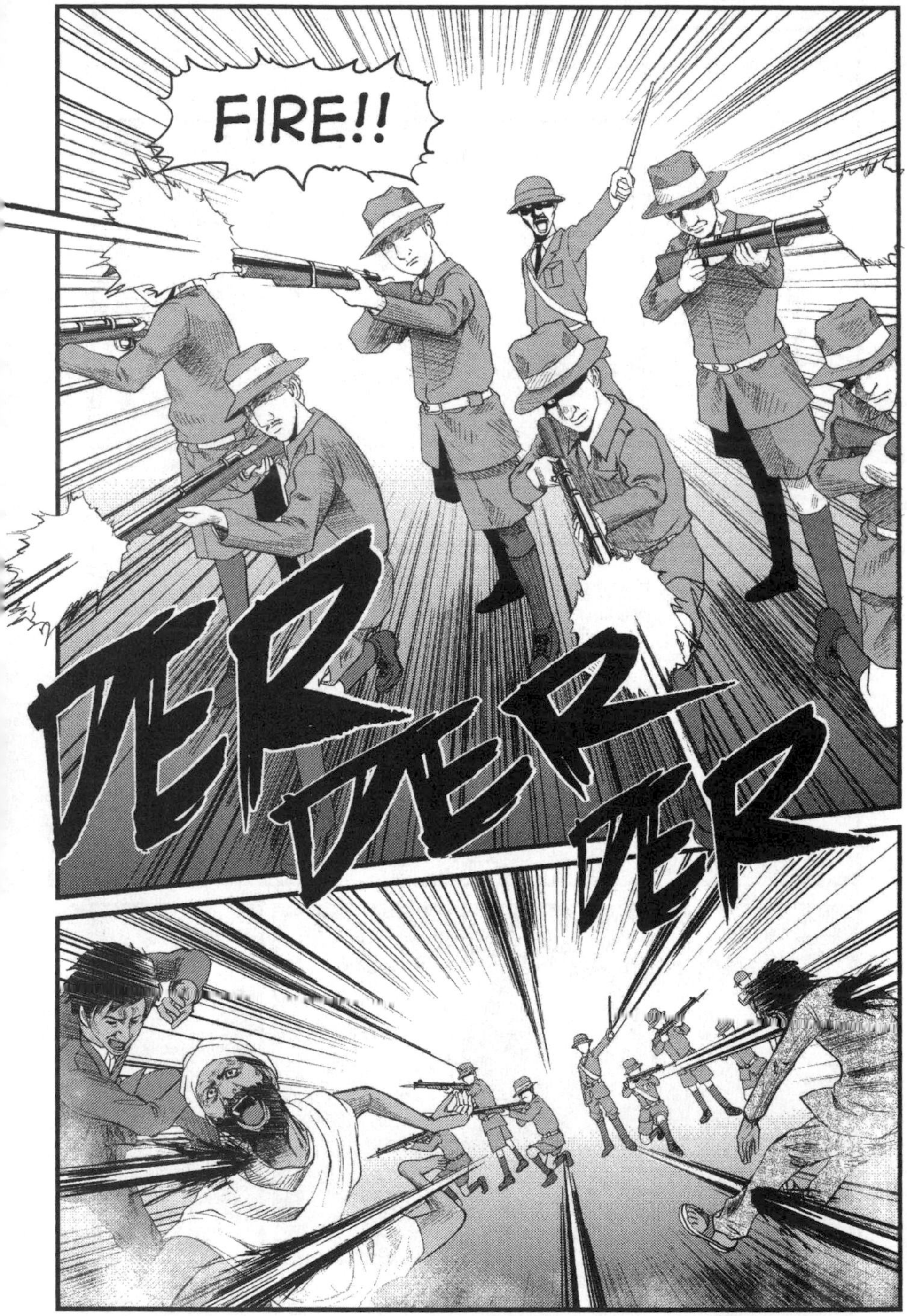
FIRE!!
DER
DER
DER

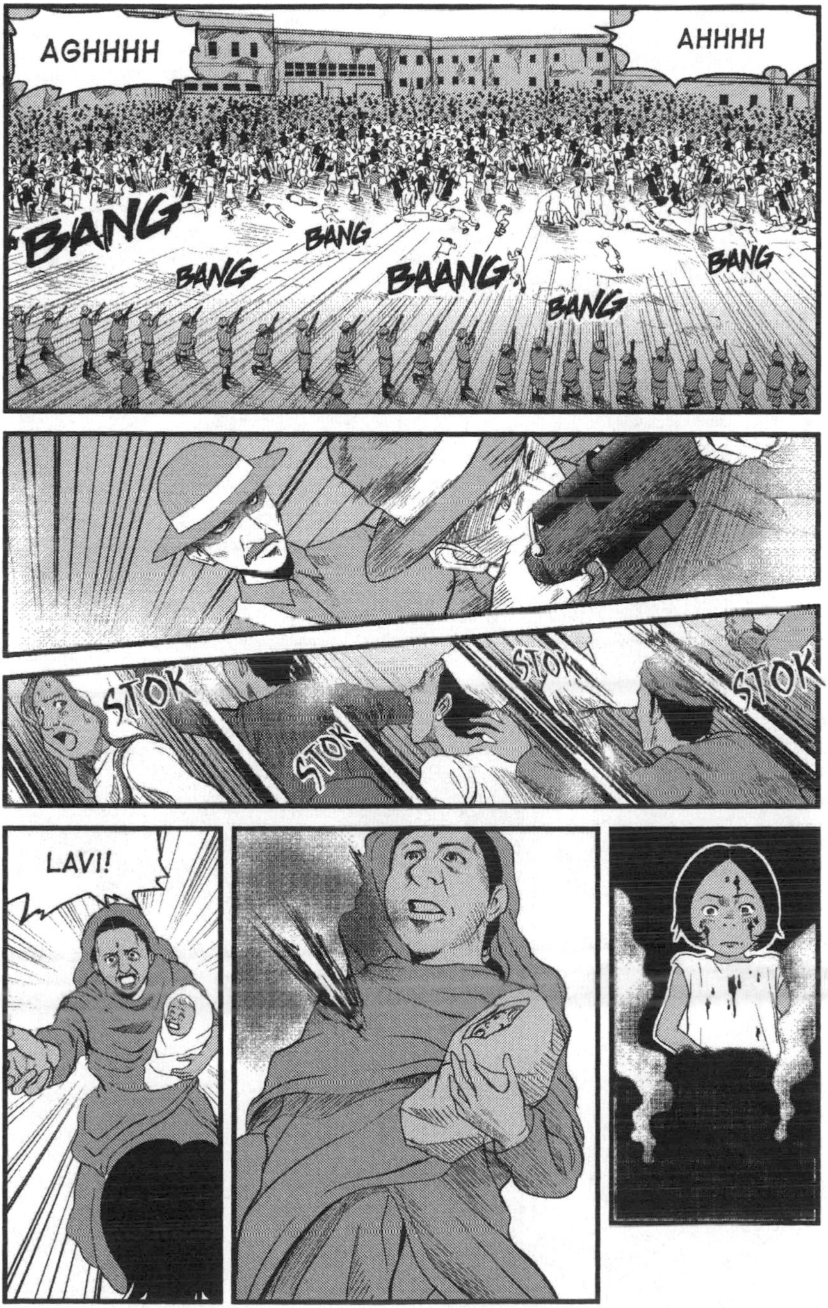
AGHHHH
AHHHH
BANG
BANG
BANG
BAANG
BANG
BANG
STOK
STOK
STOK
STOK
LAVI!

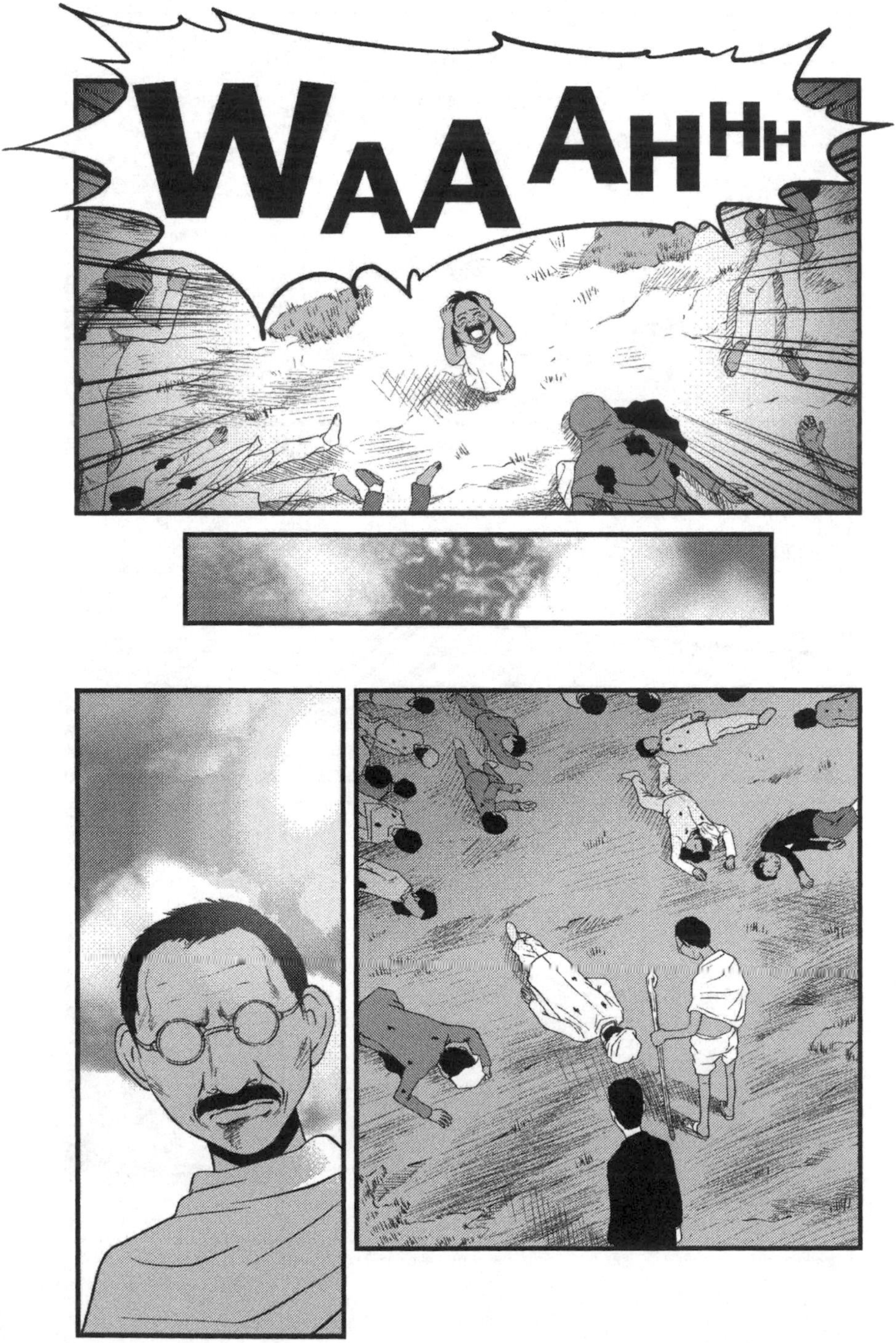
WAAAAHHH

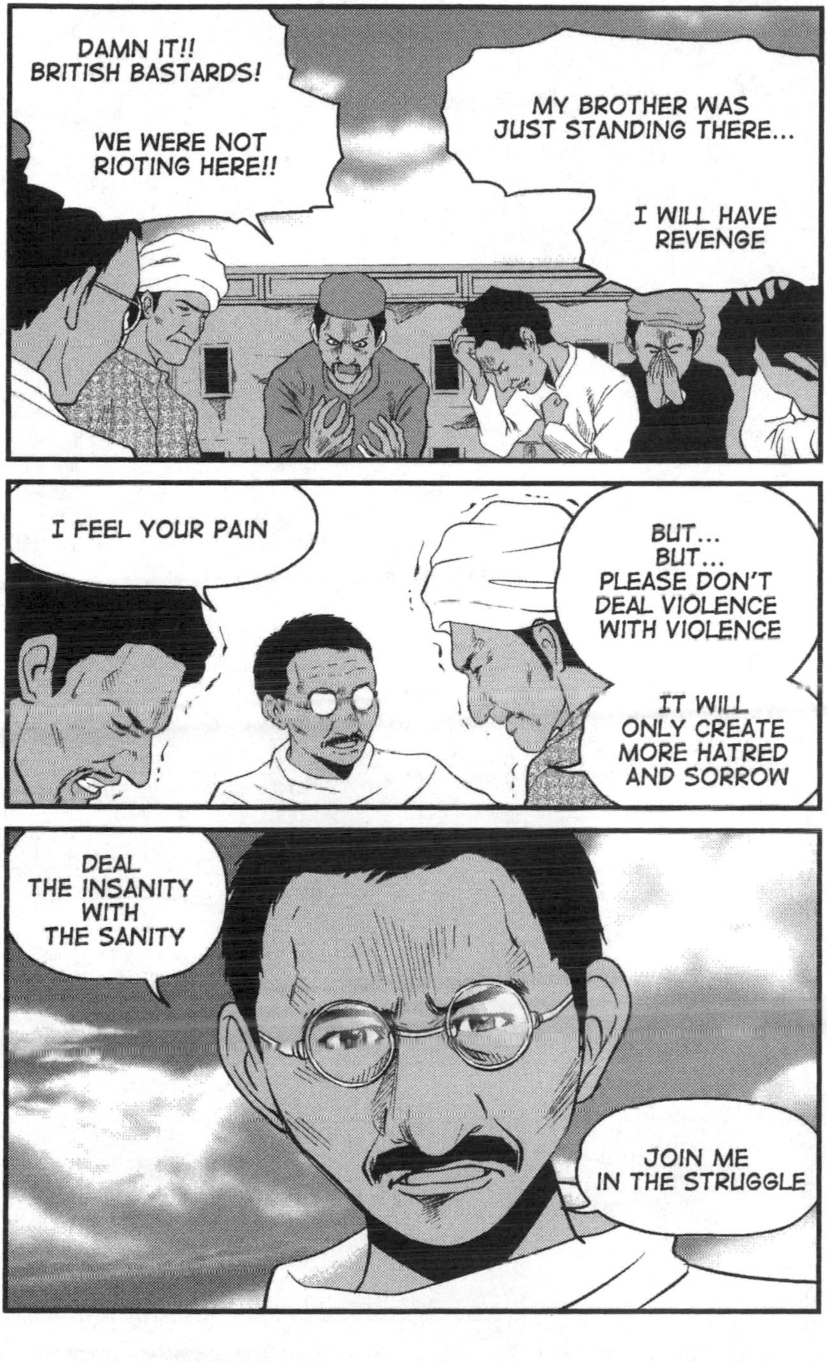
DAMN IT!! BRITISH BASTARDS!
WE WERE NOT RIOTING HERE!!
MY BROTHER WAS JUST STANDING THERE...
I WILL HAVE REVENGE
I FEEL YOUR PAIN
BUT... BUT... PLEASE DON'T DEAL VIOLENCE WITH VIOLENCE
IT WILL ONLY CREATE MORE HATRED AND SORROW
DEAL THE INSANITY WITH THE SANITY
JOIN ME IN THE STRUGGLE

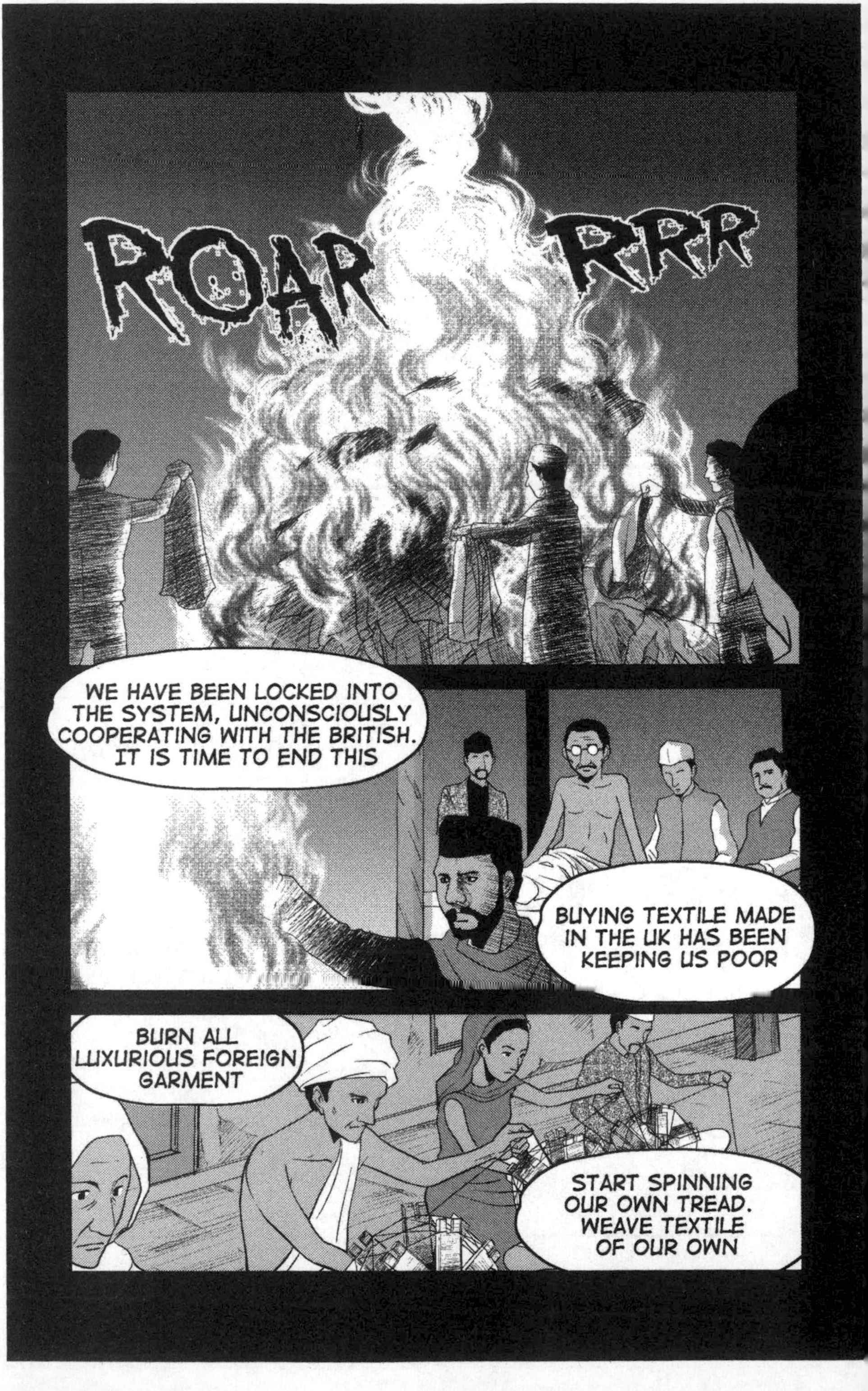
ROAR RRR
WE HAVE BEEN LOCKED INTO THE SYSTEM, UNCONSCIOUSLY COOPERATING WITH THE BRITISH. IT IS TIME TO END THIS
BUYING TEXTILE MADE IN THE UK HAS BEEN KEEPING US POOR
BURN ALL LUXURIOUS FOREIGN GARMENT
START SPINNING OUR OWN TREAD. WEAVE TEXTILE OF OUR OWN

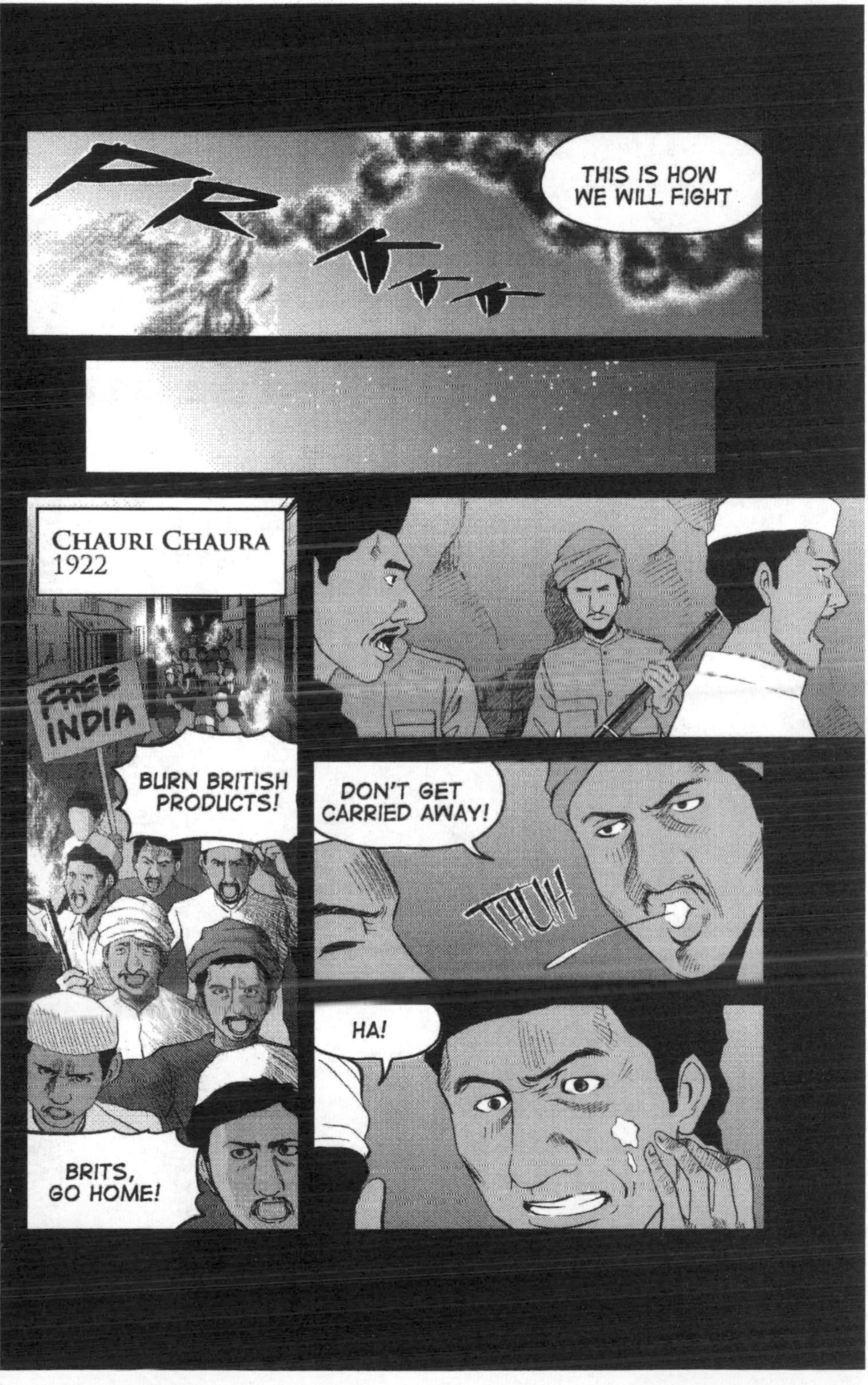
PRRRR
THIS IS HOW WE WILL FIGHT
CHAURI CHAURA 1922
FREE INDIA
BURN BRITISH PRODUCTS!
BRITS, GO HOME!
DON'T GET CARRIED AWAY!
THUH
HA!

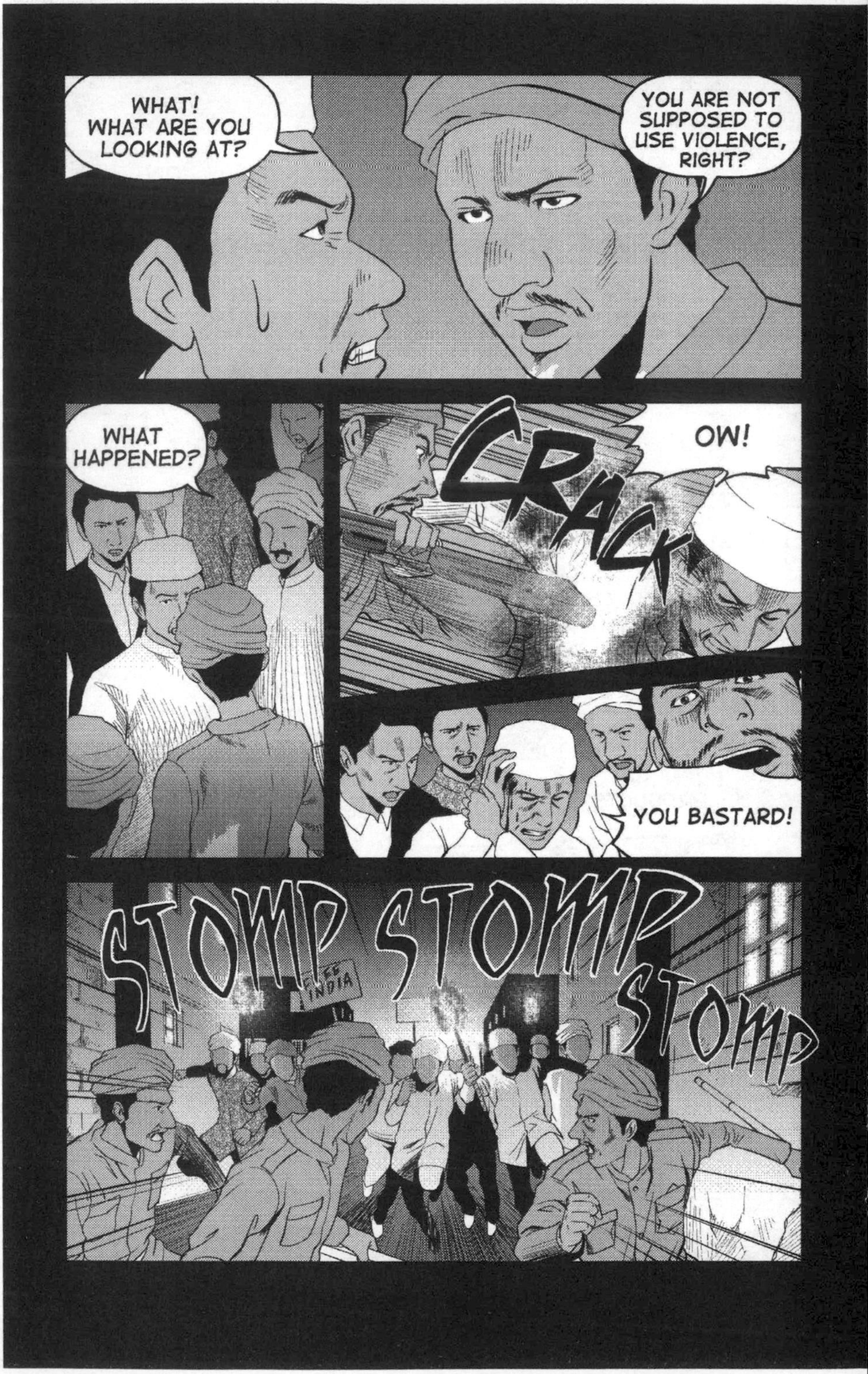
WHAT! WHAT ARE YOU LOOKING AT?
YOU ARE NOT SUPPOSED TO USE VIOLENCE, RIGHT?
WHAT HAPPENED?
CRACK
OW!
YOU BASTARD!
STOMP STOMP STOMP

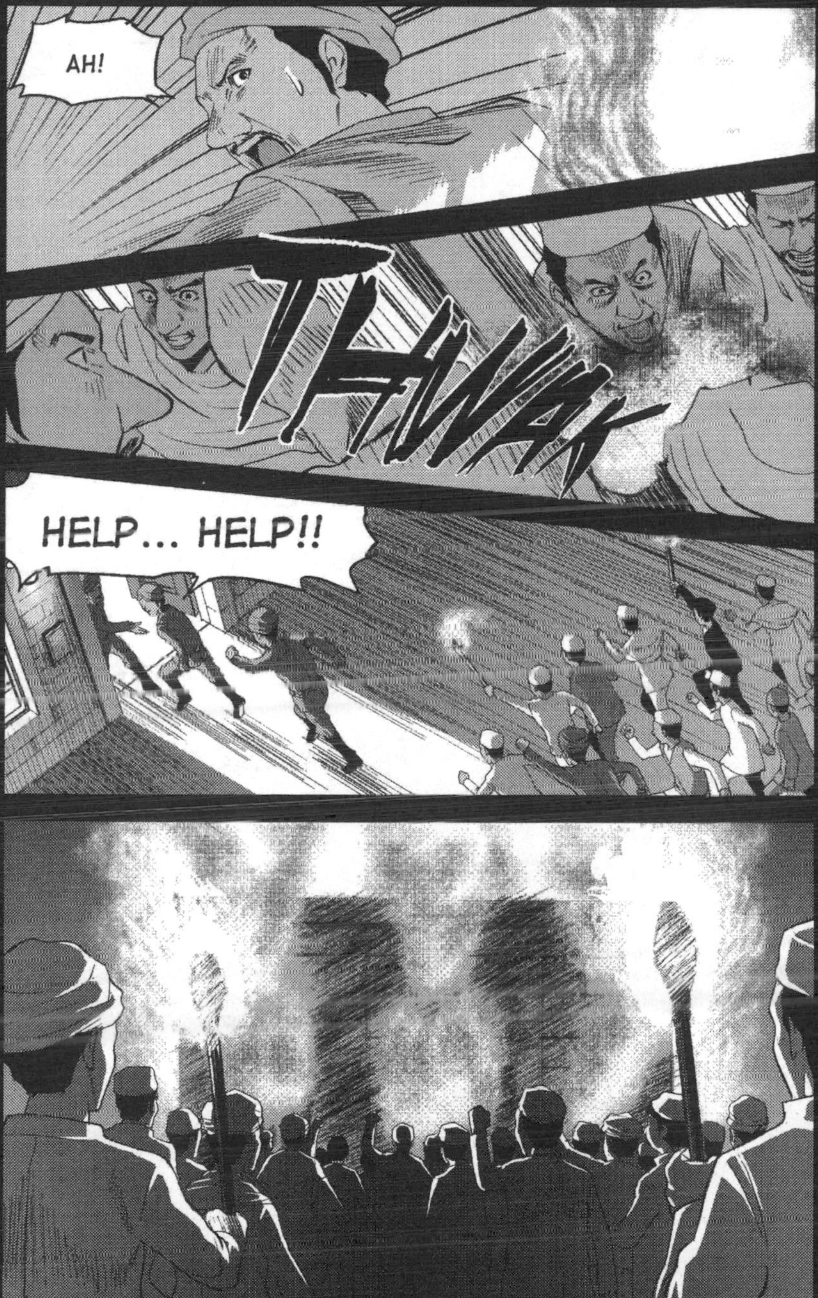

AH!
THWAK
HELP... HELP!!

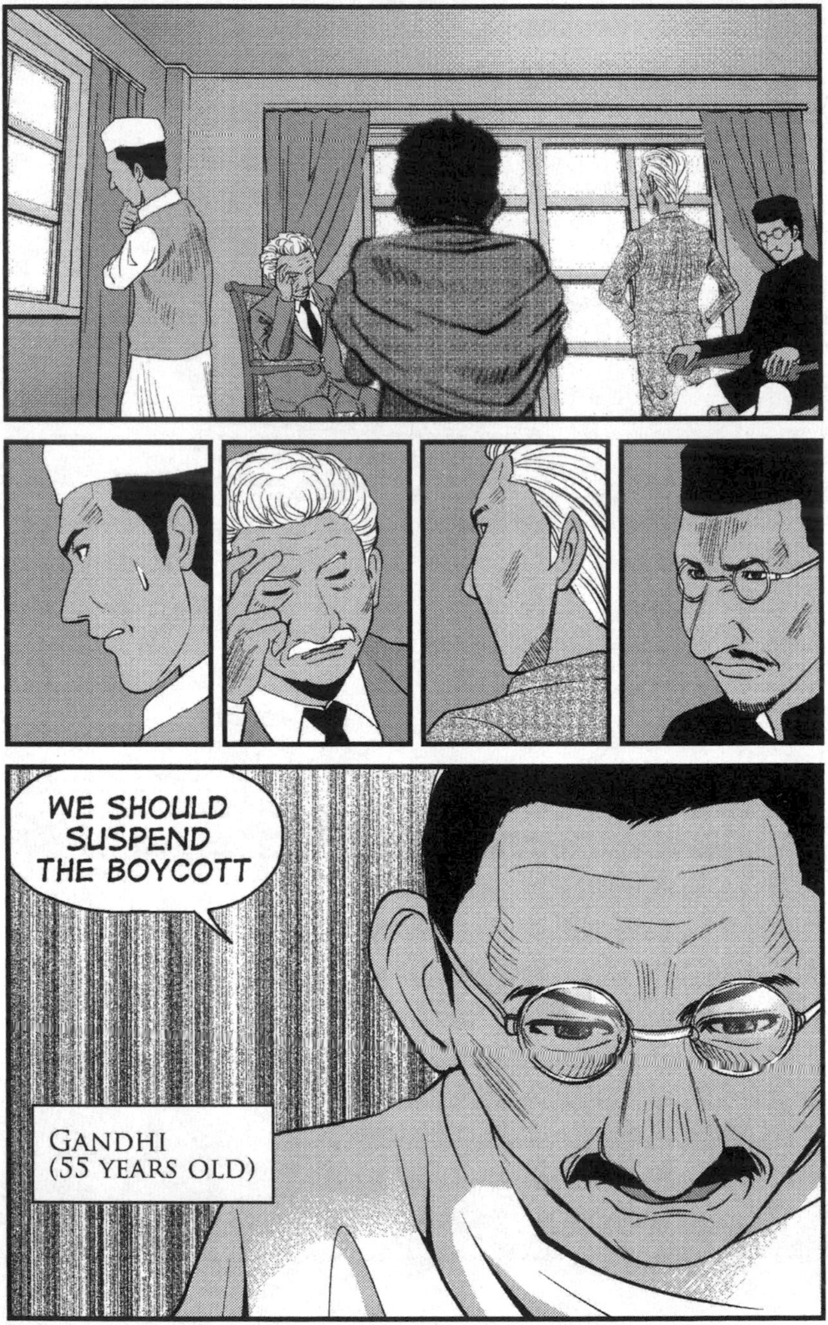
WE SHOULD SUSPEND THE BOYCOTT
GANDHI (55 YEARS OLD)

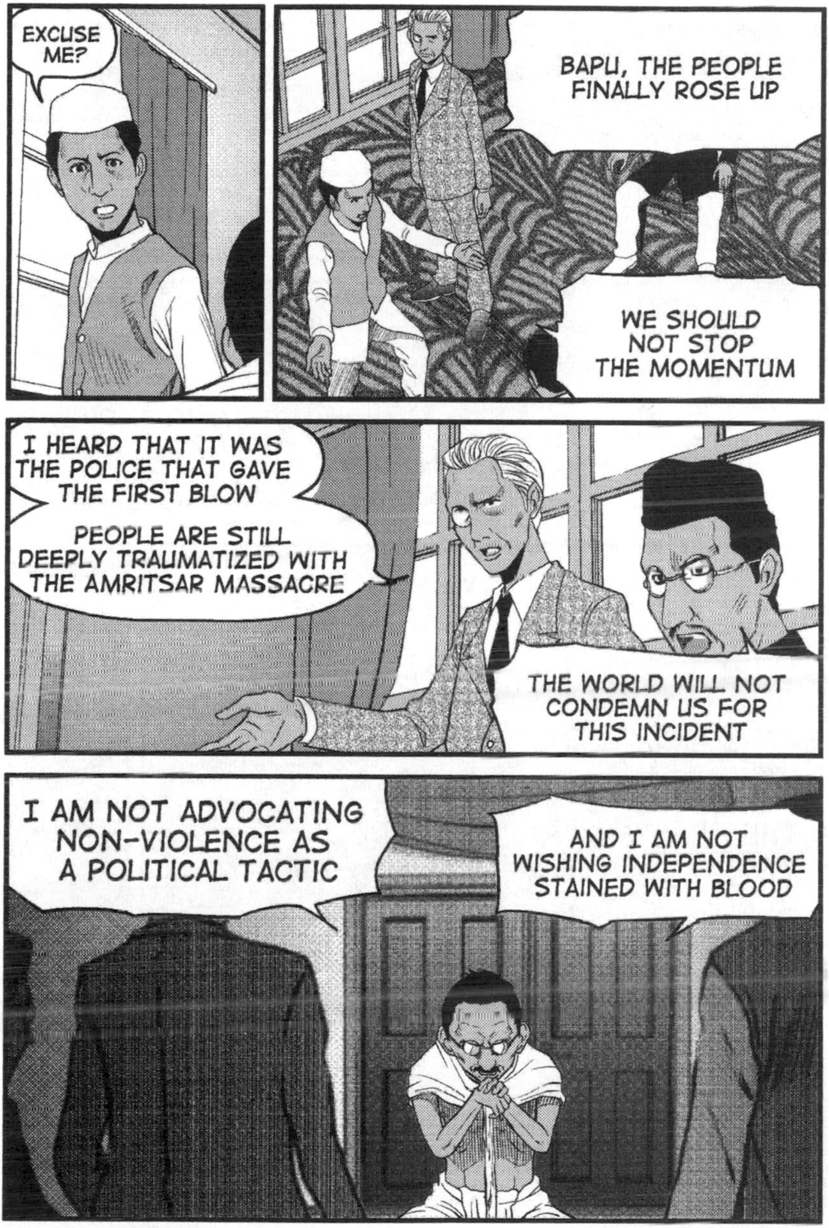
EXCUSE ME?
BAPU, THE PEOPLE FINALLY ROSE UP
WE SHOULD NOT STOP THE MOMENTUM
I HEARD THAT IT WAS THE POLICE THAT GAVE THE FIRST BLOW
PEOPLE ARE STILL DEEPLY TRAUMATIZED WITH THE AMRITSAR MASSACRE
THE WORLD WILL NOT CONDEMN US FOR THIS INCIDENT
I AM NOT ADVOCATING NON-VIOLENCE AS A POLITICAL TACTIC
AND I AM NOT WISHING INDEPENDENCE STAINED WITH BLOOD

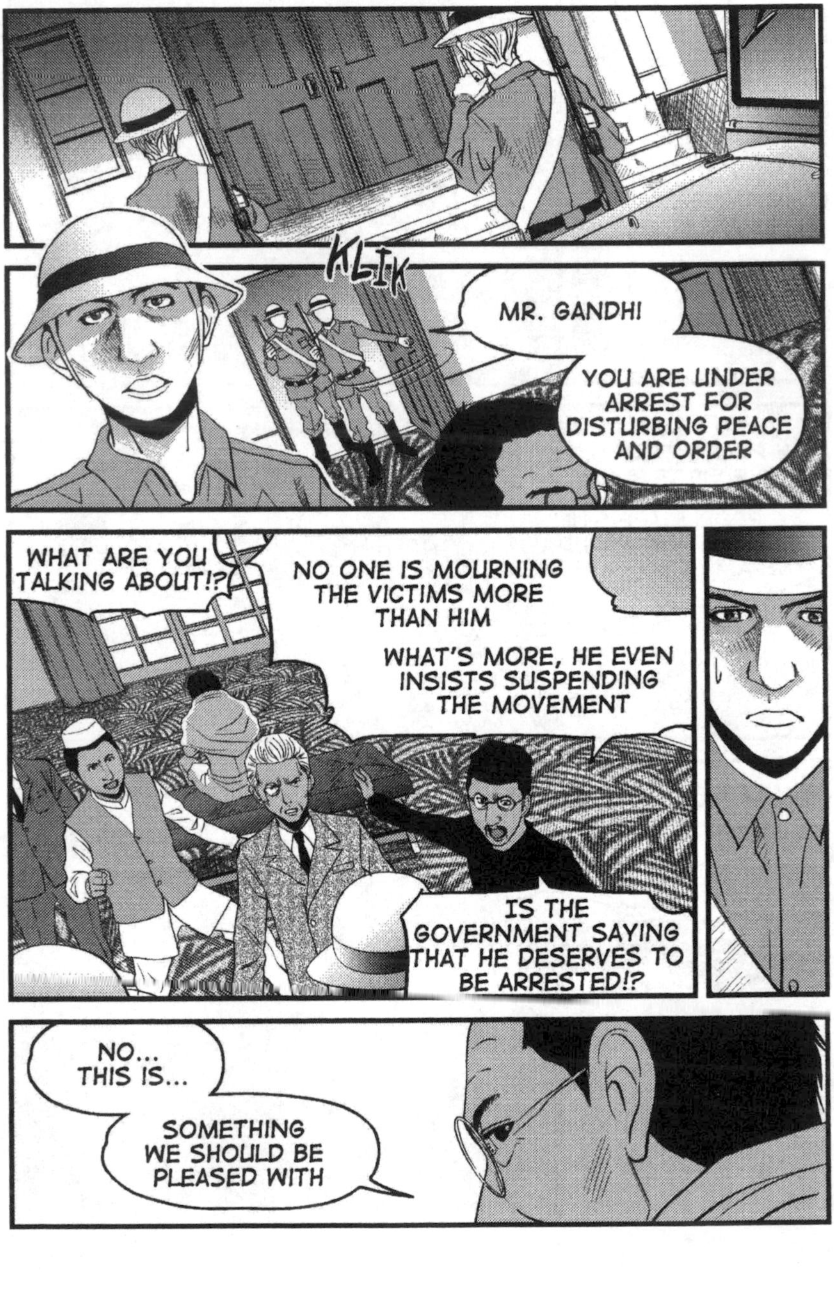
KLIK
MR. GANDHI
YOU ARE UNDER ARREST FOR DISTURBING PEACE AND ORDER
WHAT ARE YOU TALKING ABOUT!?
NO ONE IS MOURNING THE VICTIMS MORE THAN HIM
WHAT'S MORE, HE EVEN INSISTS SUSPENDING THE MOVEMENT
IS THE GOVERNMENT SAYING THAT HE DESERVES TO BE ARRESTED!?
NO... THIS IS...
SOMETHING WE SHOULD BE PLEASED WITH

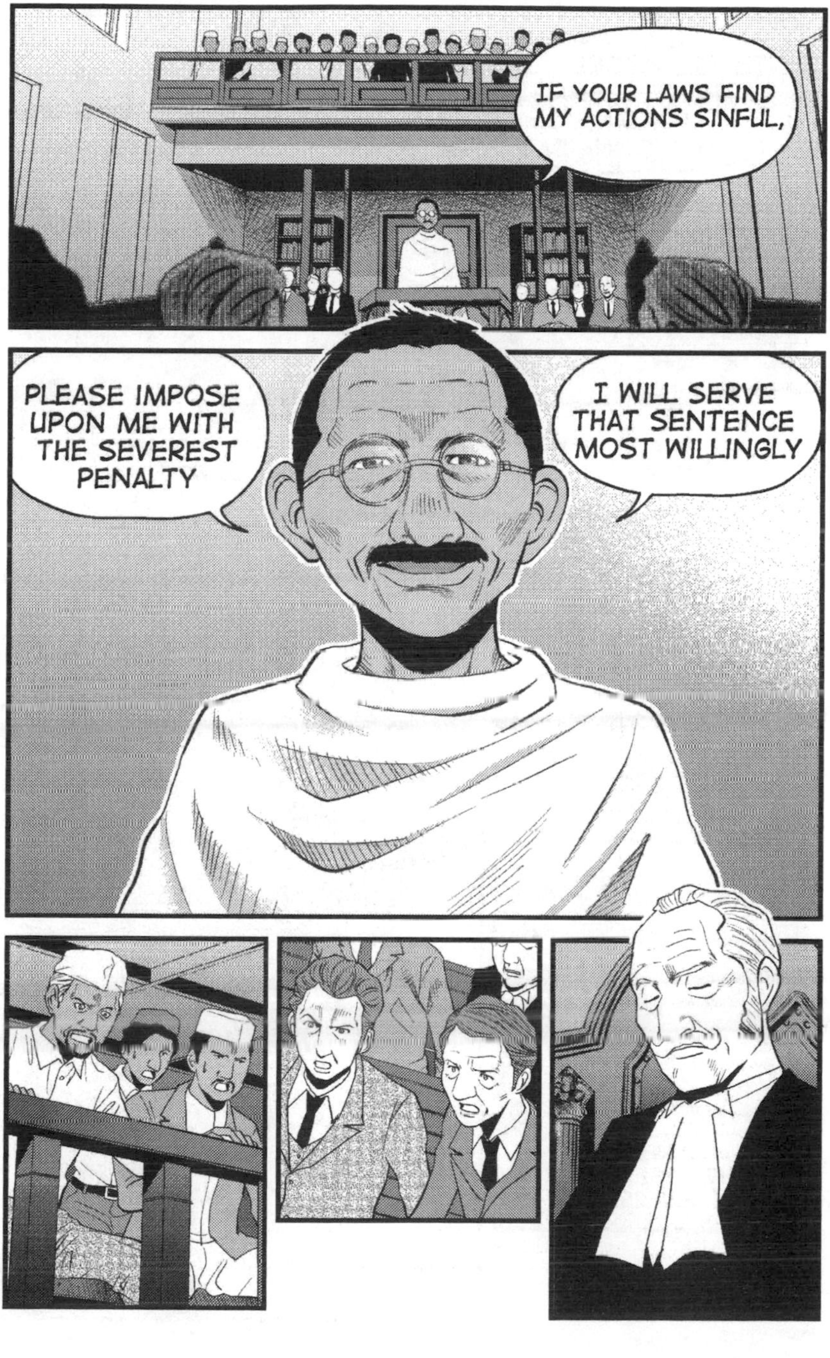
IF YOUR LAWS FIND MY ACTIONS SINFUL,
PLEASE IMPOSE UPON ME WITH THE SEVEREST PENALTY
I WILL SERVE THAT SENTENCE MOST WILLINGLY

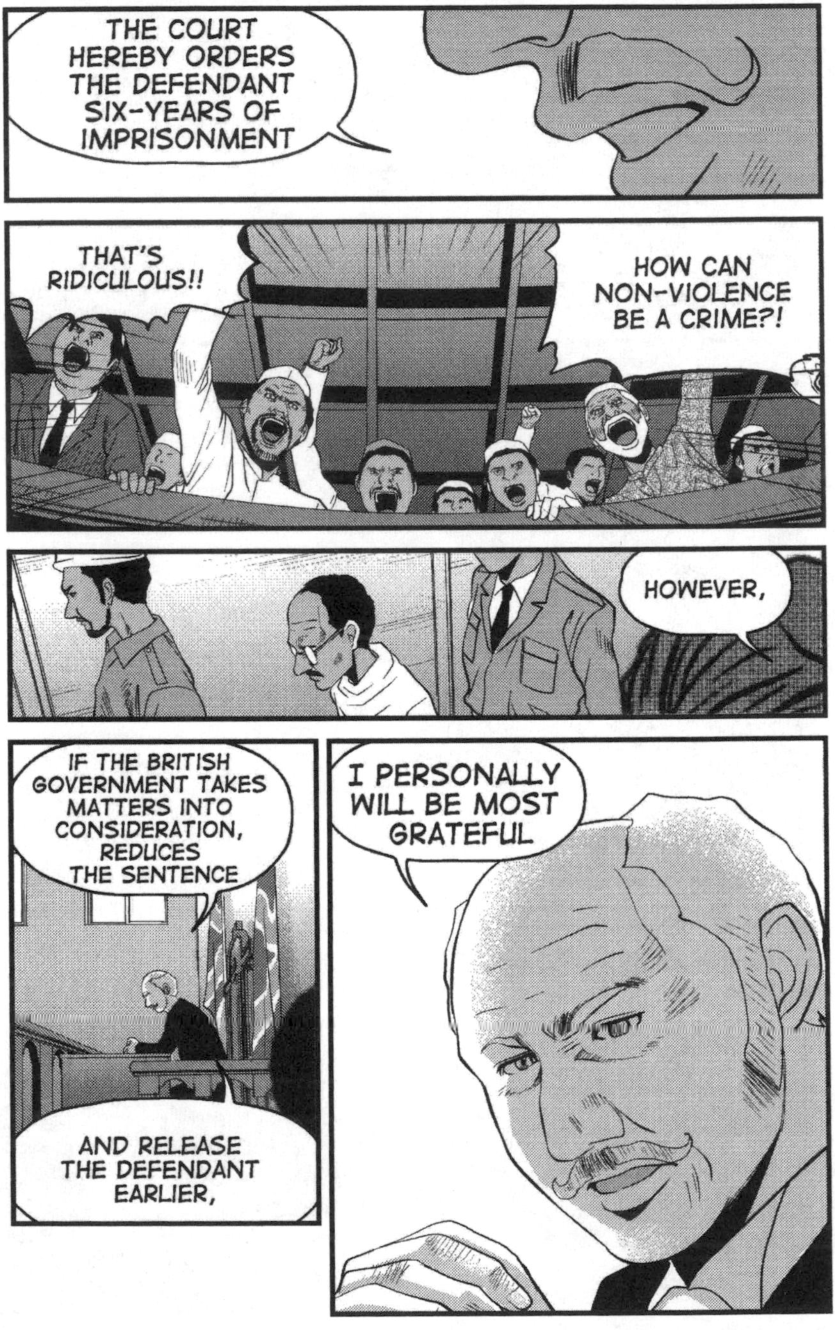
THE COURT HEREBY ORDERS THE DEFENDANT SIX-YEARS OF IMPRISONMENT
THAT'S RIDICULOUS!!
HOW CAN NON-VIOLENCE BE A CRIME?!
HOWEVER,
IF THE BRITISH GOVERNMENT TAKES MATTERS INTO CONSIDERATION, REDUCES THE SENTENCE
AND RELEASE THE DEFENDANT EARLIER,
I PERSONALLY WILL BE MOST GRATEFUL

TWO YEARS LATER, APPREHENDED WITH THE INCREASING CRITICISM, THE BRITISH GOVERNMENT RELEASED GANDHI UNCONDITIONALLY

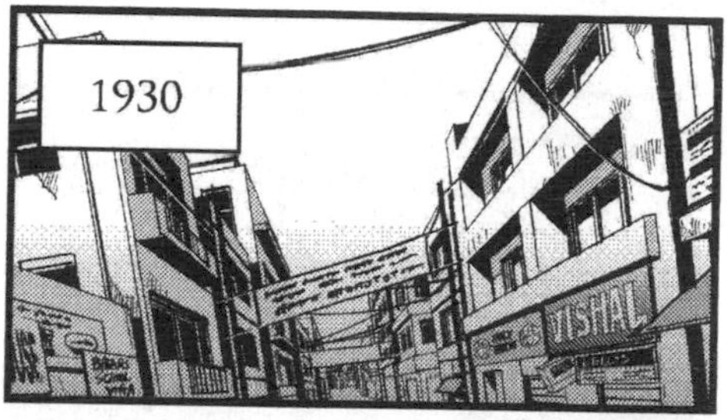
1930
VISHAL

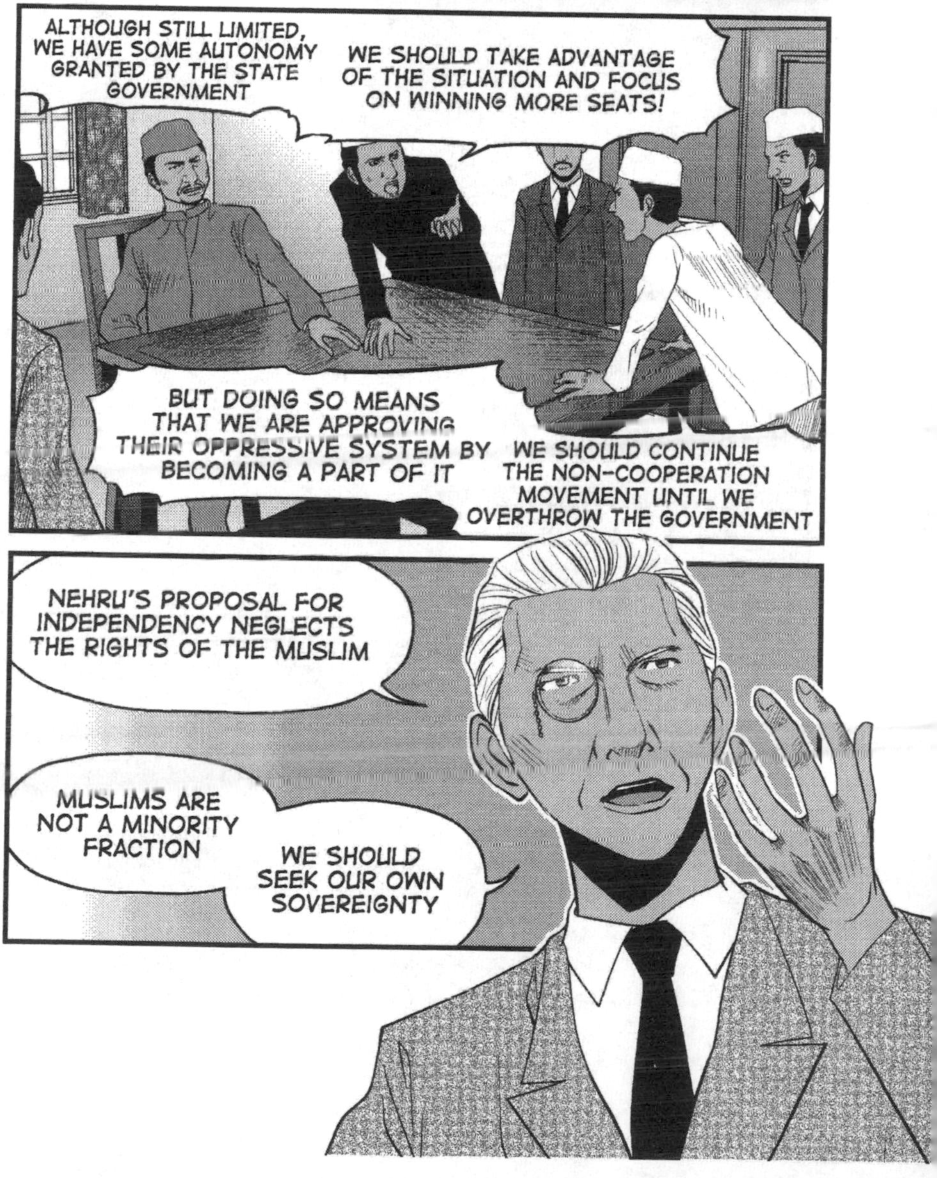
ALTHOUGH STILL LIMITED, WE HAVE SOME AUTONOMY GRANTED BY THE STATE GOVERNMENT
WE SHOULD TAKE ADVANTAGE OF THE SITUATION AND FOCUS ON WINNING MORE SEATS!
BUT DOING SO MEANS THAT WE ARE APPROVING THEIR OPPRESSIVE SYSTEM BY BECOMING A PART OF IT
WE SHOULD CONTINUE THE NON-COOPERATION MOVEMENT UNTIL WE OVERTHROW THE GOVERNMENT
NEHRU'S PROPOSAL FOR INDEPENDENCY NEGLECTS THE RIGHTS OF THE MUSLIM
MUSLIMS ARE NOT A MINORITY FRACTION
WE SHOULD SEEK OUR OWN SOVEREIGNTY

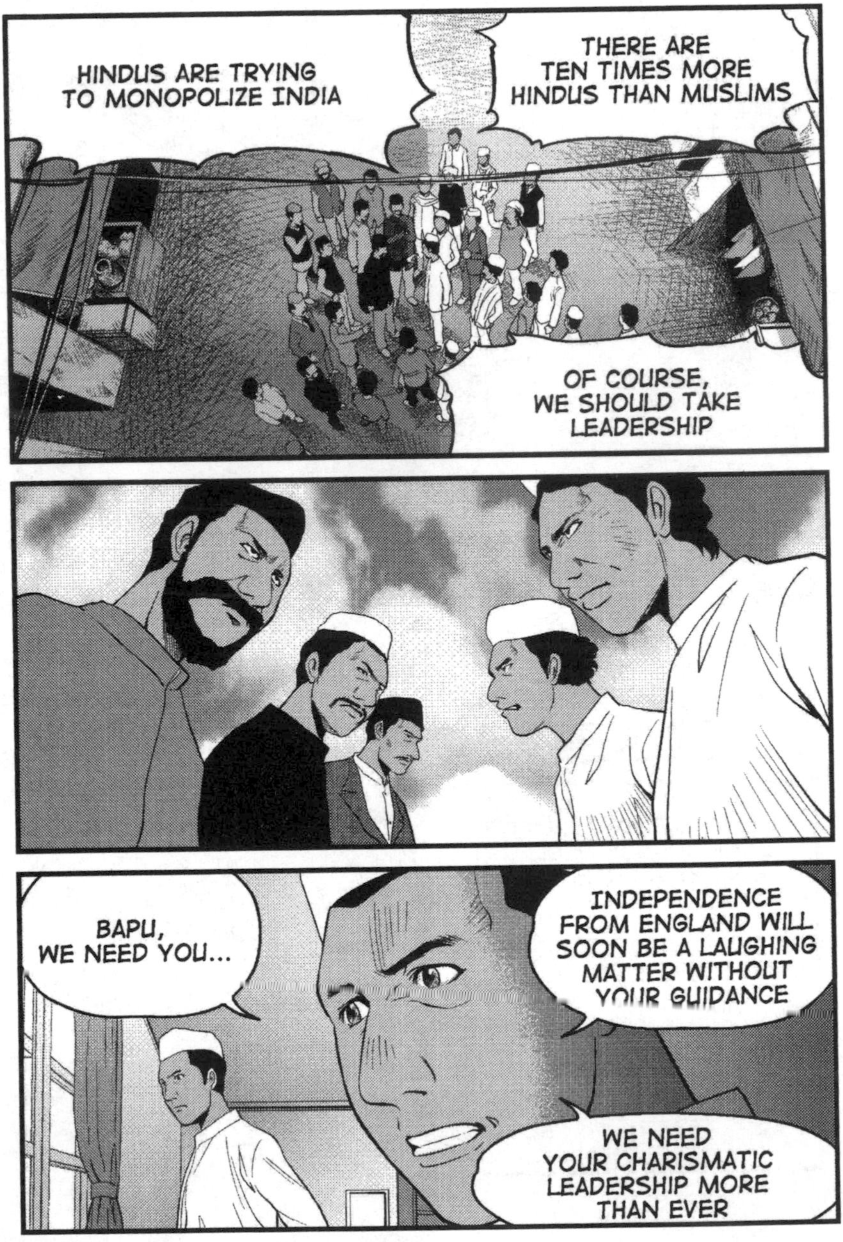
HINDUS ARE TRYING TO MONOPOLIZE INDIA
THERE ARE TEN TIMES MORE HINDUS THAN MUSLIMS
OF COURSE, WE SHOULD TAKE LEADERSHIP
BAPU, WE NEED YOU...
INDEPENDENCE FROM ENGLAND WILL SOON BE A LAUGHING MATTER WITHOUT YOUR GUIDANCE
WE NEED YOUR CHARISMATIC LEADERSHIP MORE THAN EVER

"IF THEY ANSWER NOT TO THY CALL WALK ALONE,"

RABINDRANATH TAGORE
GITANJALI

"IF THEY ARE AFRAID AND COWER MUTELY FACING THE WALL, ... OPEN THY MIND AND SPEAK OUT ALONE"

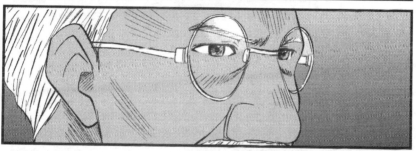

ARE YOU ALRIGHT? YOU LOOK SO SERIOUS

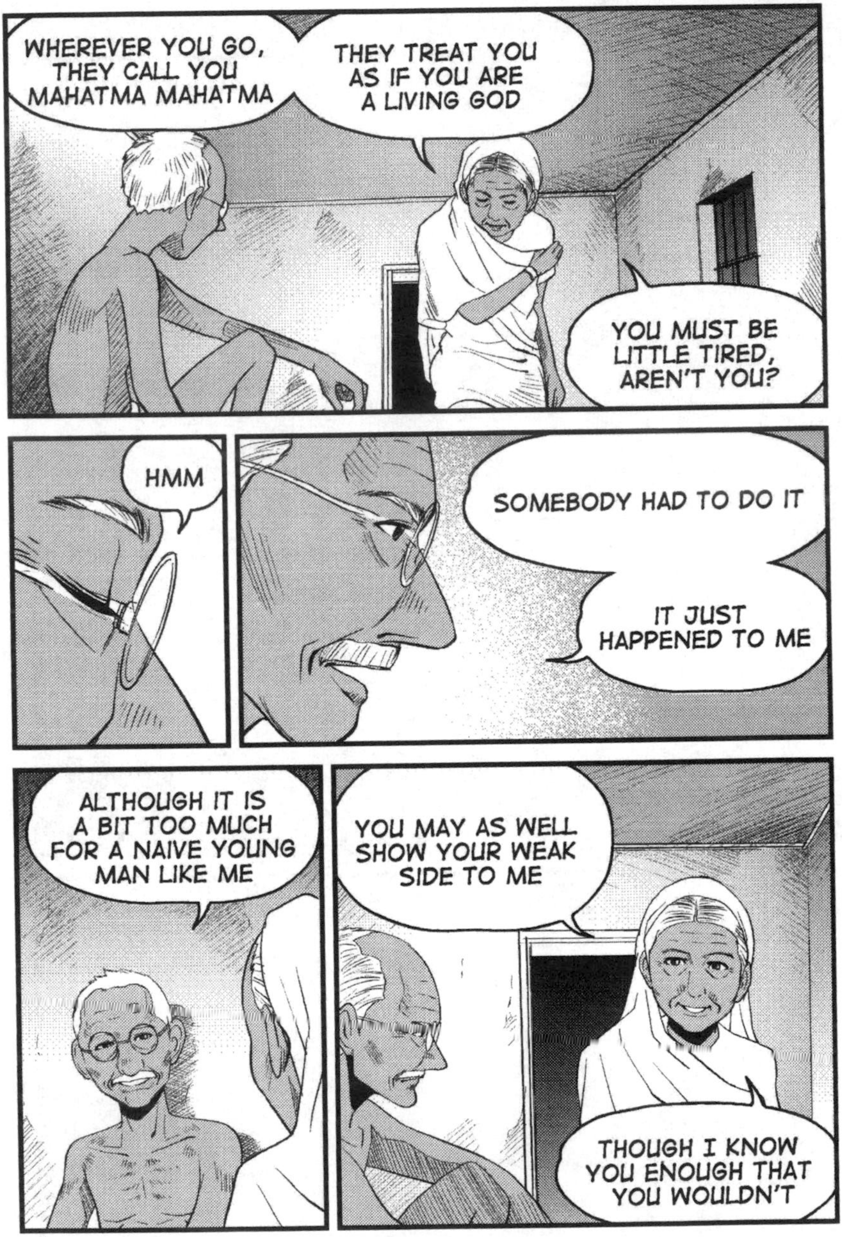
WHEREVER YOU GO, THEY CALL YOU MAHATMA MAHATMA
THEY TREAT YOU AS IF YOU ARE A LIVING GOD
YOU MUST BE LITTLE TIRED, AREN'T YOU?
HMM
SOMEBODY HAD TO DO IT
IT JUST HAPPENED TO ME
ALTHOUGH IT IS A BIT TOO MUCH FOR A NAIVE YOUNG MAN LIKE ME
YOU MAY AS WELL SHOW YOUR WEAK SIDE TO ME
THOUGH I KNOW YOU ENOUGH THAT YOU WOULDN'T

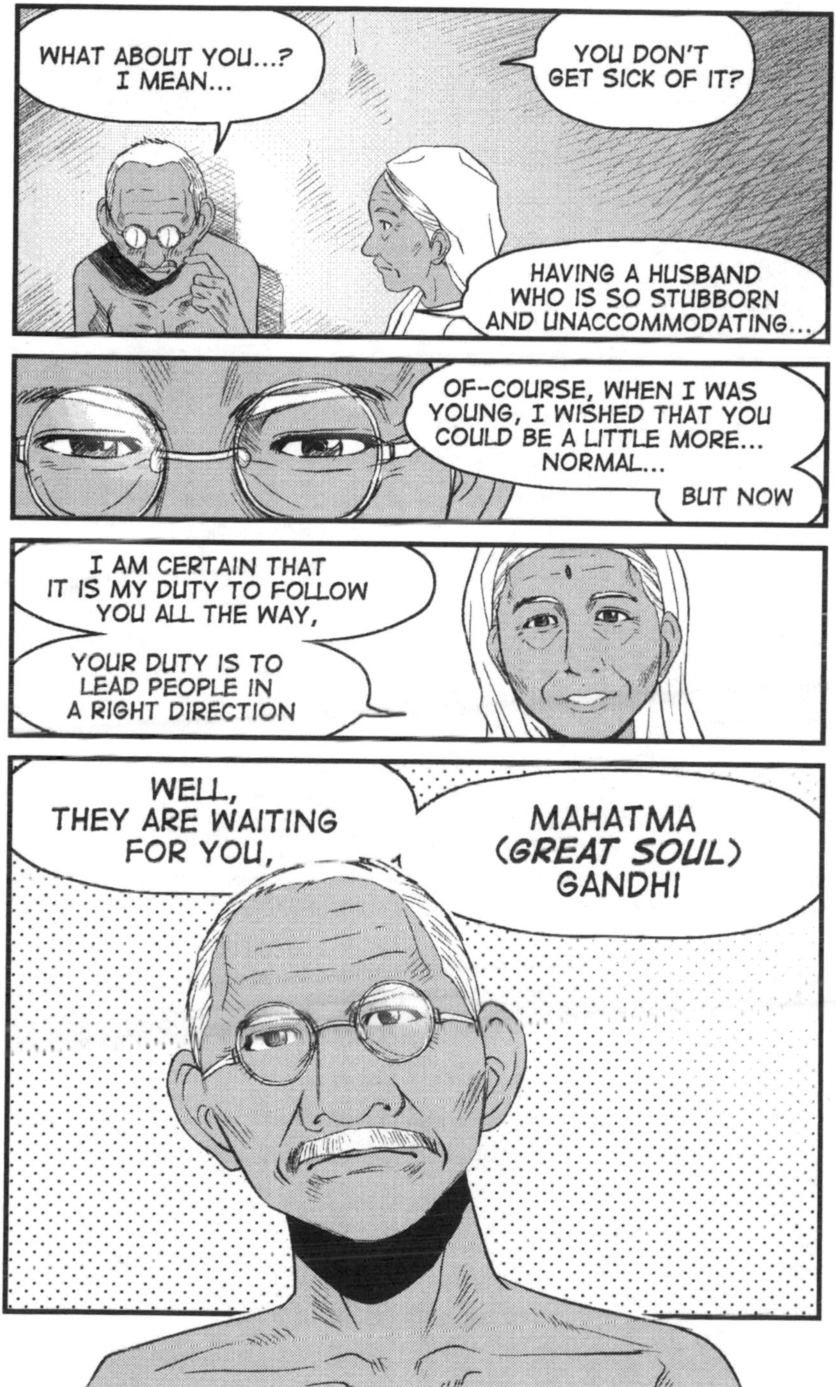
WHAT ABOUT YOU...? I MEAN...
YOU DON'T GET SICK OF IT?
HAVING A HUSBAND WHO IS SO STUBBORN AND UNACCOMMODATING...
OF-COURSE, WHEN I WAS YOUNG, I WISHED THAT YOU COULD BE A LITTLE MORE... NORMAL...
BUT NOW
I AM CERTAIN THAT IT IS MY DUTY TO FOLLOW YOU ALL THE WAY,
YOUR DUTY IS TO LEAD PEOPLE IN A RIGHT DIRECTION
WELL, THEY ARE WAITING FOR YOU,
MAHATMA (GREAT SOUL) GANDHI

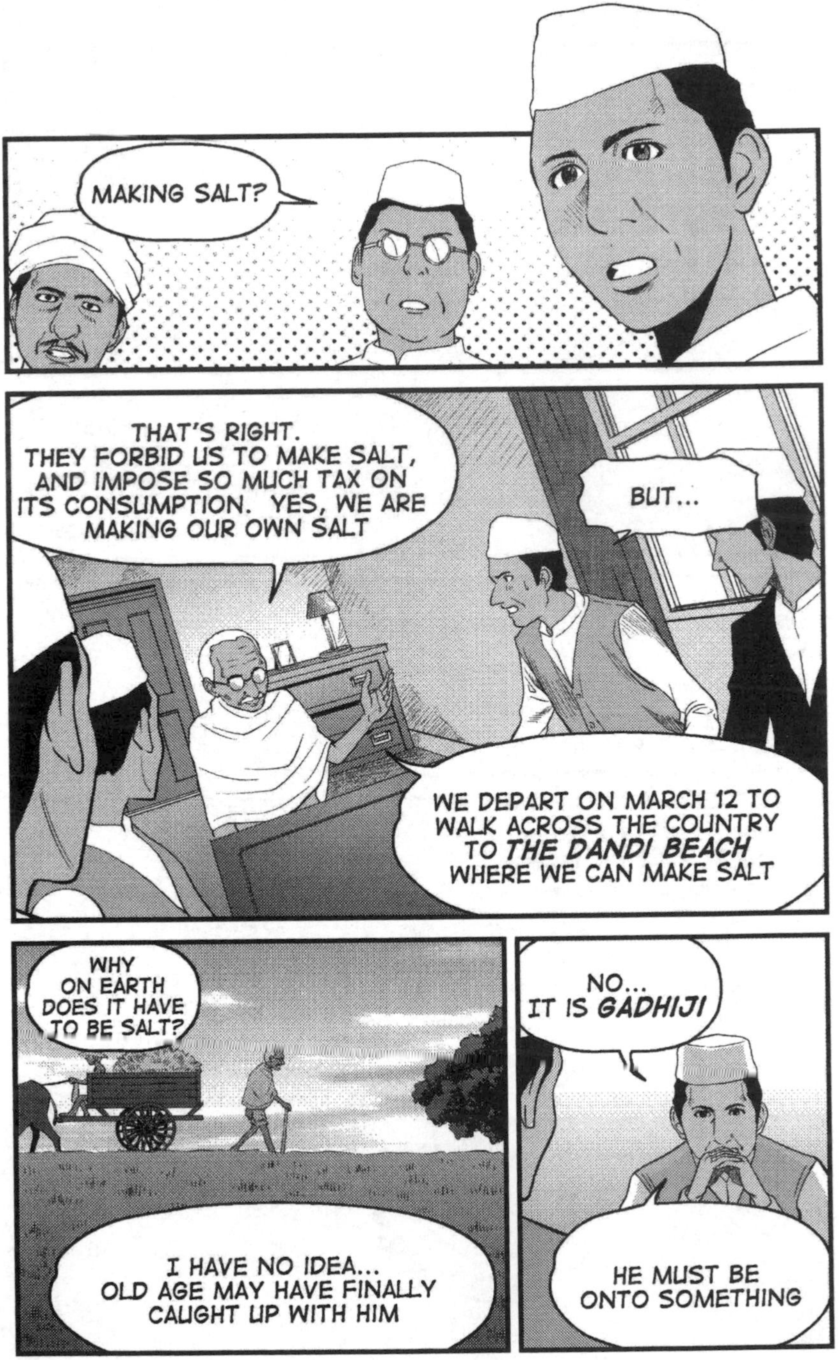
MAKING SALT?
THAT'S RIGHT. THEY FORBID US TO MAKE SALT, AND IMPOSE SO MUCH TAX ON ITS CONSUMPTION. YES, WE ARE MAKING OUR OWN SALT
BUT...
WE DEPART ON MARCH 12 TO WALK ACROSS THE COUNTRY TO *THE DANDI BEACH* WHERE WE CAN MAKE SALT
WHY ON EARTH DOES IT HAVE TO BE SALT?
I HAVE NO IDEA... OLD AGE MAY HAVE FINALLY CAUGHT UP WITH HIM
NO... IT IS *GADHIJI*
HE MUST BE ONTO SOMETHING

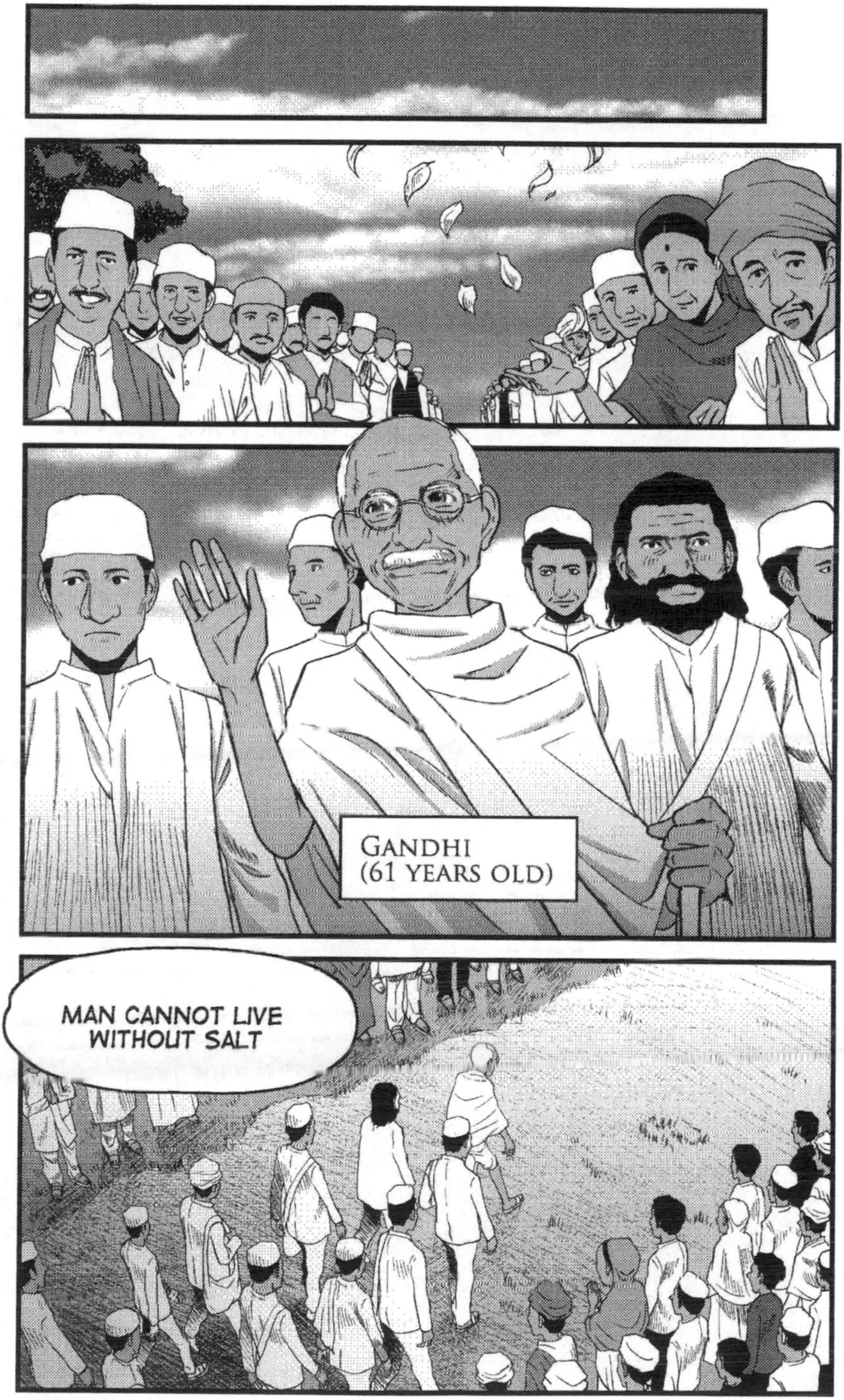
GANDHI
(61 YEARS OLD)
MAN CANNOT LIVE WITHOUT SALT

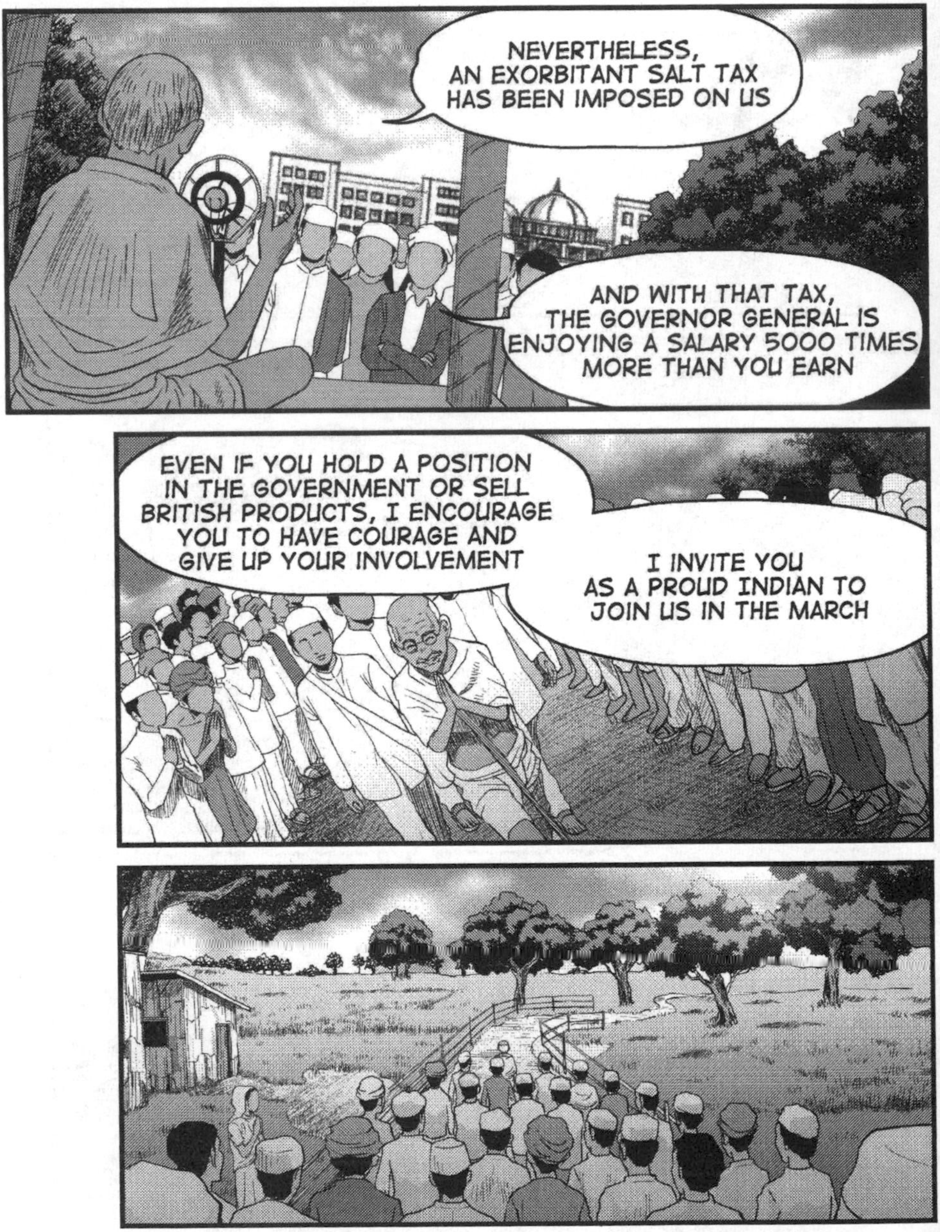
NEVERTHELESS, AN EXORBITANT SALT TAX HAS BEEN IMPOSED ON US
AND WITH THAT TAX, THE GOVERNOR GENERAL IS ENJOYING A SALARY 5000 TIMES MORE THAN YOU EARN
EVEN IF YOU HOLD A POSITION IN THE GOVERNMENT OR SELL BRITISH PRODUCTS, I ENCOURAGE YOU TO HAVE COURAGE AND GIVE UP YOUR INVOLVEMENT
I INVITE YOU AS A PROUD INDIAN TO JOIN US IN THE MARCH

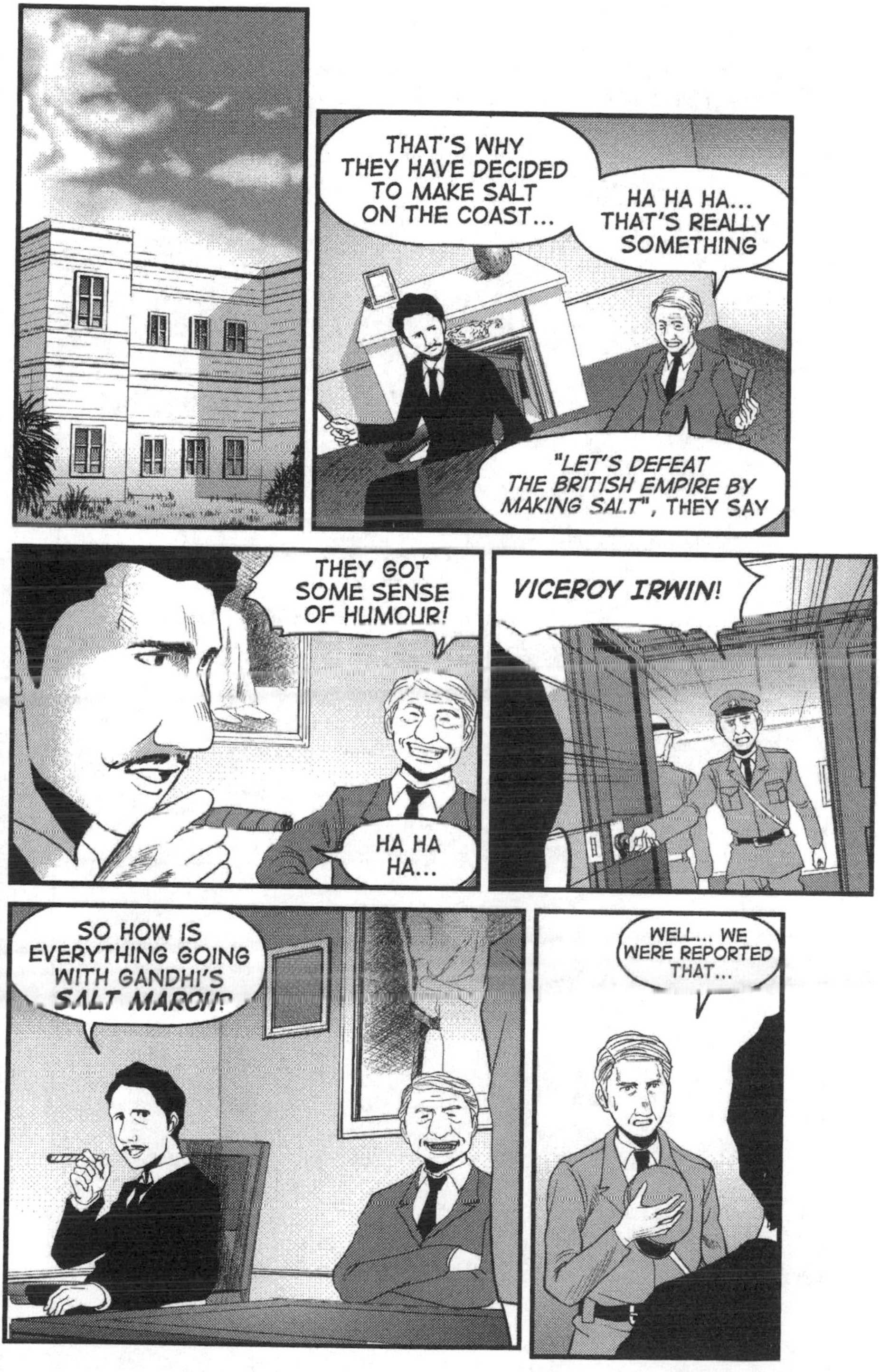
THAT'S WHY THEY HAVE DECIDED TO MAKE SALT ON THE COAST...
HA HA HA... THAT'S REALLY SOMETHING
"LET'S DEFEAT THE BRITISH EMPIRE BY MAKING SALT", THEY SAY
THEY GOT SOME SENSE OF HUMOUR!
HA HA HA...
VICEROY IRWIN!
SO HOW IS EVERYTHING GOING WITH GANDHI'S SALT MARCH?
WELL... WE WERE REPORTED THAT...

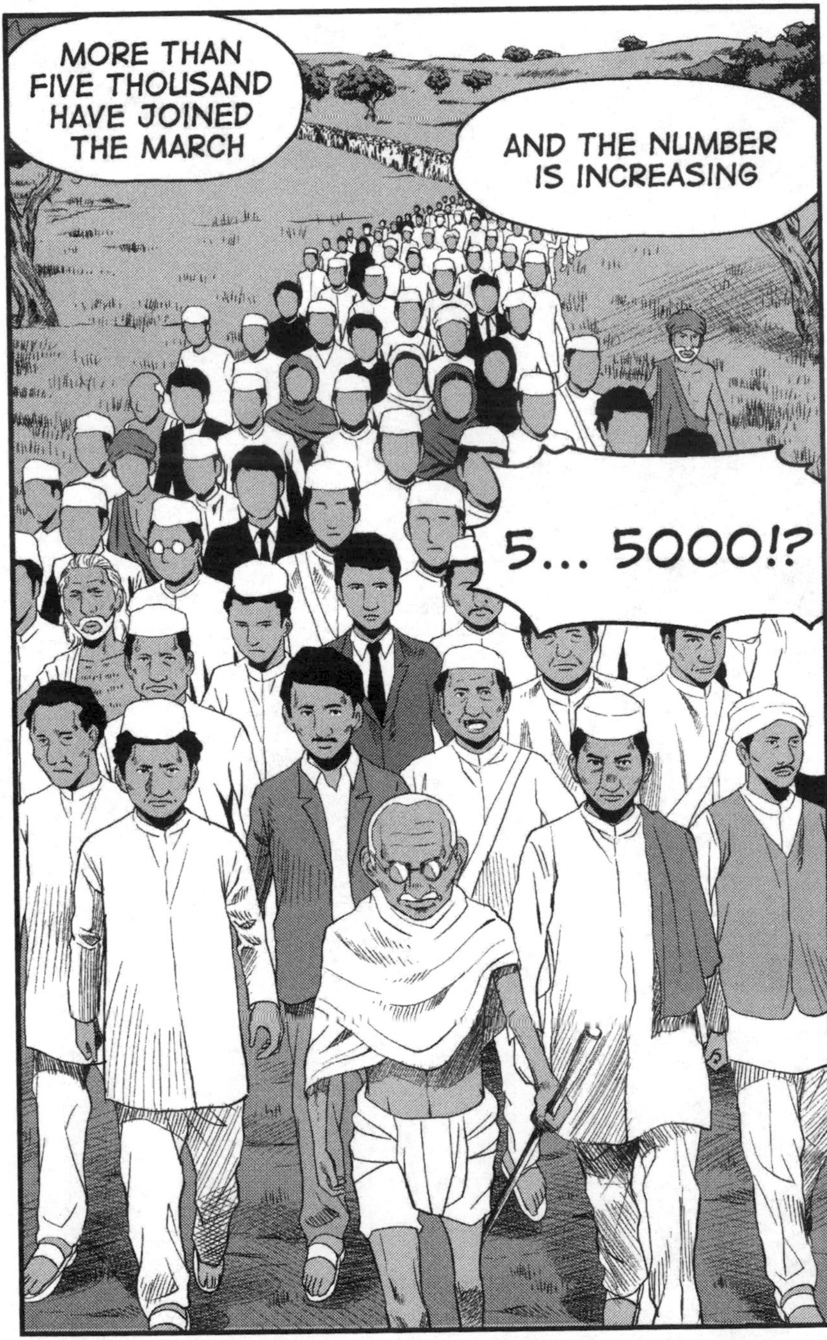
MORE THAN FIVE THOUSAND HAVE JOINED THE MARCH
AND THE NUMBER IS INCREASING
5... 5000!?

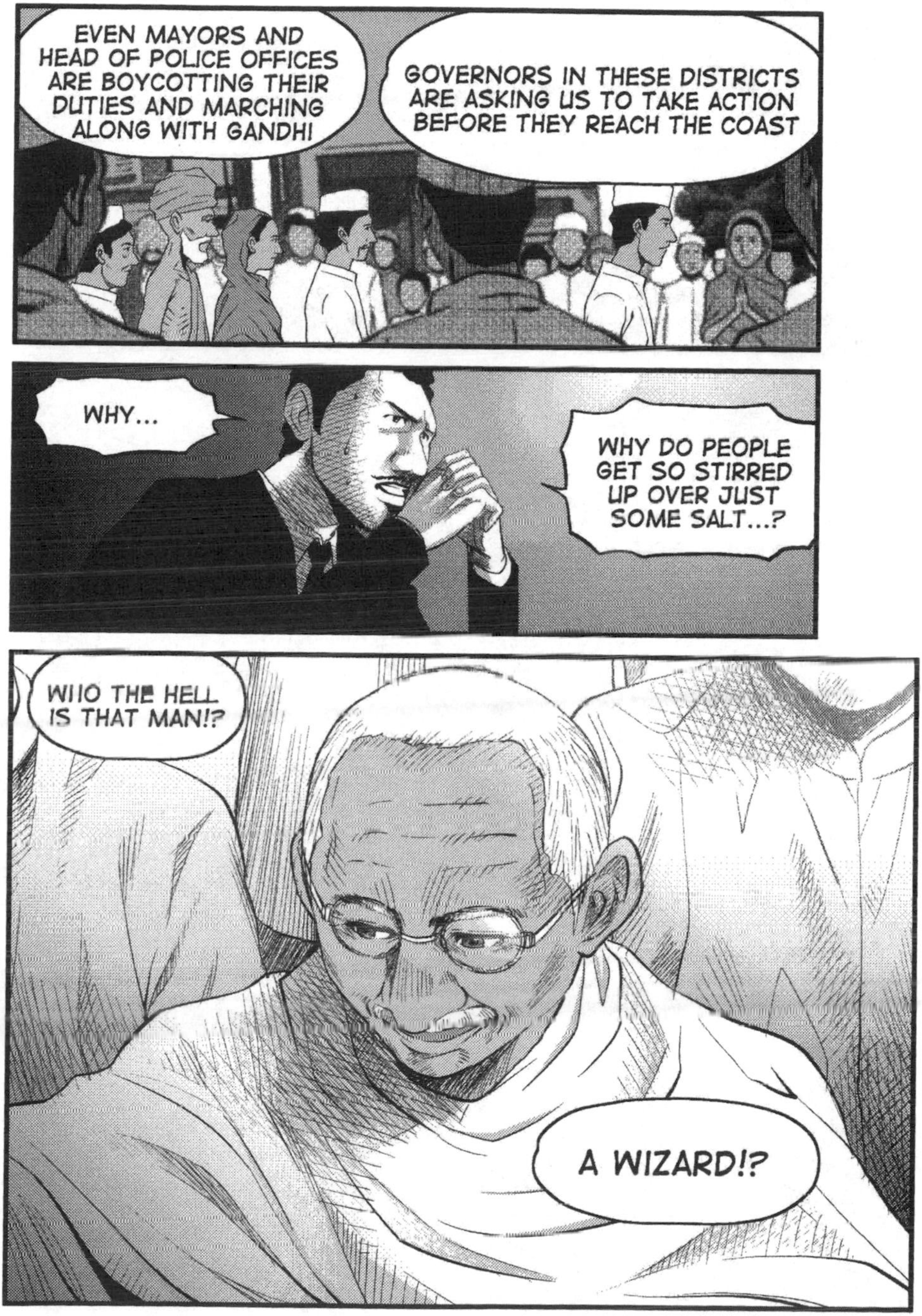
EVEN MAYORS AND HEAD OF POLICE OFFICES ARE BOYCOTTING THEIR DUTIES AND MARCHING ALONG WITH GANDHI
GOVERNORS IN THESE DISTRICTS ARE ASKING US TO TAKE ACTION BEFORE THEY REACH THE COAST
WHY...
WHY DO PEOPLE GET SO STIRRED UP OVER JUST SOME SALT...?
WHO THE HELL IS THAT MAN!?
A WIZARD!?

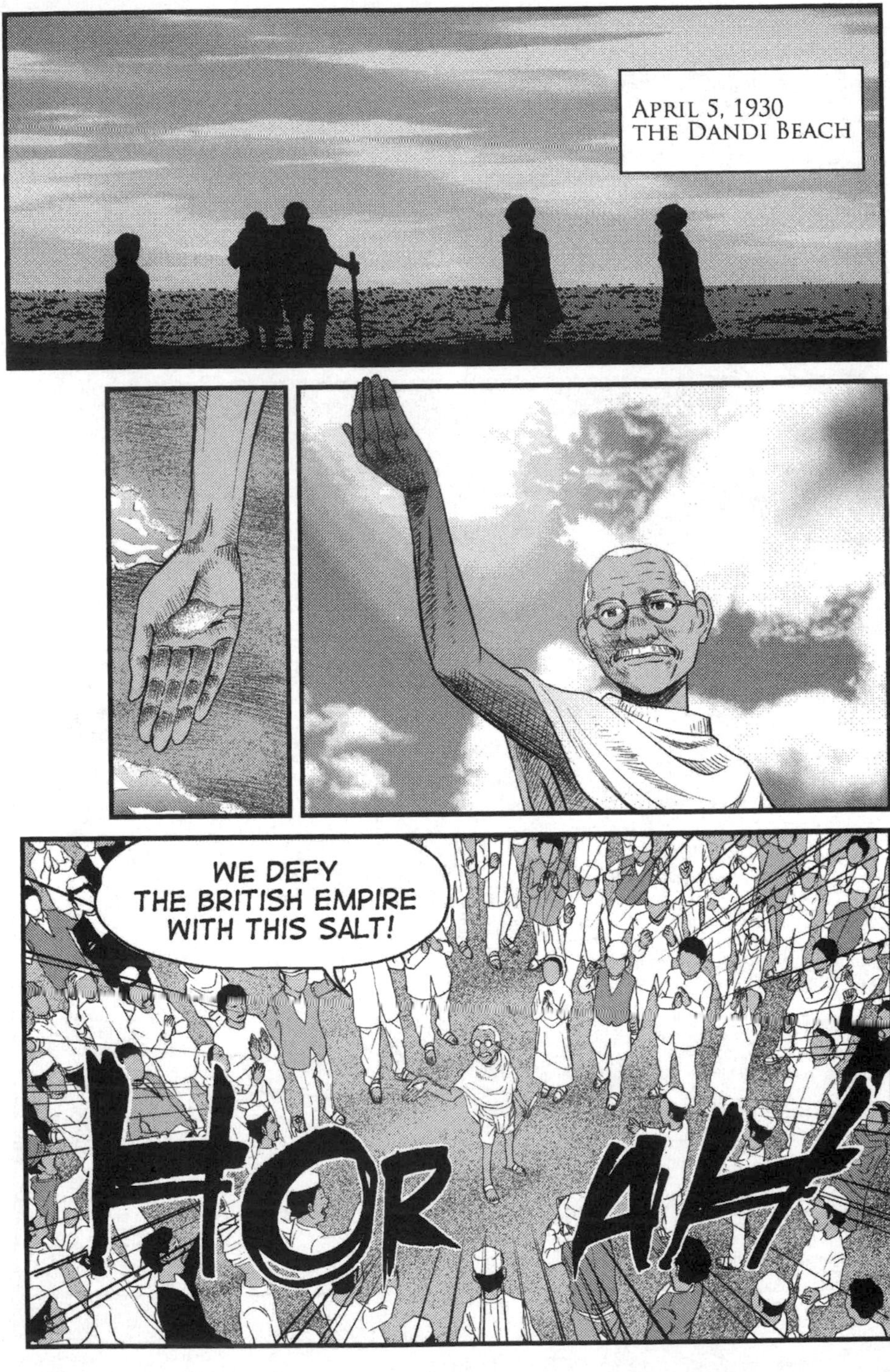
APRIL 5, 1930
THE DANDI BEACH
WE DEFY THE BRITISH EMPIRE WITH THIS SALT!
HOORAH

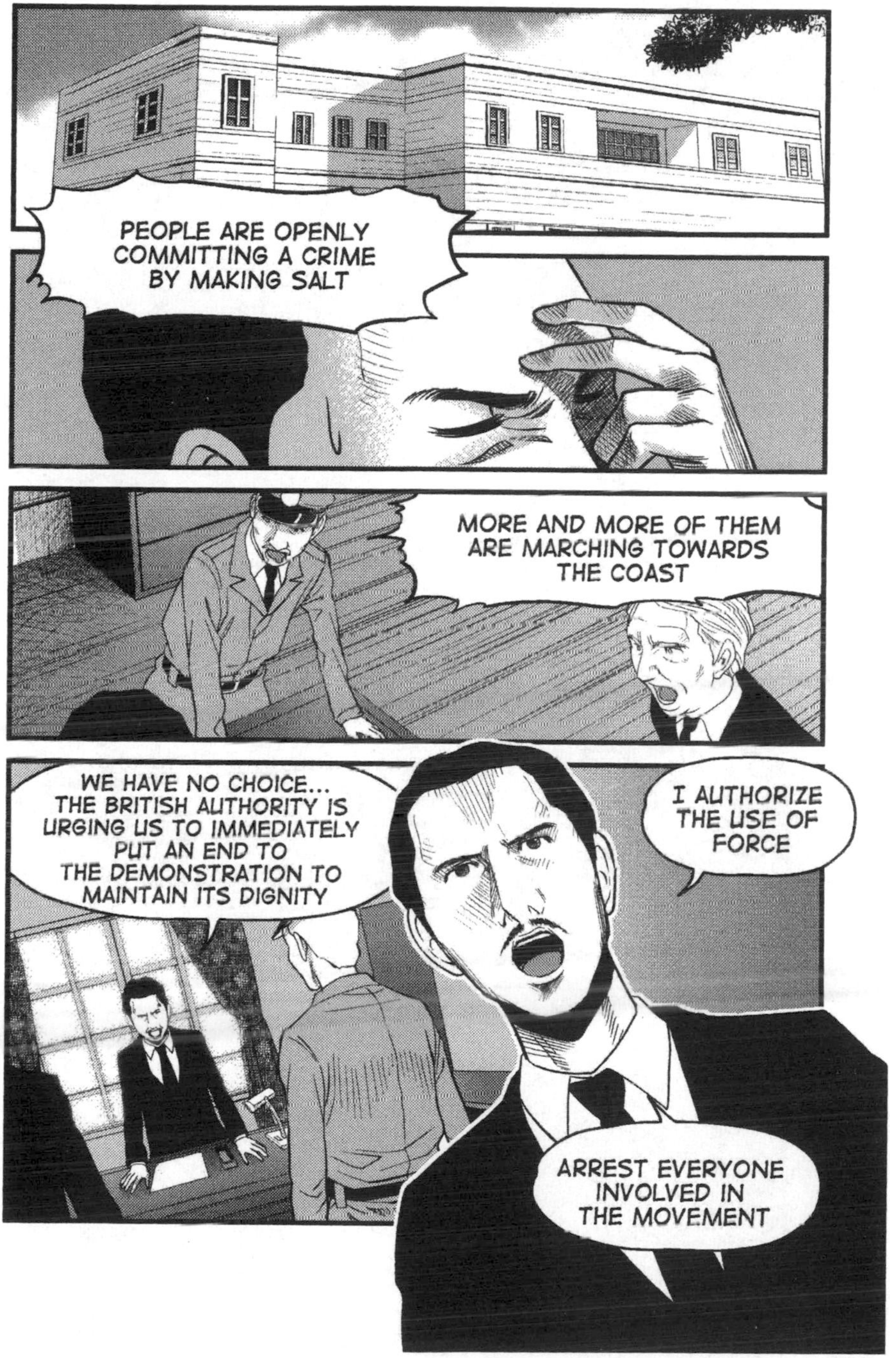
PEOPLE ARE OPENLY COMMITTING A CRIME BY MAKING SALT
MORE AND MORE OF THEM ARE MARCHING TOWARDS THE COAST
WE HAVE NO CHOICE... THE BRITISH AUTHORITY IS URGING US TO IMMEDIATELY PUT AN END TO THE DEMONSTRATION TO MAINTAIN ITS DIGNITY
I AUTHORIZE THE USE OF FORCE
ARREST EVERYONE INVOLVED IN THE MOVEMENT

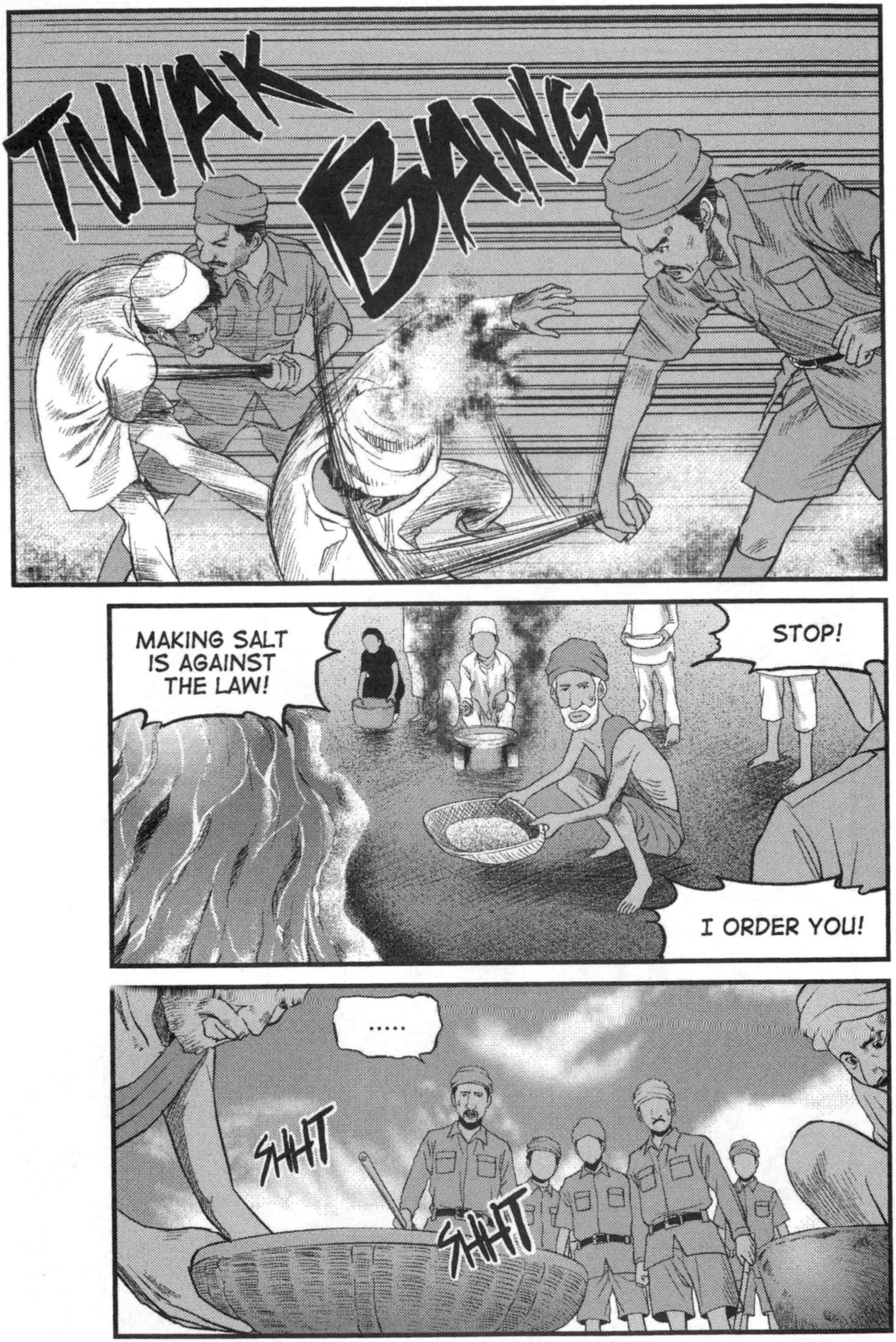
TWAK
BANG
MAKING SALT IS AGAINST THE LAW!
STOP!
I ORDER YOU!
.....
SHHT
SHHT

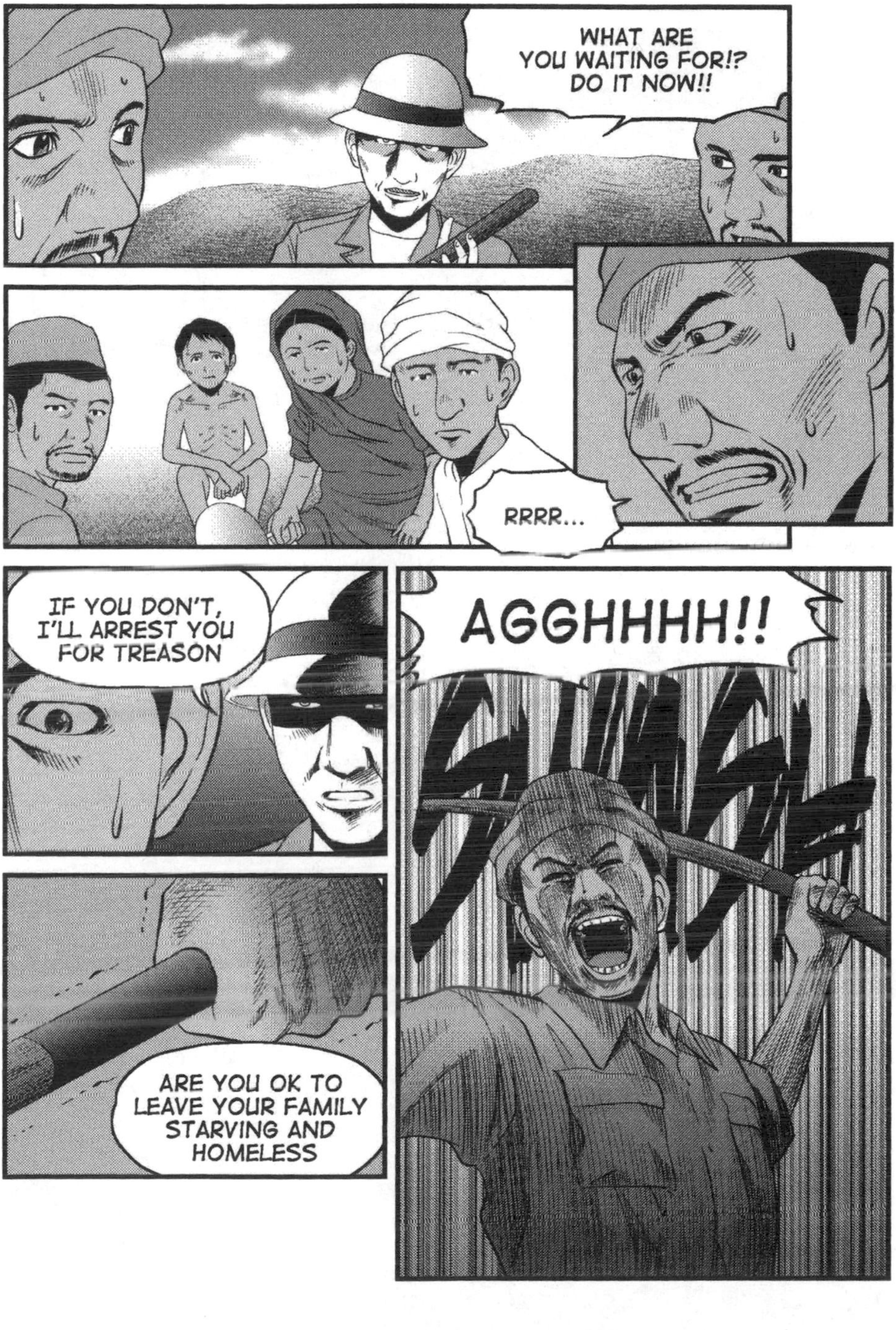
WHAT ARE YOU WAITING FOR!? DO IT NOW!!
RRRR...
IF YOU DON'T, I'LL ARREST YOU FOR TREASON
ARE YOU OK TO LEAVE YOUR FAMILY STARVING AND HOMELESS
AGGHHHH!!

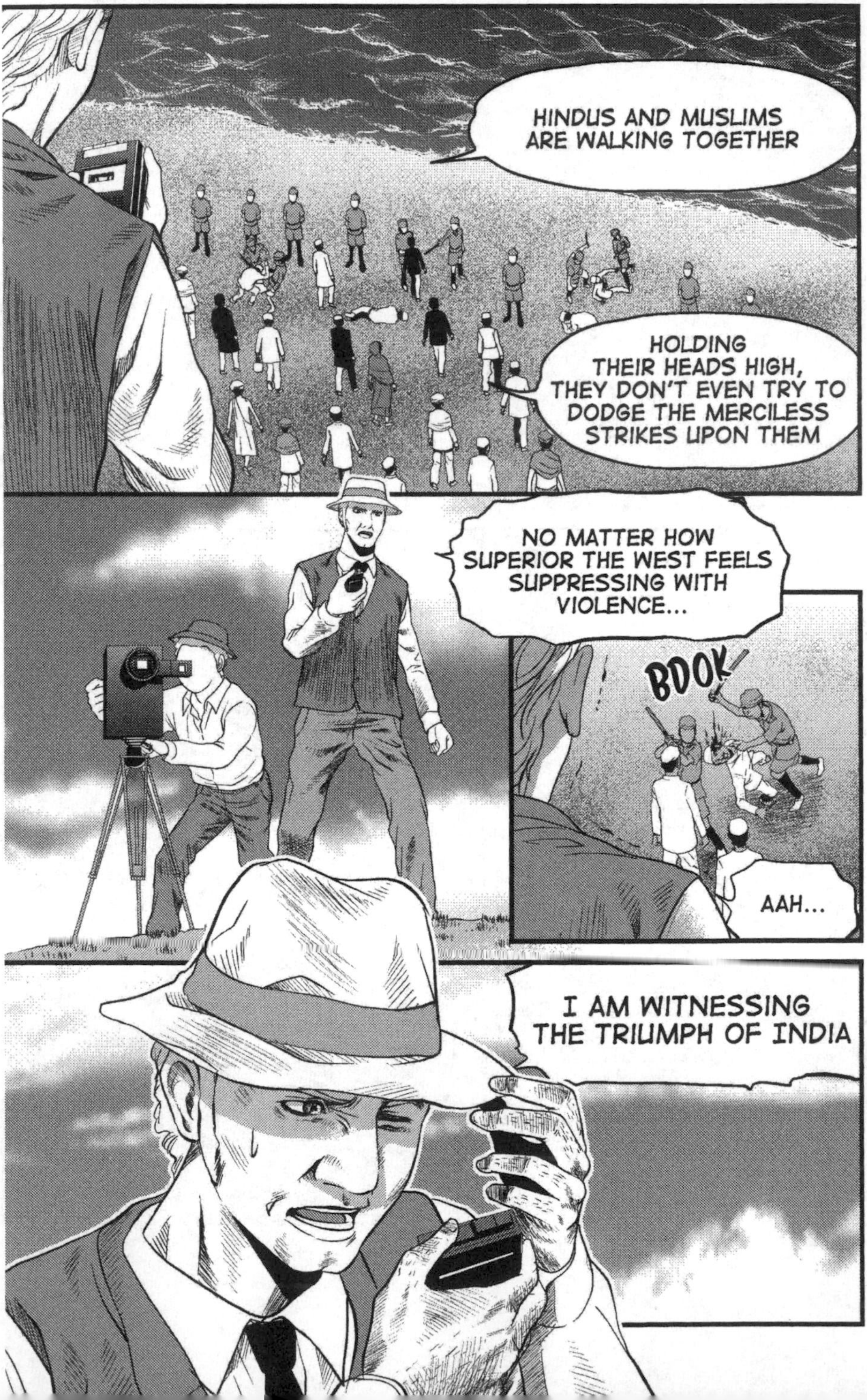
HINDUS AND MUSLIMS ARE WALKING TOGETHER
HOLDING THEIR HEADS HIGH, THEY DON'T EVEN TRY TO DODGE THE MERCILESS STRIKES UPON THEM
NO MATTER HOW SUPERIOR THE WEST FEELS SUPPRESSING WITH VIOLENCE...
BOOK
AAH...
I AM WITNESSING THE TRIUMPH OF INDIA

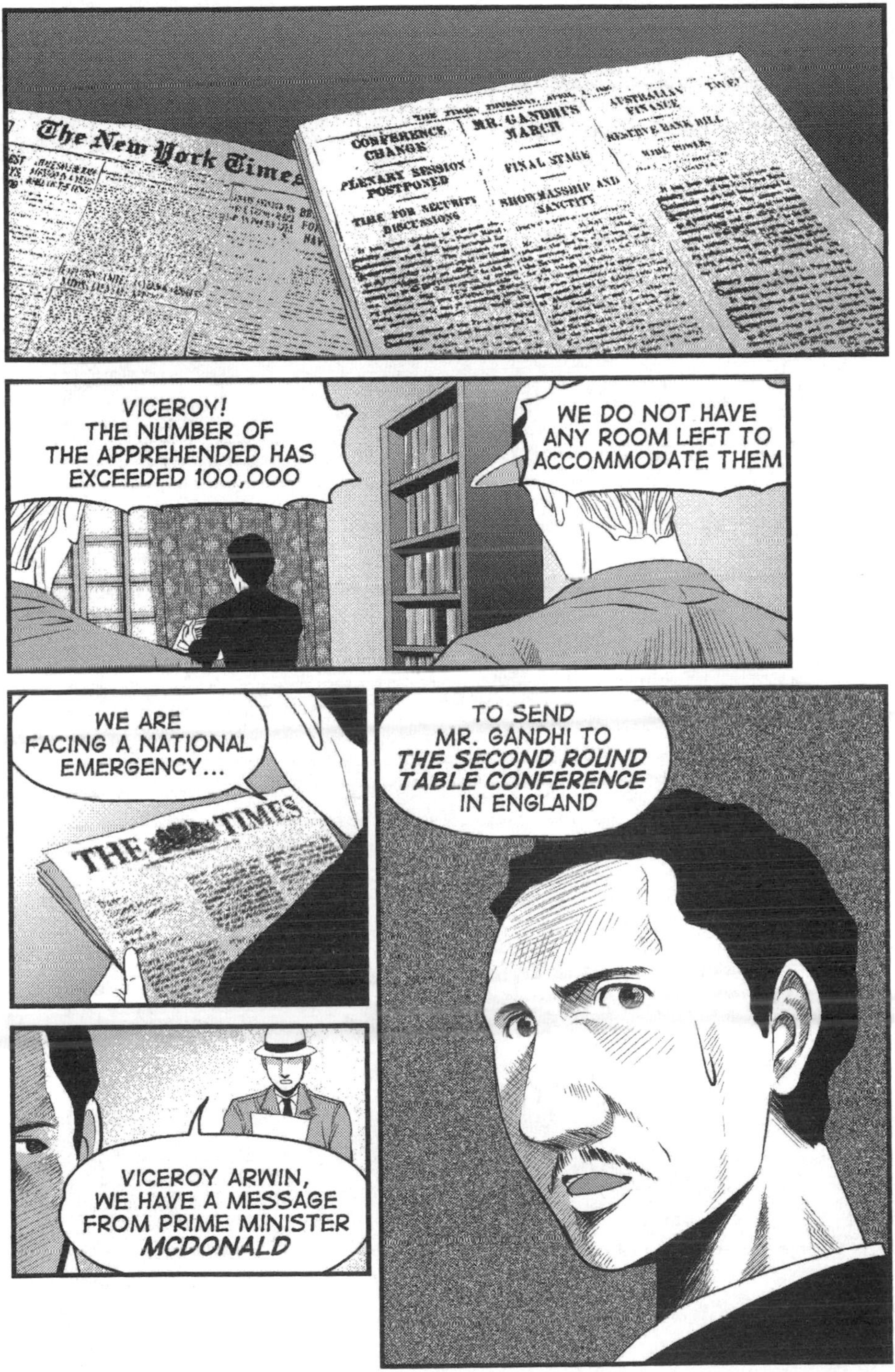
The New York Times
CONFERENCE CHANGE
PLENARY SESSION POSTPONED
TIME FOR SECURITY DISCUSSIONS
MR. GANDHI'S MARCH
FINAL STAGE
SHOWMANSHIP AND SANCTITY
AUSTRALIAN FINANCE
RESERVE BANK BILL
VICEROY! THE NUMBER OF THE APPREHENDED HAS EXCEEDED 100,000
WE DO NOT HAVE ANY ROOM LEFT TO ACCOMMODATE THEM
WE ARE FACING A NATIONAL EMERGENCY...
THE TIMES
TO SEND MR. GANDHI TO *THE SECOND ROUND TABLE CONFERENCE* IN ENGLAND
VICEROY ARWIN, WE HAVE A MESSAGE FROM PRIME MINISTER *MCDONALD*

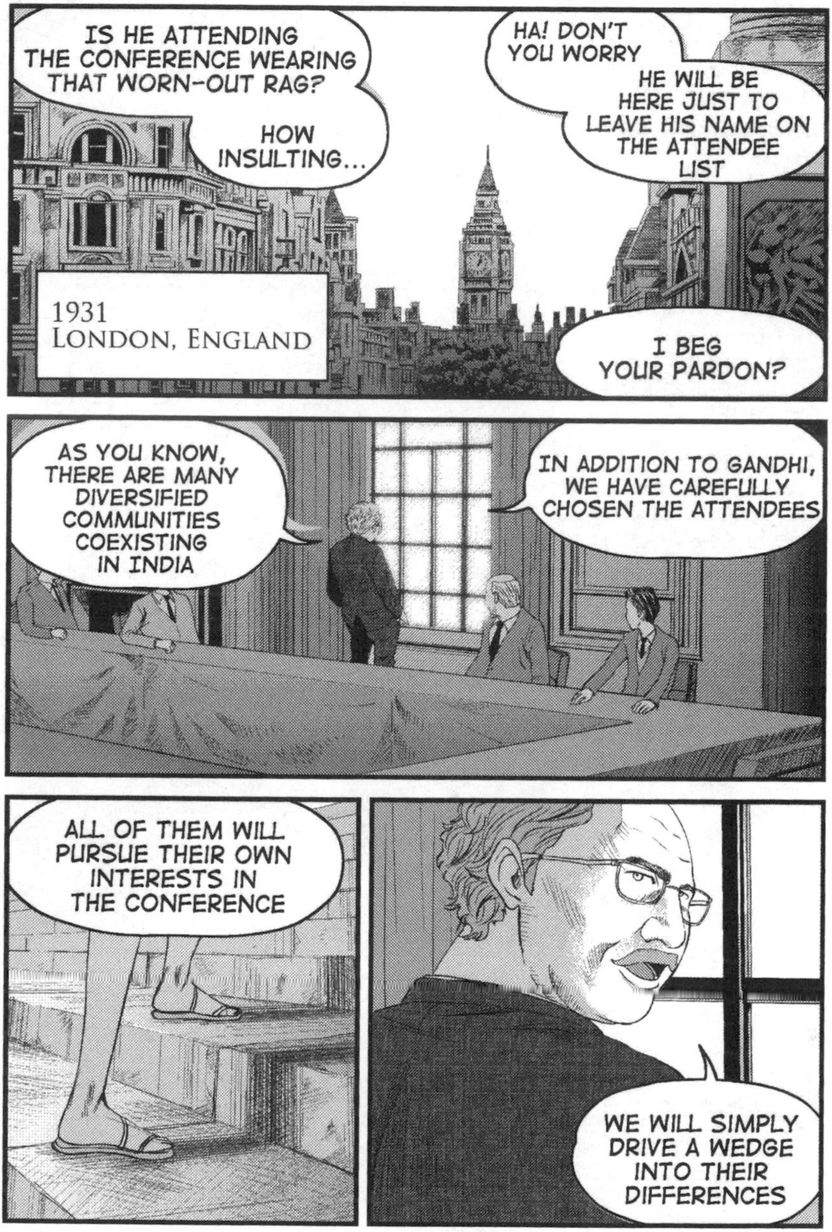
IS HE ATTENDING THE CONFERENCE WEARING THAT WORN-OUT RAG?
HOW INSULTING...
HA! DON'T YOU WORRY
HE WILL BE HERE JUST TO LEAVE HIS NAME ON THE ATTENDEE LIST
1931
LONDON, ENGLAND
I BEG YOUR PARDON?
AS YOU KNOW, THERE ARE MANY DIVERSIFIED COMMUNITIES COEXISTING IN INDIA
IN ADDITION TO GANDHI, WE HAVE CAREFULLY CHOSEN THE ATTENDEES
ALL OF THEM WILL PURSUE THEIR OWN INTERESTS IN THE CONFERENCE
WE WILL SIMPLY DRIVE A WEDGE INTO THEIR DIFFERENCES

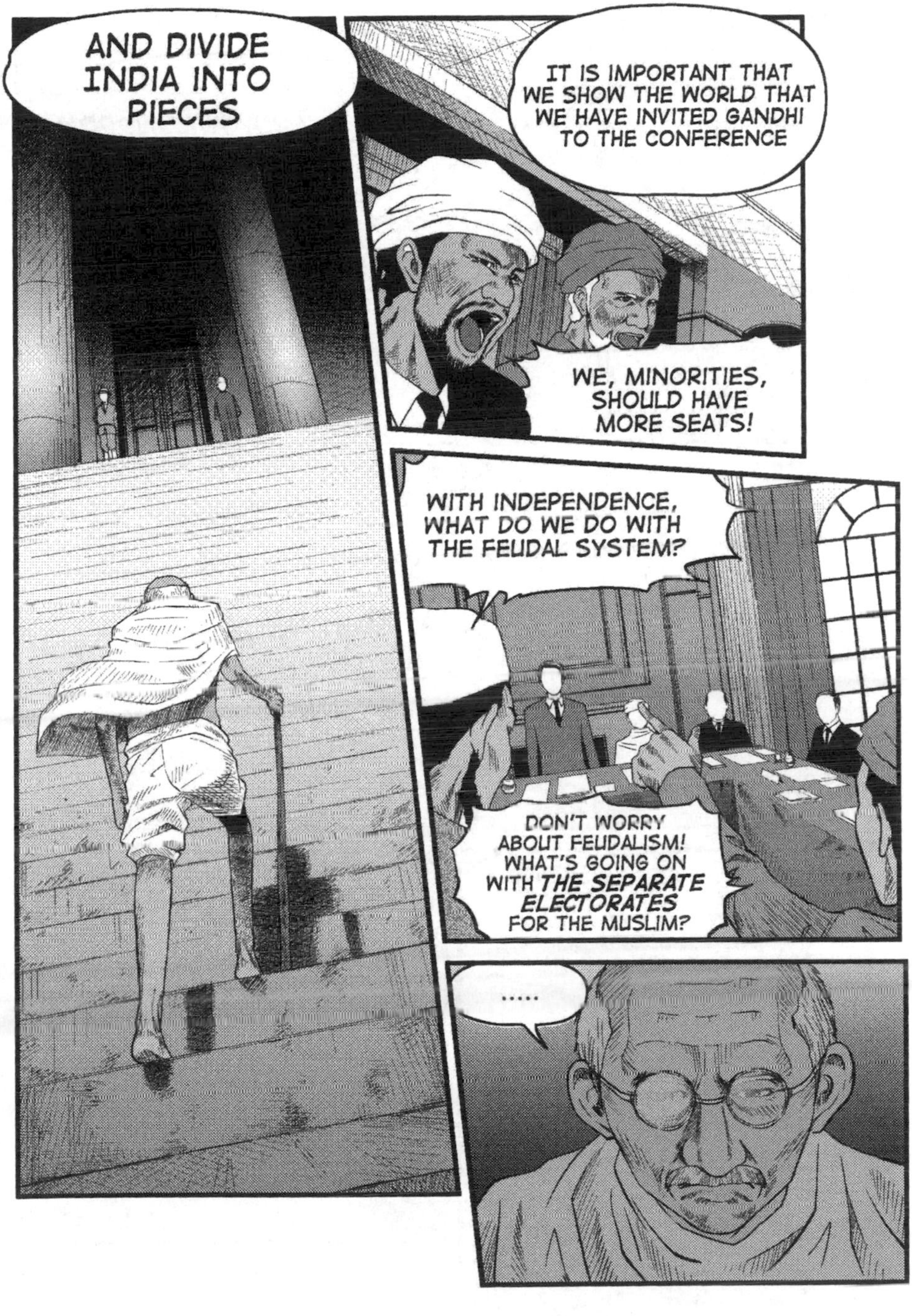
AND DIVIDE INDIA INTO PIECES
IT IS IMPORTANT THAT WE SHOW THE WORLD THAT WE HAVE INVITED GANDHI TO THE CONFERENCE
WE, MINORITIES, SHOULD HAVE MORE SEATS!
WITH INDEPENDENCE, WHAT DO WE DO WITH THE FEUDAL SYSTEM?
DON'T WORRY ABOUT FEUDALISM! WHAT'S GOING ON WITH *THE SEPARATE ELECTORATES* FOR THE MUSLIM?
.....

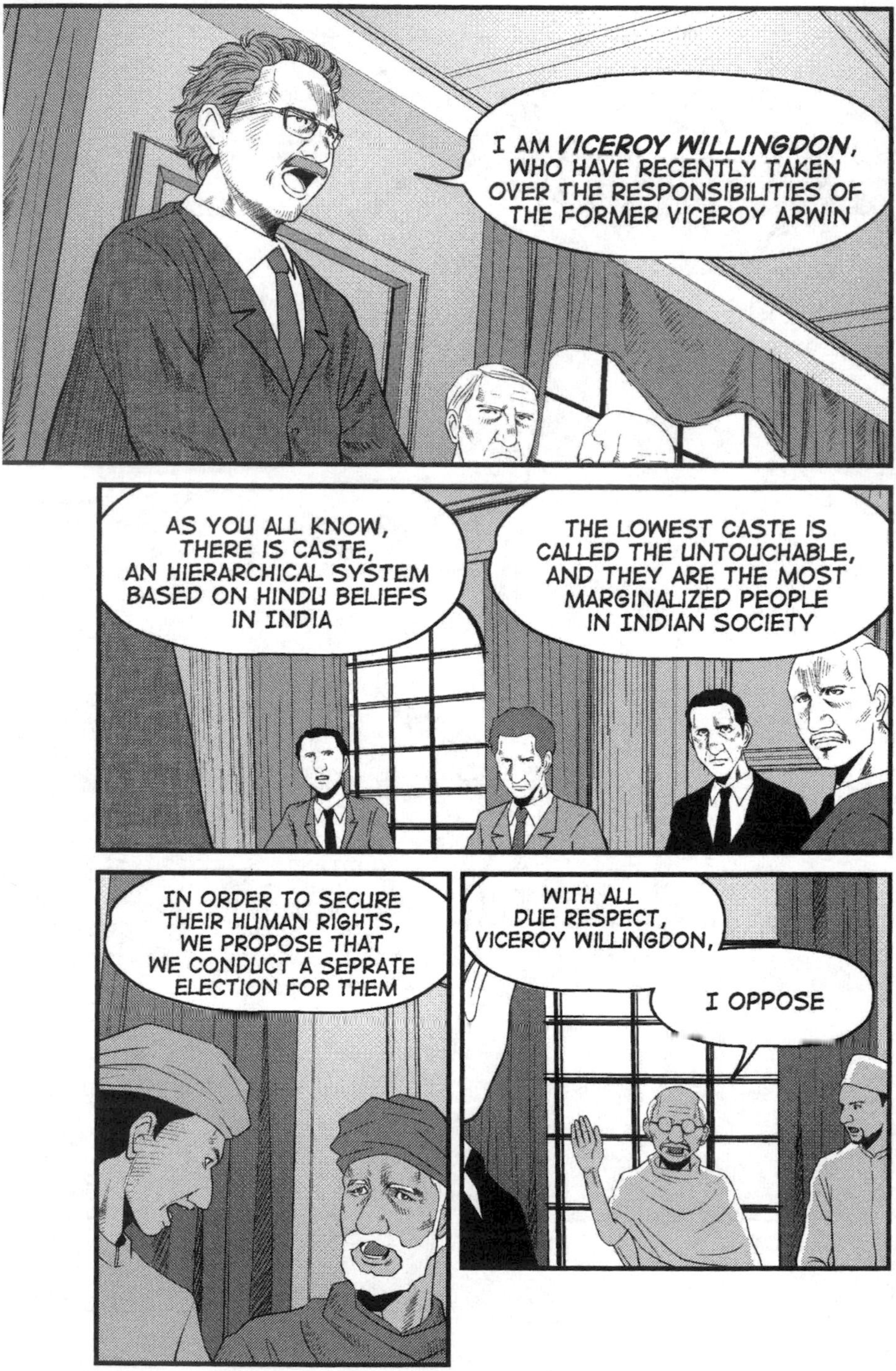
I AM VICEROY WILLINGDON, WHO HAVE RECENTLY TAKEN OVER THE RESPONSIBILITIES OF THE FORMER VICEROY ARWIN
AS YOU ALL KNOW, THERE IS CASTE, AN HIERARCHICAL SYSTEM BASED ON HINDU BELIEFS IN INDIA
THE LOWEST CASTE IS CALLED THE UNTOUCHABLE, AND THEY ARE THE MOST MARGINALIZED PEOPLE IN INDIAN SOCIETY
IN ORDER TO SECURE THEIR HUMAN RIGHTS, WE PROPOSE THAT WE CONDUCT A SEPRATE ELECTION FOR THEM
WITH ALL DUE RESPECT, VICEROY WILLINGDON,
I OPPOSE

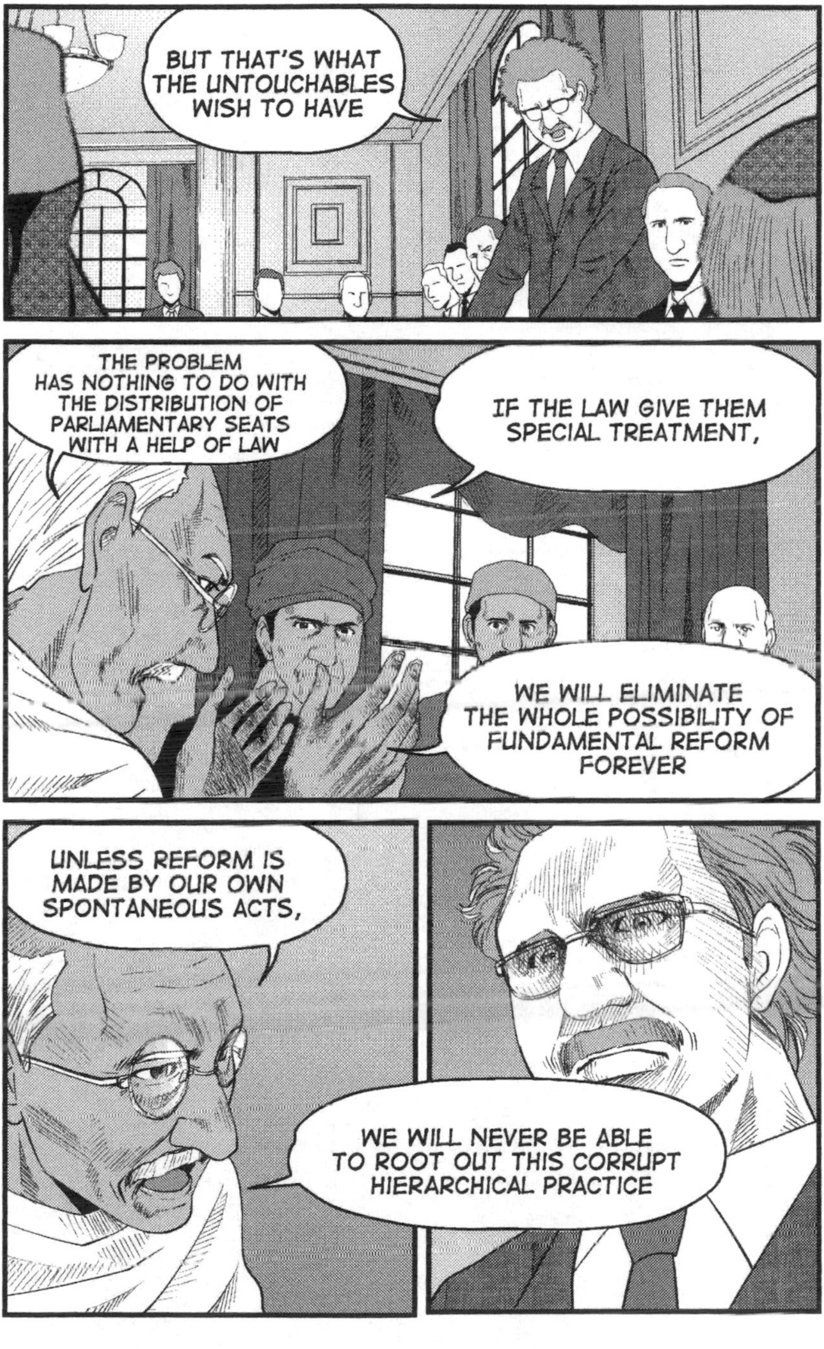
BUT THAT'S WHAT THE UNTOUCHABLES WISH TO HAVE
THE PROBLEM HAS NOTHING TO DO WITH THE DISTRIBUTION OF PARLIAMENTARY SEATS WITH A HELP OF LAW
IF THE LAW GIVE THEM SPECIAL TREATMENT,
WE WILL ELIMINATE THE WHOLE POSSIBILITY OF FUNDAMENTAL REFORM FOREVER
UNLESS REFORM IS MADE BY OUR OWN SPONTANEOUS ACTS,
WE WILL NEVER BE ABLE TO ROOT OUT THIS CORRUPT HIERARCHICAL PRACTICE

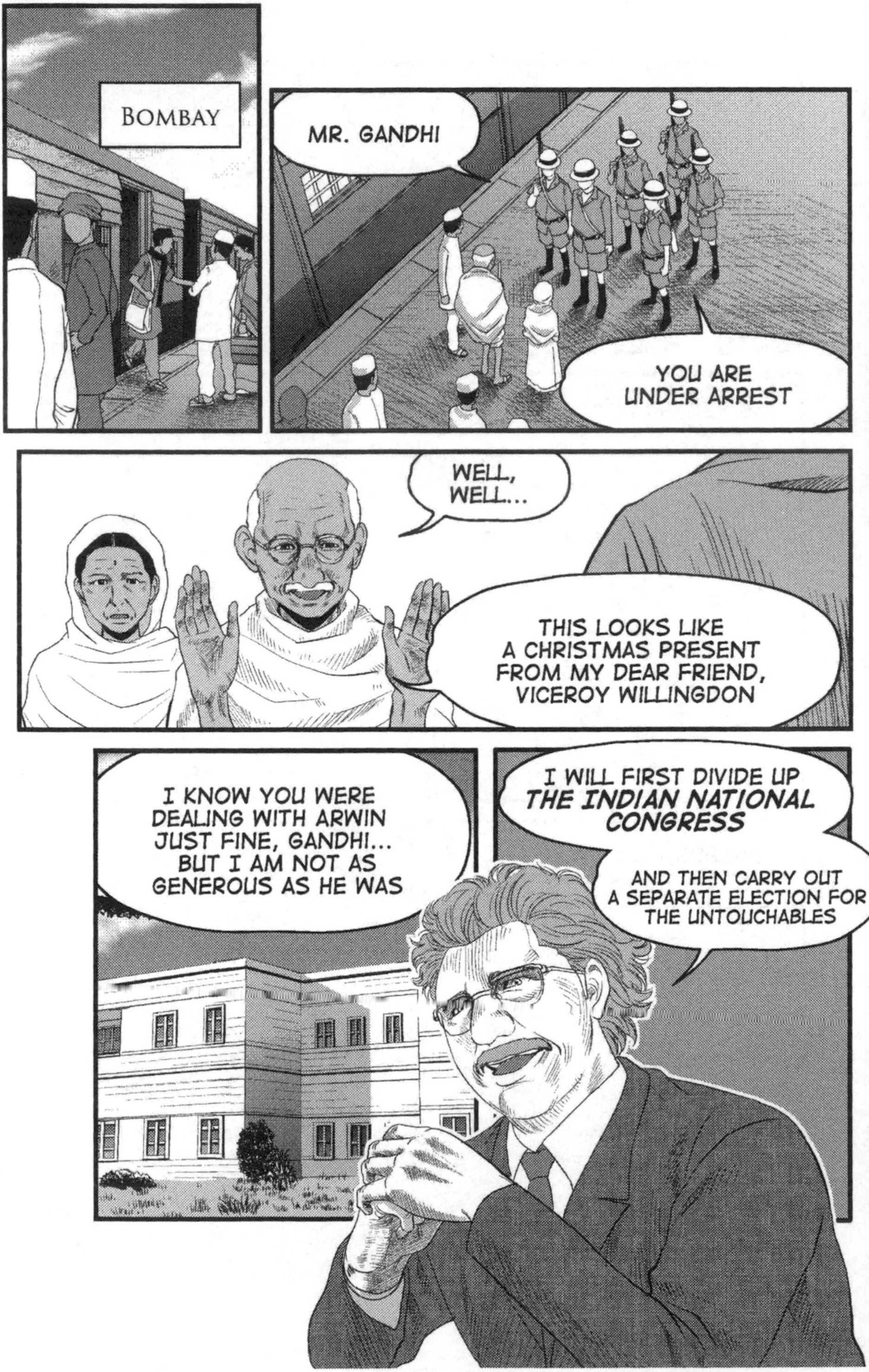
BOMBAY
MR. GANDHI
YOU ARE UNDER ARREST
WELL, WELL...
THIS LOOKS LIKE A CHRISTMAS PRESENT FROM MY DEAR FRIEND, VICEROY WILLINGDON
I KNOW YOU WERE DEALING WITH ARWIN JUST FINE, GANDHI... BUT I AM NOT AS GENEROUS AS HE WAS
I WILL FIRST DIVIDE UP *THE INDIAN NATIONAL CONGRESS*
AND THEN CARRY OUT A SEPARATE ELECTION FOR THE UNTOUCHABLES

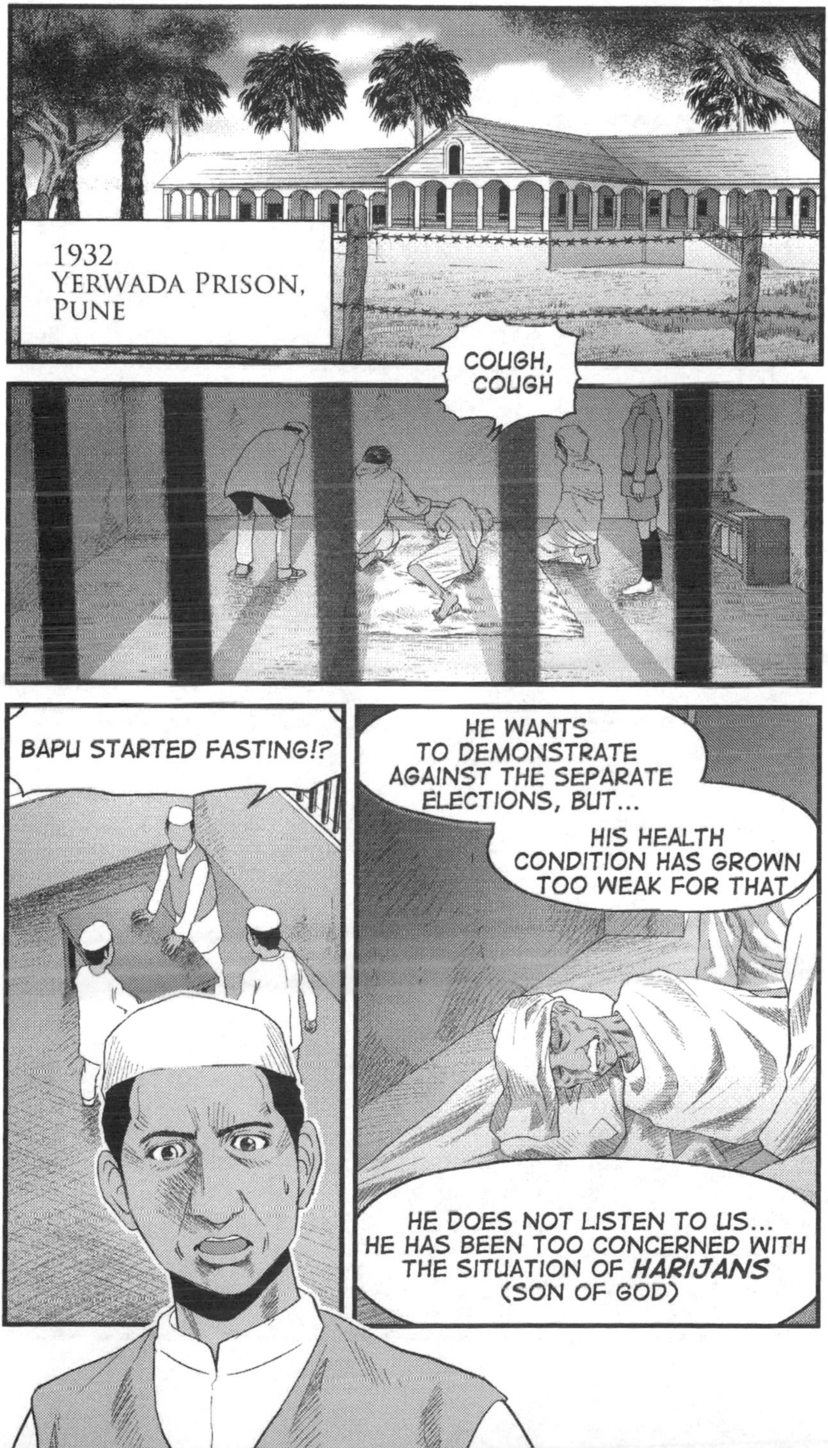
1932
YERWADA PRISON, PUNE
COUGH, COUGH
BAPU STARTED FASTING!?
HE WANTS TO DEMONSTRATE AGAINST THE SEPARATE ELECTIONS, BUT...
HIS HEALTH CONDITION HAS GROWN TOO WEAK FOR THAT
HE DOES NOT LISTEN TO US... HE HAS BEEN TOO CONCERNED WITH THE SITUATION OF *HARIJANS* (SON OF GOD)

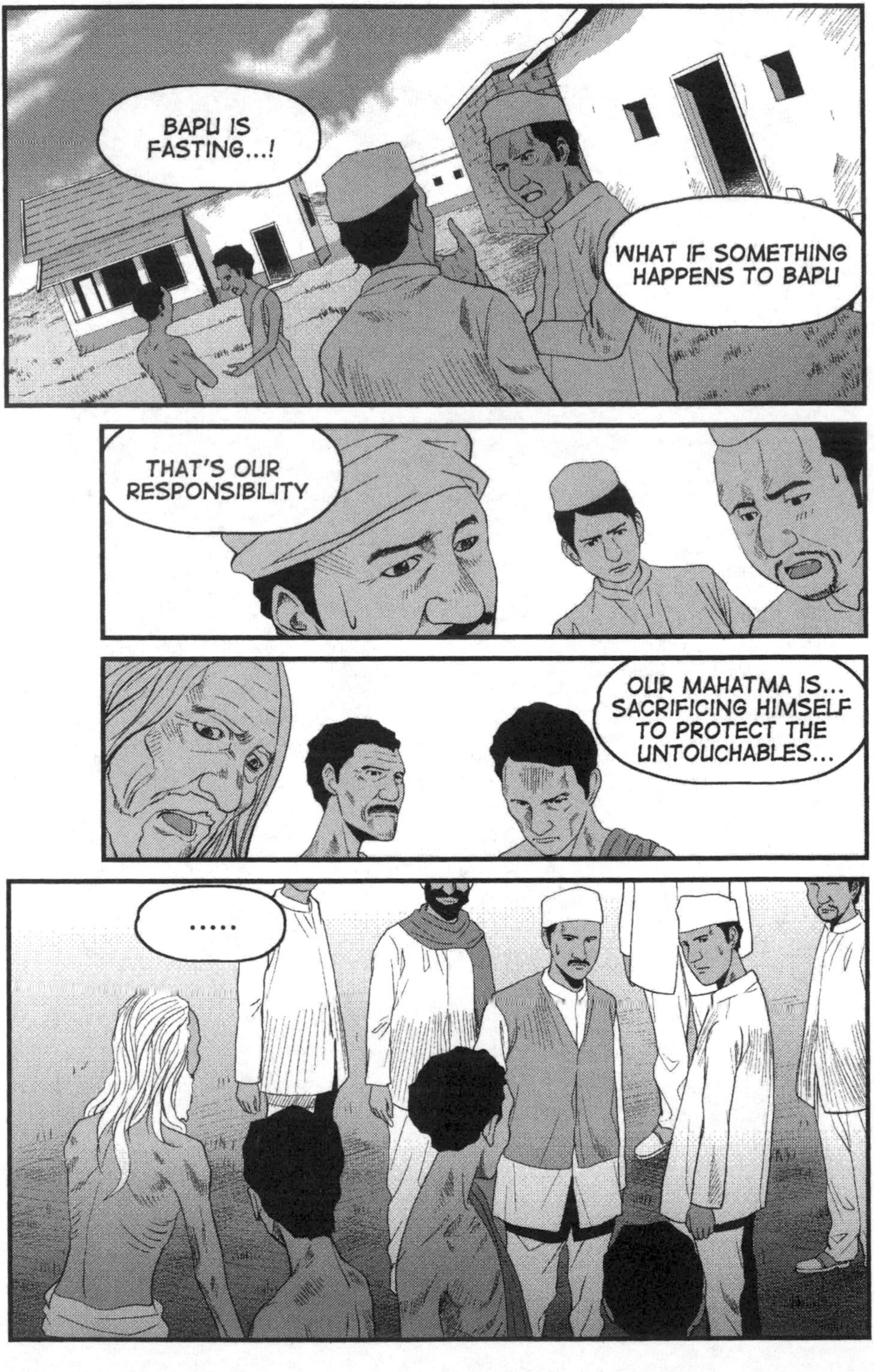
BAPU IS FASTING...!
WHAT IF SOMETHING HAPPENS TO BAPU
THAT'S OUR RESPONSIBILITY
OUR MAHATMA IS... SACRIFICING HIMSELF TO PROTECT THE UNTOUCHABLES...
.....

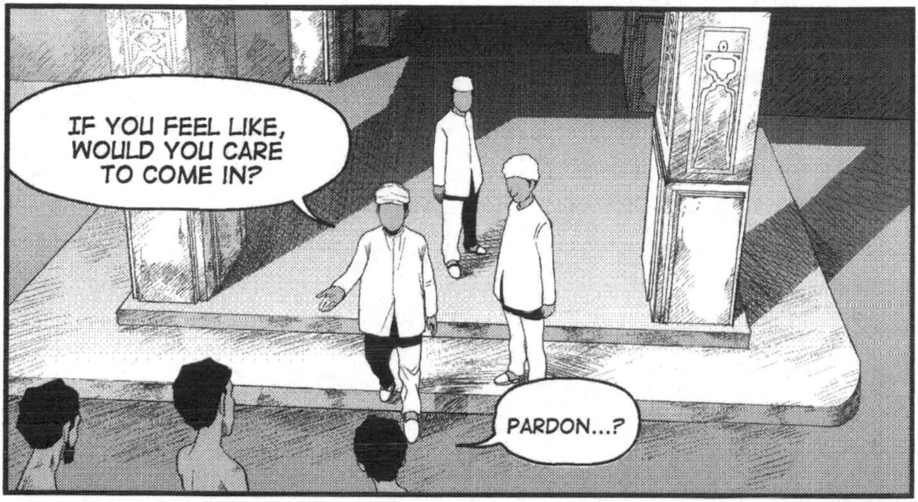
IF YOU FEEL LIKE, WOULD YOU CARE TO COME IN?
PARDON...?

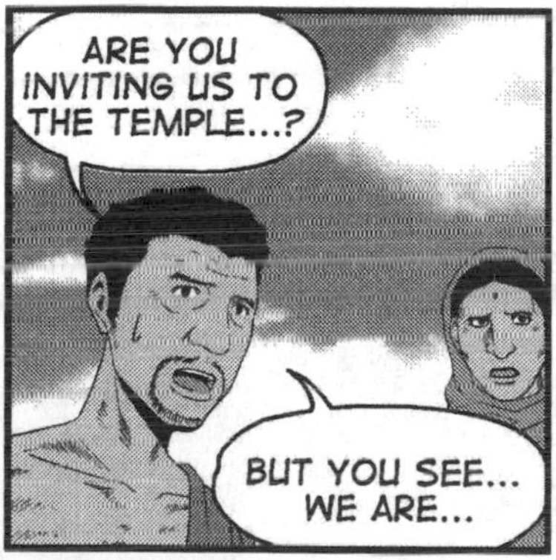
ARE YOU INVITING US TO THE TEMPLE...?
BUT YOU SEE... WE ARE...

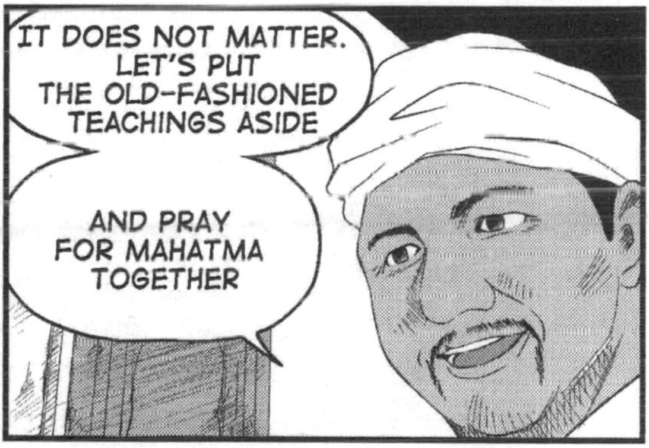
IT DOES NOT MATTER. LET'S PUT THE OLD-FASHIONED TEACHINGS ASIDE
AND PRAY FOR MAHATMA TOGETHER

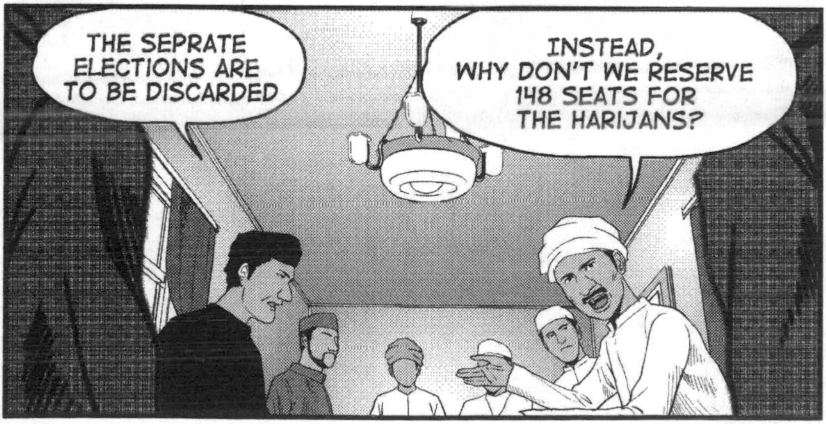
THE SEPRATE ELECTIONS ARE TO BE DISCARDED
INSTEAD, WHY DON'T WE RESERVE 148 SEATS FOR THE HARIJANS?

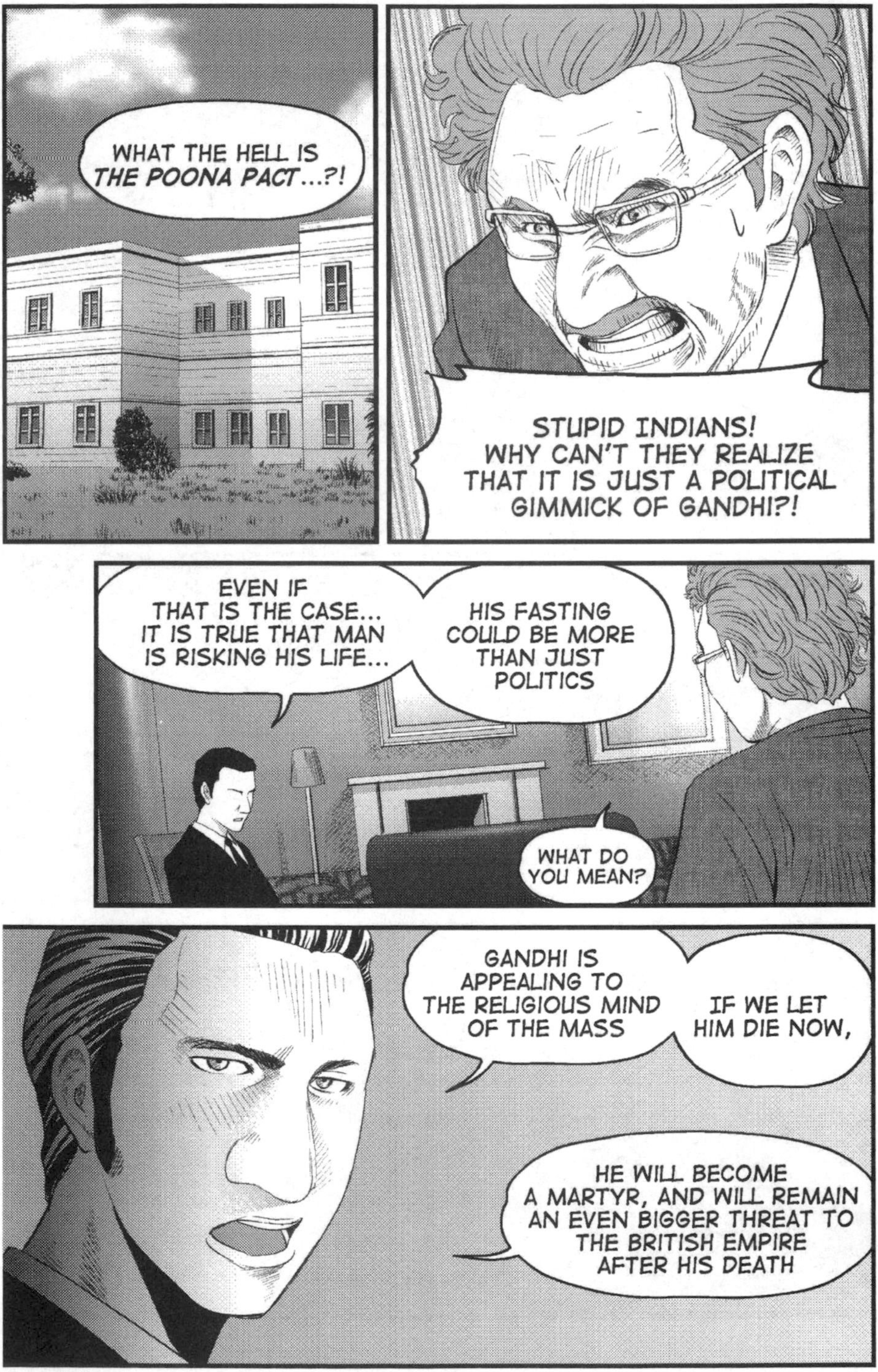
WHAT THE HELL IS THE POONA PACT...?!
STUPID INDIANS! WHY CAN'T THEY REALIZE THAT IT IS JUST A POLITICAL GIMMICK OF GANDHI?!
EVEN IF THAT IS THE CASE... IT IS TRUE THAT MAN IS RISKING HIS LIFE...
HIS FASTING COULD BE MORE THAN JUST POLITICS
WHAT DO YOU MEAN?
GANDHI IS APPEALING TO THE RELIGIOUS MIND OF THE MASS
IF WE LET HIM DIE NOW,
HE WILL BECOME A MARTYR, AND WILL REMAIN AN EVEN BIGGER THREAT TO THE BRITISH EMPIRE AFTER HIS DEATH

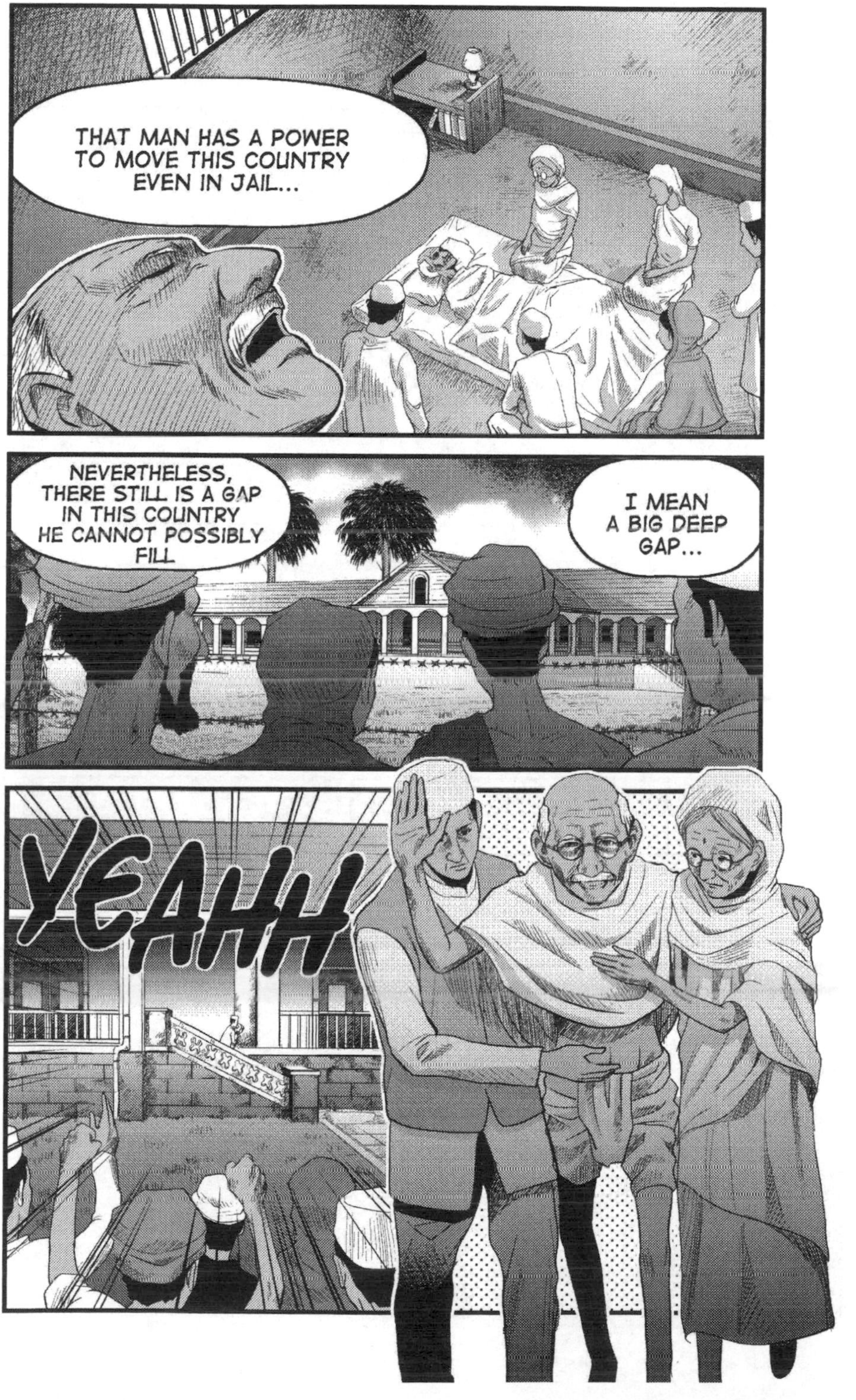
THAT MAN HAS A POWER TO MOVE THIS COUNTRY EVEN IN JAIL...
NEVERTHELESS, THERE STILL IS A GAP IN THIS COUNTRY HE CANNOT POSSIBLY FILL
I MEAN A BIG DEEP GAP...
YEAHH

GAHAK!

BAPU!!

BA!!

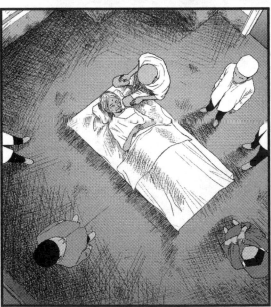

I HAVE A FAVOUR TO ASK...

WHEN I DIE, WILL YOU USE THE THREAD... YOU SPUN AND MAKE A SARI...

TO WRAP AROUND ME...

BA!

YOU HAVE BEEN RELEASED FROM THE PAINS OF LIVING

WE SHOULD BE CELEBRATING INSTEAD...

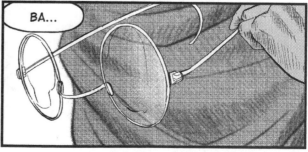

BA...

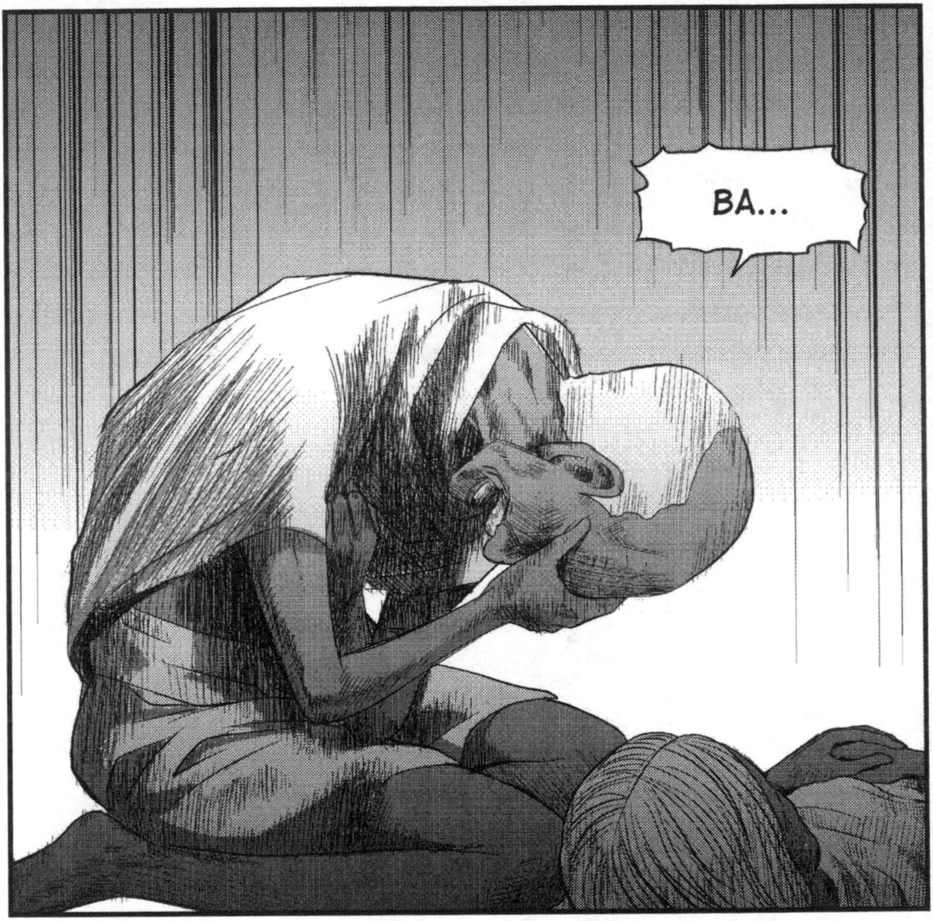
BA...

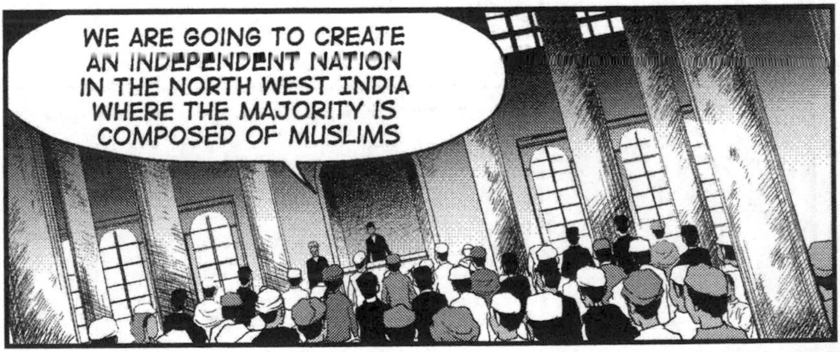
WE ARE GOING TO CREATE AN INDEPENDENT NATION IN THE NORTH WEST INDIA WHERE THE MAJORITY IS COMPOSED OF MUSLIMS

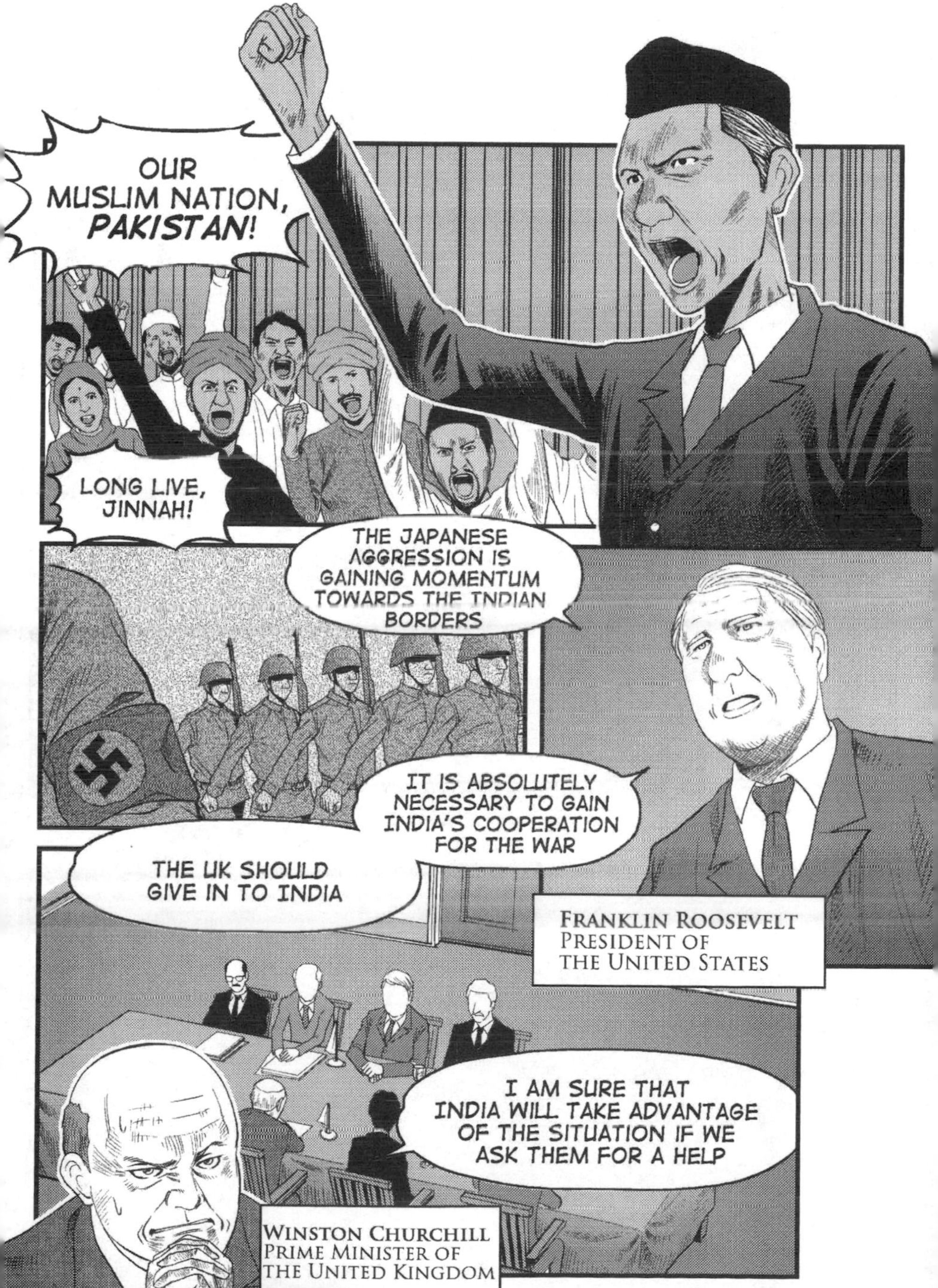
OUR MUSLIM NATION, PAKISTAN!
LONG LIVE, JINNAH!
THE JAPANESE AGGRESSION IS GAINING MOMENTUM TOWARDS THE INDIAN BORDERS
IT IS ABSOLUTELY NECESSARY TO GAIN INDIA'S COOPERATION FOR THE WAR
THE UK SHOULD GIVE IN TO INDIA
FRANKLIN ROOSEVELT PRESIDENT OF THE UNITED STATES
I AM SURE THAT INDIA WILL TAKE ADVANTAGE OF THE SITUATION IF WE ASK THEM FOR A HELP
WINSTON CHURCHILL PRIME MINISTER OF THE UNITED KINGDOM

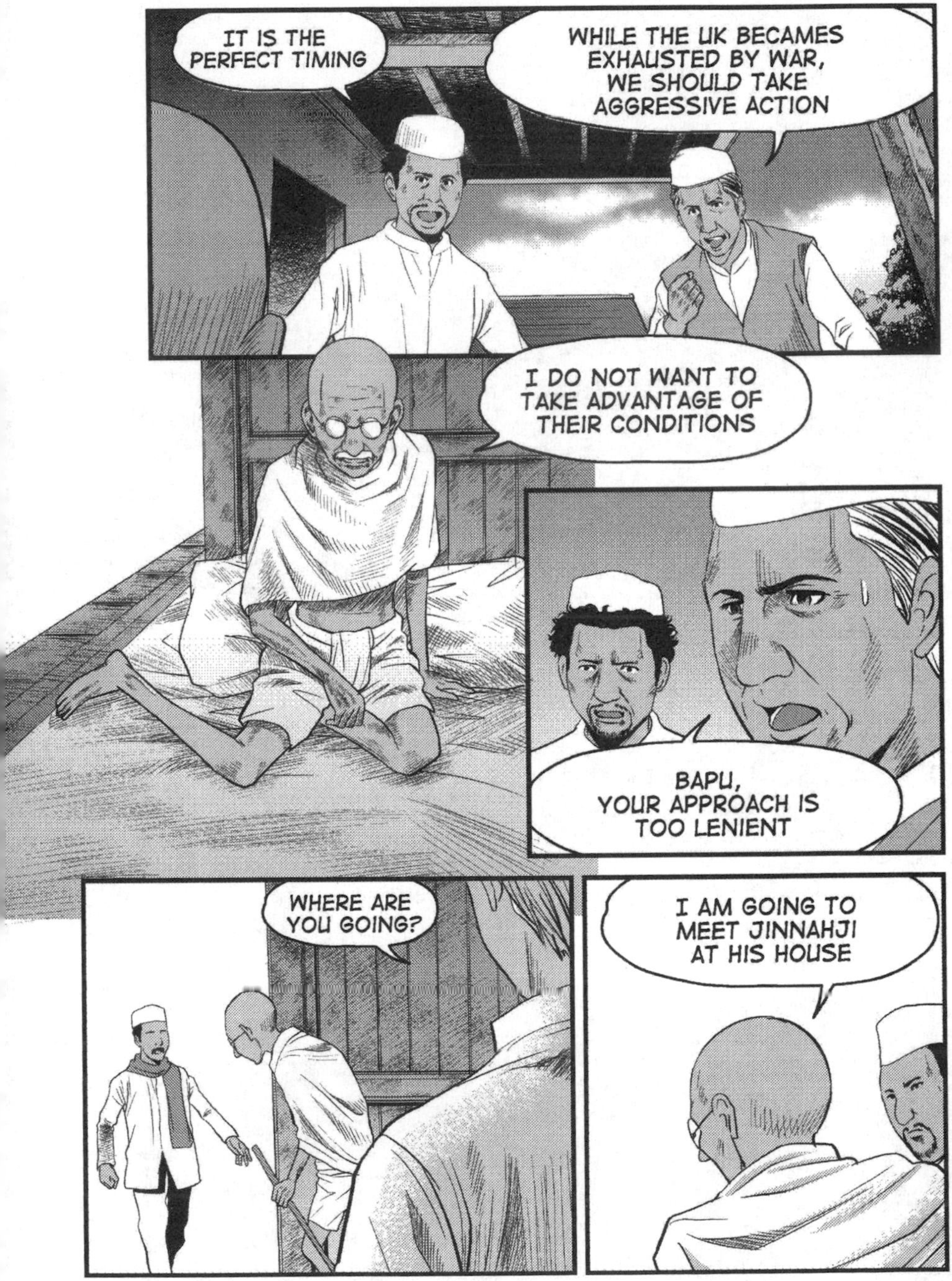
IT IS THE PERFECT TIMING
WHILE THE UK BECAMES EXHAUSTED BY WAR, WE SHOULD TAKE AGGRESSIVE ACTION
I DO NOT WANT TO TAKE ADVANTAGE OF THEIR CONDITIONS
BAPU, YOUR APPROACH IS TOO LENIENT
WHERE ARE YOU GOING?
I AM GOING TO MEET JINNAHJI AT HIS HOUSE

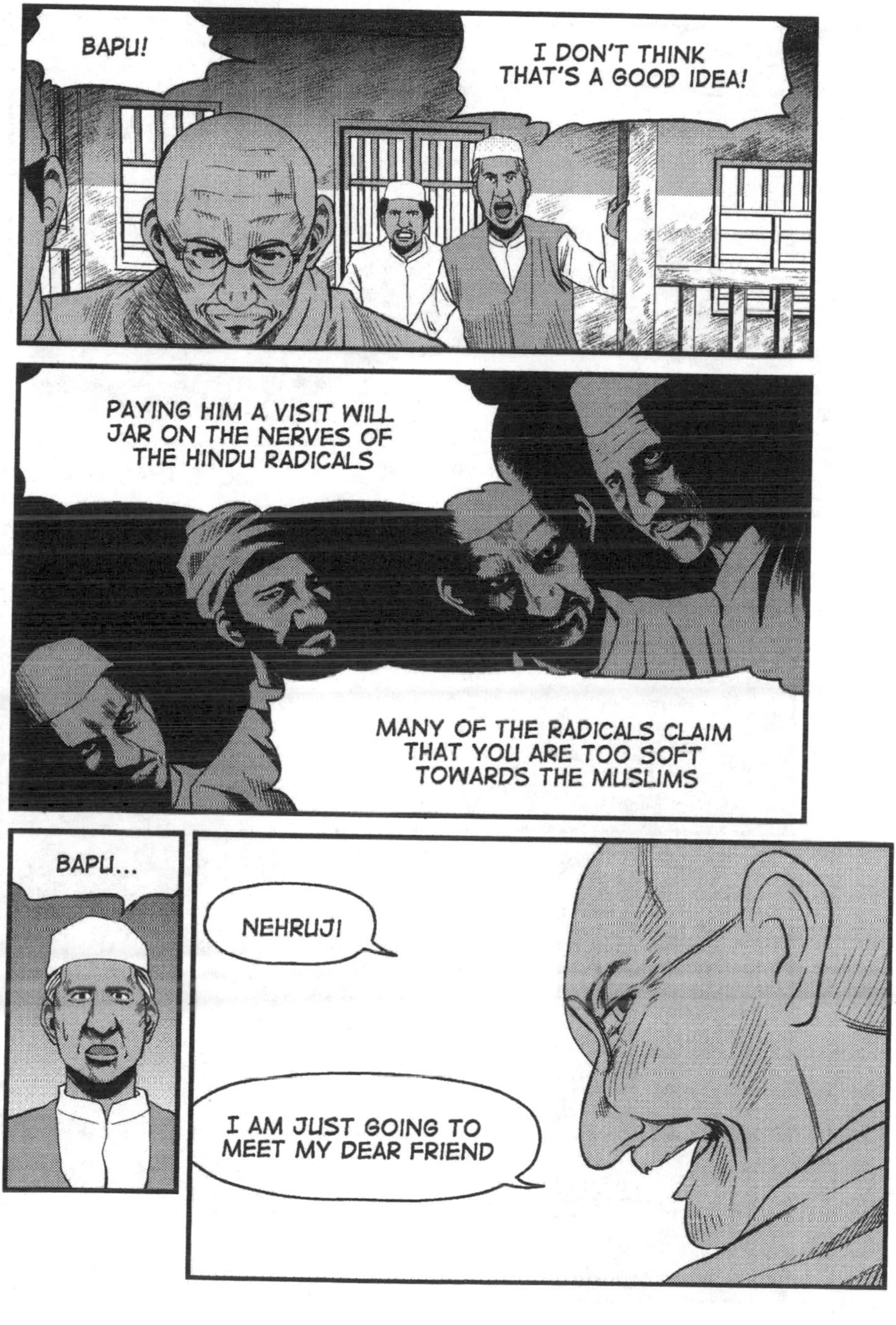
BAPU!
I DON'T THINK THAT'S A GOOD IDEA!
PAYING HIM A VISIT WILL JAR ON THE NERVES OF THE HINDU RADICALS
MANY OF THE RADICALS CLAIM THAT YOU ARE TOO SOFT TOWARDS THE MUSLIMS
BAPU...
NEHRUJI
I AM JUST GOING TO MEET MY DEAR FRIEND

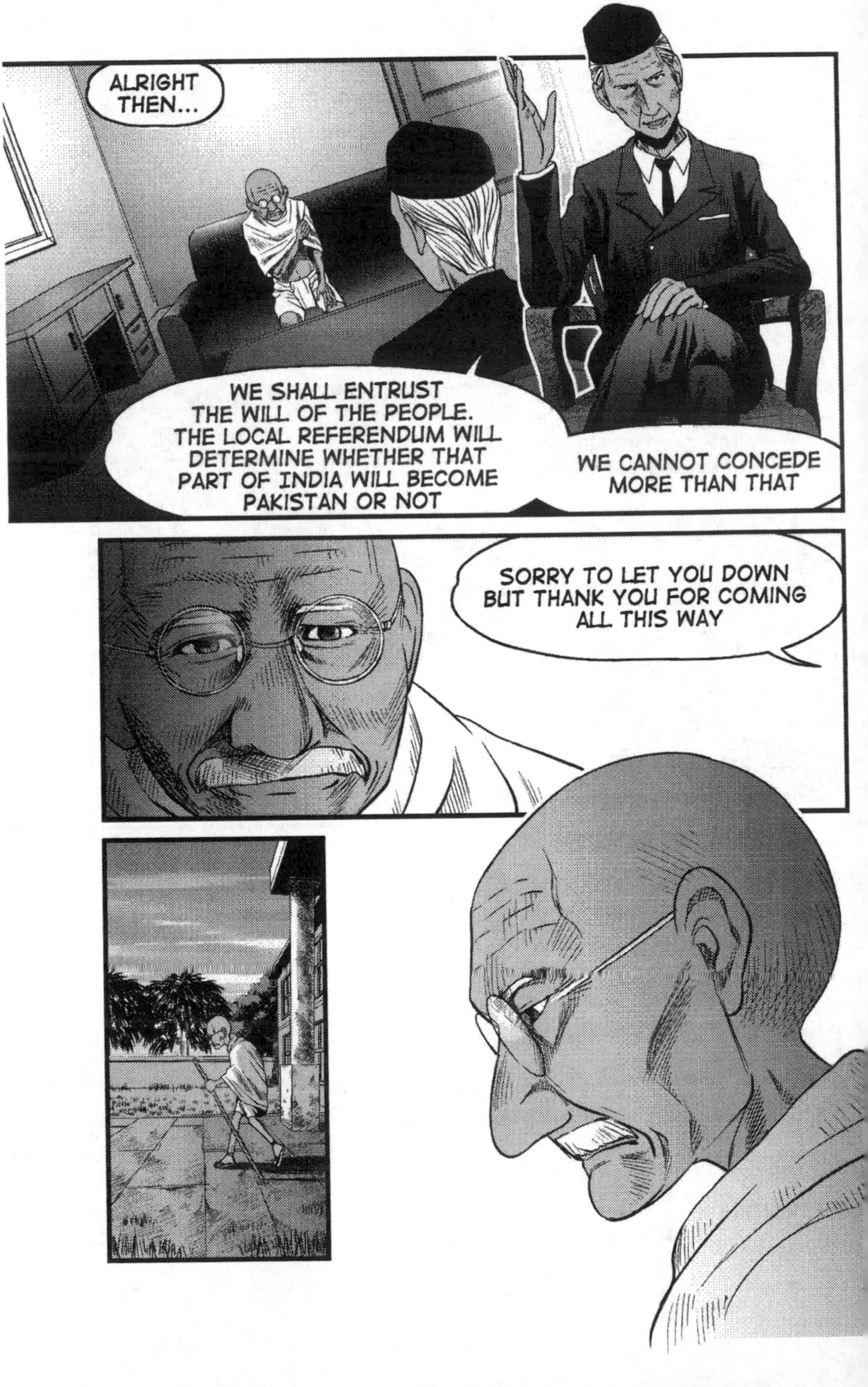
ALRIGHT THEN...
WE SHALL ENTRUST THE WILL OF THE PEOPLE. THE LOCAL REFERENDUM WILL DETERMINE WHETHER THAT PART OF INDIA WILL BECOME PAKISTAN OR NOT
WE CANNOT CONCEDE MORE THAN THAT
SORRY TO LET YOU DOWN BUT THANK YOU FOR COMING ALL THIS WAY

THE UK IS SENDING A DELEGATION...!

1946

GANDHI
(77 YEARS OLD)

THEY SAID THAT THEY WANTED TO DISCUSS ABOUT THE TIMING AND CONDITIONS REGARDING THE TRANSFER OF AUTONOMY

THE NEW PRIME MINISTER, *ATTLEE*, PLEDGED AN EARLY ACTUALIZATION OF INDIAN AUTONOMY DURING HIS ELECTION CAMPAIGN

AND IT IS OBVIOUS THAT THEY REALIZED THAT THE UK CAN NO LONGER AFFORD TO REIGN OVER INDIA

BAPU

WE HAVE OUR INDEPENDENCE!

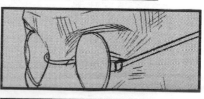

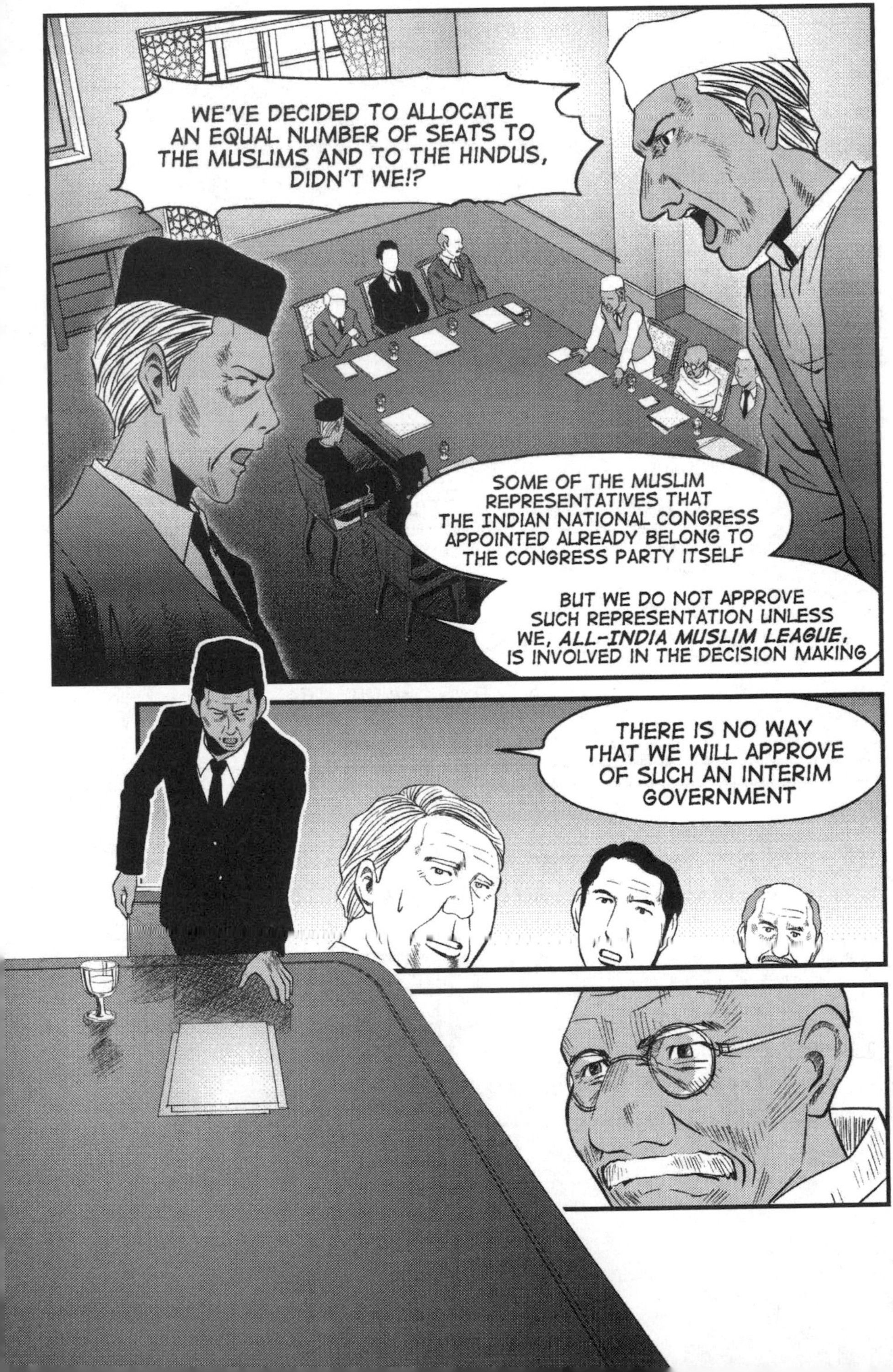
WE'VE DECIDED TO ALLOCATE AN EQUAL NUMBER OF SEATS TO THE MUSLIMS AND TO THE HINDUS, DIDN'T WE!?
SOME OF THE MUSLIM REPRESENTATIVES THAT THE INDIAN NATIONAL CONGRESS APPOINTED ALREADY BELONG TO THE CONGRESS PARTY ITSELF
BUT WE DO NOT APPROVE SUCH REPRESENTATION UNLESS WE, *ALL-INDIA MUSLIM LEAGUE*, IS INVOLVED IN THE DECISION MAKING
THERE IS NO WAY THAT WE WILL APPROVE OF SUCH AN INTERIM GOVERNMENT

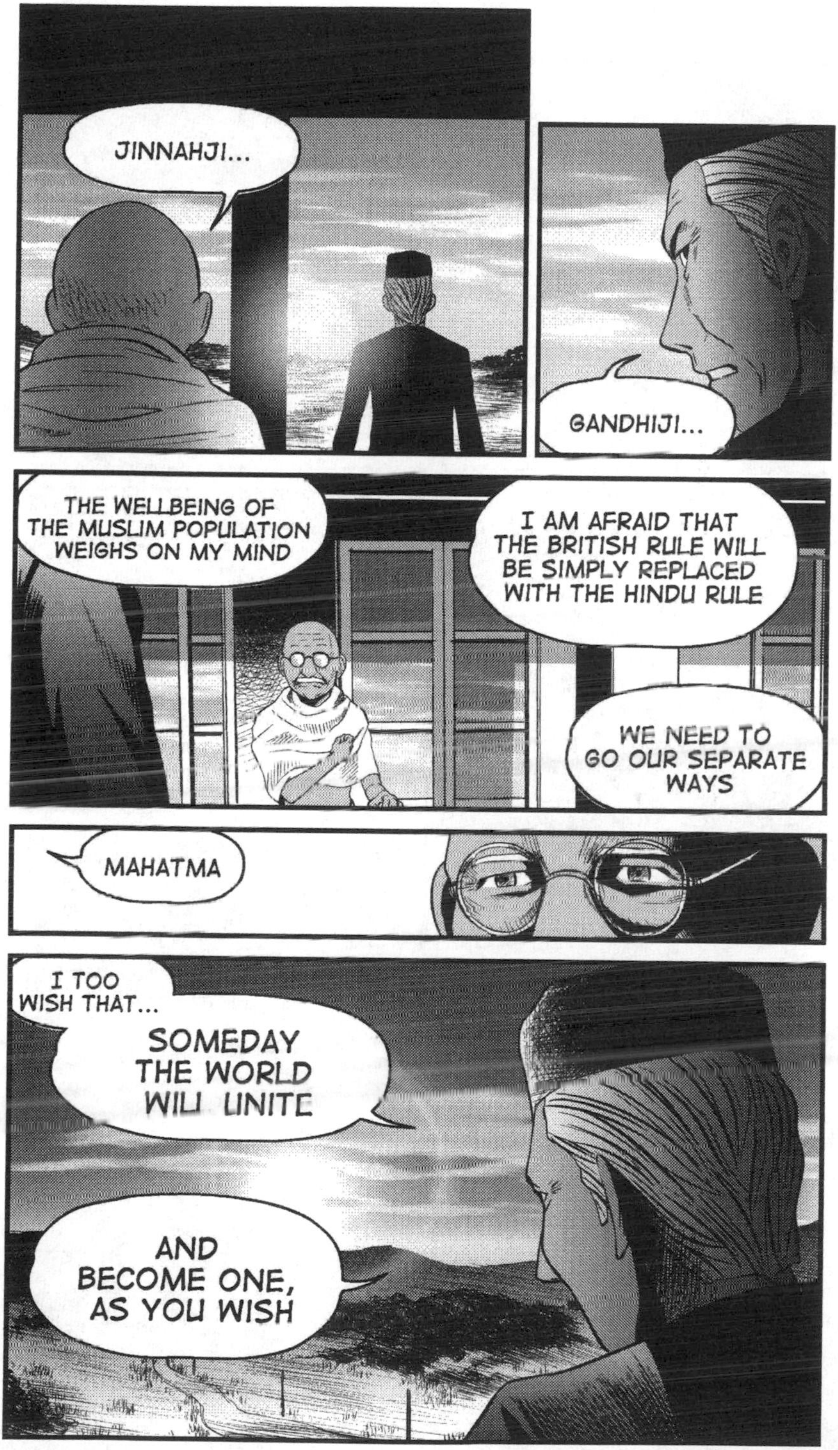
JINNAHJI...
GANDHIJI...
THE WELLBEING OF THE MUSLIM POPULATION WEIGHS ON MY MIND
I AM AFRAID THAT THE BRITISH RULE WILL BE SIMPLY REPLACED WITH THE HINDU RULE
WE NEED TO GO OUR SEPARATE WAYS
MAHATMA
I TOO WISH THAT...
SOMEDAY THE WORLD WILL UNITE
AND BECOME ONE, AS YOU WISH

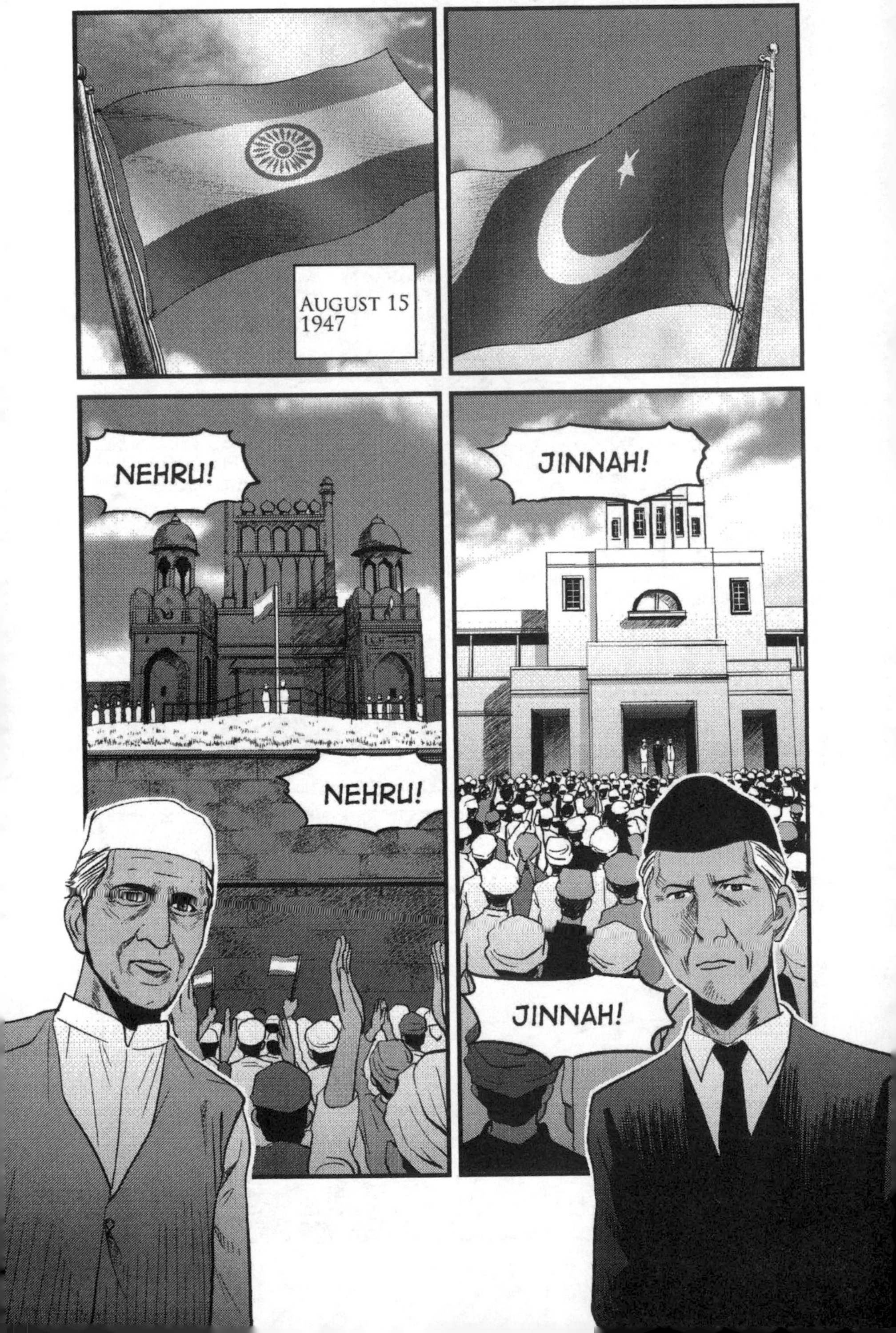
AUGUST 15
1947
NEHRU!
NEHRU!
JINNAH!
JINNAH!

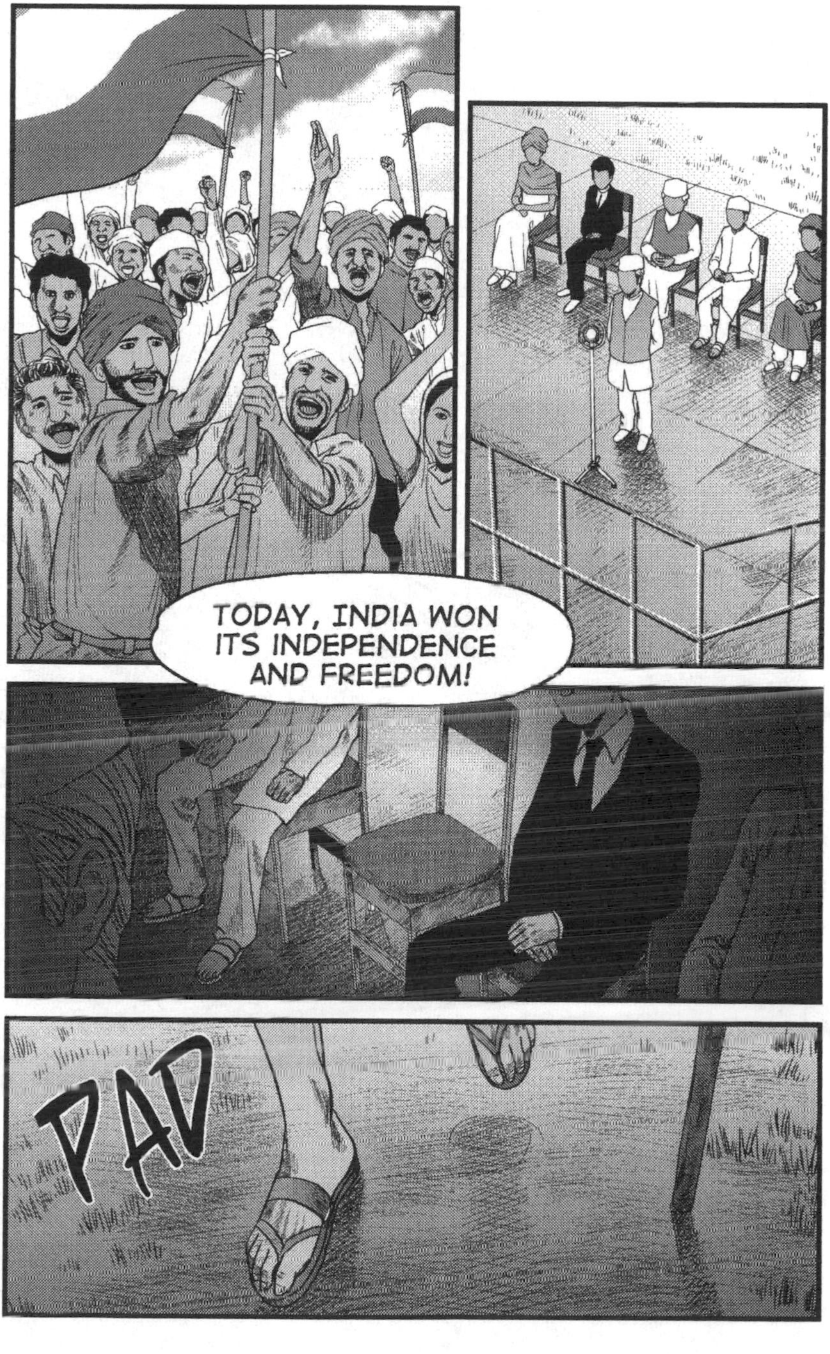
TODAY, INDIA WON ITS INDEPENDENCE AND FREEDOM!
PAD

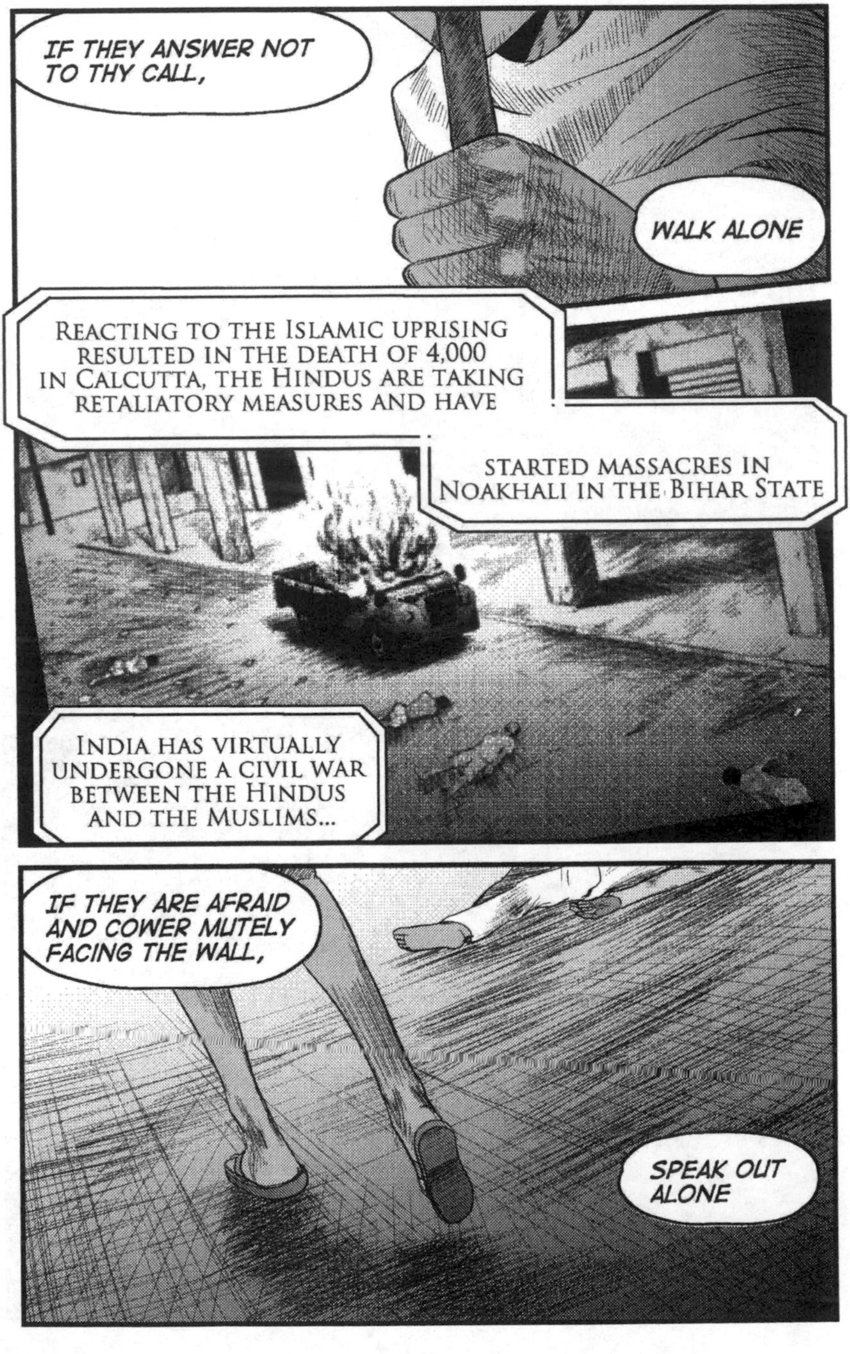
IF THEY ANSWER NOT TO THY CALL,
WALK ALONE
REACTING TO THE ISLAMIC UPRISING RESULTED IN THE DEATH OF 4,000 IN CALCUTTA, THE HINDUS ARE TAKING RETALIATORY MEASURES AND HAVE
STARTED MASSACRES IN NOAKHALI IN THE BIHAR STATE
INDIA HAS VIRTUALLY UNDERGONE A CIVIL WAR BETWEEN THE HINDUS AND THE MUSLIMS...
IF THEY ARE AFRAID AND COWER MUTELY FACING THE WALL,
SPEAK OUT ALONE

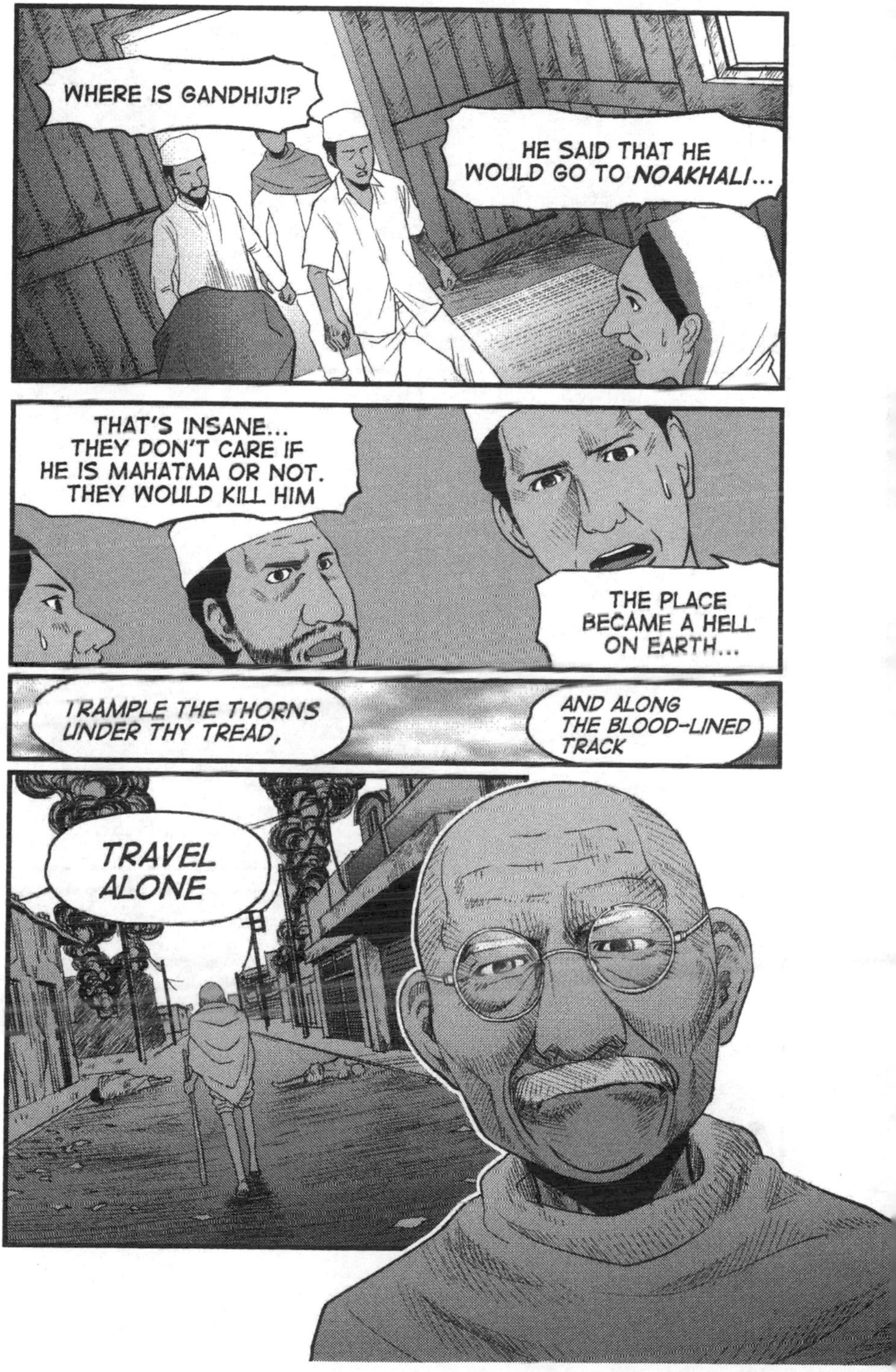
WHERE IS GANDHIJI?
HE SAID THAT HE WOULD GO TO NOAKHALI...
THAT'S INSANE... THEY DON'T CARE IF HE IS MAHATMA OR NOT. THEY WOULD KILL HIM
THE PLACE BECAME A HELL ON EARTH...
TRAMPLE THE THORNS UNDER THY TREAD,
AND ALONG THE BLOOD-LINED TRACK
TRAVEL ALONE

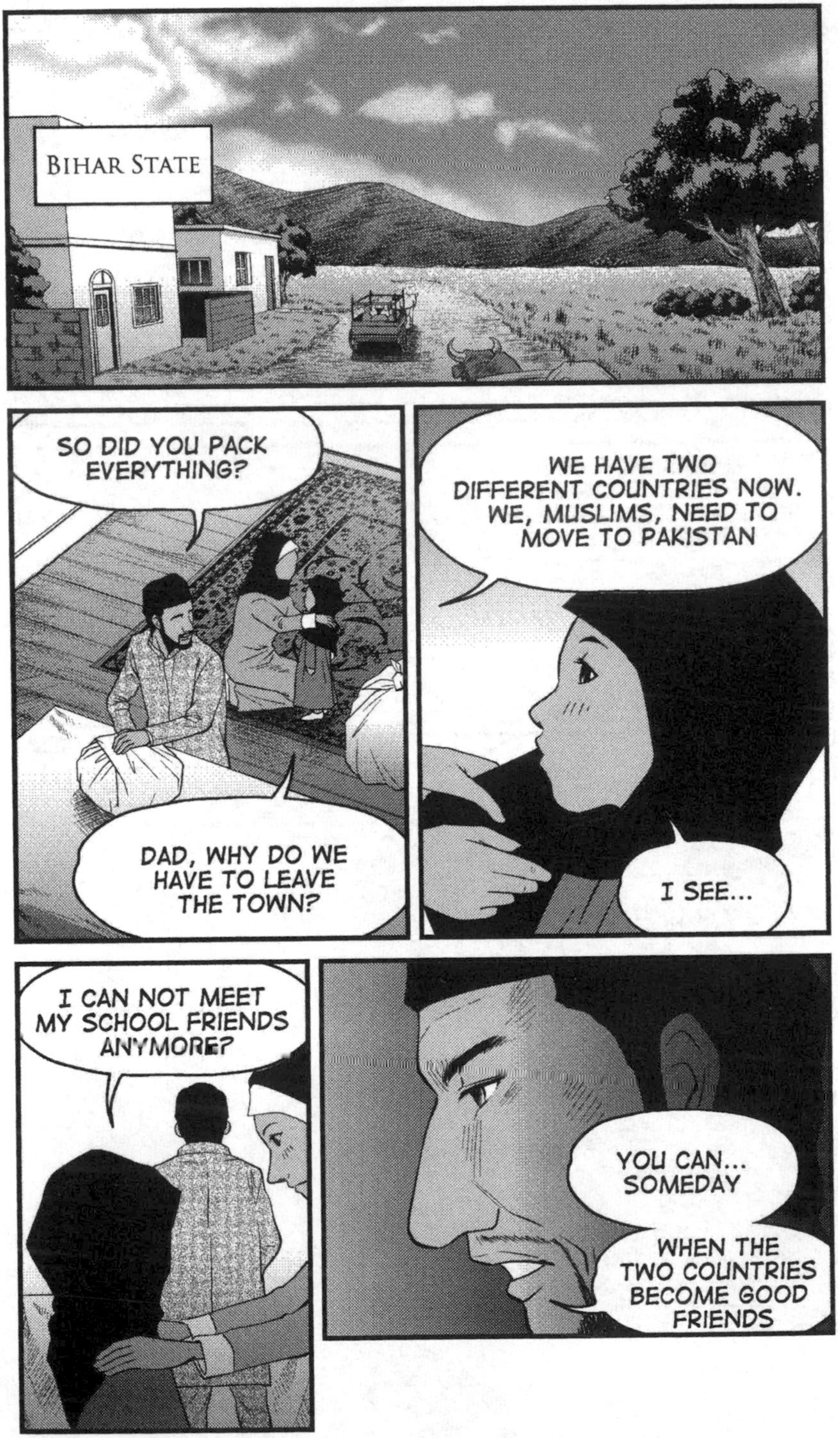
BIHAR STATE
SO DID YOU PACK EVERYTHING?
DAD, WHY DO WE HAVE TO LEAVE THE TOWN?
WE HAVE TWO DIFFERENT COUNTRIES NOW. WE, MUSLIMS, NEED TO MOVE TO PAKISTAN
I SEE...
I CAN NOT MEET MY SCHOOL FRIENDS ANYMORE?
YOU CAN... SOMEDAY
WHEN THE TWO COUNTRIES BECOME GOOD FRIENDS

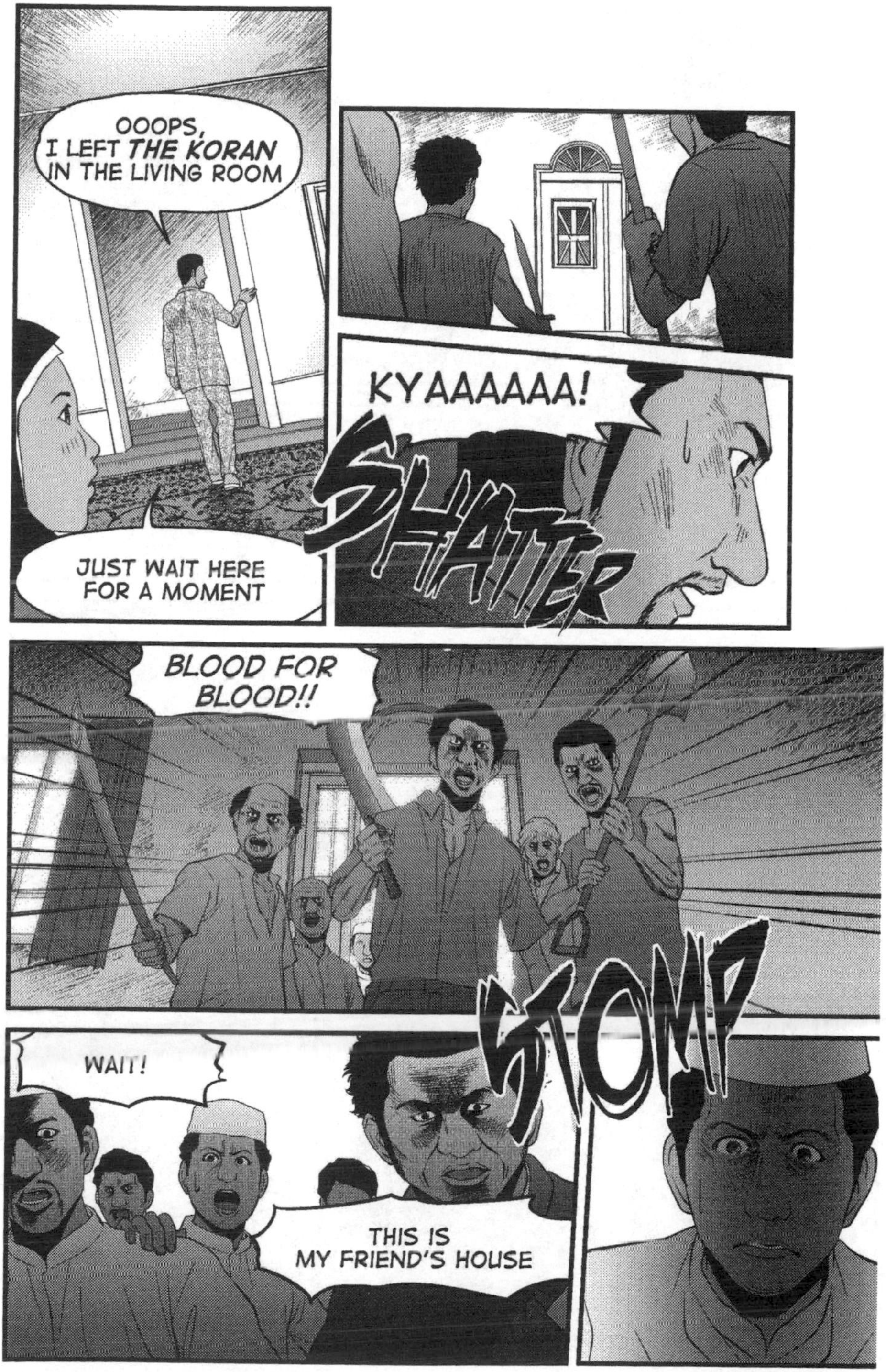
OOOPS, I LEFT THE KORAN IN THE LIVING ROOM
JUST WAIT HERE FOR A MOMENT
KYAAAAAA!
SHATTER
BLOOD FOR BLOOD!!
STOMP
WAIT!
THIS IS MY FRIEND'S HOUSE

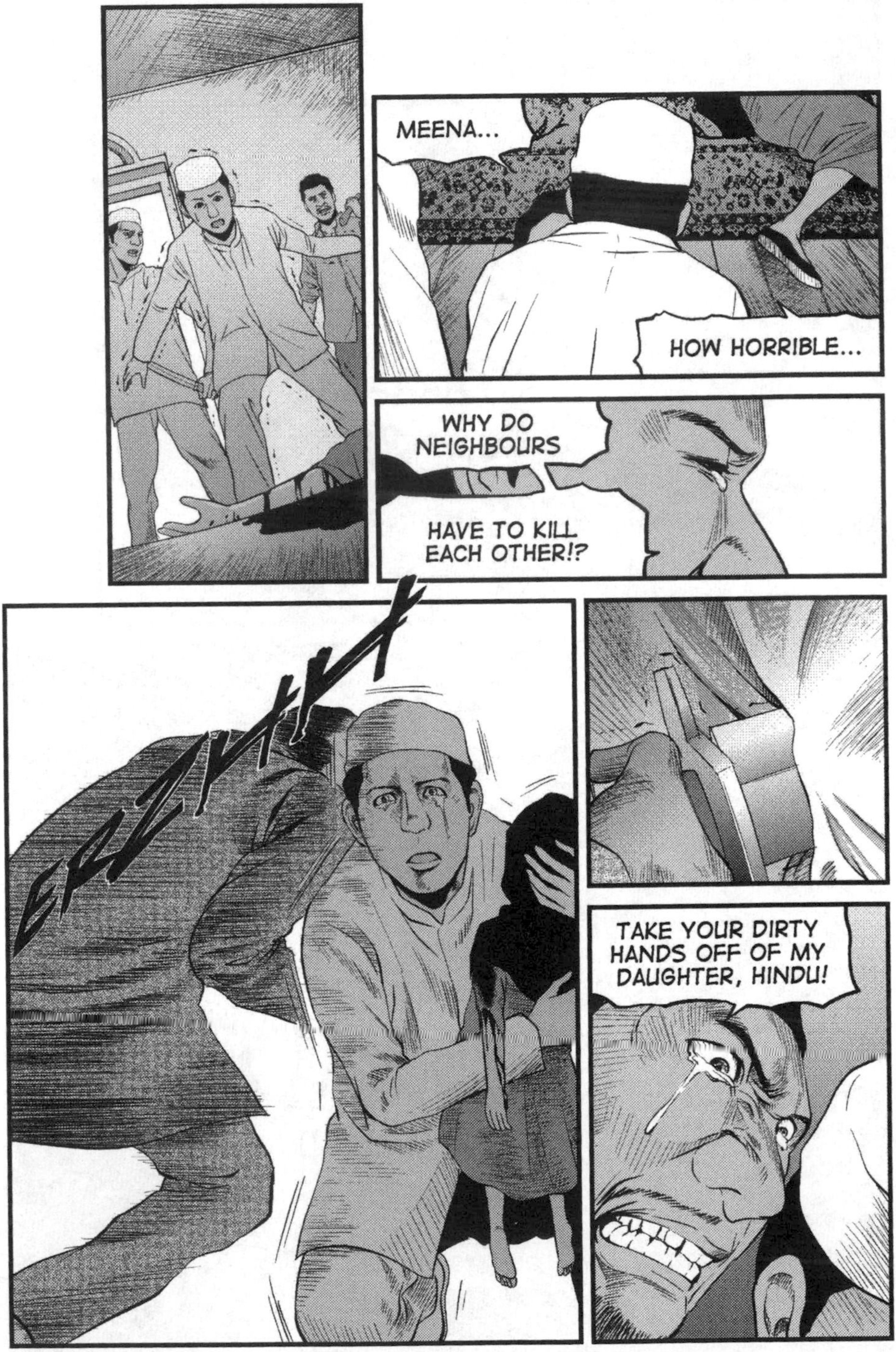
MEENA...
HOW HORRIBLE...
WHY DO NEIGHBOURS
HAVE TO KILL EACH OTHER!?
TAKE YOUR DIRTY HANDS OFF OF MY DAUGHTER, HINDU!

A... ABDULLA...

KUMAR!?

THUMP

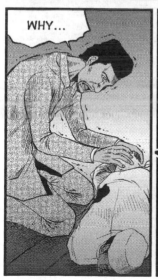

WHY...

BLOOD FOR BLOOD

RRR

RRR

GRRR

BLOOD FOR BLOOD

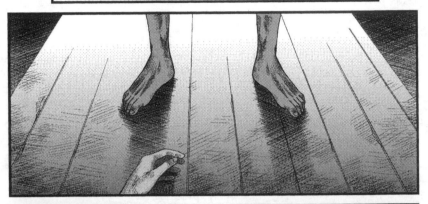

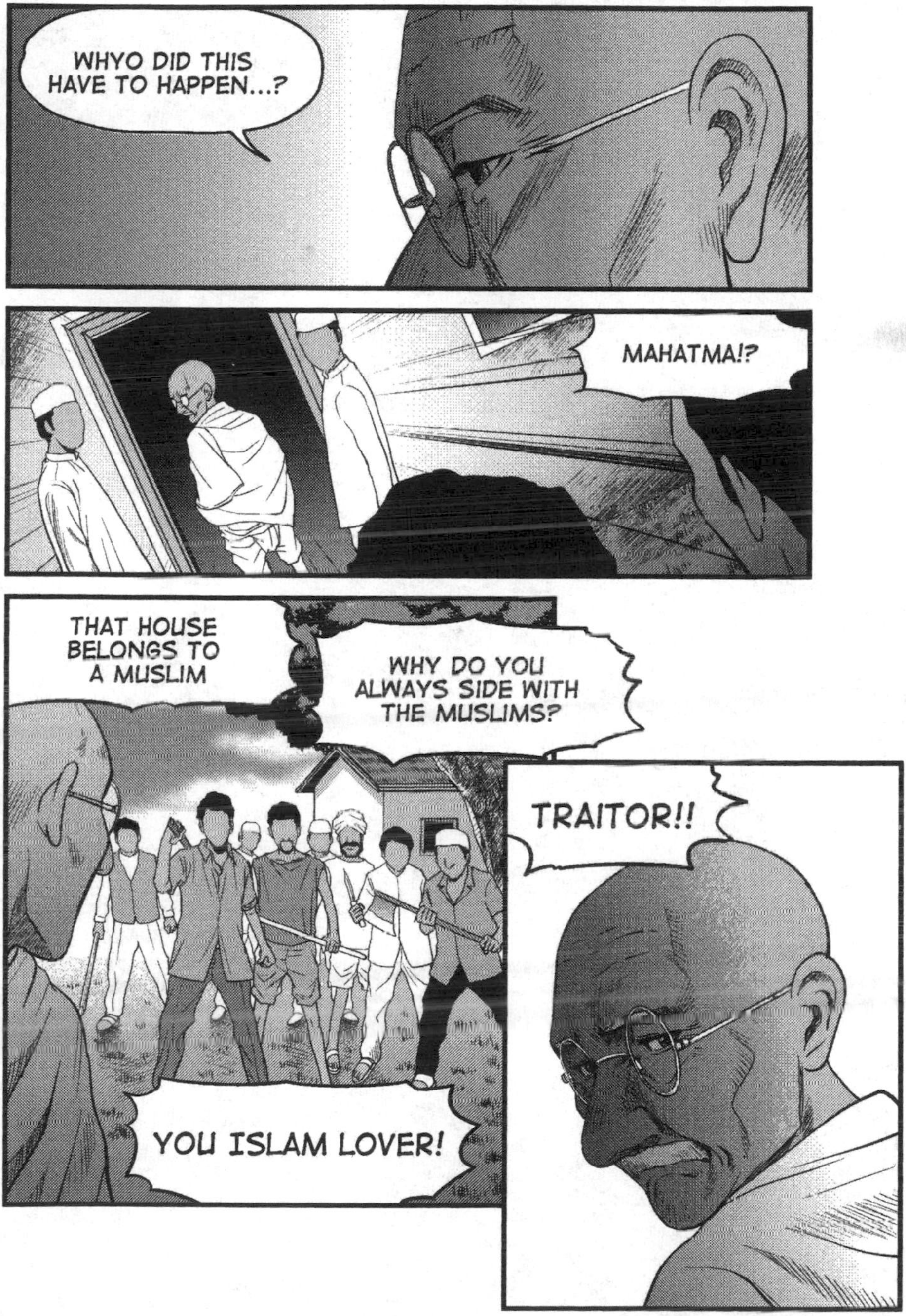
WHYO DID THIS HAVE TO HAPPEN...?
MAHATMA!?
THAT HOUSE BELONGS TO A MUSLIM
WHY DO YOU ALWAYS SIDE WITH THE MUSLIMS?
YOU ISLAM LOVER!
TRAITOR!!

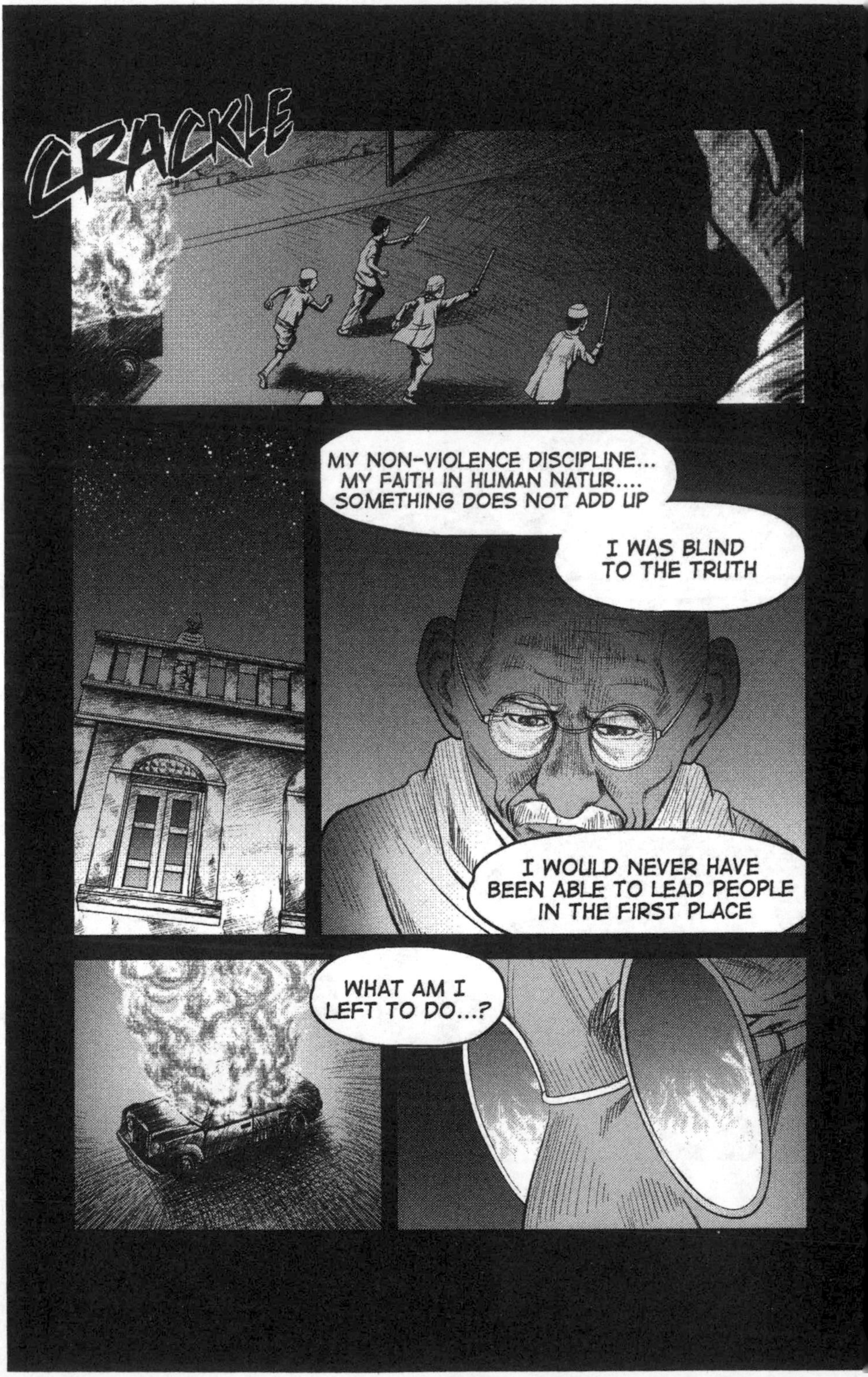
CRACKLE
MY NON-VIOLENCE DISCIPLINE... MY FAITH IN HUMAN NATUR.... SOMETHING DOES NOT ADD UP
I WAS BLIND TO THE TRUTH
I WOULD NEVER HAVE BEEN ABLE TO LEAD PEOPLE IN THE FIRST PLACE
WHAT AM I LEFT TO DO...?

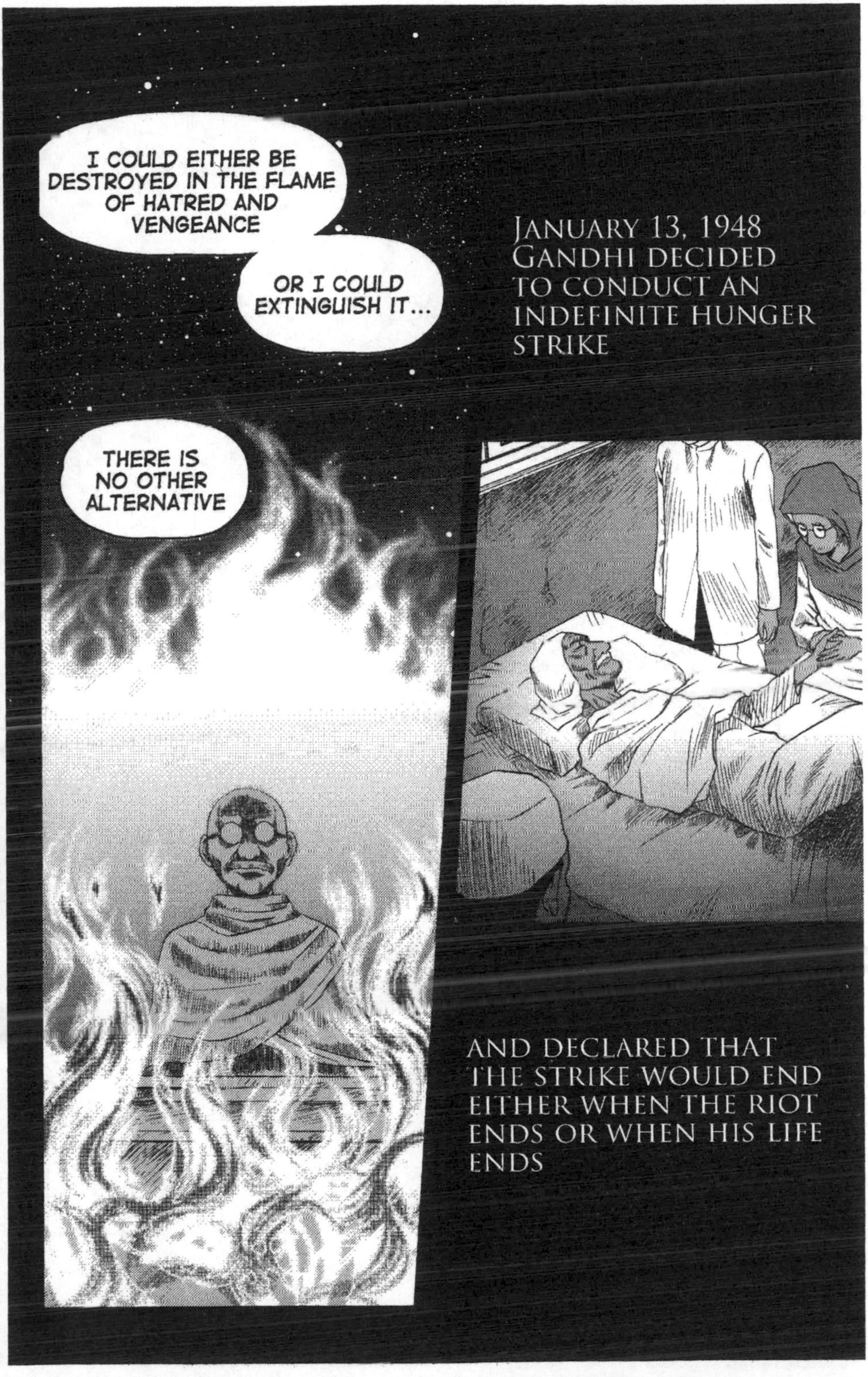
I COULD EITHER BE DESTROYED IN THE FLAME OF HATRED AND VENGEANCE
OR I COULD EXTINGUISH IT...
JANUARY 13, 1948 GANDHI DECIDED TO CONDUCT AN INDEFINITE HUNGER STRIKE
THERE IS NO OTHER ALTERNATIVE
AND DECLARED THAT THE STRIKE WOULD END EITHER WHEN THE RIOT ENDS OR WHEN HIS LIFE ENDS

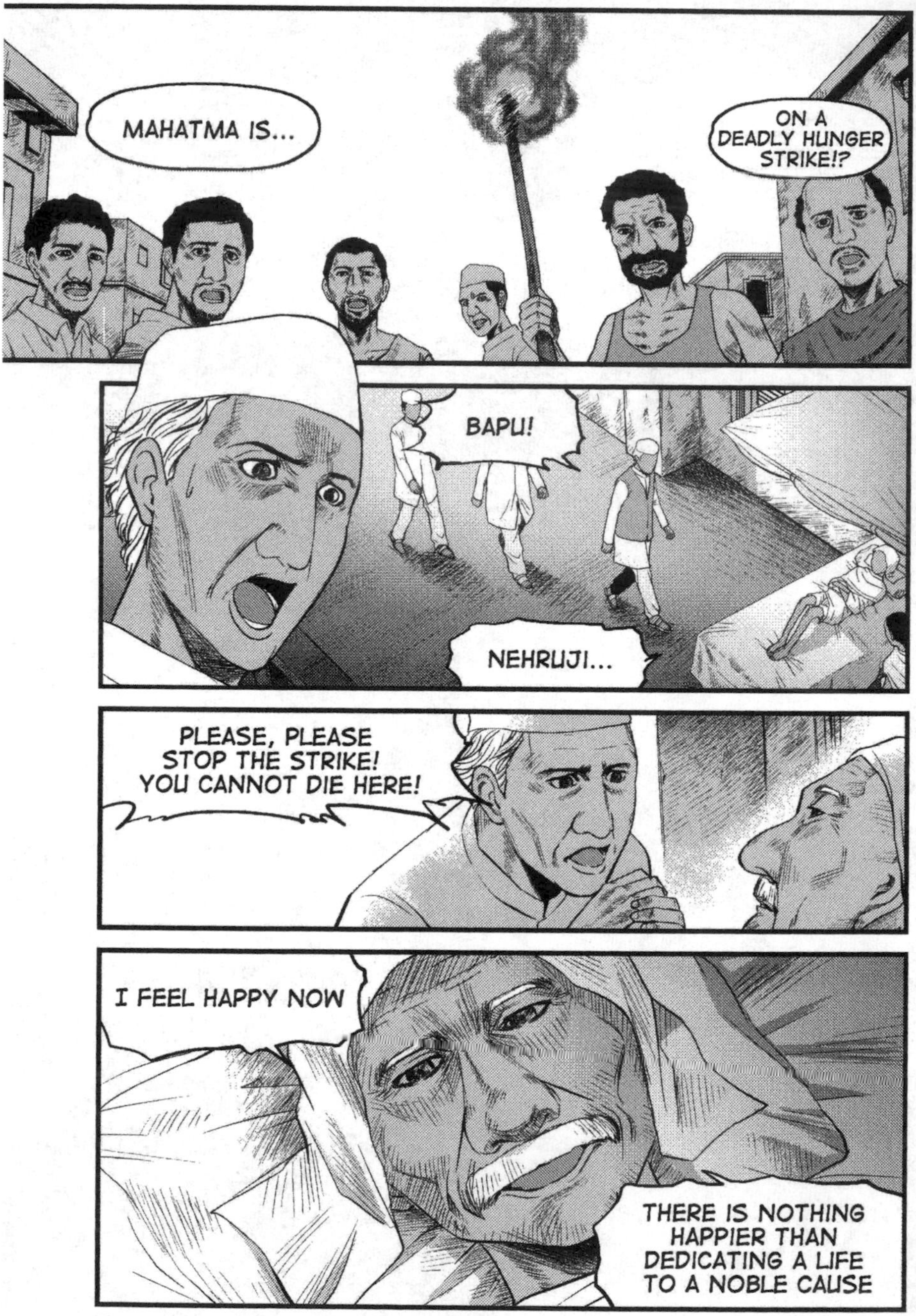
MAHATMA IS...
ON A DEADLY HUNGER STRIKE!?
BAPU!
NEHRUJI...
PLEASE, PLEASE STOP THE STRIKE! YOU CANNOT DIE HERE!
I FEEL HAPPY NOW
THERE IS NOTHING HAPPIER THAN DEDICATING A LIFE TO A NOBLE CAUSE

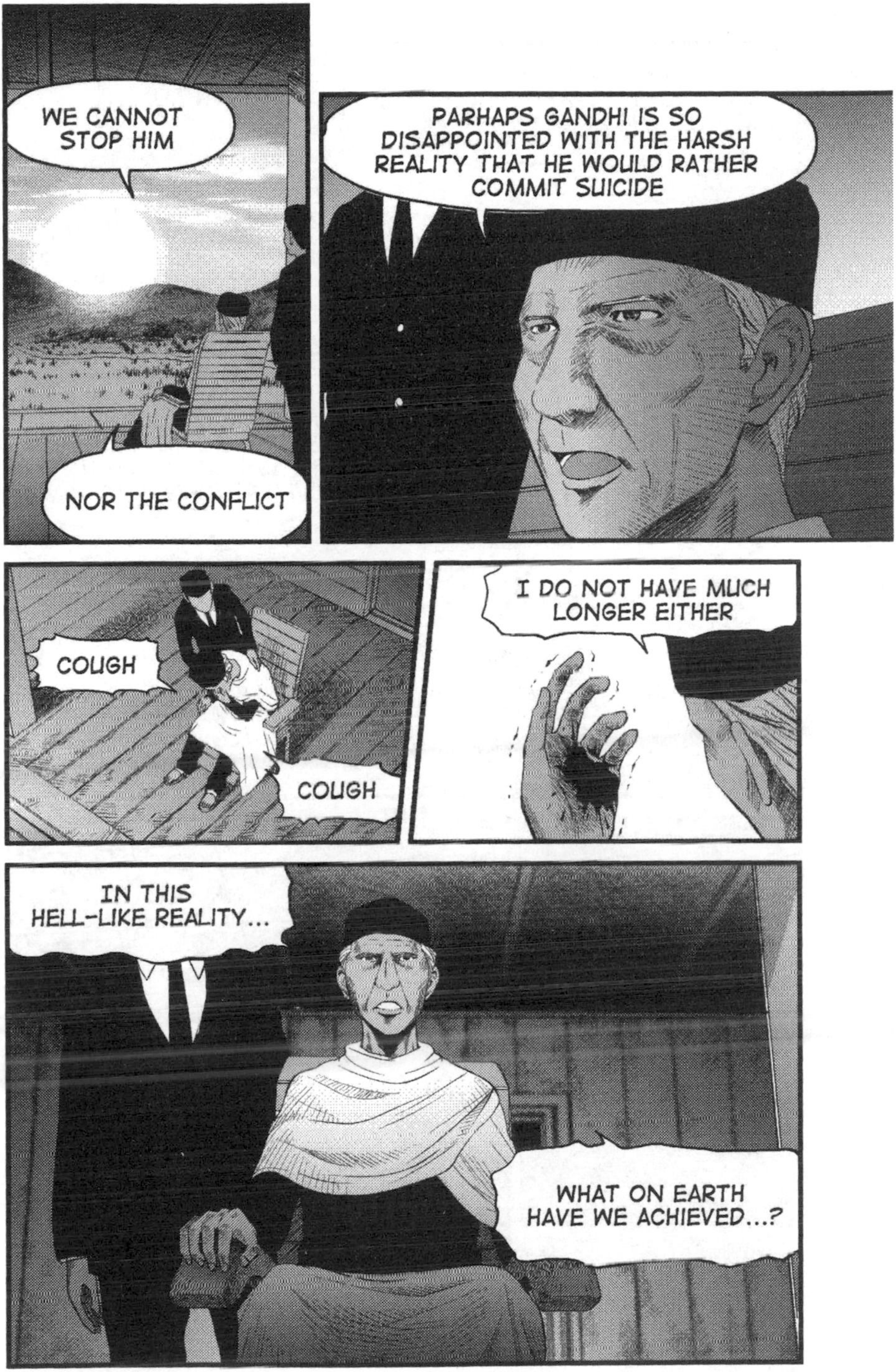
WE CANNOT STOP HIM
NOR THE CONFLICT
PARHAPS GANDHI IS SO DISAPPOINTED WITH THE HARSH REALITY THAT HE WOULD RATHER COMMIT SUICIDE
COUGH
COUGH
I DO NOT HAVE MUCH LONGER EITHER
IN THIS HELL-LIKE REALITY...
WHAT ON EARTH HAVE WE ACHIEVED...?

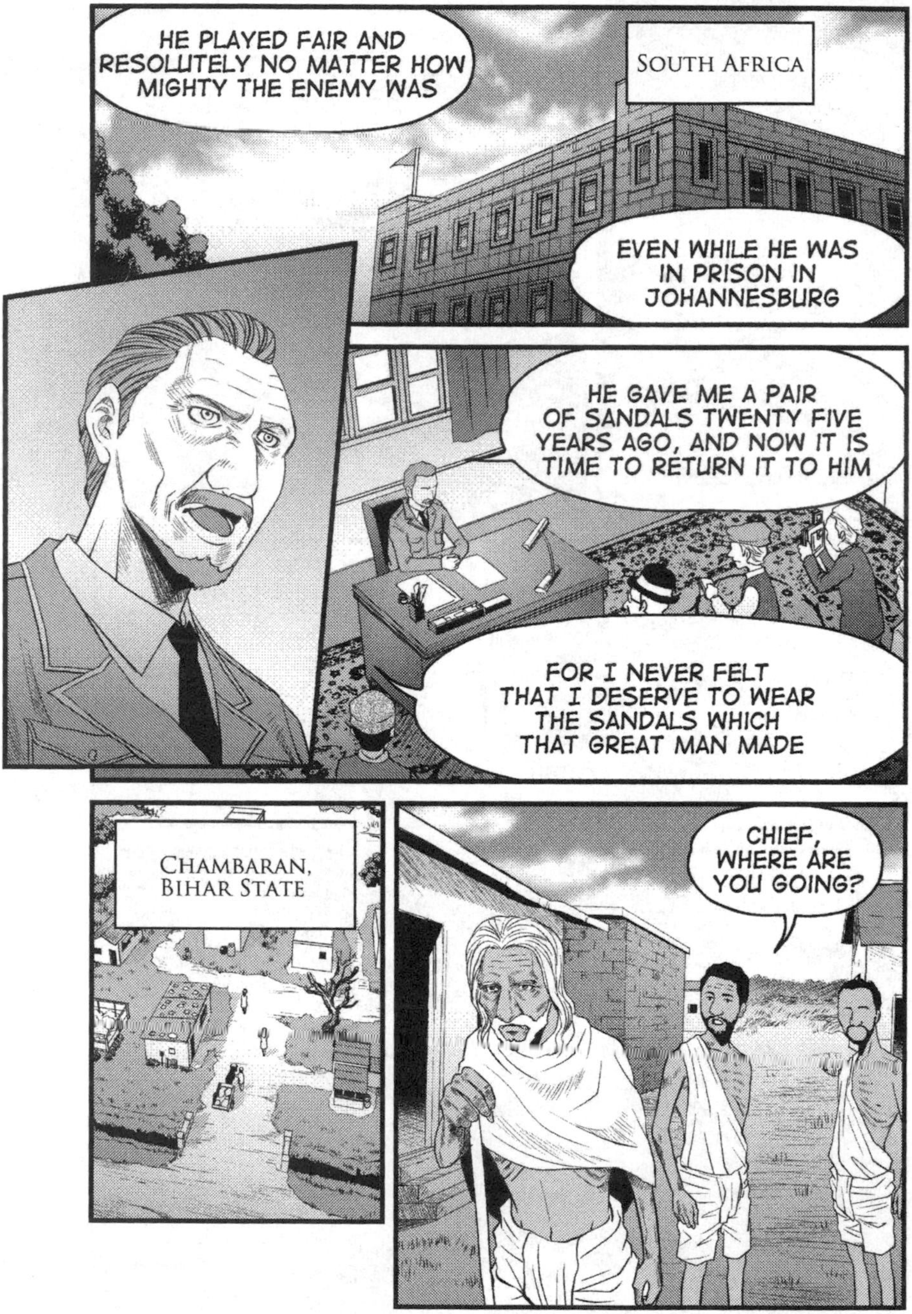
HE PLAYED FAIR AND RESOLUTELY NO MATTER HOW MIGHTY THE ENEMY WAS
SOUTH AFRICA
EVEN WHILE HE WAS IN PRISON IN JOHANNESBURG
HE GAVE ME A PAIR OF SANDALS TWENTY FIVE YEARS AGO, AND NOW IT IS TIME TO RETURN IT TO HIM
FOR I NEVER FELT THAT I DESERVE TO WEAR THE SANDALS WHICH THAT GREAT MAN MADE
CHAMBARAN, BIHAR STATE
CHIEF, WHERE ARE YOU GOING?

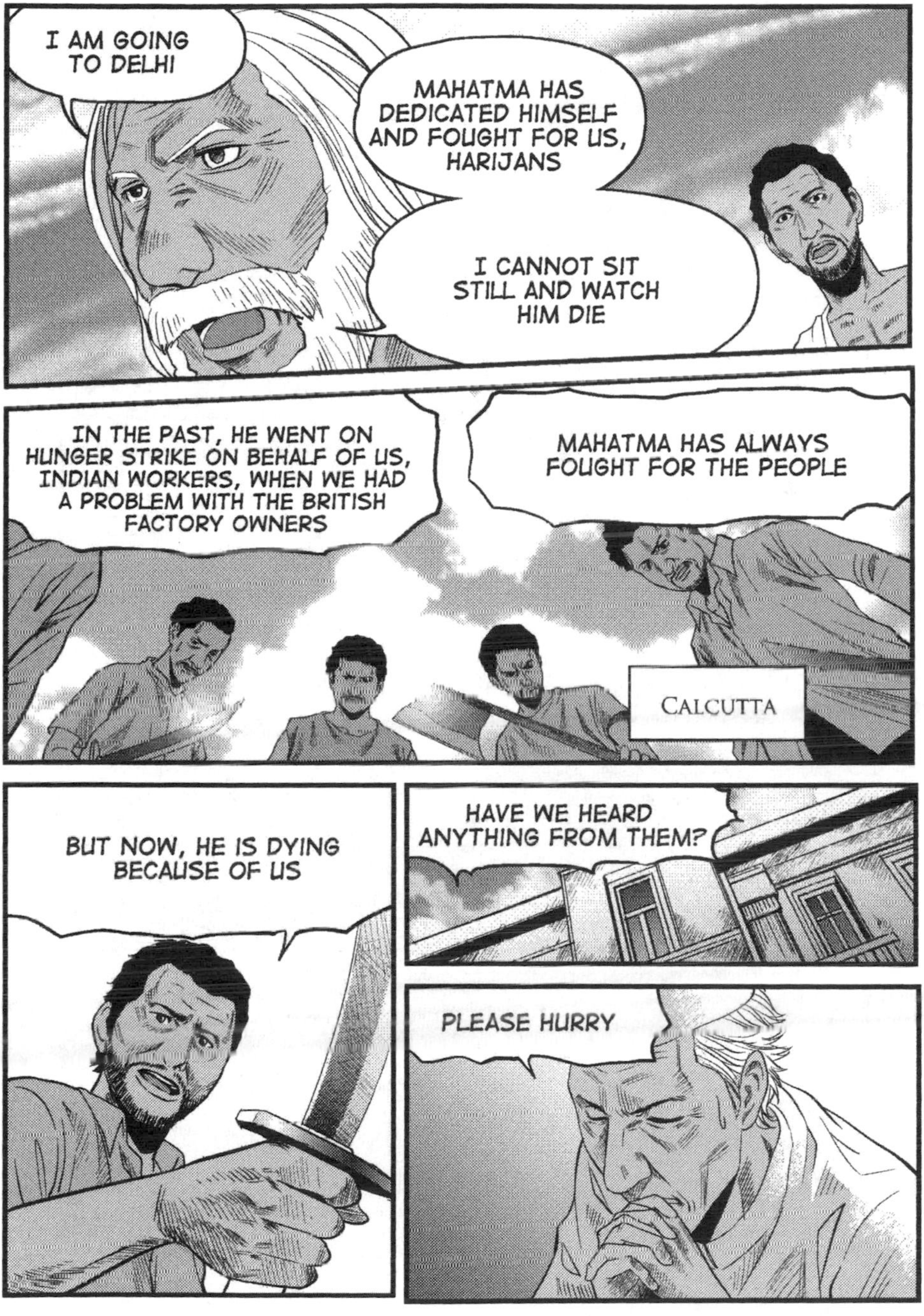
I AM GOING TO DELHI
MAHATMA HAS DEDICATED HIMSELF AND FOUGHT FOR US, HARIJANS
I CANNOT SIT STILL AND WATCH HIM DIE
IN THE PAST, HE WENT ON HUNGER STRIKE ON BEHALF OF US, INDIAN WORKERS, WHEN WE HAD A PROBLEM WITH THE BRITISH FACTORY OWNERS
MAHATMA HAS ALWAYS FOUGHT FOR THE PEOPLE
CALCUTTA
BUT NOW, HE IS DYING BECAUSE OF US
HAVE WE HEARD ANYTHING FROM THEM?
PLEASE HURRY

THE SIXTH DAY OF THE HUNGER STRIKE

BLOOD PRESSURE IS GOING DOWN. THE PULSE RATE IS LESS THAN 50.

IT MUST BE STOPPED RIGHT NOW, OTHERWISE...

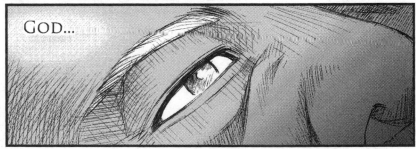

GOD...

I WONDER IF MAN CAN OVERCOME HATRED AND VIOLENCE SOMEDAY
I WONDER IF WE WAKE UP WITH TRUE LOVE FOR OTHERS
I WONDER IF TEARS OF SORROWS CAN DISAPPEAR FROM ALL MANKIND
GOD...
... BAP...
BAPU...

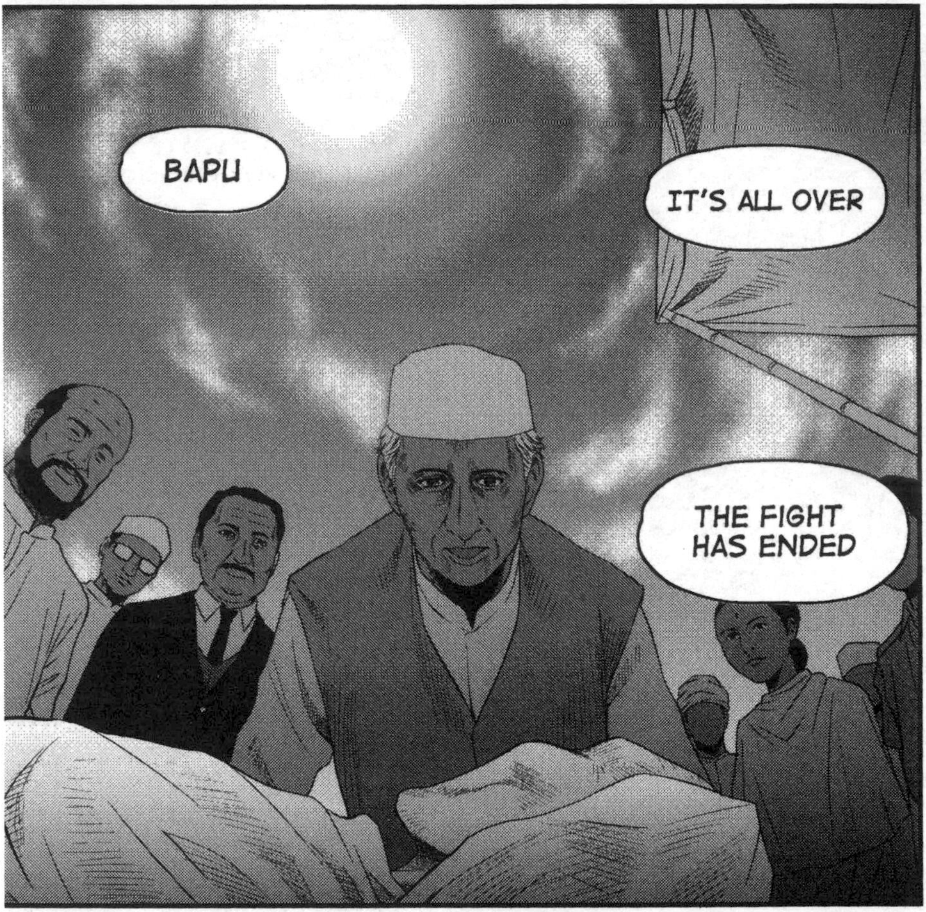
BAPU
IT'S ALL OVER
THE FIGHT HAS ENDED

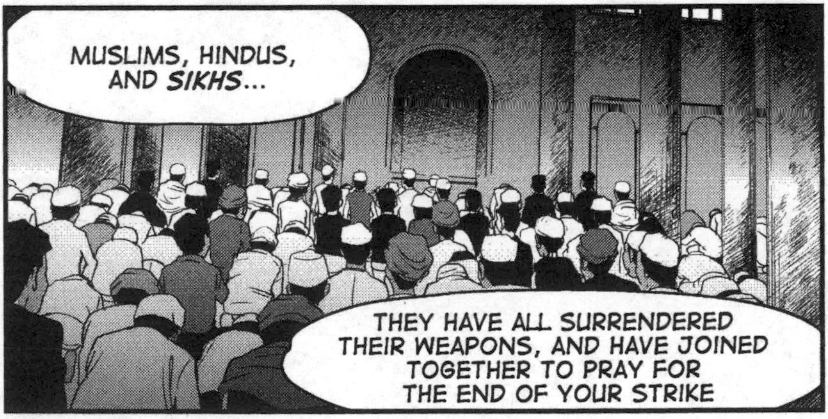
MUSLIMS, HINDUS, AND *SIKHS*...
THEY HAVE ALL SURRENDERED THEIR WEAPONS, AND HAVE JOINED TOGETHER TO PRAY FOR THE END OF YOUR STRIKE

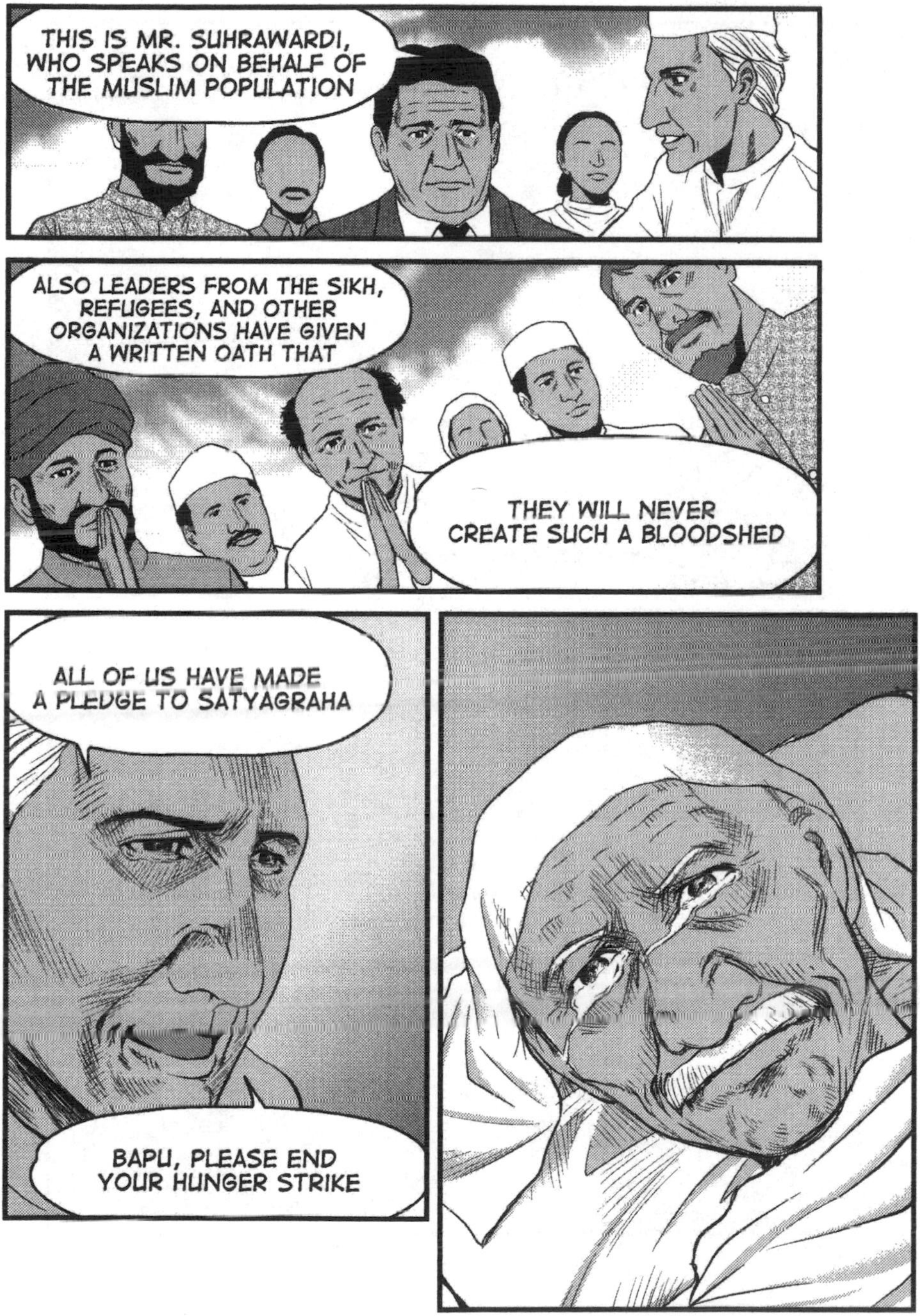
THIS IS MR. SUHRAWARDI, WHO SPEAKS ON BEHALF OF THE MUSLIM POPULATION
ALSO LEADERS FROM THE SIKH, REFUGEES, AND OTHER ORGANIZATIONS HAVE GIVEN A WRITTEN OATH THAT
THEY WILL NEVER CREATE SUCH A BLOODSHED
ALL OF US HAVE MADE A PLEDGE TO SATYAGRAHA
BAPU, PLEASE END YOUR HUNGER STRIKE

12:45,
JANUARY 18
HUNGER STRIKE
ENDED

IN FACT,
I HAVE BEEN
FASTING SINCE
YESTERDAY

NEHRUJI...

PLEASE LIVE
A LONG LIFE

AND BECOME *JAWAHARLAL*
(THE JEWEL) OF INDIA

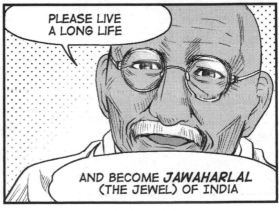

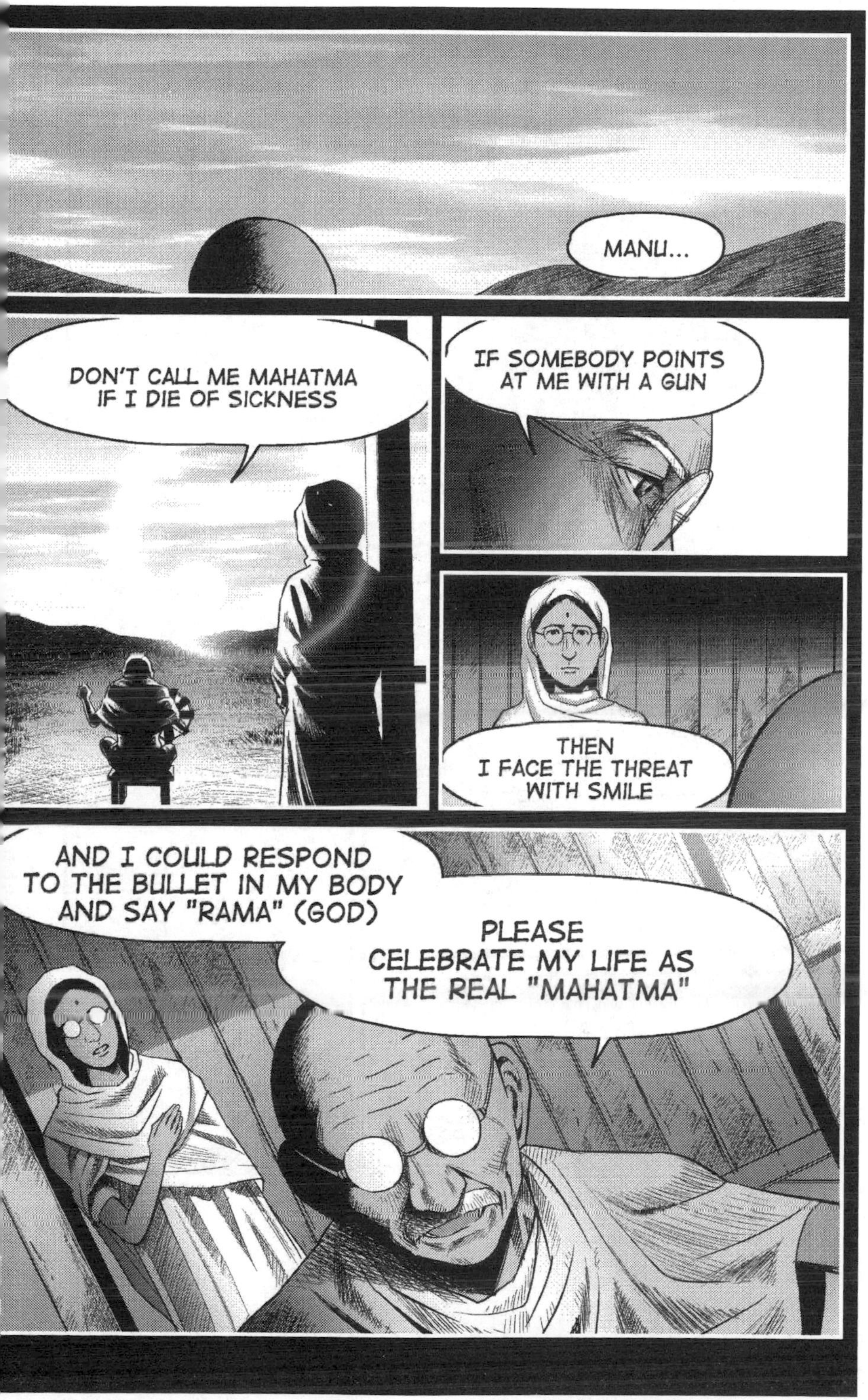

MANU...
DON'T CALL ME MAHATMA IF I DIE OF SICKNESS
IF SOMEBODY POINTS AT ME WITH A GUN
THEN I FACE THE THREAT WITH SMILE
AND I COULD RESPOND TO THE BULLET IN MY BODY AND SAY "RAMA" (GOD)
PLEASE CELEBRATE MY LIFE AS THE REAL "MAHATMA"

05:17
January 30
1948

HURRY UP, MY DEAR CRUTCHES

OR WE WILL MISS THE SERVICE

PERHAPS HE WILL NOT SUCCEED.

BAPU, LEADERS FROM KATHIAWAR WANT TO SEE YOU

LET THEM KNOW THAT WE WILL MEET AFTER THE PRAYER

PROVIDED THAT I AM STILL ALIVE

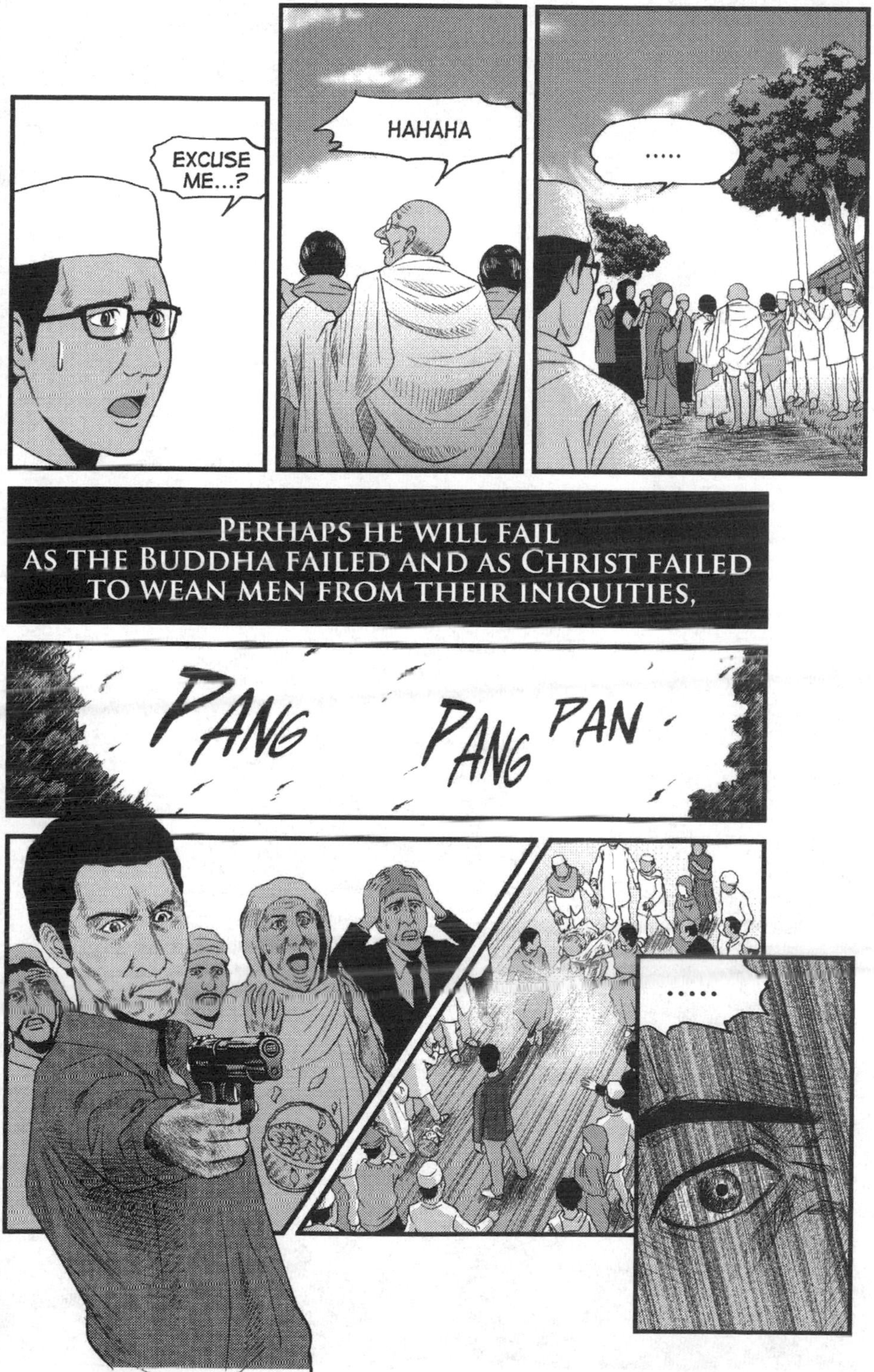
EXCUSE ME...?
HAHAHA
.....
PERHAPS HE WILL FAIL
AS THE BUDDHA FAILED AND AS CHRIST FAILED
TO WEAN MEN FROM THEIR INIQUITIES,
PANG
PANG
PAN
.....

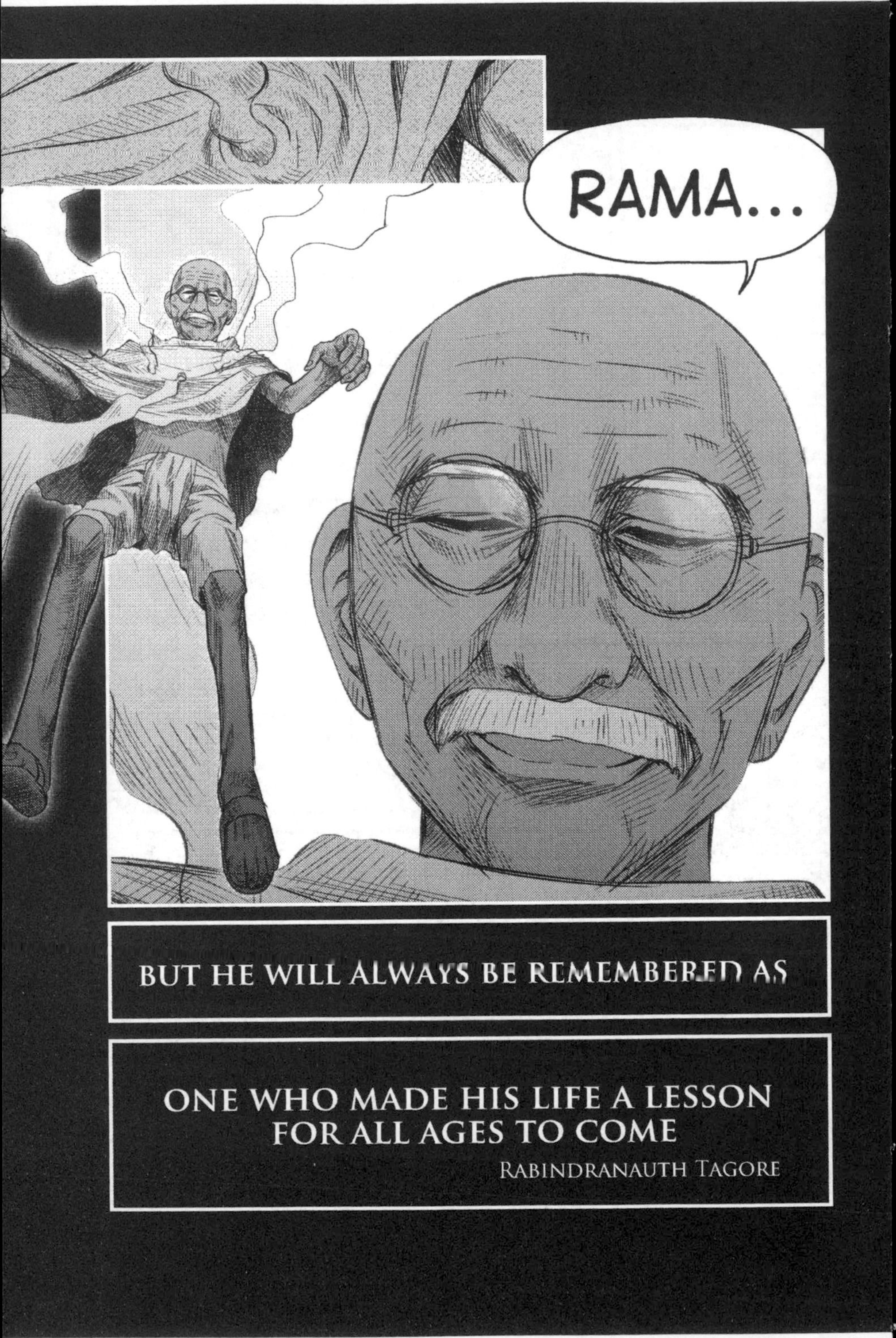
RAMA...
BUT HE WILL ALWAYS BE REMEMBERED AS
ONE WHO MADE HIS LIFE A LESSON FOR ALL AGES TO COME
RABINDRANAUTH TAGORE

Author's Note

Thank you very much for reading this book.

Upon receiving this assignment, the first thing that came to my mind as a biographer was that I wanted to draw Gandhi as a real human being.

As we all know, Mahatma Gandhi is one of the most respected and influential individuals to have ever existed, and his words and deeds have been well recorded in the history books. Because of his legendary fame, his existence has always seemed foreign and even mystical to an ordinary person like me, and his maxims have sounded rather didactic without any notable relevance to my daily life.

When I embarked on this project I conducted a thorough research to find out who this man really was. Interestingly, the more I learned about his life, the clearer it became to me that he was, just like all of us, uncertain, troubled, and unsuccessful from time to time in leading the people and keeping faith in his beliefs and ideals.

Now that I have worked on this biography and met him in my imagination, his words have become as familiar and convincing to me as those of my aging parents. I, myself, am not qualified to preach to readers how to live, but I hope that you learn something from Gandhi's life and pursuit for the truth. I firmly believe that his life itself is a meaningful message to all of us today.

Lastly, from my research of Gandhi's life, what has left the biggest impression on me is not his words but rather a photo of him with his genuinely blissful smile as he holds a baby in his skinny arms.

Kazuki Ebine
Tokyo, Japan

Bibliography

DVDs

1. *Gandhi*. Directed by Richard Attenborough. Colombia Pictures, 1982.

Books

1. Kripalani, Krishna. *Gandhi: A Life*. Orient Longmans, London, 1968.

2. Mehta, Ved. *Mahatma Gandhi and His Apostles*. Viking, New York, 1977.

Web sites

1. GandhiServe Foundation, www.gandhiserve.org.

2. Hihei Shita Gendaijin no Tamashii wo Iyashi Jyouka suru (Healing and Cleansing the Tired and Weak Spirit of Today), www.ichigenkuyou.jp (in Japanese).